Yves Guyot

Principles of Social Economy

Second Edition

Yves Guyot

Principles of Social Economy
Second Edition

ISBN/EAN: 9783744644990

Printed in Europe, USA, Canada, Australia, Japan

Cover: Foto ©Suzi / pixelio.de

More available books at **www.hansebooks.com**

PRINCIPLES

OF

SOCIAL ECONOMY

BY

YVES GUYOT

Minister of Public Works and Hon. Member of the Cobden Club

TRANSLATED FROM THE FRENCH

By C. H. D'EYNCOURT LEPPINGTON

SECOND  *EDITION*

LONDON
SWAN SONNENSCHEIN & CO.
NEW YORK: CHARLES SCRIBNER'S SONS
1892

PREFACE TO THE ENGLISH EDITION.

The author of these pages on the Principles of Social Economy is not insensible to the honour conferred on him by their presentation to the English public; nor is this honour the less gratifying because he feels that in crossing the Channel his doctrines are returning, in a sense, to the land of their birth—the land of Adam Smith, the land of Malthus, Ricardo, and John Stuart Mill; of Pelham Villiers, of Cobden and John Bright, of Fawcett, Shaw Lefevre, and Mundella. So much is his book an English book, that even where he attacks the conclusions of these masters, it is largely on the ground of facts taken from the economic development of their own country. In the matter of Economy England leads the vanguard of the nations; and it is therefore on her experience that all forward-looking eyes are fixed; while, by the thoroughness of her investigations and the accuracy of her statistics, she has opened a mine of information to which we go for the material of our economic studies, just as we go for coal to Newcastle or Cardiff, for iron to Stockton, for steel to Sheffield, for engines to Birmingham, for cloth to Leeds, for cottons to Manchester, for ships to the Thames, the Clyde, and the Mersey.

In France we are as yet far behind. In spite of the labours of a few clear-sighted and honest thinkers, like Jean Baptiste Say and Bastiat, we are still ruled for the most part by what Buckle called "the protective spirit;" what the Italian Menzotti calls "Colbertism."[1]

It would be saying too much if we were to charge the memory of Colbert with the whole responsibility of a system not of his invention, and which in his day was more or less recognised and practised in every country in Europe; but it was undoubtedly he who organised and consolidated it, expounded its theory, and attempted a rigorous and extended application of it. The system perfectly corresponded with the monarchic ideal of Louis Quatorze. Regarding himself as being, by Divine investiture, the absolute master of his subjects, the king claimed to direct all their actions—social, intellectual, and religious. This theory covered at once the

[1] *Memoirs of the Academy of Florence,* 1797.

revocation of the Edict of Nantes, the savage persecution of the lampoonists, and the trade regulations of Colbert.

To Colbert the right to labour was itself a part of the domain of the State, to be granted by it to certain privileged persons, to the exclusion of all others; and it then became the duty of the State to protect the persons thus licensed from foreign or unauthorised rivalry, and at the same time to protect the consumer against its own licensee. In the exercise of his royal prerogative, the king sold to such-and-such individuals or corporations, and no other, the right of manufacturing and selling such-and-such articles, and no other, in such-and-such places, and nowhere else. The fine for weaving stuffs out of the trade was 150 livres. Wool dyers were forbidden to dye silk or cotton; silk and cotton dyers were forbidden to dye woollen goods. The shoemakers and the cobblers, the booksellers and the bookstall-keepers, the tailors and the secondhand-clothes men, were always accusing each other of encroachment; always at strife, always at law. Colbert writes to his son, the Marquis de Clergiselay, that "all sorts of manufactures which do not at present exist in the kingdom must, if possible, be introduced." In 1662 he bought the Gobelin tapestry manufacture, getting the workmen for it from Flanders. In 1664 he granted a thirty years' monopoly of tapestry representing foliage and figures to one Sieur Hinaud, who founded the royal manufactory at Beauvais. At the same time an edict of 1664 decreed one million a year for the encouragement of manufactures and navigation. In 1673 and 1675 public money was granted for the foundation of privileged companies to carry on the slave-trade in Senegal and Guinea. Colbert began with a premium of six livres a head on the negroes taken, he ended by raising it to thirteen livres a head. He also founded the companies of the North, the Levant, and the Pyrenees.

But encouragement was not enough for the monopolists, they required the protection of coercion. The production of "French point" was made a monopoly, the industry being entirely displaced where it already existed and given to certain privileged persons. The making of it by private individuals for their own use was forbidden; and a contemporary says that Colbert carried out the change by the most violent means, imprisoning the refractory, and "dragging the young girls from their fathers' houses to toil like slaves for their bread and water." [1]

Another part of the system was, that good workmen were forbidden to go abroad. Colbert writes to the Archbishop of Lyons to arrest and bring to justice two embossed-velvet makers, who were intending to settle in Florence; and threatens the family of a

---

[1] Quoted by Pierre Clément, *History of the Protective System in France.*

French manufacturer who had gone to Lisbon, and was proposing to start a cloth factory there.

Having thus organised industry at home, Colbert proceeded to secure it from foreign competition. In a letter dated 1666 to the Intendant of Marine at Rochefort, he said, "We must always buy in France rather than abroad, even though the articles be inferior and somewhat dearer; because, when the money does not go out of the kingdom, the State gains a double advantage, since it is none the poorer for spending it."

The terms of the formula may vary, but the substance is always the same. In a memorandum addressed to the king, Colbert gives the theory of the protective system ever since: "To reduce the duty on all articles and manufactured products going out of the kingdom, and on all articles coming in which may serve as the raw material of industry, and to keep out foreign manufactures by means of prohibitive duties."

These principles were carried out in the adjustment of the tariffs of 1664; which, however, were soon found insufficient, and were doubled three years later.

Nevertheless, all this was not enough to give the required start to certain industries, and further means of encouragement had to be found. "It being the king's wish that his subjects should apply themselves to navigation," a duty of fifty sous per ton was laid on Dutch vessels, and a premium was offered on all French-built ships of more than a hundred tons. The dockyards, however, apparently remained empty, for Colbert is obliged to break his rule by granting a premium of five livres per ton to importers of ships of under 100 tons, and six livres per ton to importers of ships of over 100 tons.

Having made all these arrangements for fostering national industry and protecting it from any influx of foreign products, Colbert proceeded to protect the consumer against the manufacturer by regulating the trade corporations. An edict of 1669 declares that, the goldsmiths' and silversmiths' work having deteriorated, and being no longer of the required quality, statutes and regulations have been drawn up for the purpose of bringing it to the greatest possible perfection. The length and width of cloth were determined by authority. The cloth was to be inspected and marked on its return from the fuller, and confiscated if it did not conform to the prescribed conditions. Textile fabrics were to have so many threads to the warp and so many to the woof. A code of instructions, published in 1671, defined in 317 articles the composition of dyers' colours. The manufacturers loudly complained; but they were informed that there were great advantages in this uniformity of length and breadth in all the textile manufactures, and that the rules would continue to be rigorously applied. In 1672 it was ordained that defective goods should be exposed in the pillory with the names of the manufacturers and workmen found in default; and in case of a repetition of the offence the offender was to be put along with them. The State proved its infallibility by issuing an extraordinary number of contradictory decrees—forty-four between 1666 and 1683, and between 1683 and 1739 no less than 230.

To secure cheap bread, Colbert forbade the exportation of grain, thus destroying a main source of profit to the agriculturists. England and Holland answered his customs tariffs with a war tariff, and ceased to buy French wines. The French peasantry were in the deepest misery; the subsidised industries did not flourish; Colbert himself confesses that, multiply privileges as he would, he was always asked for more. "They never attempt," he says, "to surmount difficulties by their own efforts, as long as the king's authority will do it for them." He describes the tariffs as the "crutches" of industry, as if industry were a cripple. It had only become a cripple by leaning on its crutches and making no effort to walk alone. In spite of all his "encouragements" Colbert's companies fell to pieces one after another, like so many houses of cards. After bringing the country to the verge of desperation, he himself died in despair, and was only saved by a secret funeral from the last insults of the mob.

And yet this man had intellectual powers of the highest order; a faculty for organisation which could adapt itself equally to the projecting of vast designs and the carrying out of the most minute details, unwearying industry, unfaltering and ardent purpose. It was the system that was to blame. It was the mistaken attempt to substitute the action of the Government for individual initiative, authoritative regulation for private contract, the responsibility of the State for that of the individual, which spoilt all his fine qualities, brought disaster on all his schemes, plunged the country into distress and ruin, instead of giving it wealth and prosperity, and provoked disorder in the very endeavour to secure absolute order.

These results were enough to advertise the system as a failure. The physiocrats opposed to it the formula of Gournay, "*Laissez faire, laissez passer;*" and Turgot, on his accession to power, attempted the practical application of the principles, but failed, and fell in the struggle with the protectionist spirit. The Revolution of 1789 abolished the corporations, with all their paraphernalia, in a single night; but a momentary burst of enthusiasm was not enough to eradicate Colbertism from the French mind. It soon reappeared, under the ægis of the Revolution itself, in measures for limiting prices and preventing the buying-up of the market. It showed itself under the Empire in the police regulations to which workmen were subjected; and it was worked out on a tremendous scale in the Continental blockade. It was perpetuated under the

Restoration, the Government of July, and the Second Empire. It was supported, not only by the rich and powerful manufacturers who were the immediate gainers by it, but by the ignorant public, who, notwithstanding all the efforts of the Economists, allowed themselves to be carried away by its plausibilities. During the Revolution of 1848 it broke out afresh in the demands of the Collectivists and State Socialists, who agitated for the right to labour, for State credit, and sundry other equally indefinite advantages. To this day, in spite of the enormous industrial development which has within the last thirty years opened a new channel for the economic progress of the nations, in spite of multiplied facilities of transport and communication, and of the experiments made and the gigantic results achieved in England by the diminution of the customs, Colbertism is still endemic in France. Cured in one form, it breaks out in another. Driven from this point, it flies to that. Men of all parties agree in this—that protection is indispensable, only each has his own particular Colbertism, which he wishes to set up at the expense of the rest, since privilege necessarily implies privation. I wish to offer here a few observations on the French Colbertism of to-day.

Colbertism is like a delirium—the form of the spectre changes, the agony of terror is the same. Once it was the influx of English products that kept French Colbertism in panic fear, then it was the influx of American products, now it is the Treaty of Frankfort. Yet many of those who declaim the most loudly against this fatal 11th article, have never read its text. It amounts to nothing more than what is known as the "most favoured nation" clause.

It runs as follows:—

Art. 11.—The French Government and the German Government shall take as the basis of their commercial relations the system of reciprocity, on the footing of the most favoured nation. Under this rule are included the rights of ingress, egress, and transit, custom-house formalities, and the admission and treatment of subjects of the two countries and their agents. Provided that such favours as either of the contracting parties may have accorded, or may accord, by treaties of commerce, to States other than the following—England, Belgium, the Netherlands, Switzerland, Austria, Russia—shall be excepted from the above rule.

It is always the same old struggle of the producer to maintain prices. He wants his rivals put down; and he never perceives that he himself is a consumer to begin with, and a very large one, and that in making things dear for other people he is making things dear for himself. A manufacturer uses coal, iron, and other raw material, such as soda, for instance, which, nevertheless, according to the customhouse scale, are treated as manufactured products; he consumes, also, through the medium of his workmen, large quantities of manufactured goods—clothes, furniture, utensils, food, fuel. Every tax on any of these articles increases the expense of production. He is, therefore, compelled to sell dear. This obligation might suit him well enough if it were not that, across the frontier, and even close at hand, he finds himself surrounded by competitors, who are all doing their very best to undersell him. And yet, in spite of all their efforts, the final result of the competition of producers and merchants among themselves, the need of the consumer to buy cheap, and the general advance in mechanical conveniences of all sorts and in the means of transport, is that the price of circulating capital is constantly falling, while that of fixed capital is as constantly rising.

The most recent statistics, published since the appearance of this volume in France, show a steady continuance of this phenomenon; and every fresh investigation confirms the maxim, that "the wealth of a nation is in inverse ratio to the value of its circulating capital, and in direct ratio to the value of its fixed capital."

But if the value of lands and forests, houses and factories, and above all, the value of man, the highest kind of fixed capital, rises in proportion to the fall of circulating capital, it follows that, instead of trying to keep up prices by protective tariffs, we should make every effort to assist their fall by freeing them from imposts, which are a sort of inland customs.

But all the nations except England have followed a directly opposite course, and impeded the circulation of commodities by weighting them with a factitious dearness. Each individual wishes of course to buy at the best price for his own advantage, and to sell at the best price for distancing his competitors; and society, the nation, the State—what are they but collections of these same individuals? Yet it is held that, while it is the object of the individual to bring down prices, it must be the object of the State to keep them up. I have been speaking of the past; but it is not a question of the past; it is unhappily a question of the present, and perhaps even of the future.

All industries are tributary one to another; if therefore all industries are protected, it is obvious that each is paying for the protection of the others. If, on the other hand, some industries are protected and others not, then Peter is robbed, without compensation, to pay Paul. The unprotected industries must still pay protection prices for their raw material, their machinery, and their labour. Before he can produce, the manufacturer must begin by consuming; and the greater the production the greater the consumption; and if he cannot buy cheap, how is he to sell cheap?

The Colbertists have no idea of keeping the golden rule. They wish to exclude your produce; but if they can they will make you admit theirs. They claim protection that they may develop their exports. It seems to have escaped their notice that, if they need protection, it must be because, with every advantage of language, taste, and proximity, they have been unable to compete with foreign goods in their own country; and that if, with all these advantages, they cannot keep the home market, it is hardly to be supposed that they can secure one across the frontier.

One is ashamed to repeat such obvious truisms; and yet, as long as they are unaccepted in practice, we can but go on unfolding them and presenting them in their various aspects. It seems that it is easier to impose the tariffs than to master the theory of free trade!

The worst is, that there is not even the excuse that the theory has not been verified by experience. One nation has had the courage to act on it; and its experience has given abundant proof of the soundness of the theory.

"But England is the market of the world."

Yes; and why? Because she has opened her frontiers to the produce of all the world; because she buys, all the world over, at the lowest price, augmented only by the cost of transport. It is she herself who gains by the freedom she gives. Moreover, as everything goes to the English market, it is the English market which decides the current price; and the English merchant or manufacturer is the first to profit by the rise or fall, while those of other nations follow at a distance. It is not Havre that rules the price of cottons; it is Liverpool.

The English manufacturer, getting his raw material in the cheapest possible market, can produce at the lowest possible price, and at the same time afford the highest wages. The value of man, like that of land and buildings, rises in proportion to the cheapness and abundance of circulating capital. Yet this cheapness is the terror of the French Colbertist. His ideal is the policy of dearness.

Now for the consequences:

The very manufacturers who, in the name of "national labour," demand the exclusion of their foreign rivals, make no scruple of themselves employing foreign labour. French workmen have not perceived this inconsistency; they are so simply protectionist that they need no argument of this kind against the competition of the foreigner! They are trying to obtain the insertion of a clause in the contracts for public works forbidding the employment of foreign labour, or admitting it only under strict limitations. They are consistent. The inconsistency rests with the employers, who are willing enough to erect barriers against foreign products, but object to barriers against foreign workmen, though the one is but a corollary of the other.

I have said something of these inconsistencies in the Fourth Book of this work; but there is always more to say, for the evil goes on increasing.

The law on trade syndicates, recognising the right of the workmen to hold meetings, form associations, and concert measures for selling their labour wholesale, has not yet passed the Senate. On the other hand, the workmen and most of the Radical deputies are eagerly demanding the limitation of the working day for adults to ten hours (which is really an application of the principle of the maximum). The Senate rejects the measure; not, however, in any enlightened spirit, but on the same protectionist principles which led to the rejection of the other Bill. And yet we keep our faith in Government regulation of trade and labour! The names of liberty and equality are constantly in our mouths, but we are like liars protesting our veracity. We "protest too much." And all the while we are clamouring incessantly for new measures of tutelage and new recognitions of caste.

Ever since Political Economy has been taught by the faculties of law we have been witnessing the evolution of a new form of Colbertism. Once they despised Political Economy altogether; now many of its teachers, imbued with prepossessions derived from the old Roman and French legists regarding the omnipotence of law, adopt the doctrines of the *Catheder-Socialisten*. The example of England, however, has always stood in their way. The successes of the *Catheder-Socialisten* and of the State socialism, let alone those of Colbert himself, have hardly been brilliant enough to be quoted on the other side. They therefore hail such succour as that of Prof. Cliffe, Leslie's *Essays*, Mr. Ingram's manifesto, Stanley Jevon's *The State and Labour*, Mr. Goschen's late speech, and the observations made by Mr. Chamberlain and the members of the Philosophical Institute at Edinburgh, on "*Laissez faire*" and Government interference. England herself, they say, is abandoning the principle of non-intervention, and coming down to a sort of State socialism, and hence the outburst of demands for protection on behalf of all interests,—the protection of the men against the masters, and the masters against foreign competition,—and the mutual recriminations of commerce, industry, and agriculture, as if they formed three hostile camps!

The inquiry now on foot [1] before a committee of the Chamber of Deputies will have the advantage of showing up the economic prejudices and fallacies still in force among us.

If the Government loses here, it gains there; you cut away one tentacle, and another buds out on the instant. Every day it loses something of its religious, intellectual, or political influence over men to whom political liberty means the right to take part in the affairs of the State, to whom the liberty of the press means the right to choose your own reading, and liberty of conscience, the right

[1] February, 1886.

to think and believe without asking permission. But, on the other hand, it constantly finds a pretext for its activity in some new domain. We see it in Paris to-day, under the plea of hygienic necessity and through the medium of the municipal laboratory, interfering with the provision trade in ways as vexatious as those of Colbert himself—including public advertisement, which is but a modern form of the pillory.

This pretext of hygiène may go far. It has been used in England from time to time to stop the importation of foreign cattle. It has been used in France within the last two years to support the prohibition, by a simple ministerial decree, of the importation of American bacon. This is for fear of trichinæ. It is not proved that there has ever been a single case of trichinosis in France; and with the trenchant logic which is apt to characterise Government measures, while prohibiting bacon in the barrel from across the Atlantic, we were admitting live bacon from across the Rhine, where trichinosis is endemic. The Academy of Medicine pronounced, unanimously, but for a single vote, against the prohibition; but none the less a whole trade was destroyed by a nod of the ministerial head. Who is to be held responsible for the bankruptcy and ruin of the victims? The modern Colbertism ends, like the old, in a government by inspectors. They come into our houses now to see if their sanitary condition is satisfactory; soon we shall have them coming to see if the children's faces are washed and they are gone to school, and whether the kitchen utensils are clean or not. We shall have them prescribing our hours of sleep, and our dishes at table, like Sancho Panza's doctor—absit omen!—forbidding us this or that drink, as they did in some parts of America, and sounding the curfew, as in the good old times, because we cannot be allowed to reverse the order of Nature by turning night into day.

Let the partisans of the extension of State intervention, who are distinguished, for the most part, by their distrust of its agents, consider the consequences! The State can only act through regulations, the execution of which must be enforced by inspectors, government officials, and the police; and when these agents of the Executive begin to come in contact with the daily life of the individual, controlling his actions, intermeddling in all his affairs, the very men who have been the foremost in calling the State to their aid will be the first to turn against the system, to load its agents with recriminations, to expose their tyranny, their incapacity, their blunders; they will look back with regret on the part they have taken in bringing about the evils from which they suffer, and which, in the pursuit of their own supposed advantage, they have inflicted on others besides themselves.

Nevertheless, I have faith in the future; the encroachments of the State and of the local authorities are temporary; they cannot last long. As we go on, the consciousness of individual rights must grow more distinct, and with it must come fresh outgrowths of self-directing energy, and a more determined revolt against all measures which tend to repress or frustrate human activity. With forces like these in the field, it can be only a question of time, how soon we are to witness the overthrow of a system under which more time and strength are spent in getting leave to do a thing than in actually doing it. A man's whole energy is spent in attempting to alter the law, or to contrive that a law directed against him shall in some way serve his purposes. We find this last form of activity constantly at work among those who are subjected to indirect taxation.

What, then, are the advantages of the system? What is there to say in its favour? That the Government becomes responsible? In what way? As regards political responsibility, a minister's responsibility to his country appears, notwithstanding some few celebrated instances, to be considerably lighter than that of a merchant to those with whose money he is trading. But, to speak only of economic responsibility—when the State undertakes a department of the public service, what is its first act? To declare its irresponsibility. The Compagnie du Nord paid two million francs for a railway accident; if the State were to work the railways, it would have a fixed price for human breakages, as it has for the loss of registered letters. When a private person brings an action against the State, he comes into conflict with the entire social and political organisation, which fights him with his own money, paid to it in taxes. The attempt to substitute corporate responsibility for private responsibility ends in this,—that there is no responsibility at all. Mr. Goschen quotes a striking instance of this result. Mr. Plimsoll's Merchant Shipping Act obliged the Government to undertake the protection of the lives of seamen. Nothing has come of it, or worse than nothing. Individual responsibility has disappeared, and Government responsibility is totally ineffective. A shipwreck occurs; the shipowner cannot be blamed; the Government had passed the vessel.

Prof. Stanley Jevons, in his book on *The State and Labour*, says, "The individual is not always the best judge of his own wants and interests. He is not always able to judge for himself." We may go further; we may admit that he never is; for he is always liable to be misled by prejudice, passion, or ignorance. But Governments also are composed of men; have they no prejudices, no passions, no defects of knowledge? What has made them infallible? Prof. Stanley Jevons admits the ignorance of the State in matters of Economy; but if its knowledge is inadequate it surely ought to abstain from action. A private person may make a mistake in his calculations; but the consequences of his mistake will be limited to a very narrow area compared with the far-reaching consequences of an error committed by the State.

The city of Paris has drawn up a scale of prices intended to serve as a basis for the rate of its contracts. Little by little, this scale of prices has come to be considered as an official standard, giving the law to prices generally. The contractors take these fixed prices as the basis of their estimates in contracting with private persons. Consequently, the price of buildings goes up; the workmen, having consulted with their masters, quickly raised the rate of wages. Then the contractors, finding others who will work for lower pay, employ them, and the higher scale of wages is not paid after all. In this way two classes of workmen have come to be formed, those who work at par and those who work below par. The former detest the latter; and all demand that the city shall by its rules compel the contractors to pay invariably according to the fixed scale. The consequence will be, that the contractors will secure themselves by raising their prices; the ratepayer will pay more for a less result; the workmen will find fewer workshops open; and the demand for labour will be diminished. This is only another phase of the policy of dearness.

In France, we have before our eyes at this very moment an instance of the danger of State intervention in matters of economy. In 1878 M. Freycinet's Government, by large purchases of machinery, gave a sudden impetus to the metal-foundries and other industries. Political difficulties supervened; the Government was obliged to close, or greatly reduce, its works; a part of the machinery remains unproductive, and the purchasing power of the capital sunk in it remains unrecovered.

In the recent discussions in the Chamber on the financial crisis, two speakers only, M. Frédéric Passy and M. Lalande, ventured to take the ground of freedom of trade; all the rest showed themselves more or less tainted with Colbertism. Consciously or unconsciously, they implied the belief that a vote of the Chamber is all that is necessary to change the nature of economic conditions. The illusions I have referred to in the first chapter of this volume are not yet dissipated. No sooner does a crisis occur than everybody requires the State or the communes to set on foot great public works. Whether the work will be of any use or not, is a secondary consideration. No one seems to realise that the money spent on these works is just so much withdrawn from employment in private enterprise. The capital is sunk for the present; when will it regain its purchasing power? What if it never regains it? The supposed remedy only aggravates the evil. Yet not a voice was lifted in the French Chamber of Deputies to demonstrate this obvious truth.

Latterly, the expedition to Tonquin has been spoken of as a remedy for the crisis. Unfortunately, our experience in Cochin China goes to prove that our colonies serve rather as outlets for the capital of the French taxpayers than for the products of French industry. Colonised chiefly by Government officials, the purchases they make in France are made with the money we have just sent out to them in salaries. From this point of view they represent one of the most desperate forms of Protectionist policy.

Every measure which bears the mark of Colbertism has to be fed in the first instance out of the budget. There may be a question as to its subsequent advantages; there can be no question at all as to this preliminary sacrifice.

Again, a Protectionist measure, once adopted, is almost impossible to get rid of; it creates around it a group of vested interests which buttress it on every side, and a troop of functionaries always in arms to defend it as a personal possession. "Gentlemen," say these officers of the State, "we cannot allow the authority which has been entrusted to us to suffer in our hands." They regard the whole organisation, with all its vices and abuses, as a sacred deposit, which they cannot see impaired without dishonour.

Under the bourgeois government of the Restoration and of Louis Philippe, the nobility and the upper middle class had secured to themselves certain privileges, by means of the Protectionist system. The democracy, in attacking these privileges, took its stand on the high ground of liberty. All Oppositions do. But now the democrats are in power, and all this is changed. The privileges they despised for others, they now wish to keep for themselves. It is in the nature of things.

It is the inevitable tendency of every Colbertist measure to carve out privileges for the governing party at the expense of the governed. *Social equality is in inverse ratio to the intervention of the State.*

In proportion as the animal develops, the organs differentiate, and become more and more independent of each other. It is the same with species. The higher the type, the more marked are the individual differences. Mussel resembles mussel; but man differs from man. Two natives of Tierra del Fuego are not very dissimilar in thought and character; but every unit of our Paris population has ideas, tastes, capacities, that distinguish him from his neighbour. But the Colbertist ideal would bring down all these diversities to a dead level, would run them into a single mould, and fix the pattern once for all. It is not life, not freedom, not progress; it is mummification.

It is an anachronism too. It is an attempt to superimpose the military civilisation of a past age on the industrial civilisation of our modern times.

The system cannot but produce intellectual and moral depression. Based on privilege, it implies spoliation, provokes hatred or rebellion, leads to social warfare. If regulation affords room for official tyranny, it positively invites corruption; intrigue and fraud are the safety-valves of repressed energies.

By increasing expenditure, by diminishing the productive power of individuals, and by compelling them to struggle with obstacles on every side, it creates dearness; and dearness means famine, destitution, misery.

Alas! these things have frozen us to the very marrow of our bones; and yet we cannot give up our belief in the system, and in its salutary influence on the production of wealth. In England no one imagines that the production of wealth can gain by State intervention, but only that State intervention is required to facilitate its first distribution.

The figures recently published by Mr. Giffen,[1] and the statistics quoted in the body of this book, suffice to prove that the existing distribution is not so unjust, whatever complaint may be made of the non-interference of the State with labour-contracts, and of its refusal to protect the employers against the men, the landlords against the manufacturers. The injustice is on the other side. Colbertism, while it stimulates a factitious production, enforces a factitious distribution. It persistently sacrifices certain classes of people to certain other classes. The English corn laws, while they lasted, injured the workman by limiting the market in which he could buy his bread. The French Customhouse injures the manufacturer, by forbidding the paper-maker to buy his soda and the spinner to buy his cotton at their natural price.

But even in England, they say the distribution of wealth is unjust, and for this they blame the principle of non-intervention. But where is there any such thing as non-intervention? Does not the State everywhere intervene with its system of taxation? Is not this State interference defeating human activity? Does it not weigh down a trade here, an industry there? Does it not lay its finger on every transaction, every transfer, every exchange?

I will give an instance of one of its most flagrant inequalities.

A man's wealth may increase in two ways; either directly, by his own exertions, or incidentally, through the exertions of others. It may be entirely the result of the latter. A man owns a house on the Place de la Bourse in Paris. He has inherited it, by no effort of his own; he takes no trouble about it; he only does not sell it. Yet year by year the property rises in value. He hunts, shoots, fishes, gives himself no concern; and all the while the labour of others is creating wealth for him.

[1] *Journal of the Statistical Society*, December, 1883.

Now, if we take the average of the recent budgets in the city of Paris, we find that the octroi and other duties have brought in more than 180,000,000 fr. out of a budget of from 250,000,000 to 260,000,000. On whom are these duties levied for the most part? On the tenants.

Which brings us to this singular conclusion,—that the tenants pay almost the whole of the charges on everything that goes to increase the value of the property, and consequently to raise their own rent. They provide the rod for their own back. They pay for the privilege of having to pay.

This mode of taxation presses them on two sides; in the first place it makes the necessaries of life dear to-day; and in the second place, it threatens them with a rise in their rent to-morrow.

Then the collectivists take up the old theories as to the nationalisation of the land, which broke down so pitifully in 1848. In France, the bulk of the small proprietors are too much attached to their own plot of ground for the collectivists to think of including rural property in their schemes. They confine themselves to disposing of town property; though their arguments tell quite as much in one direction as in the other.

The solution is to be looked for, not in the merging of individual proprietorship of the soil, but in a fiscal reform such as that adopted by the Municipal Council of Paris,[1] such as that proposed by the Municipal Reform Association in England, such as that indicated by John Bright in his speech at Liverpool on the 1st of December, 1879. It is to collective effort and expenditure that fixed capital owes a great part of its advance in value; fixed capital must make good this advance, and seek recoupment for so doing indirectly by repercussion.

But whence come these inequalities? From the burdens imposed by State intervention. Remove taxation, and the inequality disappears. It is not by the augmentation of fiscal charges that we can rectify the distribution of wealth, but by their reduction. But it is impossible at the same time to reduce taxation and to increase the area of State intervention.

Then we are told that we have no pity for the ills of suffering humanity, because we object to empirical remedies which cost much and do no good. Because we refuse to raise up a new privileged class, we are accused of buttressing the privileges of the old. In France, and in many other countries, Governments, Chambers, and people all prefer to try the charlatan's receipt. "We don't know whether it will do any good," they say, "but we must do something." The doctor must never go away without leaving a prescription. The patient must have something to take, even though the whole thing may be only a question of dieting.

[1] See Book vi., ch. 2

The schools, or rather the sects, which make it their business to solve "the social question" offer us a Babel of nostrums. The Anarchists are for liberty, all liberty, nothing but liberty; only the instruments of labour are to be collective property. They do not tell us how the two ideas are to be reconciled. The revolutionary Collectivists have a different vocabulary; but there the difference ends. The moderate Collectivists are content to work by the day, line upon line, here a little and there a little; but they accept the whole principle of economic intervention with its maxima and minima, its privilege here and privation there; in fact, they hardly deserve a name of their own, for their policy is simply the policy of the French nation. They profess to be progressists; they are reversists. Collectivism is only another name for Colbertism. The worst of it is, that nobody recognises this, any more than they recognise the inconsistency in the claims of the more or less authorised leaders of the democracy, who ask at once for political liberty and economic leading-strings.

There are, however, a few who still faithfully follow the economic traditions of English Radicalism, as understood by Cobden and John Bright, by Fawcett, Mundella, and Shaw Lefevre. They would give back to the public all that has been taken from it by royal spoliation, by judicial artifice, by the greed of privileged classes, including labour itself, which, if it is no longer seized by the monarchy and parted among guilds and corporations, is still chafed and restricted by an effete legislation, by custom-house extortion, and by vexatious and oppressive taxation.

This is our Collectivism. Far from wishing to add to the old artificial restrictions, we consider it the most important part of our work to destroy them. We hold, with Buckle, that all the great reforms have consisted, not in doing something new, but in undoing something old. We would limit the action of the State to the registration and enforcement of contracts. For the rest, we ask it only to abstain from hindering the development of rights kept hitherto in the shade, but which are just stirring into consciousness and claiming their place in the light of day.[1] We allow, in virtue of what Herbert Spencer calls the law of the family, the protection of children against careless or cruel parents; but we consider the protection of the sane and able-bodied adult, which can only be undertaken at the cost of other adults, not only as a distinct act of spoliation in regard to them, but as loading them with a dead weight which must tend to repress their own energies. We hold, through all contradictions, to the belief that man develops greater strength and intelligence in managing his own affairs than in working for other people's benefit; and that of all civilisations, the

[1] An interesting example of this sort of development in England is to be found in the recent measure relating to Married Women's Property.

worst would be a civilisation in which everybody was administering for everybody else.

In a very remarkable book, called "The Statics of Civilisation," a French savant, M. Paul Mougeolle, works out these two laws:—

"Alimentary substances diminish in quantity from the equator to the pole."

"The evolution of civilisation has been in the opposite direction; it rises as it recedes from the equator towards the north."

The suggestion is very striking. At first sight we might be led to conclude that man would be richest and most powerful where food was most abundant. But it is not so; because human energy grows with the increase of difficulty in finding nourishment, and with the need of a larger amount of nourishment to maintain the body at its normal temperature. Civilisation, therefore, develops first and in its most primitive form, where living is easiest; but gradually men acquire the habit of industry; patience and energy are accumulated through hereditary transmission; they leave their original centre and press northward, to found by their ever-increasing energy a more and more advanced civilisation. For no wealth of circumstance ever produces progress. It has but one factor—man.

Every measure which tends to enfeeble the energy of man, and to reduce his responsibility, is an arrest of development. Those who promote measures which substitute the action of the State for that of the individual, are not favouring the evolution of humanity; they are paralysing it.

Three years ago I pointed out, in the concluding chapters of this volume, that the great question which presses on all the nations, whatever their form of government, now, at the end of the nineteenth century, is the apportionment of the duties of the State and the rights of the individual. All the movements of thought and of events which have since been taking place around us drive me more and more forcibly to the conviction that this is indeed the great problem which lies before the thinkers of all nations.

(Signed)

YVES GUYOT.

Paris, 1884.

TABLE OF CONTENTS.

BOOK I.
ECONOMIC SCIENCE, ITS NATURE, OBJECTS, AND METHODS.

CHAPTER		PAGE
I.	On Method in Economic Science	1
II.	The Materials of Economic Science	18
III.	Economic Psychology	26
IV.	Definitions	29
V.	Value	35
VI.	The Object of Economic Science	41

BOOK II.
THE CONSTITUENTS OF VALUE.

I.	Economic Tendencies of Man	45
II.	Capital	48
III.	Fixed and Circulating Capital	50
IV.	Nomenclature of Fixed Capital and Circulating Capital	53
V.	The Place of Fixed and Circulating Capital in the Work of Production	54
VI.	Space	58
VII.	Time	60
VIII.	Exchange	64
IX.	Circulation	66
X.	Résumé	67

BOOK III.
VALUE OF FIXED AND CIRCULATING CAPITAL.

I.	An Economic Contradiction	68
II.	The Measure of Value	72
III.	Money	77
IV.	Relative Values of Fixed and Circulating Capital	94
V.	The Relation of Space to the Value of Capital	109
VI.	The Relation of Time to the Value of Capital.—Price of Credit	117

BOOK IV.
THE VALUE OF MAN.

CHAPTER		PAGE
I.	POPULATION	123
II.	PROFESSIONS AND OCCUPATIONS	142
III.	THE VALUE OF MAN	151
IV.	THE ORGANISATION OF HUMAN INDUSTRY	177
V.	THE PRIVILEGES OF MASTERS	180
VI.	THE RIGHT TO LABOUR, AND THE ORGANISATION OF LABOUR	182
VII.	EXCEPTIONAL CONDITIONS OF LABOUR	186
VIII.	THE LABOUR MARKET	192
IX.	CO-OPERATION	211
X.	CONCLUSION	215

BOOK V.
EXPERIMENTAL ECONOMICS.

I.	LANDED PROPERTY	217
II.	COMMERCE	230
III.	COMMERCIAL CRISES	239
IV.	BANKS	249
V.	PUBLIC COMPANIES AND ASSOCIATIONS	262

BOOK VI.
THE FUNCTIONS OF THE STATE.

I.	STATE INTERVENTION IN ECONOMICS	270
II.	THE REVENUES AND EXPENDITURE OF THE STATE	275
III.	THE PROVINCE OF THE STATE	286

CONCLUSION.—CHARACTERISTICS OF ECONOMIC PROGRESS . . . 292

BOOK I.

ECONOMIC SCIENCE,

ITS NATURE, OBJECTS, AND METHODS.

CHAPTER I.

ON METHOD IN ECONOMIC SCIENCE.

I AM led to treat of Method in Economic Science at the outset of my work, partly by the confusion which, as we shall find, exists in people's minds, and partly by some recent discussions on the subject.

M. Courcelle Seneuil has rightly observed, that political economy,—or, more accurately, economic science,—is the first branch of social science which has been carefully, steadily, and successfully studied.[1]

It has existed as a science for only one century. Quesney, Turgot, and the physiocrats had a glimpse of some of its laws. The great work of Adam Smith appeared in 1776. Jean Baptiste Say, in his "Traité d'Economie Politique" and his "Cours d'Economie Politique," was the first to lay down clearly, though not without some verbal inaccuracies, the method which economists should follow.

"In political economy," he says,[2] "as in physics, as indeed in everything, we have framed systems before establishing truths; that is, gratuitous conceptions and mere assertion have been given forth as truth. Later on, we have applied to this science the method which has contributed so much since the time of Bacon to the pro-

---

[1] *Journal des Economistes.* "Situation de l'Economie Politique," Sept. 1877, p. 326.
[2] *Discours Préliminaire.* This did not appear till 1826.

gress of all the others, namely, the experimental method,[1] the essential feature of which consists in admitting as true only those facts the truth of which has been demonstrated by observation and experiment, and as constant truths only such conclusions as can be naturally drawn from them; a method which altogether excludes that deference to authority and precedent which, in science as in morals, in literature as in government, interposes between man and the truth.

"But do we really know all that is meant by this word 'facts,' which is so often used?

"It seems to me that it means both things which are, and things which happen; and this introduces at once two orders of facts; it is a fact that such and such a thing is thus, and it is a fact that such and such an event has happened in such a manner.

"Things which are, if they are to serve as a basis for sound reasoning, must be seen as they are, under all their aspects and with all their properties. Otherwise, while thinking to discuss the same thing, we may be discussing two different things under the same name.

"To the second order of facts, namely, things which happen, belong the phenomena which appear when we observe how things take place. Thus it is a fact that when metals are exposed to a certain amount of heat they melt.

"The way in which things are and happen constitutes what is called the nature of things; and the correct observation of the nature of things is the sole foundation of all truth.

"Hence spring two classes of sciences: the sciences which we may call descriptive, and which consist in naming and classifying things, like botany and natural history; and the experimental sciences, which inform us of the reciprocal action of things on each other, or, in other words, the connection between cause and effect; such are physics and chemistry.

"These latter require the study of the inner nature of things, for it is in virtue of their nature that they act and produce these effects; it is because it is in the nature of the sun to be luminous, and of the moon to be opaque, that when the moon passes in front of the sun the sun is eclipsed. Sometimes a careful analysis suffices to make known to us the nature of a thing; in other cases it is completely revealed to us only by its effects; and in any case observation is

---

[1] Say ought to have said, method of observation. Claude Bernard has well distinguished between the two methods in the following passage: "The name of observer is given to one who employs simple or complex modes of investigation for the purpose of studying phenomena as they occur in nature; the name of experimenter is given to one who employs simple or complex modes of investigation in order, for some purpose or other, to alter or modify natural phenomena, and to reproduce them under circumstances or conditions under which they do not occur in nature."

cecessary, when we cannot have recourse to actual experiment, to confirm what analysis has taught us.

"These guiding principles will help us to distinguish two sciences which have almost always been confounded: political economy, which is an experimental[1] science; and statistics, which is only a descriptive science.

"Political economy, as it is now studied, is altogether founded on facts; for the nature of a thing is as much a fact as its consequences. The phenomena, the causes and consequences of which it seeks to make known, may be considered either as general and constant facts, which under like circumstances are always the same, or as isolated facts, which indeed also take place in obedience to general laws, but where several laws, acting simultaneously, modify without destroying each other; like the fountains in our gardens, where we see the laws of gravity modified by those of equilibrium, without therefore ceasing to work. Science cannot pretend to reveal all these modifications, in their daily repetition and infinite variety; but it lays bare the general laws, and illustrates them by instances which every reader can substantiate for himself.

"Statistics can only make us acquainted with facts which have actually taken place. . . . They may gratify curiosity, but cannot usefully satisfy it, so long as they do not indicate the origin and consequences of the facts they record; and when they do, then they are not statistics, but political economy.

"Political economy is established on immovable foundations the moment the principles which serve as its bases are proved to be rigorous deductions from incontestable facts.

"In truth, general facts are founded on particular facts; but we can select those particular facts which have been the best observed the best recorded, and of which we ourselves have been the witnesses, and when the results have been found to be constantly the same, and solid reasoning shows why they have been the same, when the very exceptions are but the confirmation of other principles as clearly proved, then we are justified in giving these results as general laws. A new particular fact, if it be isolated, if the reasoning fails to show its connection with its antecedents and its consequences, is insufficient to shake a general law; for who can say but that the difference observed between the two results may have been due to some unknown circumstance? . . . In political economy it is a general fact that the interest on money varies with the risk run by the lender. Am I to conclude that the principle is unsound because I have seen hazardous loans at low interest? The lender may have been unaware of the risk; gratitude or fear may have compelled him to make a sacrifice: the general law, disturbed in a

---

[1] Say meant, "inductive."

particular case, will have resumed its sway the moment the perturbing influences have ceased to act.

"Besides, how few individual facts are satisfactorily proved, and how few of these have been observed with all their attendant circumstances; and even supposing them to be well authenticated, faithfully observed, and accurately described, how many there are that prove nothing, or prove the reverse of what they were intended to establish!

"It is idle to oppose practice to theory. What is theory, if not the knowledge of the laws which bind the effect to the cause, fact to fact? Who can be better acquainted with the facts than the theorist, who knows them under all their aspects, and knows, too, the relations which subsist between them? And what is practice without theory but the employment of means without knowing how or why they exist? It is simply a dangerous empiricism, by which we apply the same methods to cases which are alike only in appearance, and which tend to results quite other than those we are seeking.

"In order, then, to arrive at the truth, we must know, not many facts, but the essential and influential facts, must regard them under all their aspects, and, above all, must draw from them just conclusions, and make sure that the effects ascribed to them are really caused by them and by nothing else.

"Some persons, at home in other sciences, but strangers to this, imagine that there are no positive ideas except the mathematical verities, and the exact observations of natural science. They fancy that in the moral and political sciences there are no constant facts and indisputable truths, and that they are therefore not sciences at all, but merely more or less ingenious individual hypotheses. These men of science found their belief on the disagreements of those writers who treat on these subjects, and on the real extravagances of some of them. As to extravagances and hypotheses, what science is without them? Chemistry, physics, botany, mineralogy, physiology, what are they but the lists in which opinions encounter each other, just as in political economy?

"Each party sees indeed the same facts, but classifies and explains them in its own way; and let it be observed that in these debates we do not find all the true men of science on the one side, and all the charlatans on the other. Leibnitz and Newton, Linnæus and Jussieu, Priestley and Lavoisier, de Saussure and Dolomieu, were all of them first-rate men, and yet they could not agree. Did the sciences they professed not exist, because they disagreed?

"In the same way, the general laws of which the political and moral sciences are composed exist in spite of disputes. So much the better for those who, by judicious and repeated observation, can discover these laws, can show their connection and deduce their consequences. They spring from the nature of things as certainly as do the laws of the physical world; they are found, not imagined; they govern those who govern others, and they can never be violated with impunity.

"The general laws which control the course of things, take, as soon as they come to be applied, the name of principles.

"Political economy, like the exact sciences, is made up of a small number of fundamental principles, and of a great number of corollaries or deductions from these principles. It is important to the progress of the science that its principles should flow naturally from observation; each author afterwards increases or diminishes at pleasure the number of inferences, according to the end he has in view. The more this science is extended and perfected, the fewer the inferences it will be needful to draw, because they will be readily apparent; every one will be in a position to find them out and apply them for himself.

"There are, no doubt, in the social state, evils which are in the very nature of things, and from which it cannot be freed entirely; but there are many others which it is not only possible, but easy, to remedy. Several passages in this book will go to prove this; I might even add that amongst almost all nations many abuses might be rectified without the smallest sacrifice on the part of the privileged persons who profit, or think they profit, by them."

In the whole of this passage there is hardly anything to reprehend. I have quoted it because, published in 1826, and written probably still earlier, it has answered beforehand some of the questions lately raised in England and Germany.

In England it has been affirmed that economic science has not, up to the present time, been anything more than a deductive science; and the question has been seriously mooted whether it is a science at all.

In Germany they claim to have invented a national economy based on a so-called historic method.

Lastly, in France there are men deeply impressed with social miseries, who think that in order to heal them, it suffices to sum up their own aspirations in a maxim; and men, on the other hand, who refuse to acknowledge any sphere for the economist at all.

I will proceed to a brief statement and examination of these questions.

Mr. Ingram, the President of the Economic Section at the meeting of the British Association at Dublin in 1878, put forth a manifesto,[1] in which he declared that political economy had no future, practical or scientific. He acknowledged meanwhile that it had a certain utility.

[1] *The Present Position and Prospects of Political Economy.*

Mr. Ingram charges the economists,—

1st. With having separated the study of facts relating to wealth from other social phenomena;

2nd. With having given to many of their conceptions a metaphysical and dangerously abstract character;

3rd. With having misused deduction in their researches;

4th. With having been too positive in the enunciation of their conclusions.

While, on the one hand, economic science is charged with being deductive, on the other hand, M. Cournot, in a book published in 1838, entitled, *Recherches sur les Principes Mathématiques de la Théorie des Richesses*, a German author, M. Hagen (1839), and within these last few years, Mr. Stanley Jevons and M. Léon Walras, have endeavoured to make it a mathematical science.[1]

The mathematical process consists, as we know, in extracting and isolating some extremely simple and general notions, which are regarded as axioms, and then deducing, apart from any observation or experiment, all the inferences which can be drawn from them. But this leads us into the most monstrous errors.[2] Mathematics may serve as accessory methods, as a system of checks, they may be employed to define and formulate certain relations; they may fill a useful part analogous to diagrams. But it is a vain attempt to substitute in economic science the mathematical for the inductive method.

At the same time, in the course of his paper, Mr. Ingram abandons his first charge, and he does well, for it will not stand examination. Economists have been in error, not in limiting themselves too narrowly, but in not limiting themselves enough. A science, to exist, must be specialised, otherwise everything includes all, and you may build up an encyclopedia on a grain of salt.

As to the second charge, we have seen that the method indicated by J. B. Say is the real inductive method. Mr. Ingram acknowledges[3] that Adam Smith's work is full of facts, and that he assigns an important place to induction. Senior says, "Political economy is greedy of facts." It is true that Ricardo based his theories on abstractions; but J. B. Say had already, in 1826, pointed out this vicious tendency. If Mr. Ingram thinks himself the first to have discovered it, he is a little late in the field. Speaking of Ricardo, J. B. Say said, " Condillac has judiciously remarked that a process of abstract reasoning is an arithmetical calculation, only with other symbols. But an argument does not furnish, any more than an equation, the data which in the experimental sciences are indis-

---

[1] The *Journal of the Statistical Society* published in June, 1878, a bibliography of works applying mathematical theory to political economy.

[2] See Yves Guyot, *L'Inventeur*, p. 264.

[3] Page 23.

pensable for arriving at the truth." He accuses Quesnay and his friends of having "begun by laying down abstract generalities."

That there may have been disciples of Ricardo who did nothing but make deductions, is possible, but that is their own fault; the science itself is not involved in their error.

Still, after having complained of economic science as relying too much on the deductive method, Mr. Ingram and Mr. Cliffe Leslie are not fortunate in invoking the authority of Auguste Comte. They are doubtless not aware that Comte, in his *Politique Positive*, founds the whole science of sociology on the deductive method. He has adopted the system of Gall, has assigned to man eighteen faculties, without even attempting to verify this statement *à posteriori*, has then divided these faculties into emotional and intellectual, and has determined in favour of the subjection of the latter to the former. Mr. Ingram, in rushing into the subjectivism of Comte in order to escape the abstractions of Ricardo, has been simply an unconscious Gribouille.

Mr. Bonamy Price has all at once been avised to propound to himself this question, "Is political economy a science?" and to answer, "No."

This is modest on the part of a Professor who has long filled the chair of political economy at Oxford, since it is virtually saying to his pupils, "It is not a science I have taught you, it is not a science I am teaching."[1] But is his reasoning equal to his modesty? His arguments are four in number.

1st. "Political economy has neither created nor discovered the means of satisfying the wants of mankind." True; but mankind ate bread before chemistry had made known its composition, or physiology had studied the phenomena of assimilation. Men walked, built houses, raised weights with the lever, before they framed physical theories or studied the laws of gravity. They blew glass before they knew of silicates. Are we to say, that because men have done all this without being chemists, physiologists, or physicists, that therefore chemistry, physiology, and physics are not sciences? Science is everywhere preceded by empiricism.

2nd. "The object of political economy is to make common sense the supreme controller of industry and commerce."

I quote this sentence because Mr. Bonamy Price attaches much importance to it; but it means nothing. Objective philosophy has long since abandoned the idea of common sense. If Mr. Bonamy Price means to say that the object of political economy is to formulate laws so exact that every one shall be obliged to accept and apply them, he is contradicting his own thesis. This is the very object of science as science, namely, to proclaim undeniable truths.

---

[1] *Chapters on Practical Political Economy*, ch. i., 1878.

3rd. Mr. Bonamy Price says again, "The majority of men do not study chemistry and astronomy. They know that these pursuits are above them. But they know too that these sciences contain information extremely important to them, and they are ready to follow the rules they lay down, without trying to account for them. The dyer and the intelligent farmer go for help to the chemist. The seaman takes observations of the sun and moon, and consults his almanack. It is quite otherwise with political economy. Every one thinks he understands economical questions as well as, or rather better than, the economists." What does this prove? Why, the infatuation of ignorance under one of its forms.

4th. "The truths enunciated by political economy are truisms." It is the same with all scientific laws. The legendary M. de la Palisse is the patron of all men of science. They content themselves with recording facts as clear as this, "A quarter of an hour before his death he was still alive." Those who are reckoned greatest among them do but establish facts which every one might have seen, but which they alone have seen. Their merit has lain in substituting intentional for accidental observation.

In Germany, political economy has always ranked with the Parliamentary Sciences (those which have the State for their object). It is one of the forms of administration, and nothing more. The Germans may have made some statistical monographs, but until the last few years they have played no part in economic science.

In the matter of jurisprudence, every one knows the characteristics of the German historical school, represented by Savigny, Eichhorn, Grimm, and Hugo. It is the fatalist school; an institution or a law exists, and, since it exists, it is right. This school confounds necessary and constant facts, without which humanity and the world could not exist, with accidental and contingent facts, which might very well never have taken place.

M. Roscher wishes to do for economic science what Savigny has done for jurisprudence, and announces, with much sound of trumpet, the application of the historic method to the study of economic science. To hear him, one would think that no economist before him had ever opened a volume of history, and yet Adam Smith did not avoid the examination of historic facts. His work contains elaborate historical analyses on banking, on the various agricultural systems, and the difference in the increase of wealth among different peoples.

We find the same in J. B. Say. So far from ignoring the past, they have both of them testified to its frequent violation of economic laws, and to the frightful disorders and miseries which have resulted from it. Besides, are past facts only to be examined? Do not the facts which are passing under our eyes strike us still more forcibly? Are they not easier to examine, to estimate, and to control? Do not most of the facts of the past appear to us as shrouded in a sort of mist? Not only are we uncertain as to their causes and effects, we hardly know the facts themselves.

But the Germans use the term "historical method" as a means of exclusion. They will recognise none but individual facts; they imagine that they can thus find the happiest solution for such and such a practical problem; as to general facts, on which general laws may be based, they refuse to admit them.

Professor Held, of the Bonn University, calls on the economists to give up, once for all, the search after natural laws.

Then what are they to seek for? The *Oatheder Socialisten*,[1] the Socialists of the pulpit, admit no laws except those made by Government; and these they regard as having unlimited authority. M. Schmoller, a Strasburg professor, puts it plainly, "The State can do everything, since it can make the laws."

Such has indeed been the claim of all autocrats; but it is hardly worth while to be a professor, and assume an air of profundity, in order to formulate an idea long ago mastered by the pettiest African tyrant.

Messrs. Hildebrand of Jena and Knies of Heidelberg, and M. Emile de Laveleye of Liége, who has made himself their spokesman in France and Belgium, support the same theory in terms more or less distinct. They all demand a stronger intervention of the State in economic matters—"in order to invigorate public spirit," says M. Held, not perceiving that, generally speaking, the stronger the State, the feebler is public spirit. M. Wagner goes so far as to deny to the individual the right to come and go, to change his residence from one commune to another, or to marry, without leave; with Marlo and Schöffle, he would give the State power to fix the number of households, and the number of children in each, though he omits to say what course should be taken to bring about this last result.

Prince Bismarck, in his discussion on the German tariff, has shown himself the most powerful of the *Catheder-Socialisten*.

They seem to me to resemble in some respects M. Rondelet, who has published a book called *Du Spiritualisme en Economie Politique*, and M. de Metz-Noblat, professor of the faculty of law at Nancy, who has placed as a motto at the head of his *Cours d'Economie Politique*,[2] this text from St. Matthew, "Seek first the kingdom of God and His righteousness, and all other things shall be added unto you." Such absurdities discredit only their authors, they prove nothing against economic science.

What then is the difference between these Catheder-Socialisten,

[1] The name was applied to this school of economists by M. Oppenheim, a member of the Prussian Parliament, in a pamphlet published in 1872.
[2] 2nd edition, 1880.

whose doctrines Prince Bismarck upholds in Parliament, and the Socialists, whom he persecutes with proscriptive animosity?

It is simply this, the former would apply the forces of the State chiefly to the advantage of the governing classes, the latter to that of the working classes. At bottom, both hold the same doctrine, and are under the same illusions as to the functions of the State.

Prince Bismarck was not deceived on this point, as is clear from his avowal of his relations with Lassalle.[1] Lassalle proposed to found associations for production by the assistance of the State; the State was to regulate the labour of the nation, as labour is regulated in a large factory.

It is always the substitution of the State, the collective entity, for individual initiative and individual energy. The idea is not new. The *Catheder-Socialisten*, with all their pretensions, have said nothing that all the protectionists, all the communists and socialists who rely on authority, had not said before.

I will take the latest representative of these last, in whom they find their highest expression—the late M. Louis Blanc. His sojourn in England did not modify the ideas he held in 1848; and in his speech at Nîmes on the 28th Sept., 1879, he showed that he still held to his idea of the *Organisation of Labour*.

I will not just now examine his speech further than as regards its method, and in the very first lines I find the following assertion, "Adam Smith, Turgot, and all the great economists were honest enough men, but they made the mistake of studying economic phenomena as they were, without concerning themselves with what they should be." And then he is angry with Adam Smith and J. B. Say because they say that the price of labour is fixed by the relation of supply to demand; that in the social relations this price depends on the proportion subsisting between the number of labourers and that portion of the general wealth which is destined for the remuneration of labour. Certainly, this has been said; and M. Louis Blanc anathematises the economists who have said it!

But either these facts are true or they are false, and it was M. Louis Blanc's business to determine which.

Now, M. Louis Blanc does not dispute the truth of these facts, he admits it. "The economists have explained very learnedly how things actually happen, but they have not inquired how they ought to happen. They have made political economy a purely descriptive science. They have described, with much accuracy, how wealth is created, distributed, and exchanged in modern societies; but they do not trouble themselves to inquire whether it is justly apportioned."

Here we have a confusion between a statement of existing facts

---

[1] Reichstag, 17th Sept., 1878.

and a conception, more or less correct, of right and justice. If economists had indeed arrived at the results indicated by M. Louis Blanc, their task would be ended. Unfortunately, they are far from having formulated all the laws which govern the production and distribution of wealth. It is much to have formulated a few of them. It may be that they are hard and cruel, but can we therefore deny that they exist? No; for M. Louis Blanc himself recognises their existence, though he seems to insinuate that we should disregard them. But what would he say of a mechanician who, in constructing a machine, should disregard the laws of statics and dynamics, under the plea that they only hindered him?

The Germans are logical in their way, for they declare these laws to be false; though they have to confine themselves to the assertion, for as soon as they begin to argue, they are compelled to admit that they are true. But has M. Louis Blanc any process for violating these laws without entailing by their infraction the destruction of wealth itself? Have the economists, in affirming the truths which he himself admits, said that mankind should do nothing to better its condition? It is just the reverse; whenever they have proposed an application of economic science, that application has had for its object the increase of the wealth and well-being of the majority. I speak here of the masters of the science, without troubling myself about some more or less reactionary economists, reactionary, not because they were economists, but in spite of it; for the first act of political economy was the annunciation of human progress.[1]

M. Louis Blanc, and many of those who assume with him the name of "Socialists," and make the extinction of the "proletariat" the only social question,[2] create for themselves a very noble and generous ideal of justice, but one very much beyond the reality. They have the idea of a blissful future, analogous to that of the millennialists.[3] In many of their conceptions there is a sort of transformation of the religious idea. They dream of a future life perfect as that of Paradise; they speak of it with the enthusiasm of faith; they excommunicate those who doubt whether the negation of economic laws is the best means of attaining it, as the faithful excommunicated the philosophers; and they neglect the practical means of bringing it about.

Let us distrust this social mysticism; nothing can come of it but mad enthusiasm and bitter disillusion.

It would be well if those who seek to appease the wants of humanity with words representing more or less ambiguous subjective ideas, at least knew what they were talking about.

Did not M. Tolain once say that political economy does not

---

[1] Turgot, Speech on Progress, 1750.   [2] Speech at Nîmes.
[3] See *Etudes sur les Doctrines Sociales du Christianisme*, by Yves Guyot, 2nd edition.

concern itself with the distribution of wealth?[1] Yet Adam Smith declares that his book on *The Wealth of Nations* looks into "the causes which have improved the productive faculties of labour, and the order in which its products are naturally distributed among the different classes of people." J. B. Say defines political economy as, "The science which shows how wealth is made, distributed, and consumed." And Rossi says, "Political economy is the science of wealth."

The law of supply and demand, the most indisputable ever formulated by political economy, is one which concerns the apportionment of wealth rather than its production.

Now let us turn to the other side.

Those who look on themselves as forming the ruling classes, commonly speak of the ignorance of workmen; and, in order to promote their economic education, laws are made against associations, against meetings, and against the press; a likely way to instruct the people, truly, to deprive them of the means of information and experience! Their "Socialist Utopias" are spoken of with disdain, they are told that they do not know what they want, and, as a last argument, they are threatened with force—a convenient mode of shortening the discussion.

Those who speak thus are Bachelors of Arts, perhaps, or Licentiates of Law; but is their knowledge of economy necessarily any better than the workman's?

A knowledge of Latin does not make an astronomer, nor a knowledge of Greek roots a chemist; and, to be an economist, it is not enough to be what is called in polite society "a well-informed person."

It is a very just remark of Herbert Spencer's,[2] that, as regards economic science, the ignorance of ignorant people, and the ignorance of people who are called well-informed, is just about equal. "There is no connection between the ability to parse a sentence, and a clear understanding of the causes that determine the rate of wages. . . . By kings, peers, members of Parliament, mostly brought up at Universities, trade had been hampered by protections, prohibitions, and bounties. . . . Yet of all the highly-educated throughout the nation during these centuries, scarcely a man saw how mischievous such appliances were. Not from one who devoted himself to the most approved studies came the work which set politicians right on these points, but from one who left college without a degree, and prosecuted inquiries which the established education ignored, Adam Smith. . . . In recent days those who have most clearly understood the truths he enunciated, and by persevering exposition have converted the nation to their views,

---

[1] Conf. *La République du Travail*, 20th April, 1879.
[2] *Political Essays: Parliamentary Reform.*

have not been graduates of Universities. While, contrariwise, those who have passed through the prescribed curriculum, have commonly been the most bitter and obstinate opponents of the changes dictated by politico-economical science. . . . In all this important direction right legislation was urged by men deficient in the so-called best education; and was resisted by the great majority of men who had received this so-called best education!"

This ignorance of economic questions on the part of politicians is still more striking in France than in England.

In 1848 there were four chairs of political economy in France. In England they were already numerous. The great Universities have their professors of political economy, and extend their courses of lectures all over the country.[1] In France, the lectures on political economy given in the Faculties of Law are, for the most part, utterly inadequate. And where else are there any given? and by whom?

Our French statesmen, far from being troubled at this ignorance, plume themselves on it. It is the old story; the grapes are sour. And then, to make up for it, they join with the Utopists in holding the economists responsible for the difficulties in which they find themselves.

The most intelligent assemblies are not free from this error. Dupont (of Nemours) wrote to J. B. Say, "As soon as a question of commerce or finance arises in the Assembly, they always begin with some violent invective against the economists." The habit has not been lost. Political financiers, who concern themselves very little with augmenting the general wealth, and very much with serving private interests, find no contempt too great for the economists. M. Claude (of the Vosges) has not hesitated to make this solemn declaration: "In political economy there are no principles, but only interests." M. Thiers' sarcasms on this "tedious literature" were inexhaustible.

The attacks of Utopists and Conservatives only serve to show their ignorance, not only of economic science, but also of the aim and method of science itself.

It is not the astronomer's business to consider whether it would be better if the sun were nearer or farther from the earth, or if he turned round her, instead of her turning round him. Nor is it the chemist's business to consider whether carbonic acid and carbonic oxide are noxious gases that ought not to exist. It has never been thought desirable to make Newton responsible for tiles falling on people's heads.

Economists, however, are held answerable for the laws which

[1] My friend James Stuart, Professor of Mechanics at Trinity College, Cambridge, has organised lectures on political economy, with syllabus and examinations, in almost all the manufacturing towns in England.

they discover. Because they have discovered them, they are supposed to have created and invented them, in order to enjoy the satisfaction of aggravating the sufferings of the poor, or of annoying the parasites who regard their privileges as prescriptive rights.

Their fate is that of all who tell unpleasant truths; people bear a grudge against them for their frankness. The position of sincere economists is the more difficult, because they are placed between two opposite classes of prejudices. We give two examples.

1st. The law of Malthus. It is false, as I shall easily show further on; but he thought it true. This law sums itself up into this: population increases in geometrical progression—1, 2, 4, 8, 16, etc., while production increases in arithmetical progression—1, 2, 3, 4, 5, etc.

If this law were true, it must be received as such; but without considering whether it is right or wrong, many people make Malthus out a monster, an ogre, an apostle of infanticide, and his name is held in abhorrence.

It is true that Malthus gave certain directions as to the application of his law; but if his law were true, we could not do better than follow them.

2nd. The economists have destroyed the notion of the balance of trade, and demanded free trade. Many large manufacturers, who treat workmen who ask for State protection as Socialists and Anarchists, demand in their turn the levying of prohibitory duties on foreign articles similar to those they produce. They admit the operation of economic laws when it is in their favour, but oppose it when it tells against them. Thus the economists stand between two fires. Most people are still possessed with the idea of a social alchemy; they think that the economist must have the secret of making gold, of creating wealth. If he modestly replies, that such is not his business, and refuses to occupy himself with these chimeras, he is charged with egoism, and held responsible for all the ills inherent in our nature. There is nothing left for the economists but to adopt as their motto these words of La Mettrie, " Write as though thou wert alone in the universe, and hadst nothing to fear from the jealousy and prejudice of mankind; else thou wilt assuredly miss thine aim."[1]

And in applying this maxim, they must bear in mind the rule given by Benjamin Constant, "A principle admitted to be true must not be abandoned, whatever may be its apparent danger."

Nearly every great step in the progress of science or art has been the complete subversion of what was before believed. I will give only a few instances. Science has advanced only by substituting the inductive method for the scholastic, which was the exact opposite.

[1] Preface to his *Œuvres Philosophiques*

It was long believed that science consisted in seeking the why; it only began to have a well-defined existence when it confined itself to seeking the how. Mankind thought for ages that the earth was flat, and the heavens round, and the earth motionless, and the sun turning round her. Science has proved just the contrary.

Let us take another subject. It is one of the glories of Voltaire to have substituted for the history of Providence the history of mankind, and to have shown that the golden age lies, not behind us, but before. We might give similar instances in all classes of knowledge.

With regard to economics, Montaigne did but give expression to a general prejudice, when he said, "There is no gain to one, without loss to another." Many still hold this to be true; economic science has proved it false.

Whenever our imports exceed our exports, we still hear it said, "The balance of trade is against us." Now economic science proved nearly a century ago that the wealth of a nation only grows while the balance of trade is against it.

At the present day many economists and most financiers think that commercial crises are owing to over-production. We shall see that they are due to over-consumption.

Most publicists who have turned their attention to fiscal questions have thought, up to the present time, that the best system of levying taxes is to tap the revenues of a country at the point where they take the shape of articles of consumption. M. Menier has proved that they must be tapped at their source, which is capital.

These examples will suffice to show that progress in economic science for the most part implies the subversion of existing prejudices. But these prejudices are far-sighted enough to understand, that each new economic law, as it is evolved, will receive applications which will not only disturb erroneous ideas, but also interfere with certain interests; there is, therefore, against every fresh economic truth, a coalition of prejudices and interests. In order to triumph over this coalition, it must be enunciated with force and clearness; but the greater the force and clearness of the enunciation, the more terrified will be the outcry against it.

Still, those who seek the truth alone have one satisfaction, and it is this. Their assailants always rely in their attacks on the very truths they have demonstrated. If you try to lessen or restrict competition for your private benefit, you are not denying the truth of an economic law; you are only trying to turn it to your own advantage.

There are others, equally numerous, who will say to you, "That is good in theory, but bad in practice;" and who oppose these terms one to the other; as if all practice were not the result of theory! Only, those who call themselves "practical people" usually act according to some unconscious and inconsequent theory, of which they perceive only fragments.

In mechanics also, we have theory and practice, but no mechanician would think of saying, "I shall avail myself of a practice at variance with theory." On the contrary, is it not his aim, by polish of surface and accuracy of bearings, to make his machine as nearly as possible theoretically perfect? Are there two systems of chemistry or physics, one practical and the other theoretical?

If we say to these practical people, "You assert that the effect is not to be traced to its cause, that all observation of the different data of a problem is to be avoided, and that half its co-efficients may be disregarded with impunity," they will of course repudiate any such idea, and yet, this is just what their protests against theory amount to.

In the beginning, arbitrary acts and despotic will alone were recognised; later on, laws were sought for in the physical as in the social world; it is now high time to formulate these laws. "Our acts," says Mr. Brassey[1]—himself a practical man, "have outstripped our knowledge and impede our progress. We must generalise them, and put them in order."

In economic science, as in all others, we have to deal with entities. Prejudice has taken this form in practice as in theory, and it has come to this, that we fight as much over words as over things.

In short, the great difficulty to be overcome is the confusion which always exists between incidental and permanent interests.

Economic science is charged with never having set the whole question at rest. But it is the same with all sciences. They solve one question, only to put another.

No doubt economic science is still very imperfect; yet no one will say that the application of it has impoverished the people, or that its object has been to increase their burdens, to check the distribution of raw material and products, to diminish the public wealth, or to encourage smuggling. Moreover, the men who call themselves practical, while they denounce and abuse the consequences of its teaching, are compelled to bow before them.

M. de Tocqueville has related, not altogether with approval, the great part played by the economists in the French Revolution.[2] "These economists have left less conspicuous traces in history than the French philosophers; perhaps they contributed less to the approach of the Revolution; yet I think that the true character of the Revolution may best be studied in their works. The French philosophers confined themselves for the most part to very general

---

[1] *Work and Wages*, p. 8.
[2] *The State of Society in France before the Revolution*, by A. de Tocqueville, translated by H. Reeve.

and very abstract opinions on government; the economist without abandoning theory, clung more closely to facts. The former said what might be thought; the latter sometimes pointed out what might be done. All the institutions which the Revolution was about to annihilate for ever were the peculiar objects of their attacks; none found favour in their sight. All the institutions, on the contrary, which may be regarded as the product of the Revolution, were announced beforehand by these economical writers, and ardently recommended. There is hardly one of these institutions of which the germ may not be discovered in some of their writings; and those writings may be said to contain all that is most substantial in the Revolution itself. . . .

"Yet these were men, for the most part, of gentle and peaceful lives, worthy persons, upright magistrates, able administrators; but the peculiar spirit of their task bore them onwards.

"The past was to these economists a subject of endless contempt. 'This nation has been governed for centuries on false principles,' said Lebronne; 'everything seems to have been done by haphazard.' Starting from this notion, they set to work; no institution was so ancient or so well-established in the history of France that they hesitated to demand its suppression, from the moment that it incommoded them or deranged the symmetry of their plans. One of these writers proposed to obliterate at once all the ancient territorial divisions of the kingdom, and to change all the names of the provinces, forty years before the Constituent Assembly executed this scheme.

"They had already conceived the idea of all the social and administrative reforms which the Revolution has accomplished."

Herbert Spencer, speaking from another point of view, says without exaggeration,[1] "Adam Smith, from his chimney-corner, dictated greater changes than prime ministers do. A General Thompson who forges the weapons with which the Anti-Corn-Law battle is fought—a Cobden and a Bright who add to and wield them, forward civilisation much more than those who hold sceptres. Repugnant as the fact may be to statesmen, it is yet one which cannot be gainsayed. Whoever, to the great effects already produced by Free-trade, joins the far greater effects that will be hereafter produced, not only on ourselves, but on all the other nations who must adopt our policy, must see that the revolution initiated by these men is far wider than has been initiated by any potentate of modern times. As Mr. Carlyle very well knows, those who elaborate new truths and teach them to their fellows, are now-a-days the real rulers—'the unacknowledged legislators'—the virtual kings. From afar off, those who sit on thrones and form cabinets are perceived to be but the servants of such."

[1] *Political Essays*, "Representative Government."

Economists have even been taunted with their want of practical success. "You, who treat of the science of wealth, have you been able to turn it to your own advantage?" Figaro answered long ago, "We need not own things in order to talk about them."

We are in a railway train. How many of us understand the mechanism of the engine that drags us along? The fireman who feeds it could not take it to pieces. The driver, who knows that raising a particular lever or opening a particular tap will stop or start his engine, or send it backwards, is often ignorant of the physical and mechanical laws he applies, while the man of science, who, from the depths of his laboratory, can foretell the exact results produced, would be much perplexed if he had the train to drive.

The little grocer and the great manufacturer, the petty moneychanger and the great financier, lose, gain, buy, sell, and speculate, without taking account of what it is they are doing; they succeed or fail without so much as knowing what wealth is, any more than M. Jourdain knew that he was talking prose. Most of them act by instinct,—that is to say, by incomplete reasoning. They could not express their reasons, because they have never analysed them. We see how confused their replies are when they are called upon to give evidence. The masters of political economy, those who have the decisive influence which De Tocqueville and Herbert Spencer exert, are not Rothschilds; it is a surgeon like Quesnay, a solitary professor like Adam Smith, a journalist like J. B. Say or Charles Dunoyer, or a man who has sacrificed his own to the public interest, like Cobden, who ruined himself twice over, and was only saved by public subscriptions of £70,000 and £40,000. Bentham himself, who has exercised so immense an influence on the England of the nineteenth century, had no place on the Treasury bench.

CHAPTER II.

THE MATERIALS OF ECONOMIC SCIENCE.

It is useless to deny that the application of scientific method to economic science, presenting, as it does, the greatest difficulties, has often been achieved, even by the masters of political economy, with little skill, and under the influence of preconceived ideas. There are more sources of error in economic science than in any other. J. B. Say, for instance, is wrong in saying "The component parts of Society are not the result of artificial organisation, but of natural structure." At the present moment they are the result of both. The ideal pursued in the application of political economy is to substitute a structure based on natural laws for a structure which, up to the present time, has been distorting and violating those laws in order to benefit some at the expense of others. You make a reservoir on a hill-top, and so prevent the water from flowing down into the valley; you do not thereby violate natural laws; but you apply them in order to arrive at an artificial result. It is thus that governments and peoples have understood the application of economic laws. They have everywhere set up barriers to hinder the circulation of utilities.

When Quesnay, following De Gournay, repeated the formula "Laissez faire, laissez passer," it meant, "Respect natural law. Do not try to disturb the natural order of the production and distribution of wealth. It is the first formula of an art which, renouncing *à priori* reasoning, has learnt to confine itself to the application of existing laws.

I admit that some economists, with the best intentions, have come to it with prepossessions foreign to the object of the science itself. Instead of seeking truth, they have tried to establish theories. Bastiat, for instance, wrote his "Harmonies économiques" in answer to Proudhon's "Contradictions économiques." "In this work," he said, "I have attempted to show the harmony of the laws of Providence which regulate human society." He endeavours to justify Providence against the reproaches of malcontents by proving that all is for the best, in the best of all possible worlds. Here Bastiat is but a disciple of Pangloss. It reminds one of Sforza's ironical saying, "How marvellously my cousin Charles VIII. and I agree! We both want the same thing—Milan!"

But have the physicists, the chemists, the physiologists, never made similar declarations? Have they never mixed up theological prejudice with scientific research? It seems to us that it was not as a physiologist pure and simple that M. Pasteur combated the theory of spontaneous generation; he combated it also in the name of morals and religion. Providence is not yet expelled from the Académie des Sciences; and M. de Coste showed some courage when, wishing to conciliate all opinions, he rendered homage "to eternal matter and its eternal Author." It is true that economists have not all been free from prejudice, bias, and passion; but have other men of science been always free from them? Their errors tell against the men, not against the science. We should study them for our warning; and so much the more carefully, as the investigation of economical questions is open to still greater chances of error.

It must also be confessed that since the great works of Adam Smith and J. B. Say, there has been a pause in political economy. Far be it from me to deny the value of a number of excellent works which have been written in France and in England; but they have been too often but paraphrases or commentaries on the works of the masters. They lose themselves in subtle refinements, and have thus fallen into an economic conventionalism, instead of acquiring fresh vigour by observation.

What, then, are the materials which the economist has at his disposal, and what is their value?

The facts of history? Shall we go back to the estimate made by order of Charles VII., in which France, which at that time comprised some 15,000 square leagues, is credited with 1,700,000 cities, towns, and villages? In England there is the same uncertainty. Edward III. obtained from Parliament in 1340 a subsidy of £50,000 sterling. It was reckoned that this sum, divided among the parishes, would average £1 2s. 4d. per parish. Each parish actually paid £5 16s. For, instead of 45,000 parishes, there were only about 9,000—one-fifth of the number! The error was repeated in 1775. In the reign of George III., the House of Commons having rated each parish at £1 2s., it was thought that the sum total would amount to £50,000. It was afterwards found that there had been a mistake of four-fifths!

It is on Statistics that political economy must depend for the greater part of the materials for its work. According to Achenwall, who seems to have been the first to use the word in Germany (1749), "the entire body of all that is really noteworthy in a State forms its constitution in the most general sense of the word; and statistics are the summary of the constitution of one or more States."

Since then the meaning of the word has become more restricted. "Statistics," says Berry, "essentially consist in the methodical enumeration of varying elements, of which they determine the mean."

In reality, statistics are simply the record of certain phenomena. J. B. Say truly says, that it is practically impossible to speak of statistics without adding the limitation "in such a place" or "at such a time."

According to M. Moreau de Jonnès, the science of statistics consists in making the greatest possible number of similar observations and taking the average of the numbers obtained. According to M. Guillard, it is "the science which is composed of all such observations as are capable of being reduced to an average numerically expressed."

But what are the questions which can properly be dealt with by statistics? Nine congresses of statisticians have never yet been able to decide.

No statistics are worth anything unless they are based on large numbers. Quetelet goes so far as to say that "the accuracy of the results varies as the square root of the number of observations;" so that the degree of accuracy is to the number of observations as 1, 2, 3, 4, etc., to 1, 4, 9, 16, etc. He ascertained this fact by a ballot of black and white balls. There is a tendency among some statisticians to use averages a little too much. Michelet asked Moreau de Jonnès for a description of the battle of the 10th of August, 1792, of which he had been a witness. The statistician gave the numbers of those killed by cannon, by gunshot, and by the sword, and added " Average, x,"—giving the figure.

Averages are all very well; but how are we to know the limits of variation of the figures on which they are based?

We take the average price of grain for ten years. One of those years may have been a year of actual famine, and yet the average may have been no higher than usual. Look at the averages of French commerce for the years 1867–1876. Who would ever have guessed from this the frightful disasters of 1870?

In 1856 the Minister of Public Works asked the railway companies what were the hours of work of their drivers and stokers. The averages were given him. In 1865 the companies were called upon, in a fresh circular, to give not only the average but also the maximum. They evaded the question, in order to avoid confessing that there were maxima of 18, 24, and even 38 hours!

Averages do not take everything into account. Yet people who are not accustomed to study these questions say, "Look at the figures! I go by the figures," as if there were nothing more to be said. They assert the infallibility of figures, forgetting that they are mere signs without any intrinsic value of their own. They ought to ask "What lies beneath them? Who groups them? What phenomena have really determined them?"

The compilers of statistics have, so far, generally belonged to one of two classes. Either they have been mere clerks, to whom the work has been a weariness, and who have consequently done it hap-hazard, troubling themselves very little about checking and verifying the materials collected, or even correcting the misprints and gross arithmetical errors which catch the eye of every one who has the misfortune to consult official documents; or else they have been interested persons who, for the purpose of proving something or other, have had recourse to the art of manipulating figures.

It was once discovered that the increase of population in France was at its highest between 1802 and 1806.[1] In the same volume of the "*Annuaire du bureau des longitudes*," it is perplexing to find that the average length of life in France is at the same time thirty-six years, and thirty-nine years seven months.

We are taught, at the most rudimentary stage of arithmetic, that only like things can be added together. Yet in statistics we often find the tonnage of sailing vessels and that of steamships added together, though one of the latter would represent something like four of the former.

---

[1] See Guillard, *Eléments de Statistique Humaine*, p. xvi.

How are the agricultural statistics made up? What value is it possible to assign to them, when so many cultivators do not know the exact quantity of their crops themselves? Again, in comparing the average prices of wheat per annum, it is necessary to know whether they are calculated for the ordinary year or for the agricultural year, which is reckoned from the 1st of August to the 31st of July.

Statistics are useless unless the conditions are constant. But the conditions—often from quite unavoidable circumstances—almost always vary. For instance, in consulting the statistics of the foreign commerce of France, we must, if we are to form a correct estimate, take into consideration the increase of territory in 1859, and the decrease of territory in 1870. Again, the advance in articles of commerce is reckoned by millions of francs. But the value of these articles varies, and if we are to have an accurate estimate, we must take these variations into account. This little consideration is for the most part overlooked. M. Keller, in a great agricultural speech on the 14th of February, 1880, showed in his own argument what consequences may be entailed by the neglect of such considerations. "There has been a great loss on silks," he said, "since 1860. This loss now amounts to 250,000,000 francs. There is a loss of about 100,000,000 francs on the exportation of wines and brandies." Now, on examining the actual quantities, this is what we find: in 1857 the exportation of wines and brandies amounted to 2,460,000 hectolitres; in 1876 it reached 3,245,000 hectolitres. In 1859 the hectolitre was reckoned at 104 francs; in 1876 at 76 francs only. The same with silk: in 1859 it amounted to 146 francs per kilogramme; in 1876 to 105 francs only. For ribbons, the estimate for 1879 was 178 francs; and for 1876, 111 francs. Taking into account the difference of prices, the amount of our exports must be raised by more than 500,000,000 francs. Besides, the figures are not always made up in the same way. In 1863 the cost of packing was deducted from the estimate, which reduced it by about twenty per cent.

A table is drawn up with the view of proving a certain point, and it appears to prove it. The unwary admit the evidence without question. The sceptic, who has learnt by experience to distrust statistics, says, "Let us see what lies beneath these figures, and whether this result is not due to quite other causes than those to which it is generally attributed." And he is seldom wrong. I will cite but one example. The English Admiralty published tables to show that where the Contagious Diseases Acts have been put in force the diseases to which they relate have diminished. All at once, from the beginning of 1873, a very noticeable diminution began to bo observed. The partisans of the Acts were triumphant. "See how the Acts have diminished disease!" they said. Not in the least. What the figures proved was not a diminution, but only a dissimulation of disease. For in that year they had adopted the ingenious method of stopping the pay of soldiers and sailors who confessed themselves diseased.

Suppose we show those gentlemen who believe in nothing but figures the following table, which gives the number of houses and the population of a certain town :—

1801	16,508 houses	128,833 inhabitants.
1861	13,298 ,,	112,063 ,,
1871	7,000 ,,	74,732 ,,

"The place is going to ruin," they would say. Not exactly, for the table refers to the city of London, which can hardly be supposed to be going to ruin. We must look not only at the figures, but at what lies beneath them. Whence comes this apparent decadence of the city of London? It comes from the fact that public buildings, railway stations, banks, and offices of every description have been erected, that wide streets have been opened and the means of communication improved, so that more than two thousand houses, full of noise and motion during the day, are deserted at night. The greater the amount of business in the city the fewer are its inhabitants; and while the number of freemen possessing the city franchise is ever on the increase, the number of residents is as constantly decreasing.

Figures, then, assuming that they are accurate, and that the conditions on which they are based remain invariable, may indicate certain phenomena, but they do not indicate the causes of those phenomena. They must be made to speak; "we must open their mouths," as Herr Rümelin says, with German boldness of metaphor.

As a warm partisan of the use of diagrams, I am surprised that they have not become more common since Playfair applied them, in 1789, to the phenomena of economics. I have myself used them in popular lectures and scientific demonstrations; and I use them here, to make certain demonstrations more striking and evident, and to give the reader a better grasp of certain proportions. But it must be remembered that the expression of relative quantities by relative lengths does not make the statement itself any the more accurate; it only expresses it in a particular manner.

Diagrams have in some cases the further advantage of indicating the maxima and minima as well as the average, thus giving a complete view of all the elements of the question, and showing at a glance how the average has been obtained.

This is the extent of their functions. It is a misuse of language to speak of their application to political economy or statistics as "the diagrammatic method."

The physiologists have sphygmographs for registering pulsation, pneumographs for registering respiration, and myographs for registering muscular action; the meteorologists have self-registering rain-gauges; the physicists register the intensity of electric currents by means of the rheograph; but the statistician has no such means for the mechanical registration of phenomena. Our diagrams only serve to show more clearly relations which might be established, though less plainly and easily, by long demonstrations; but we cannot make experiments like the physiologist; we have to take the facts as they come, and to content ourselves with the meagre information too often given by indolent officials or by politicians interested in falsifying it.

As to Committees of Inquiry, they are no doubt admirable things, so long as you take them for what they are worth. Official inquiries never can come to anything. How is the inferior to put himself in opposition to his superior? Unless he is dominated by a passion which throws suspicion on his evidence, it would take courage of the most difficult kind to venture to tell the truth in the face of failure, suffering, and perhaps prospective ruin. We cannot expect every man to be a hero.

As to Government inquiries, we know them well. When you see an inquiry set on foot by the Ministry, or by some department of the public service, you know pretty well what the object is. They want to prove that all is going well in the best of governments. If, notwithstanding every effort, the inquiry goes to prove just the contrary, nothing is easier than to break it off on the ground that it is disorganising the service. I will cite but one case, because it was so flagrant that it upset a minister—the inquiry into the Prefecture of Police, commenced by M. Gigot as a sop to public opinion, and broken off by M. de Marcère because it proved just what it was desirable not to reveal. A shorthand writer was present at its sittings; but sure I am that its proceedings will never be published.

It is the same with economical inquiries. The committee charged with the revision of the German customs tariffs was presided over by Herr von Varnbühler, who, not caring to fall foul of Prince Bismarck, assigned the subjects for reports in such a manner that those of least importance were entrusted to the free-traders, while the more important were reserved for the Protectionists. In France, the Chamber of Deputies appointed a committee to examine the general customs tariff. The persons chosen to serve on it were manufacturers and persons representing large industrial constituencies. The persons interrogated by them were the representatives of these industries. Their evidence came to this: that they met with competition from abroad, and that they would rather be without it. Whereupon the committee, some of whom were in exactly the same position, while others had influential constituents similarly involved, declared that the interest of the country demanded the suppression of foreign competition, and the granting of privileges to certain native producers. This they call protecting the national labour. And then simple-minded people say, "These are practical men; they know what they are about."

Quite so. But then there is nobody more dangerous than the practical man. He sees nothing but his own immediate interest, which is, in this case, to get the duty raised so as to benefit by the difference. He sees that every rise in the tariff is a net gain to him, the amount of which he can approximately calculate. Do not demand so much of his self-denial as to look a little farther and inquire how these gains are to be reconciled with the general interest!

But, further, those very men who, like Dickens' hero in "Hard Times," ask so freely for facts, commonly judge according to preconceived theories. England is the very home of Committees of Inquiry, and nowhere, I think, are they carried out with more entire good faith or a sincerer desire to discover the truth. Here is Herbert Spencer's estimate of them:—[1]

"Before making or altering a law, it is the custom to appoint a committee of inquiry, who send for men able to give information concerning the matter in hand, and ask them some thousands of questions. These questions and the answers given to them, are printed in large books and distributed among the members of the Houses of Parliament, and I was told that they spent about £100,000 a year in thus collecting and distributing evidence. Nevertheless, it appeared to me that the ministers and representatives of the English people, pertinaciously adhere to theories long ago disproved by the most conspicuous facts. They pay great attention to petty details of evidence, but of large truths they are quite regardless. Thus, the experience of age after age has shown that their State management is almost invariably bad. The national estates are so miserably administered as often to bring loss instead of gain. The Government ship-yards are uniformly extravagant and inefficient. The judicial system works so ill, that most citizens will submit to serious losses rather than run risks of being ruined by lawsuits. Countless facts prove the Government to be the worst owner, the worst manufacturer, the worst trader: in fact, the worst manager, be the thing managed what it may. But though the evidence of this is abundant and conclusive—though during a recent war the bunglings of officials were as glaring and multitudinous as ever; yet the belief that any proposed duties will be satisfactorily discharged by a new public department appointed to them, seems not a whit the weaker. Legislators, thinking themselves practical, cling to the theory of an officially regulated society, spite of overwhelming evidence that official regulation perpetually fails.

"Nay, indeed, the belief seems to gain strength among these fact-loving English statesmen; notwithstanding the facts are against it. Proposals for State control over this and the other, have been of late more rife than ever. . . . Suppose the shareholders in a railway company were to elect, as members of their board of directors, the secretary, engineer, superintendent, and traffic-

---

[1] Essay on Representative Government.

manager, and others such, should we not be astonished at their stupidity? Should we not prophesy that the private advantage of officials would frequently over-ride the welfare of the company?"

Tell all these truths in a committee of the Chamber charged with nominating a commissioner of customs, and see what great eyes they will make at you, and how impossible they will find it to understand you.

But setting aside human nature, and supposing that every man, once made a deputy and put on a commission, will sacrifice his own interests to those of his country, still there is one thing more to be said; the specialist sees nothing but his own speciality.

Fix your eye on the field of a microscope. You will see very interesting things quite imperceptible to the naked eye; but then you will not see a very long way round.

CHAPTER III.

ECONOMIC PSYCHOLOGY.

ANOTHER difficulty in the application of method in economic science, is the pyschological question.

Whatever the Catheder-Socialisten may maintain, the study of political economy cannot be limited to one nation. We might as well say that natural phenomena could be limited to one nation, and that the pressure of the air did not act on the barometer in the same way in Germany as in England. Still, man himself is not everywhere the same, and a native of Tierra del Fuego does not think like a West European of the nineteenth century.

I do not dispute that there are in our centres of civilisation men and women whose intellectual development is far superior to the more primitive types of human civilisation, nor do I say with Voltaire that "differences are external, man is everywhere man." On the contrary, the differences are considerable, the human type is susceptible of the widest variation. And yet Voltaire is not wholly wrong.

Mr. Francis Galton took the likenesses of six people on one negative, each of whom sat for only one-sixth of the time necessary for taking a single portrait. The features common to two or more of them came out with exaggerated clearness, the rest were more or less dimly indicated. He then threw several distinct portraits on the same screen, by means of magic lanterns, in such a manner that they were exactly superposed one on another. The common features came out so strongly, that the rest disappeared; the image obtained was extremely clear. He tried the experiment with faces of different races, and a general human type was obtained.

This experiment substantiates an undeniable truth. The organisation is the same in all men, their differences arise from a more or less advanced development. Now this similarity of organisation implies similarity of wants. Every man needs food and drink, fears the inclemency of the seasons, is solicited by appetites, has selfish and unselfish feelings of varying intensity, and, lastly, has that instinct of self-preservation, without which he would soon perish.

This instinct of self-preservation, this need of development common to all organised beings, and which constitutes the power of resistance in the struggle for existence, is called in man, *egoism*.

M. Held answers that man is not egoistic. If he were not, he would long ago have ceased to be. M. Held adds that man does not always know his best interests. Granted; but the mistaken form of the wish does not alter its egoistic nature. Economic science, which deals, not with the morality of motives, but with their effects as productive or destructive agents, necessarily regards man as a purely egoistic being, notwithstanding the protest of Lange, who takes exception to the view as materialistic.

But we are told that this conception is false, and that Adam Smith was right in regarding sympathy as a motive equal to self-interest. Is there not in man, alongside of his selfishness, some unselfishness? Does he never think of anything but buying, selling, and balancing advantages, and even then does he always consult his own interest as a buyer? Is he not affected by other influences, such as idleness, habit, affection, vanity, or vices such as drunkenness? Is not idleness, in the eyes of a Neapolitan, a higher utility than comfort, and does not the Irishman sacrifice future comfort to the present enjoyment of gossiping, sauntering, and drinking, while the Scotchman is happier at work than at rest? In studying commercial crises, must you not take into account the apathy, the love of routine, which hinders the re-investment of capital? On the other hand, look at the history of railways in England—a country which is generally supposed to know its multiplication table. Did they not have the railway mania there, which swallowed up such a mass of capital? How are you going to explain all these manias for loans to bankrupt States which have swallowed up millions paid down on 'Change in London and Paris, while *bonâ-fide* industries in England and France were wanting investors? or by what economic law will you account for the gaming instinct which introduces such uncertainties into economic relations?

Even among manufacturers, bankers, men whose sole object in life seems to be to make money, you will find, as among other men, that what is usually looked upon as the chief motive of human action is in truth but a secondary one. Does the great manufacturer, does the banker, worth his millions, risk his fortunes and his peace of mind in new enterprises, simply in order to gain fresh thousands? With the one, it is an irrepressible restlessness of activity, with the other it is the passion of speculation, and with all it is a motive infinitely higher than the desire to gain money for its own sake. Again, do you count for nothing the influence of fashion, which can ruin or create a manufacture at a stroke, or monomanias for knick-knacks or pictures, which set a fictitious value on objects neglected yesterday, and forgotten to-morrow?

All this is true; but, none the less, acquisition is a permanent and universal law of human nature. War, art, science, as well as labour and commerce, are but different expressions of this need, which is itself the result of the instinct of self-preservation. Its intensity may vary with the individual and his surroundings. Each is satisfied more or less easily, sets his ideal higher or lower, makes greater or less efforts. The most capable of progress are those in whom the satisfaction of one desire is the birth of another.

Ricardo has pointed out the other economic motive of man; he is not only eager to acquire, but he wishes to acquire with the least possible trouble. In a word, from the economic point of view, man obeys two impulses—the desire for wealth, and the aversion to labour.

This aversion to labour often puts him to much greater effort and danger than the labour itself would have done. He makes war in order to reap the fruits of others' labour, and to get slaves who may do his own. A bad bargain, perhaps, but the two motives we have just mentioned lie at the bottom of it. At another stage of civilisation, this aversion to labour impels him to invent machines, to gain by saving, without labour, the possibility of enjoying accumulated wealth.

In a word, every want is created by a wish. Utility is an essentially subjective phenomenon. The pursuit of utility shows itself in objective phenomena; and it is with these phenomena that economic science has to deal.

Utility being subjective, there is no need to inquire, with Lange, whether man is always capable of discerning his true interest. I think a thing is useful to me, and therefore it is so. Economic science is essentially unmoral. It has not to concern itself with the quality of human sentiments and needs and passions. It regards with equal impartiality the passion of the black man for glass beads, and of the white man for diamonds. It admits music as a utility, because many people like the emotion it stirs up in them. Every desire is a want, and everything that satisfies a want is a utility. *Economic science deals with the laws which govern the efforts of man in the pursuit of utility.*

It takes account, indeed, of the friction, the obstacles, the apparent contradictions which have been introduced into the application of these laws by contradictory habits, passions, and motives; but with these psychological phenomena themselves it does not concern itself in the very least.

CHAPTER IV.

DEFINITIONS.

WE proceed to determine the phenomena which it is the object of economic science to study.

Few economists have followed Voltaire's advice, "Define your terms." Still, in order to be understood, it is necessary to have a common language!

My definitions will not always agree with those generally accepted; an author has a right to use his terms as he pleases, only he must comply with two conditions, he must offer definitions not less, but more precise than those previously received, and he must always use them strictly in the sense he has assigned to them.

Unfortunately, the terms which form as it were the keystone of Economic Science are used in very different senses. Sometimes their meaning varies in the same author. This is so with Adam Smith. J. B. Say attempted a remedy, but some of his definitions are extremely questionable. Malthus observed the want of precise definition. "There seems to be little agreement," says he, "on the meaning to be given to the terms wealth, capital, productive labour, and value, or on what is to be understood by real wages, profit, labour, etc." He himself wrote a long monograph on *Definitions in Political Economy*, in the course of which he quite forgot his subject.

That man has wants, is a matter of daily observation which hardly needs be insisted on.[1]

A want is a desire to procure enjoyment, and to avoid exertion and suffering.

Nothing is created, nothing is lost—such is the great formula of modern science. Man does not create objects; but, in order to satisfy his wants, he creates utilities.

According to M. Courcelle-Seneuil, who here follows Ricardo, Malthus, and Sismondi, "A want in any economic sense is a desire having for its object the possession and enjoyment of some material thing."[2] But I "want" to be defended by an advocate. Is this not a "want" in an economic sense?

M. Courcelle-Seneuil says again, "All useful material things,

---

[1] See for philosophical analysis of "want," Letourneau, *Phyiologies des Passions, la Sociologie* ; André Lefèvre, *La Philosophie*, pp. 538-540.
[2] *Traité d'Economie Politique*, vol. i., p. 25.

appropriated to the use of man, are wealth." But are not health, strength, and intelligence, a sort of wealth?

Besides natural agents appropriated to the use of man, there are utilities resulting from a certain order established in the relations of the individual, whether with himself or with others. Health is a utility; the public safety is a utility.

According to M. Courcelle-Seneuil's theory, the physician would have no right to his fees, nor those who govern the country to their salaries. It is true that the latter, instead of insuring the public safety, are often the first to endanger it; but the taxes are not paid on that understanding.

M. Courcelle-Seneuil may answer that health and safety are both very material things. I have no objection; only he must define his terms "possession and enjoyment of a material object," so as to cover this somewhat extended meaning.

I need not here inquire how the individual can act on himself. I shall content myself with saying what every one admits, that the object of all education is to increase the power, muscular or intellectual, of the individual.

The tournaments of the Middle Ages were fairs, where the knights came to exhibit their strength and valour. Observe the propriety of the word *valour;* the stronger they were, the greater their value.

At the present time, what are we doing in our literary and scientific meetings, in our art exhibitions, or even in addressing ourselves directly to the public, but exhibiting the value which has accrued to us from our intellectual exertions?

I go one step further. Man finds a utility, not only when he satisfies a want, but also when he saves himself a pain. Every satisfaction of a desire, every alleviation of a pain, represents a value. MacCulloch,[1] indeed, says that if political economy were to treat of the production or the distribution of everything that is agreeable to man, it would include all other sciences; that the best encyclopædia would then be the best treatise on political economy. Health is a useful and pleasant thing, medicine ought therefore to be inserted in the catalogue of the science of wealth. Civil and religious liberty are eminently useful; political science must therefore be comprehended in the science of wealth. A great actor's playing is agreeable; therefore discussions on the stage must be included; and so on. But MacCulloch has put his point badly. It is not a question of medicine, or dramatic art, of civil or religious liberty, but of their economic effects. The doctor has a value, the actor has a value, civil and religious liberty themselves have a value. No one will deny the economic effects of the revocation of the Edict of Nantes.

[1] "Political Economy," an article published in the supplement to the *Encyclopædia Britannica*.

J. B. Say puts it perfectly.[1] "The industry of a physician, of a public administrator, of a judge or an advocate, satisfies wants so imperative, that without their labours society could not exist. The fruit of their labours is so real, that they are procured at the price of material products." In opposition to the term "material product," he calls the outcome of the physician's industry a "non-material product." The distinction is false, for we cannot create matter itself, and therefore can only create non-material products; or rather there are no products at all, but only utilities; and utilities include all kinds of interchangeable services. These services have an exchange value; they are bought or sold. The physician, for instance, is a contractor for cures.

But Charles Dunoyer[2] has pointed out the contradiction which exists among the majority of authors, who speak of labour which does not embody itself in a material object, as non-productive; and yet who all recognise the utility of the productive result of this so-called non-productive labour. MacCulloch is no exception to this. After the passage I have quoted, he nevertheless, in the same treatise, includes under the name of productive labour all the different kinds of advantages to which he had at first refused that title; and in his *Principles of Political Economy*, he gives the following definition of wealth [3]:—"Wealth designates all articles or products which are necessary, useful, or agreeable to man, and which, at the same time, are endowed with an exchangeable value." "Products," observe, not "material products,"—an error with which Malthus does not fail to reproach him.

J. S. Mill declares that "the skill, the energy, and perseverance of the artisans of a country, are reckoned part of its wealth, no less than their tools and machinery."[4] He defines wealth as "all useful or agreeable things which possess exchangeable value.[5] But, with an inconsequence not uncommon with him, he recurs to the matter to say,[6] "I shall, therefore, in this treatise, when speaking of wealth, understand by it only what is called material wealth, and by productive labour, only those kinds of exertion which produce utilities embodied in material objects."

"Can services be called wealth?" asks M. Courcelle-Seneuil, and he comes to the conclusion that "the idea of wealth everywhere carries with it that of purely material objects."

Let us go back to the origin of the word. With the Germans, *Reich* means power, and *Reichthum*, riches; among the Latins, both

---

[1] *Traité d'Economie Politique*, Book I., chap. xiii.
[2] *Dictionnaire d'Economie Politique*, Art. "Production."
[3] *Principles of Political Economy* (MacCulloch), Part I., p. 5.
[4] *Principles of Political Economy* (Mill), Book I., Chap iii., par. 3.
[5] *Ibid.*, Preliminary Remarks.
[6] *Ibid.*, Book I., Chap. iii., par. 3.

meanings were expressed by the word *opes;* in Spanish, rich and powerful men are alike called *ricos hombres;* while the English word means, first welfare, and then riches.

"Wealth is power," says Hobbes. The two are synonymous. He is rich who, having many services to exchange, can obtain many utilities. The inventor is rich; or the author is rich; and their wealth often shows itself in the most material manner. A people which can render great services to other peoples is rich. Are not the great French physicians, the great French actors, a part of the wealth of the country?

Lord Lauderdale gave a good definition of wealth when he included under the term "all that man desires as likely to be useful or agreeable to him."[1]

It must be understood from henceforth, that *wealth is utility.*

This distinction is important, for we shall see further on to what fantastic conclusions economists have been led who have made it consist in value.

According to them, since natural utilities tend to diminish value, the more a man has at his disposal, the poorer he is, economically speaking.[2] Artificial utilities alone constitute wealth.[3] With a curious application of the doctrine of final causes, they say, "Nature grants freely to men certain utilities which all enjoy equally."[4] "Nature places at the disposal of production, air, sunlight, water; these are unappropriated natural agents."[5]

This is an error; utility exists only in relation to man, it has no meaning apart from him; the term itself implies appropriation.

"Land," J. B. Say says, "is certainly not the only natural agent endowed with productive energy, but it is the only one, or almost the only one, which can be possessed. The water in the rivers and sea, the air, the sun, are likewise productive forces, but fortunately no one can say—'They belong to me; pay me for the services they render you!'"

Again an error; all is appropriated. Is the sunshine of no account in the selling of houses or land, or in the letting of an apartment or a garden? Do not the hotel-keepers of Nice and Pau make it pay? Where would the vineyards be without it? and what do you mean when you speak of a plantation as being well situated? Is not the sea appropriated the whole length of its shores, do not the very vessels appropriate its surface as they pass? Do not its harbours make the wealth of towns? It is so thoroughly appropriated that its appropriation forms the subject of complicated agreements. Look at Newfoundland with its fisheries!

---

[1] An Inquiry into the Nature and Origin of Public Wealth, 1804.
[2] See chap. v., Definition of Value.
[3] See Passy's *Dictionnaire d'Economie Politique,* Art. "Utilités."
[4] *Ibid.*   [5] G. de Molinari, *Cours d'Economic Politique,* vol. i., p. 44.

As to the air, it is appropriated jealously enough in the towns. You prefer a house in an airy situation; and building land varies in value according as it is more or less exposed.

A nation counts its climate among its riches,—and with the more reason, as it often forms the principal item thereof. In defending its territory, the nation defends its sunshine.

The term utility implies the idea of appropriation by means of exchange.

But we spoke just now of health as a utility; is health susceptible of exchange? Certainly. Do you not pay the doctor and the druggist for it? Granted, you say; it has a value for me, but it has no value for any one else, therefore it is not capable of exchange.

Well; I admit that my health has no value for other people, but it has for me; it is a utility which I have so appropriated, that it has become a part of myself. I can buy it, and do buy it every day, and that pretty dear. I can even sell it; for my health forms part of my powers, of which I can lend the use or sell the product.

Exchange does not imply identity, but reciprocity and diversity, of services. Health is a utility to me, and I buy it of the doctor for a sum of money, which is a utility to him.

Man acts in order to procure himself utilities. He even acts in order to procure himself the negation of action—sleep;—for he buys opium.

All action, the object of which is to procure some utility, implies effort more or less severe, more or less deliberate, more or less agreeable. This effort is labour.

Sometimes the object to which the labour is applied is man himself, or rather certain parts of him. The wrestler develops his biceps, the singer his voice, the dancer her legs; those who give themselves to intellectual work of any kind,—mathematicians, accountants, novelists, men of science,—develop their brains. Sometimes it is something external. The labourer tills the ground, the fisherman catches fish, the miner digs coal, and so on.

Labour has for its result, either a change,—physical, chemical, or physiological,—in the condition of matter, or a change of place.

We must here guard against an error into which English economists have fallen, which the Protectionists are always repeating, and which does not seem to offend public opinion. It is this: "All wealth is derived from labour." "Labour constitutes the wealth of a people," said M. de Saint-Cricq, the Minister of Commerce; and the phrase is still dinned into one's ears in every economic discussion.

But if so, wealth should be proportionate to the amount of labour. Now the less fertile the earth, and the ruder our contrivances, the heavier is the labour needed to procure us utilities. Therefore wealth is in inverse proportion to the fertility of the soil and the progress in mechanical arts. The surest way to wealth would be the cultivation of the Sahara or Greenland. M. Cunin-Gridaine, another Minister of Commerce, suggests a machine for increasing, instead of diminishing, manual labour, in order to find employment for the workmen!

Every one is acquainted with Sismondi's hypothesis. He imagines a machine, the handle of which should be placed in the hand of the king or minister, who works it without effort, and it performs the tasks which now take so many millions of men, and the men have nothing to do but look on with folded arms.

Sismondi held that this would be the ruin of the country, and many people think so still, in spite of the economists; so that M. Allain-Targé was not alone in his error when he said, "We are a labouring democracy living by our work. Labour must be defended."[1]

It is a mere confusing of good and ill, pain and pleasure, the means and the end. Labour is an effort having for its object the giving of satisfaction. The effort is the ill, and the satisfaction is the good. Mankind exerts itself to lessen effort and augment satisfaction. This is why, the apologists of labour notwithstanding, it has not ceased to invent machines the purpose of which is to put an end to labour; and every one finds himself the better for them. We do not live by labour, but by the results of labour; our ideal is to procure the maximum of utility with the minimum of effort.

Under whatever form it presents itself, labour is the application of our faculties to the satisfaction of our wants. It may be defined as *the effort necessary for the appropriation of utilities.*

But we may procure utilities possessed by others by giving them other utilities in exchange. The sick man cannot cure himself singlehanded; he buys of the physician the utility of which he is the owner, namely, his skill and science, by the aid of another utility, usually gold. Nobody makes his own coats and shoes. He buys them in exchange for other utilities, of which he is the possessor.

Exchange is the relation of utilities among themselves.

SUMMARY.

Every desire is a want. Everything which conduces to the satisfaction of a want is a utility.

Utility depends upon appropriation.

Wealth is the general mass of utilities.

Man appropriates utilities by his own exertions, or by exchange.

Exchange is the relation of utilities between themselves.

[1] The Chamber of Deputies, Feb. 17, 1880.

CHAPTER V.

VALUE.

WE have now to find a definition of the term "value."

It is not without reason that Bastiat says that "the theory of value is to political economy what numeration is to arithmetic."[1] Professor Perry says, "This word indicates and delimits the sphere of Political Economy." Proudhon calls it the corner-stone of the economic edifice. Stuart Mill is more reserved; but he too says, "The question of value is fundamental."[2] However, after saying "We must begin by settling our phraseology," [3] he omits this fundamental definition.

No other expression in the language of economy has provoked so much discussion. This or that definition has even given rise to disputes as to the question of priority. Nevertheless, the question is so far from being settled, that the late Professor Stanley Jevons declared he would give up the use of the word altogether; but he substituted for it another phrase, "rate of exchange," which he confessed did not satisfy him after all.

Professor Thornton tells the following characteristic anecdote,[4] "Most members of the Political Economy Club must be familiar with an anecdote of Sydney Smith, who, not many months after joining the Club, announced his intention to retire; and, on being asked the reason, replied that his chief motive for joining had been to discover what Value is, but that all he had discovered was, that the rest of the Club knew as little about the matter as he did."

Adam Smith has not given a definition of the word, but has accompanied it with two distinct qualifications which give it two completely opposite meanings.[5] "The word value, it is to be observed, has two different meanings, and sometimes expresses the utility of some particular object, and sometimes the power of purchasing other goods which the possession of that object conveys. The one may be called 'value in use'; the other, 'value in exchange.' The things which have the greatest value in use have frequently little or no value in exchange; and, on the contrary, those which have the greatest value in exchange have frequently little or no value in use."

Stuart Mill remarks on this last sentence,[6] that the word use is there employed, not in the sense in which political economy is con-

---

[1] *Harmonies Economiques*, chap. v.
[2] *Principles of Political Economy*, Book III., chap. i., par. 1.
[3] *Ibid.*, par. 2.
[4] Article in *Contemporary Review*, Oct., 1876, "Cairns on Value."
[5] *Wealth of Nations*, vol. i., p. 36, 5th edition.
[6] *Principles of Political Economy*, Book III., chap. i. par. 2.

cerned with it, but in that other sense in which use is opposed to pleasure.

But Adam Smith's definition is unsound all through.

If the value of a particular object means its utility, then air and water, which are of the greatest utility, should be of the greatest value. Now this is not the case, except under certain circumstances. This contradiction Adam Smith perceives, and introduces the other term, exchange value, which in this case destroys the first, since the two values are often contradictory.

Nevertheless, many economists have put up with this contradiction, and amongst them M. Blanqui. According to him, the distinction established by Adam Smith has the advantage of bringing out the peculiar character of exchange value, the only kind of any importance in business transactions, because it is the product of human labour.

This reasoning is wrong; for we exchange things because they are useful, not because they are the products of human labour. I buy a hill where I can build a windmill. The hill has a value for me, and yet its former owner had spent no labour on its construction.

Ricardo[1] perceived Adam Smith's error clearly enough; but he himself fell into that of Blanqui. Speaking of utility, he says, "This is not the measure of exchange value, although it is essential to it." The reservation was wise; but having made it, he goes on to speak of labour alone as the basis of value. "The value of a commodity," says he, "depends on the amount of labour necessary to its production." Here crops up the error pointed out by J. B. Say. You work thirty years to produce an epic poem. If there is no demand for it, if it is of no use to anybody, it has no value, notwithstanding the amount of labour you have expended on it. There is no value without utility.

Ricardo's error springs from the confusion which we have already pointed out between effort and utility, labour and its result.

In order to avoid the same difficulty, Storch makes value dependent on opinion, and Senior, on rarity.

All these definitions are true in part; but none of them gives the real and precise sense which ought to be attached to the word "value." These economists have seen but one element in value, whereas it is really composed of several.

Value is neither labour, nor utility, nor rarity.

A has great muscular force, which he has developed by exercise. He has a weight to lift. He lifts it unaided, by his own strength; his strength is a utility to him. B is weaker than A. He has the

---

[1] *Principles of Political Economy*, chap. i.

same weight to lift. He cannot lift it alone, and he asks A's help. A's strength, a utility possessed by him, is of value to B.

But B has a fountain, which supplies him with water. This water is a utility to him. A has no water. He says to B, "In exchange for the utility of my strength which I give you, give me water, which has a value for me, as my strength has a value for you." "*Do ut des.*"

In a word, man possesses utilities. The mutual relations of men alone lend value to these utilities.

Traffic is not a thing carried on by nerves and muscles, by air, water, and the other natural forces and agents which serve the use of man; it is a thing carried on between man and man; therefore value is a human relation.

Rossi, who censures Adam Smith's definition, is mistaken in saying, "Value is the relation which exists between things and the wants of man. If a thing is adapted to our needs, there lies its value."[1]

Not so. There lies its utility. Its value is determined by exchange.

B is thirsty. He has water. He pays nothing to nature for quenching his thirst. But A pays for the water he drinks, because it belongs to B.

Adam Smith, Senior, and J. B. Say look on value as a relation between two objects. H. Passy says that value is "a relation of quantity between exchanged products."[2] But why products? Have services and exertions no value?

Value is not a relation between two things; it is a relation between two individuals. Carey defines it thus:[3] "Value is the measure of the resistance to be overcome in order to procure the articles necessary for our wants; that is, the measure of the power of nature over man."

If we were in the position of Robinson Crusoe, this definition would be correct; but Crusoe's position was an exceptional one. He calculated the value of things by the effort it cost him to acquire them; we, on the other hand, calculate the value of things less by the efforts we must make than by the utilities we must give in exchange.

MM. Bastiat, Charles Dunoyer, and R. de Fontenay, having observed these facts, conclude from them that utilities furnished by natural agents have no value. Human services alone have value; and Bastiat sums up the theory in the following formula:—Value is the relation of two interchanged services.

---

[1] *Cours d'Economie Politique*, vol. i., chap. iii.
[2] *Dictionnaire d'Economie Politique.*
[3] *Principles of Social Science*, vol. i., p. 177.

But Bastiat and the non-materialist economists decline to admit that every human service is composed of three things :—
1st. Utilities furnished by nature, as nerves, muscles, brains, air, water, etc. ;
2nd. The effort implied in doing these services ;
3rd. The want of the service on the part of the person served ;—for every service implies a want.

Having thus neglected to analyse the materials of which every service is composed, MM. Bastiat and R. de Fontenay declare that the sole basis of value is the exertion which the service rendered costs or saves ; that value does not attach to the utility of things, but always to that of human services ; that "natural agents can lay claim to nothing of the nature of value in the work of production."[1]

In order to maintain this assertion, Bastiat launches into a series of subtle demonstrations. He says, "I am in want of water, and the spring is a league from the village. I, therefore, take the trouble of going every morning to fetch a supply of water, for it is in water that I find those useful qualities which have the property of alleviating the form of suffering called thirst. Want, effort, satisfaction, all are there. I recognise utility ; but as yet I know nothing of value. But, as my neighbour also goes to the spring every morning, I say to him, "Save me the trouble of the journey ; do me the service of carrying the water for me. Meantime, I will do something for you ; I will teach your child to spell." He sees that this is an advantage for both of us. Next, I say to him, "Your child worries me, I would rather do something else for you ; you shall go on carrying the water for me, and I will give you five sous." If this is agreed on, the economist may say, without fear of mistake, "The service is worth five sous." Later on, my neighbour no longer waits to be asked. He knows by experience that I want the water every day, and he becomes a water-seller. Now we begin to say, "The water is worth five sous." But has the nature of the water really changed ? Has the value, which just now was in the service rendered, become materialized, so as to be incorporated with the water ?"

No ; but Bastiat here supposes the spring to belong to no one, so that the only thing to be paid for is the labour of carrying. But suppose some one appropriated the spring, and imposed a charge on the water taken from it, will not the water itself have a value as a utility, and will not this utility be paid for ?

Bastiat takes another example. "I am walking by the sea-side. I light by chance on a superb diamond. I am now in possession of an article of great value. Why of such value ? Because I am about to confer a great boon on humanity, or because I have

[1] *Harmonies Economiques*, chap. v.

devoted myself to long and hard labour? Neither the one nor the other. Why, then, has this diamond such a value? Because, of course, the person to whom I give it up will think I have done him a great service."

And he winds up by saying, "The value is not in the diamond; it is simply in the services given and received on account of it, and it is fixed by agreement between the contracting parties."

Very good; but if the diamond did not exist, there would be no contracting parties, and no services exchanged. Utility is subjective. It is clearly not in the diamond itself, it is in the attribution of utility to the diamond by certain persons; but this utility is inseparable from the diamond; the service rendered by the person in possession of the diamond is attached to the diamond itself. In the two examples just cited, the term "service" is employed by Bastiat in two different senses; in the first it represents labour, and in the second, demand.

M. R. de Fontenay says, in support of Bastiat's theory,[1] "The high price of Clos-Vougeot has been dinned into our ears. But look at the neighbouring summits of the Côte d'Or, with their piles of greyish chalk and their vines, covered like craters by the heaps of stones, which they have thrown up, one by one, from their bosom. The wine extracted with so much labour from the soil sells at only two or three sous the bottle. Hence it is that Clos-Vougeot is worth six or eight francs. To all who have understood what we have just said, this reply will be final."

It will not be final to the wine-growers, who are much put out by their wine not selling at more than two or three sous the bottle, while that of the neighbouring vineyards realises six or eight francs. What it does prove is, that the same amount of labour produces wholly different results, according to the quality of the natural agents to which it is applied. Are not the physical conditions which give the wine its value of three sous or six francs, absolutely independent of human industry? Since there is this difference in the value of the products, you cannot say that the natural utility of the soil, which is the cause of this difference, has no value.

M. de Fontenay asserts, it is true, that the high price of Clos-Vougeot is the remuneration of the fruitless labour applied to other lands. But if this were true, the other proprietors must profit by it. Now Clos-Vougeot is owned by a particular proprietor, who alone benefits by the utility attaching to the happy situation of that district.

It is clear that the buyer, in paying a high price for the wine of this particular proprietor, takes no account of the fruitless efforts of other people; he never troubles himself about it. Clos-Vougeot is a wine which takes his fancy, and one of which the supply is

---

[1] *Du Revenu Foncier*, p. 257.

limited. The proprietor raises his price, not in proportion to the effort and outlay of the other wine-growers, but according to the offers made him, and the urgency of the demand. It is impossible to separate the utility of the natural agent from the service which it enables man to render.

Let us go a step further. One man is a good worker, but he has an ill-developed brain. He grinds away doggedly, and yet he makes but an indifferent lawyer, or doctor, or artist. He never produces anything of more than ordinary value. Another man is more fortunately endowed; with the same, or even a less, amount of labour, he turns out products of a higher quality, at least in the eyes of the consumers. His brain-power is a birthright for which no credit is due to him, yet its utility has an unquestionable value!

A natural agent can have no value, except under two conditions:
1st. It must be possessed by a human being;
2nd. Another human being must feel the want of it.

In the midst of a desert, air has no value. In a city, every house-owner possesses a certain quantity of air; and this air is felt to be of such value that its enjoyment is assured to him by law.

Electricity distributed through the atmosphere has no value; but a man may construct a battery, disengage the electricity, and, if I want it, sell it me at a given price. This electricity, then, has a value.

Adam Smith distinguishes between value in use and value in exchange, because, says he, "the natural agents most indispensable to life, as the heat of the sun, air, water, are useful, but have no value." For the same reason, Bastiat assumes that the utility inherent in natural agents has no value.

Both these errors spring from want of observation.

Smith and Bastiat, in their country walks, observed that no one contested the enjoyment of the sunshine with them; but Smith ought to have known that when Englishmen pay their fare to Nice, Pau, or Rome, they are paying for the sunlight which they want; and Bastiat ought to have known that if the Médoc district lay under London sunshine, it would never make its fortune in wines, nor sell a few acres for millions of francs.

Again, they hold that water has no value. Yet this question of water-supply is not yet solved for most European towns. It is almost everywhere wanting. Have they never noticed, in reading the Bible, how the water question crops up at every turn? Whence comes the celebrity of Mecca? From the famous wells of Zam-Zam, the wells of Ishmael. In all the Arab legends, in the records of old feuds between tribe and tribe, this question is everywhere prominent. [The importance of the possession is proportionate to its rarity and its utility.]¹

¹ See *Histoire des Prolétaires*, by Yves Guyot and S. Lacroix, vol. i., p. 341, and above, Book I., chap. iv.

Every natural agent, very natural force possessed by one man, and which another man thinks useful to him, has a value.

A man possesses a lock of hair of a woman he loved, and he says, "This souvenir has a great value for me." He is right in adding "for me." He would do still better to say, "a great utility." The souvenir has, in fact, no value, so long as no one else wants it.

M. de Molinari, therefore, was wrong in saying, "Value exists independently of exchange; exchange proves, but does not create it." No. Utility exists independently of exchange; but value is only a relation between the possessors of utilities.

Value, then, should be defined as *the relation of a utility possessed by one person to the need of another person.*[1]

CHAPTER VI.

THE OBJECT OF ECONOMIC SCIENCE.

I will here give my reasons for calling this work "Principles of Economic Science," and not "Principles of Political Economy."

True as it is that the value of words depends on the sense in which they are used, and not on their etymology, it is sometimes useful to recall their derivation.

Economy comes from οἶκος, house, and νόμος, rule. The ancients did not distinguish very closely between the arts and the sciences. Xenophon says, "Economy is a science like medicine, like bronze-founding, like architecture." And he defines it thus, "It is the science by which a man can increase his house." To this noun we prefix a derivative of the word πόλις, city or society; so that, etymologically, Political Economy is simply the art of augmenting the resources, wealth, and fortune of a society.

Art has everywhere preceded science. Science is the ascertaining of the mutual relations of phenomena, while art is the application of these relations to the satisfaction of human wants. Medicine, for instance, is but the application of physiology and biology. The confusion between art and science in the study of economic phenomena is expressed in the phrase *Political Economy*.

This term was used for the first time at the head of an old French treatise published by Mountchrestien de Watteville, in 1615. Quesnay and his friends, although they had taken the name of *Physiocrats*, adopted this word and spread it. Adam Smith took it from them, and used it without examination. He considers[2] that "Political Economy, considered as the science of a statesman or legislator,

---

[1] I first published this definition in 1869.
[2] *Wealth of Nations*, Book IV.

proposes two distinct objects; first, to provide a plentiful revenue or subsistence for the people, or, more properly, to enable them to provide such a revenue or subsistence for themselves; and secondly, to supply the State, or commonwealth, with a revenue sufficient for the public services. It proposes to enrich both the people and the sovereign." Rousseau had given a similar definition of it in the *Encyclopédie*.

J. B. Say makes some reservations. In the very title of his *Traité d'Economie Politique*, he describes its object as being the knowledge of the laws which control the formation, distribution, and consumption of wealth. The second title of his book is, "A Simple Exposition of the Manner in which Wealth is Made, Distributed, and Consumed." In his *Cours d'Economie Politique* he reverts to this definition, and says,[1] "It may be seen, even in this work, that all social interests are comprised within the sphere of this science. Since it has been shown that non-material properties, like personal gifts and acquired faculties, form an integral portion of social wealth, it has also been found that Political Economy, which might seem to have had for its object only material good, embraces the whole social system."

The less advanced a science is, the less defined are its limits. These words of J. B. Say prove how vague his idea of Economic Science still was, and what a confusion existed in his mind between its laws and their application. The same defect is still more marked among the Germans who have occupied themselves with this subject.

M. Cauwès, Professor of Political Economy in the Faculty of Law at Paris, rejects "pure political economy," and wishes to make it a "moral science."[2]

Ricardo and Malthus attempt no definition, and Rossi, while he discusses several, offers none himself.

Stuart Mill defines Political Economy[3] as, "the science which treats of the production and distribution of wealth, so far as they depend upon the laws of human nature."

Mr. Fawcett[4] says: "Political Economy is concerned with those principles which regulate the production, the distribution, and the exchange of wealth."

Senior, to avoid all confusion, says, "The economist must not give a single word of advice; his object is not to recommend one measure, or to dissuade from another, but to establish general principles."

MacCulloch also says, " We may define Political Economy as the

---

[1] *Cours d'Economie Politique*, Considérations Générales, p. 41.
[2] *Cours d'Economie Politique*, vol. i. p. 9.
[3] *Essays on some Unsettled Questions in Political Economy*, p. 133.
[4] *Manual of Political Economy*, p. 4. 5th edition.

science of the laws which govern the production, accumulation, distribution, and consumption of articles or products which are necessary, useful, or agreeable to man, and which possess at the same time an exchangeable value."

MacCulloch himself, however, has mixed up questions of the application of the science with the science itself; and indeed almost all the economists, Stuart Mill included, have committed the same error.

We, for our part, shall begin by considering Economy as a pure science, and seeking the laws which regulate the relations between human wants and the utilities which satisfy them; and we shall afterwards confine ourselves to showing how they have been applied.

M. Courcelle Seneuil drew attention to the necessity of making this distinction, and even proposed to accentuate it by calling the pure science, "Plutology," or the science of wealth, and the applied science "Ergonomy," or the law of labour.

But as these two words have not found admission into the language, it will be better to employ words already in use, explaining at the same time the precise meaning to be attached to them.

It is not necessary to create fresh words; but in order, as far as possible, to avoid all confusion, it would be well, in treating of these systems from a purely scientific point of view, to omit the word "political," which distinctly suggests its treatment as an applied science. "Under the word house," says Xenophon, "we include all that a man possesses." In that case, οἶκος and νόμος would signify the regulation or ordering of things possessed by man. The science itself, then, should take the title of "*Economic Science;*" whilst its various applications might be known as political, social, or financial economy, and so on.

MM. Alglave and Leroy-Beaulieu are not wrong in demanding that political economy should be taught in the Faculties of Science, and regarded as a natural science.[1]

All the definitions which I have quoted contain some errors. For instance, Economic Science is not the science of the production of wealth. The science of the production of wealth is mechanics, physics, chemistry, which produce wealth by enabling man to modify the condition of natural objects. Economic Science has only to do with human relations, resulting from the necessity of satisfying the wants of man.

Exchange is the mutual relation of utilities between themselves.

Value is the relation of a utility possessed by one person to the want of another person.

Economic Science is the study of these relations,—that is, of the

---

[1] Sitting of the Société d'Economie Politique, 4th April, 1874.

elements which constitute value. MacCulloch was not wrong in proposing to define it as *the science of values*.

The object, then, of Economic Science is to ascertain the laws which regulate the relations of natural agents utilised by individuals, acting independently of any forces which could interfere with those relations.

Or, more concisely, *Economic Science is the science of value.*

BOOK II.

THE CONSTITUENTS OF VALUE.

CHAPTER I.

ECONOMIC TENDENCIES OF MAN.

MAN finds himself in face of two objects, external to himself,— matter and force. They may become utilities to him, if he knows how to appropriate them to his needs.

This appropriation may be brought about by the aid of,—

1st. Changes in the condition of matter, whether chemical or physiological;
2nd. Changes of place;
3rd. Changes of time;
4th. Changes of ownership.

Let us consider, to begin with, how the first transformations are effected.

Among the chalks of the Beauce are found flints, artificially cut and shaped. It appears, then, that even so early as the Tertiary epoch there existed a creature which attempted to provide itself with tools. Geologists call him Tertiary Man. But M. Mortillet has given him his true place as the precursor of man.

Go back as far as we may in the history of humanity, and we still find in man, or in the animal which comes nearest to man, this tendency to make tools. Man has been defined as the toolmaking animal. This definition is clearly incomplete, but it is not otherwise incorrect. The characteristic is so marked, that, in distinguishing the various phases of prehistoric civilisation, we designate them by their tools, the Stone Age, the Bronze Age, etc.

Now turn to the natives of Tierra del Fuego; their tools are so primitive that the women are forced to plunge into the water to catch mussels, while the men are sleeping. They use dogs to help them in catching the otter. Their food-supply is so precarious, that they are sometimes driven to eat their women.

Four things characterize this period: the insufficiency of tools; the use of animals as tools; the use of women as tools; and the want or inadequacy of foresight.

The imperfection of his tools retards man's progress. Improve his implements, and you raise his grade of civilisation. It also discourages foresight; for while man is so impeded in his exertions to procure indispensable nourishment, he cannot find time either to improve his implements or to save a stock of food sufficient to secure him from the constant pressure of hunger.

The only efficient implement he has is the dog. Him he has fairly subjugated; and he makes him work for him, and catch otters.

His other implement is woman. We shall see the same thing reproduced in various stages of civilisation.

Man detests exertion. The strongest therefore obliges the weakest to work, and takes the produce for himself. The first to find herself under these conditions is woman. She begins by being the slave of man. The degree of civilisation is in inverse ratio to the subjection of woman.

Slavery has originated in the same way. The conqueror has arrogated to himself the right of having wants, and he imposes on the conquered the duty of satisfying them. The slave is regarded as the most convenient, the most productive, of tools. Almost every people, starting with this idea, has tried, not to work for itself, but to conquer others, and thus to get slaves who may work for it. Thus the slave is a living tool.

In the first stage of civilisation, man is a hunter and fisher, and his implement is an arrow or a hatchet.

In the second stage, he is a shepherd. He has been able to subjugate animals, or at least to collect them round him; they are the instruments which furnish him with milk, meat, and wool.

The agricultural stage comes next. Here man takes the earth as his instrument of labour. He has discovered by observation that by burying grain at a given time, he will reap a harvest at another time. He has foresight now. He has learnt to keep back part of his crops for seed. He has learnt to wait.

Last of all comes the industrial stage, in which man utilises all those forces of which he once ignored the nature and existence, but which science has now revealed to him. For many centuries he uses wind or water as a motive power; later on, he learns the use of steam, electricity, and the hoarded heat of the sun; but it is but a new phase of the same phenomenon, the perpetual endeavour of man to add to his own force the force of implements.

All these stages may co-exist among the same people, but the predominating one will give its name to the rest. And the token of the economic superiority of one people over another is, that it has more efficient instruments, and is therefore better able to appropriate natural agents to its wants.

There are fishermen in England and France to-day, as there were under the earliest civilisation; but they have boats and fishing tackle, they have contrivances unknown to the savages of Tierra del Fuego, and, following the general movement of production, they are beginning to replace the sail and oar by steam, which they now use for drawing up their nets.

The chase is now become a mere accessory in the business of production, and its importance is fated to decrease more and more. In populous and cultivated lands, game is reared like poultry; and so perfect is the weapon of destruction, that, left to themselves, the game have no chance of escape.

No doubt we still have flocks and herds; but the Hebrew patriarchs would be considerably surprised if they could find themselves in an English stable or a Normandy pasture. The breeding, rearing, and produce of cattle, whether for labour or for the supply of meat and milk, are calculated to a nicety. A bullock is a machine, constructed to give a return proportionate to the amount of fuel furnished to it under the form of food. The whole thing is a mechanical problem.

So, too, with regard to agriculture, machinery tends more and more to supersede human exertion. Animals were first employed; these are replaced to-day by steam, to-morrow by electricity. Agriculture is still in many respects empirical; but the farther we go, the more the earth becomes an instrument of labour like all other tools. We reckon what we have put into it; we calculate what it ought to return.

These general facts prove beyond dispute that the industrial stage is absorbing all the others. Its characteristic feature is the power and precision of its tools.

From these observations it results that man, in his contest with nature, progresses,—

   1st. *In appropriating natural agents to the satisfaction of his wants and the saving of labour;*

   2nd. *In adapting natural agents to facilitate indirectly the satisfaction of his wants.*

CHAPTER II.

CAPITAL.

MUCH discussion has arisen among economists as to the name to be given to the natural agents thus appropriated; and I will here briefly pass in review the theories to which it has given rise, since the truths of a science acquire fresh salience by the exposure of its errors.

The physiocrats regarded the soil as the source of all wealth. This error was excusable in their time. They had not seen what wealth can be evolved from the transformation of heat into steam. But it is an outcome of this error, that modern economists still attribute to the soil a peculiar economic character.

M. Coquelin says,[1] "All economists, except a few writers of little weight, are agreed in including under the name of capital only those values which have been created and accumulated by the hand of man, and excluding land and the instruments given by nature."

This restriction is admitted by Rossi and M. Joseph Garnier.[2] "Land and labour are primitive forces; capital is the result of human industry."

M. Joseph Garnier has given a table in which he divides what may be called the stock-in-trade of society into three categories, designated as follows:—

"1st. Unappropriated natural instruments, including the sea, public watercourses, the atmosphere, the heat of the sun, and the other forces of nature, physical, chemical, or mechanical, which lie at every one's disposal.

"2nd. Appropriated natural instruments, including *land* and *labour*.

"3rd. Appropriated *artificial* or *acquired instruments*; *i.e.*, capital.

He distinguishes capital as material or non-material.

"*Material capital* comprises all products, as provisions, seed, raw materials, manufactured products, tools, warehouses, buildings, cattle, money, etc., resulting from previous industry; and also includes the capital employed in the improvement of land, and forming part and parcel of the land improved, thus giving it the double character of a *natural* and an *acquired* instrument.

"*Non-material capital* includes trade-connection, scientific processes, knowledge of all sorts, scientific, literary, artistic, etc.,—this last constituting *intellectual capital*."

[1] *Dictionnaire d'Economie Politique*, vol. i., p. 273.
[2] *Traité d'Economie Politique*.

According to this table, land (including under this term watercourses, mines, and so forth) represents appropriated natural instruments; but coal and iron ore, both of which are raw material, represent appropriated artificial instruments. Further, the substances put into the soil, and forming part and parcel of it, are capital, but the land itself is not. A drain-pipe is capital; but J. B. Say himself admits that it would be no easy task to decide whether a tree planted by man would be a natural or an artificial instrument.

But is not all appropriation the result of human industry? And if so, then, by M. Garnier's own definition, appropriated land must be capital, like any other natural agent.

The worst, and at the same time the most widely received definition of capital, is that of James Mill, "Capital is accumulated labour." If so, capital can be created by turning somersaults in the air. The squirrel in its cage is creating capital. And what in the world can he mean by "accumulated labour"?

The distinction made by other English economists is somewhat more intelligible.

Capital, according to Malthus, is "a portion of property devoted to the production and distribution of wealth."

According to J. S. Mill, it is "wealth applied to a reproductive use." According to Mr. Banfield,[1] it is "the portion of goods which nature has given us, or which we have accumulated by abstinence." M. Rossi adopts these ideas, and makes capital "not only produce saved," but also "produce destined for reproduction."

But, from the point of view of economic science, these distinctions only serve to complicate the question. It is hard to distinguish between those appropriated articles which are intended for reproductive use, and those which are not. For instance, food is often very clearly capital employed in reproductive labour.

J. B. Say, in sore perplexity, makes another distinction.[2] "When a man builds a dwelling-house, he derives from it no product which he can actually carry to market; but he derives from it a very appreciable product, since he can sell its use at any time (as he does when he lets it at a rent); or he can consume it himself (as when, instead of letting the house, he lives in it). This portion of his capital, then, is not unproductive, although it does not go to the creation of any material product."

He comes to the conclusion that some capital is productive of utility, and some of enjoyment; but where, in the language of economy, is the line to be drawn between enjoyment and utility?

Bastiat says simply,[3] "The capital of a nation consists in its wealth of materials, provisions, and instruments."

---

[1] *Organisation of Industry.*
[2] *Cours d'Economie Politique*, part 1, chap. xi.
[3] *Harmonies Economiques*, chap. vii.

"Capital," says M. Courcelle-Seneuil,[1] "is nothing but the sum of wealth existing at a given time in a given space or in the possession of a given person. Capital, then, is, in some respects, synonymous with wealth, since both appellations are applied to the same objects, regarded generally and without distinction."

In a word,—

Every natural agent appropriated by man is a utility.

Every utility is capital.

The capital of an individual is the general mass of utilities possessed by him.

If I am asked, "But health, which you have described as a utility, is that capital?" I answer with another question, "Is a sick man worth as much as a sound man?"

But a surgical operation, is that capital? It is an exchange of capital; the science embodied in the surgeon, and the need of health in me.

CHAPTER III.

FIXED AND CIRCULATING CAPITAL.

ALL economists, from Adam Smith downwards, have divided capital into fixed and circulating capital. By what criterion are they to be distinguished? Adam Smith gives none. He confines himself to the following classification.[2]

"Fixed capital, of which the characteristic is, that it affords a revenue or profit without circulating or changing masters. It consists chiefly of the four following articles,—

"First, of all useful machines and implements of trade which facilitate and abridge labour.

"Secondly, of all those profitable buildings which are the means of procuring a revenue, not only to a proprietor who lets them for a rent, but to the person who possesses them and pays that rent for them; such as shops, warehouses, workhouses, farmhouses, with all their necessary buildings; stables, granaries, etc. These are very different from mere dwelling-houses. They are a sort of instruments of trade, and may be considered in the same light.

"Thirdly, of the improvements of land, of what has been profitably laid out in clearing, draining, inclosing, manuring, and reducing it into the condition most proper for tillage and culture. An improved farm may very justly be regarded in the same light as those useful machines which facilitate and abridge labour, and by means of which an equal circulating capital can afford a much

---

[1] *Traité d'Economie Politique*, vol. i., p. 47.
[2] *Wealth of Nations*, vol. ii., p. 9, 5th edition.

greater revenue to its employer. An improved farm is equally advantageous and more durable than any of those machines, frequently requiring no other repairs than the most profitable application of the farmer's capital employed in cultivating it.

"Fourthly, of the acquired and useful abilities of all the inhabitants or members of the society. The acquisition of such talents, by the maintenance of the acquirer during his education, study, or apprenticeship, always costs a real expense, which is a capital fixed and realised, as it were, in his person. Those talents, as they make a part of his fortune, so do they likewise of that of the society to which he belongs. The improved dexterity of a workman may be considered in the same light as a machine or instrument of trade which facilitates and abridges labour, and which, though it costs a certain expense, repays that expense with a profit.

"The third and last of the three portions into which the general stock of the society naturally divides itself, is the circulating capital; of which the characteristic is, that it affords a revenue only by circulating or changing masters. It is composed likewise of four parts,—

"First, of money.

"Secondly, of the stock of provisions which are in the possession of the butcher, the grazier, the farmer, the corn-merchant, the brewer, etc., and from the sale of which they expect to derive a profit.

"Thirdly, of the materials, whether altogether rude, or more or less manufactured, of clothes, furniture, and building, which are not yet made up into any of those three shapes, but which remain in the hands of the growers, the manufacturers, the mercers and drapers, the timber-merchants, the carpenters and joiners, the brick-makers, etc.

"Fourthly, and lastly, of the work which is made up and completed, but which is still in the hands of the merchant and manufacturer, and not yet disposed of or distributed to the proper consumers; such as the finished work which we frequently find ready-made in the shops of the smith, the cabinet-maker, the goldsmith, the jeweller, the china-merchant, etc. The circulating capital consists in this manner of the provisions, materials, and finished work of all kinds that are in the hands of their respective dealers, and of the money that is necessary for circulating and distributing them to those who are finally to use or to consume them.

"Of these four parts, three,—provisions, materials, and finished work,—are, either annually or in a longer or shorter period, regularly withdrawn from it, and placed either in the fixed capital, or in the stock reserved for immediate consumption."

J. B. Say, Stuart Mill, MacCulloch, MM. de Molinari, Courcelle-

Seneuil, and Stanley Jevons have all restricted themselves to simple commentaries on Adam Smith's classification. M. Courcelle-Seneuil winds up with[1] "This distinction is not indisputable in theory, and often by no means easy to recognise in practice."

Is the distinction, then, to be regarded as a scholastic refinement, or as a solid reality?

In order to answer this question, I must remind the reader that we have observed in the appropriation of natural agents to the wants of man a double character.

1st. The appropriation of natural agents by man for the immediate satisfaction of his wants.

2nd. The appropriation of natural agents to facilitate indirectly the satisfaction of his wants.

Look at the facts; a man has a hook for catching fish. This hook will always be of use to him as a fish-hook. Should he lose it, he will catch no more fish. But what does he want the fish for? Either to sell or to eat. If he eats it, it is still of no use to him, unless it undergoes certain chemical changes amounting to a complete transformation. If he sells it, it is none the less transformed, so far as he is concerned, for it is turned into money, cocoa-nuts, brandy, etc.

Take an implement more highly finished than the fish-hook,—say a steam-engine. It is of use only so long as all its gear and machinery remain intact. On the other hand, the coal supplied to its furnace is useful only on condition of its conversion into motive force.

Again, take a cotton-mill. The cotton goes in as cotton-wool, it comes out as cotton-yarn; in order to produce this utility it has undergone a physical change, while the spindle by means of which this transformation is effected can, on the contrary, be of no use at all, except by remaining exactly as it was.

The cotton-yarn loses all its utility to the spinner if it is not transformed into money or other products. Like other commodities, it has no utility unless it be transformed afresh by way of exchange.

From these observations, it appears that there is a real criterion between fixed and circulating capital.

The following criteria were first established by M. Menier in 1874, in his work, *Théorie et Application de l'Impôt sur le Capital*.

Fixed capital consists of all such utilities as yield their products without changing their nature.

Circulating capital consists of all such utilities as change their nature in yielding their products.

---

[1] *Manuel des Affaires*, p. 88.

Or thus,—
Fixed capital produces utilities without transforming itself.
Circulating capital produces utilities only by undergoing transformation.
Or, still more simply,—
Fixed capital is the tool.
Circulating capital is the raw material and the product.

CHAPTER IV.

NOMENCLATURE OF FIXED CAPITAL AND CIRCULATING CAPITAL.

THIS criterion established, it becomes very easy to distinguish what is fixed and what is circulating capital.

The soil must remain as it is if it is to produce utilities. No doubt it will become exhausted, unless a certain number of its component elements be renewed; but then, if those component elements have been exhausted, the soil is no longer what it was before. It must be restored to its identity. The soil, therefore, is fixed capital.

On the other hand, the crops, which are destined to be sold or eaten, are circulating capital. So is the part reserved for seed, for it can only be utilised by losing its identity.

Among animals, those kept for labour or enjoyment are fixed capital. A pig intended for salting is circulating capital. The cock is fixed capital, the capon is circulating capital.

Machines, furniture, household utensils, objects of art,—in short, all instruments productive of utility, whatever form they may take, —are fixed capital.

All raw material, all manufactured products intended for sale, are circulating capital.

As to money, it is fixed capital to the legendary miser, who spends his life in counting his gold; but other men are not in the habit of keeping it to look at. On the contrary, they no sooner have it than they hasten to convert it into houses, lands, food, etc. Money is simply an organ of transmission, a means of exchange. It is, by its very nature, circulating capital.

But what of bonds and shares?

The question shows that the public does not yet realise the exact nature of these things. Shares are nothing but fractions of a title, they are simply a claim to a part-proprietorship. The property may be fixed or it may be circulating capital, as it happens; the shares are not capital at all, they only represent capital.

So with bonds; they are mortgage-deeds, usually secured on

fixed capital. Now every mortgagee is a co-proprietor in the property which forms the security. It is this fixed capital which produces the annual sum necessary to pay the interest on the advance.

Private individuals may reckon their bonds and shares among their fixed capital, since they produce a very real utility; but it is giving them another character than their true one of simple documents, fractional titles to property; it is confounding the sign with the thing signified.

The following utilities, then, are fixed capital:—

Soil,	Mines,	Buildings,
Machinery	Implements,	Ships,
Carriages,	Animals put to use,	Household utensils.
Furniture,	Objects of art,	

The following are circulating capital:—

Raw material, Articles of commerce, Money.

CHAPTER V.

THE PLACE OF FIXED AND CIRCULATING CAPITAL IN THE WORK OF PRODUCTION.

No one will dispute that tools augment the power of man. The day he learnt to use the lever, he was enabled to apply more force with less exertion. The day he tamed the dog, he was enabled to do with the dog's help what he could not have done without it. These truths are practically undeniable. I may, however, draw attention to the fact that it is not so long since a good many people debated whether machinery was useful; and some working men still have their doubts on this point. I shall explain further how this prejudice has arisen.

It is enough for my present purpose to point out the following fact. According to the experiments made for ascertaining the horse-power of steam, the strength of one horse is equal to that of seven men. One horse-power of steam is equivalent, at the current rate, to that of three draught-horses, or twenty-one men.

Now, in 1878, out of nearly 2,800,000 horses, 2,200,000 were used for draught. The total power would equal that of 15,400,000 men.

There was 3,024,000 horse-power of steam, equalling the power of 63,504,000 men. This force, moreover, is continuous, so that the figures may be doubled, trebled, even quadrupled, without exaggeration.

Four horses draw a plough; they are doing the work of twenty-eight men. While they are ploughing the furrow, the twenty-eight men may be employing their strength, some as joiners, some as masons, some as professors; whilst others again may be doing nothing. At the end of the day, the same quantity of land will have been ploughed as if the twenty-eight men had all been ploughing it. If, instead of the four horses, four horse-power of steam had been employed, it would have saved the exertions of eighty-four instead of twenty-eight men, and set them free for some other employment. They might have folded their arms and looked on, and the result at the close of the day would have been the same as if they had been toiling all the time without a moment's respite. That boiler, that valve, those pistons, that coal and water, represent eighty-four cheap, active, and indefatigable slaves.

Tools tend to reduce human effort to a minimum.

If, by means of a tool, a man can obtain in a quarter of au hour results which he could not otherwise obtain in twenty hours, the use of the tool will have given him all the rest of the time to do what he likes with. In the same way, if a machine can produce the same quantity of utilities as the labour of twenty-one men, then we have twenty-one men set free to attend to the production of something else.

Thus, three million horse-power of steam represents the exertions of sixty-three millions of men. These men would have been engaged in the mere production of motive force, and in nothing else. Introduce the use of steam, and you have gained the motive force; the sixty-three millions of men can apply themselves to the production of something else.

In France, for instance, work is done which would take sixty-three millions of men to do it, and the sixty-three millions of men do not exist.

Moreover, the energies thus set free may in their turn act on other tools, no less powerful than those which have set them at liberty; one horse-power of steam supplies the place of twenty-one men, but this horse-power is not the only one. The energy of these twenty-one men may spend itself in the use of tools every one of which in its turn liberates the energies of ten, twenty, or a hundred men.

Hence we draw the conclusion,

Human effort is productive of utilities in proportion to the power of its tools.

Here we encounter a new factor.

From the hand-shaped flint to the flint fixed in a wooden haft is a great stride, and from this stone hatchet to the steam-engine is a

From the day it first occurred to man to fix his flint in a wooden handle, the process has gone on repeating itself. The tool he has made helps him to make another.

The lids of many thousands of saucepans and kettles must have been raised by the escaping steam, much to the annoyance of housewives, before a young man of the last century, an intuitive observer, perceived the full meaning of this fact, and invented the steam engine. But, once invented, the steam-engine is reproduced indefinitely, and with fresh improvements every day. It is itself employed in its own reproduction.

Thus: *The effort necessary to produce a given result varies inversely as the power of the tool.*

The energy set free by the use of the tool varies directly as the power of the tool.

A tool, once produced, may be reproduced indefinitely, and may itself, directly or indirectly, aid in the reproduction.

I shall be told that the cotton-spindle is not used in reproducing itself. No; not directly; but indirectly it helps to clothe the workman who reproduces it.

I shall be told that a picture is an instrument of enjoyment, and that nevertheless it cannot be reproduced indefinitely. That, too, is strictly true; but why is the original so valuable, and the copies of so little relative worth, if not because the latter are so easily produced? Michael Angelo's "Last Judgment" is to art what Watt's engine is to industry.

To this productive faculty of the finished instrument must be added another characteristic, that of durability.

An implement lasts a year, two years, ten years; a road lasts a century or two; a harbour or railway, if kept in repair, lasts indefinitely; a house lasts for a variable period. The new fixed capital does not destroy the old. Thus there is an accumulation of fixed capital.

We have embraced all such tools as produce utilities more or less subjective under the term *fixed capital.*

Now, fixed capital produces utilities in only one way, viz., by absorbing raw material, and converting it into products.

With the man of the Stone Age, the expenditure of raw material is considerable in proportion to the product. He must live long days before he can provide himself with a stone hatchet, and during these days he must eat; food is his raw material; the consumption is great, and the result small. The search for circulating capital—food, is an hourly anxiety; for the slenderer his fixed capital, the more difficult he finds it to procure circulating capital. But when, little by little, he has succeeded in obtaining fixed capital enough to allow of his obtaining circulating capital beyond his immediate wants, he has time and energy at his disposal for attempting to increase his fixed capital.

Compare the hunger-driven pre-historic man with the man of our modern civilisation!

Our industry consumes circulating capital in the form of food for thousands of men, and in the form of materials, stone, iron, coal, etc., and this consumption goes on for considerable periods of time. For what purpose? For the purpose of constructing a house, a ship, a railway, etc., which shall afterwards serve to economise human effort and save the consumption of food and other circulating capital for some other work. Hence:—

The consumption of circulating capital is in inverse ratio to the power of the tool.

A kilogramme of coal represents 8,000 calories.[1]

One calorie equals 425 kilogrammètres,[2] therefore one kilogramme of coal represents $8,000 \times 425 = 3,400,000$ kilogrammètres.

One horse-power yields $75 \times 3,600 = 270,000$ kilogrammètres per hour.

In a steam-engine consuming one kilogramme of coal per hour per horse-power, the proportion between the labour exerted and the numerical equivalent of the heat given out is $\frac{270000}{3400000} = 0 \cdot 08$.

The steam-engine consumes a raw material, coal, which it converts into force. This force again results in a product. The loss is as yet considerable; progress will consist in reducing it.

A goods-engine at the present day fed with one-eighth the fuel, yields fourteen times the force that Stephenson's engines did in 1825. The proportion is as 1 : 112.

According to Mr. Mundella,[3] the number of tons of coal used in the production of one ton of pig iron were, nine in 1787, three in 1869, and two in 1876.[4]

This saving has been effected by the improved construction of furnaces, the improved arrangements of bellows, and the greater utilisation of heat. This rate of progress has been outstripped in the conversion of iron into Bessemer steel, by the regenerating furnace, and by the Siemens direct process.

Thus, by means of improved machinery, more utilities are produced at less cost than formerly.

Industrial progress consists in obtaining the highest possible inverse ratio between the consumption of circulating capital and the return yielded by fixed capital.

[1] The term *calorie* expresses the amount of heat required to raise one kilogramme of water one degree centigrade.

[2] The kilogrammètre is the French dynamometric-unit, answering to the English foot-ton.

[3] *Journal of the Statistical Society*, March, 1878.

[4] The diagrams in this volume have been made out by M. Prosper Guyot, director of the *Correspondance Scientifique et Agricole*.

In the multiplication of circulating capital, the effort is in inverse ratio to the power of the fixed capital.

The multiplication of circulating capital is in direct ratio to the power of fixed capital.

We are unable at present to determine, at least in the majority of cases, the exact rate of this proportion; later on it may be possible to ascertain it, when statistics may have furnished more certain information than that we at present possess.

But of what character is the consumption of most of this circulating capital, whether raw material or produce?

Man consumes food; and while he consumes it he is building his hut or making his tools; in doing so, he is converting circulating capital in the form of food into fixed capital in the form of a hut or tools. In a more advanced stage of civilisation, we find him converting raw material of all kinds,—food, coal, minerals, and so forth,—into roads, bridges, harbours, and locomotives. We may say, then, that—

Circulating capital, with the exception of money, has a constant tendency to be converted into fixed capital.

CHAPTER VI.

SPACE.

WE have just examined the action of fixed and circulating capital in changing the condition of matter.

We find it just the same with the changes of place to which matter is subjected.

We repeat, the partisans of final causes notwithstanding, that matter and force alone lie at the disposal of man. His exertions alone convert them into utilities.

Man does not find in one place all the various objects which minister to the satisfaction of his wants. He gets his cotton from the United States, and his coal from England. He brings these two species of raw material together; and when they are transformed into products, he brings these products within reach of the consumers who want them.

A want once recognised, if the utility which will satisfy that want cannot be brought within reach of a man, the man must go within reach of the utility. The sky of Nice cannot be transported into a London fog, so the Englishman goes to Nice for his sunshine.

The principal factor in this problem is space.

I borrow the following figures from M. Perdonnet, who has specially interested himself in the means of transport.

A horse of average strength, going at a foot-pace, ten hours out of the twenty-four, cannot carry on his back more than 100 kilogrammes. The same horse, harnessed to a vehicle, will carry, or rather draw, for an equal distance on an ordinary macadamised road, 1,000 kilogrammes, and on a tramway without sharp curves or heavy gradients, 10,000 kilogrammes.

Further, in 1840, waggons conveying merchandise did from three to four kilomètres an hour easily, and, travelling eight hours in the twenty-four, accomplished from twenty-eight to thirty kilomètres a day. The express goods service, using relays, made from sixty-five to seventy kilomètres per day.

The expense of construction of macadamised roads, from ten to twelve mètres broad, would be on an average twenty thousand francs per kilomètre, and the annual cost of repair five hundred francs.

The making of the great railway lines in France has cost 503,000 francs per kilomètre. A goods engine like the *Engerth* costs 107,000 francs. But this locomotive draws forty-four waggons, each laden with ten tons of merchandise, at a speed of thirty kilomètres per hour. Thus it performs in one hour a longer journey than a common carrier's cart would do in a day, and in two hours almost as much as the express goods service; and in twenty-four hours as much as would take the former twenty-four days, and the latter twelve days; while to the 440,000 kilogrammes drawn by the locomotive must be added its own weight of 62,000 kilogrammes.

This locomotive, which can run 300,000 kilomètres without getting out of repair, consumes in drawing this load sixteen kilogrammes of coal per kilomètre in summer, and eighteen in winter. The expense, including wages, duty, cost of coal, water, oil, grease, waste, lighting, and the repairs of engines and tenders, amounts on an average to 1 fr. 10 cents.

Let us look into these facts. A man could not carry more than thirty or forty kilogrammes at the most. A horse will carry a hundred—three times as much. The horse costs his keep and training; but these advances are reimbursed by his labour, which replaces that of the man in the proportion above named. It is true, that in order to obtain this result, the man has had to make some exertion in advance.

Next, the man makes a wider step in advance;—he not only trains the horse, but he makes a road; but while he is making the road, he must eat; he must therefore have laid up circulating capital for his own consumption while he is creating the fixed capital. He knows what he is about; he is converting his food into roads, in order to get more out of his first fixed capital, the horse. Once the road is made, the horse will no longer carry a hundred kilogrammes, he will draw a thousand. The effort of the man becomes less and less, for a greater and greater result.

More or less unconsciously, he follows out this system. He spends at last 500,000 francs per kilomètre on roads which formerly cost only 20,000. These 500,000 francs represent for the most part the consumption of coal, iron, and food,—circulating capital which has been turned into embankments, tunnels, and rails. The effort expended in advance is so great as to seem absurd, and yet nothing can be more reasonable, since it has proportionately diminished the effort made in the long run. By means of a definite amount of completed labour, he has saved an indefinite amount of labour in the future.

Here we find another confirmation of the laws already stated:—

Industrial progress consists in obtaining the highest possible inverse ratio between the consumption of circulating capital and the return yielded by fixed capital.

Circulating capital, with the exception of money, has a constant tendency to be converted into fixed capital.

CHAPTER VII.

TIME.

ANOTHER economic factor, and one far too much neglected, is time.

Prehistoric man must have taken a fortnight, perhaps a month, to fashion his hatchet; and however inured he might be to hunger, he could not live all that time without eating.

He must therefore have absorbed circulating capital in the shape of food, to be transformed into fixed capital in the shape of a stone hatchet. This is an advance of capital.

The more developed the civilisation, the more considerable is the advance of capital required. One kilomètre of railway costs 500,000 francs; that is to say, during a space of three or four years an amount of circulating capital equivalent to that sum is spent in food for man and beast, in coal for the steam engines, and in materials. Now this fixed capital does not turn into an immediate utility the circulating capital it has consumed. We have first to wait till it is completed, and when it is completed, it is only by little and little that it returns the equivalent of the utilities absorbed by it.

We have shown that circulating capital has been advanced. This advance is called credit. It minimises time, just as transport minimises space. We define it thus:—*Credit is the advance of circulating capital.*

This circulating capital is consumed in various ways; but, as we have seen, the greater part of it will be converted into fixed capital.

But it may be said, Credit produces nothing. No more does transport. But credit shortens time, just as transport shortens space.

A has a capital of fifty thousand francs; with this money he can buy a factory of Z, which he pays for in part only; he buys coal of Y, which he will pay for in three months, when he has had time to make and sell the products. Every one else does the same in his own case. If it were not the custom to give credit, Y would not have let A have the raw material, A could not have gone on with the manufacture, and the product would never have existed.

But if Y had not had the raw material, it is clear he could not have given A credit for it. Credit, like transport, always exists in connection with something, and is inseparable from it. Transport, in bringing together raw materials of different kinds, and putting them within reach of the consumers, has as its indisputable consequence the multiplication of capital; and it is the same with credit.

Credit does not by itself immediately augment the amount of existing capital, but it does augment the producing power of that capital.

In an active civilisation, this results in a repercussion which indefinitely multiplies the original capital. A consumer buys at three months and sells at three months, which makes six months, and so on. This multiplication, applied daily and hourly to the millions of individuals who produce and consume, represents an immense power of production. It is useless to cavil at it; it is impossible to deny it.

Although Stuart Mill himself attests these effects, he laughs at people who speak of an extension of credit as though it were a creation of capital, whereas credit is only permission to use the capital of another person.[1] But if Stuart Mill is right, these people are nevertheless not altogether wrong. An extension of credit is equivalent to an extension of capital, for it places at the disposal of those who have it an amount of capital which they would not otherwise have had. Credit does not always imply the actual use of another person's capital; it sometimes means a mere guarantee or bail. A capitalist opens a credit with a manufacturer who, on the strength of it, enters into certain engagements; if his affairs prosper, he may never have recourse to the capital represented by his credit. Credit, then, in this case, is a real extension of capital.

Again, credit is an extension of capital, because it is a saving of time. To produce fixed capital, such as a railway, for instance, I must spend 500,000 francs per kilomètre in articles of food and clothing for the workmen, in stone, iron, and other circulating pital, which is thus withdrawn from circulation. Supposing it

---

[1] *Principles of Political Economy*, Book III., chap. xi., par. 1.

to be a French railway, it is calculated that it will repay the capital advanced, with interest, in ninety-nine years.

Take a bill of exchange, discounted at three months. This bill enables me to procure circulating capital; raw material, which, transformed into products, will enable me to meet the bill at maturity. Whence does this bill derive its value? From the assurance that it will be paid at the date specified. Thanks to this bill, I have been able to procure for myself the "capital of another person," to use it, and to transform it into capital of a higher value; all which I could not otherwise have done. Here we have not a mere shifting of capital, but an extension of capital.

"But," it will be urged, "if credit produces an extension of capital, an indefinite extension of credit will produce an indefinite extension of capital."

This objection only establishes my point. The effect of credit being to absorb circulating capital into fixed capital, it follows that too great an extension of credit will provoke a too rapid absorption, and so the equilibrium is disturbed, and the circulating capital required for utilising the fixed capital becomes scarce.[1]

Stuart Mill himself admits that credit has an acquiring power similar to that of money.

It is the advantage of credit, that it puts at the disposal of those who will use it to the best advantage capital which the apathy or inaptitude of its possessors might have rendered unproductive.

In this way, the late Mr. Bagehot has pointed out the principal function of Lombard Street. There are quiet people in the country who accumulate money, and there are active people who use it; Lombard Street negotiates between them.

This question of credit was so ill understood, even within comparatively recent times, that J. B. Say wrote, "It is better, whenever possible, to work with one's own capital."

The answer to this is, as Mr. Tooke says,[2] "The power of acquisition of merchants who have capital and credit extends far beyond anything people can imagine who have not a practical acquaintance with the speculation-market. If a man with a reputation for possessing sufficient capital for his business and enjoying good credit in his trade, foresees a rise of price in the article in which he deals; if he be favoured by circumstances at the outset and in the course of his speculation, he may effect enormous purchases, out of all proportion to his capital."

Mr. Bagehot goes further still.[3] "In every district small traders have arisen, who discount their bills largely, and with the capital so borrowed, harass and press upon, if they do not eradicate, the old

---

[1] See Book IV., *Commercial Crises*.
[2] *Inquiry into the Currency Principles*.
[3] *Lombard Street*, p. 8.

capitalist. The new trader has obviously an immense advantage in the struggle of trade. If a merchant have £50,000 all his own, to gain 10 per cent. on it he must make £5,000 a year, and must charge for his goods accordingly; but if another has only £10,000, and borrows £40,000 by discounts (no extreme instance in our modern trade), he has the same capital of £50,000 to use, and can sell much cheaper. If the rate at which he borrows be 5 per cent., he will have to pay £2,000 a year; and if, like the old trader, he make £5,000 a year, he will still, after paying his interest, obtain £3,000 a year, or 30 per cent. on his own £10,000. . . . In modern English business, owing to the certainty of obtaining loans on discount of bills or otherwise at a moderate rate of interest, there is a steady bounty on trading with borrowed capital, and a steady discouragement to confine yourself solely or mainly to your own capital."

At the same time, credit gives a democratic character to production; it puts personal activity in place of capital; it does away with the great old families of "merchant princes;" in fact, at the present day we may almost say that whoever has an idea which seems likely to turn out profitable, can obtain capital. I say "seems likely," for he need not be right in his expectation; he need only make others believe that he is right. Credit is from *credere*, to believe.

Credit is quite a modern institution. Formerly there was only the classic usurer, who put out his capital on hazardous ventures, and made it his business to squeeze enormous profits out of the embarrassments of other people. The money-lender was a person quite by himself, one to whom no other employment was open,—a Jew, perhaps; and he was rarely to be met with in real life. Even now, in many countries, the capitalist cares only to hoard his money, without attempting to get any interest upon it. The popular legends about hidden treasure bear witness to a universal instinct, still to be found in Asia, Africa, and South America, and even among some of our own French peasantry. Macaulay gives a vivid picture of the embarrassment of the merchant of the 17th century, who has made money, and does not know what to do with it. He tells us that during the interval between the Restoration and the Revolution, the wealth of the nation had rapidly increased. Thousands of merchants discovered, on taking stock at Christmas, that after having provided out of the year's incomings for their domestic expenditure, there still remained a surplus. What to do with this surplus was for many of them a question not easy of solution. In the 17th century, a lawyer, a doctor, a retired merchant, who had put by a few thousand pounds, was often much embarrassed to find some safe and profitable investment for them. The father of the poet Pope was a city merchant; when he retired from business he took with him a box containing twenty thousand pounds, from which he drew from time to time the amounts necessary for keeping house.

Hence arose those prejudices against interest on money which are now beginning to disappear. Proudhon, whose only importance as a writer consists in his having appropriated and set forth in an attractive light all the chimæras of all the utopists who played on the credulity of the masses about the middle of the present century, exclaims, "My philosopher's stone is absolute freedom of credit. If I am deceived in this, socialism is a vain dream." I remember my amazement when, in 1868 and 1869, I heard this question of gratuitous credit discussed at length in public meetings. The disciples of Proudhon offered it as a universal panacea. As a matter of fact, interest is based on two indestructible facts,—firstly, the price of time; secondly, security against risk.

The borrower pays for the service rendered him. If he does not choose to pay for it, he should not ask for it. Those who wish to abolish interest on money must begin by abolishing the borrower.

The object of all these combinations of credit is to save time, and to stimulate the more and more rapid formation of new capital, just as all combinations for the purpose of transport aim at minimising space. And these two systems of combinations work together towards the same result, the system of credit serving in effect for the transport of capital all over the world, while modern means of transport, by facilitating and accelerating the circulation of circulating capital, facilitate and accelerate its realisation.

A railway consumes in the making hundreds of millions of francs in food and clothing for workmen, in fodder for horses, in coal for the engines employed, in rails and sleepers which have themselves absorbed in the making a quantity of circulating capital.

After a time these expenses are refunded, and this refunding we call amortisation.

Amortisation is the reimbursement of the circulating capital absorbed by fixed capital.

Thus :—

Credit is the advance of circulating capital.

Credit does not immediately augment the amount of existing capital, but it does augment the producing power of that capital.

CHAPTER VIII.

EXCHANGE.

I HAVE defined value as *the relation of the utility possessed by one person to the needs of another person.*

Exchange is the relation of utilities between themselves. According to the Roman classification, *Do ut des ; facio ut facias ; do ut facias ; facio ut des.*

A Frenchman of the nineteenth century needs shoes, clothes, wine, bread, meat, coffee, sugar, fish, vegetables, music, news, security, etc. His wants are more varied than his aptitudes; he would find it a hard matter to make all these articles himself. The country he lives in is not suited to the production of all this raw material; nor has he at his disposal the machinery, the motive power, the skill, the land, necessary for obtaining the manufactured product. I need not insist further. Everybody sees how impossible it is that each should provide for all his wants himself. Formerly it was a maxim in agriculture, that a piece of land should suffice for itself; that is, that it should produce all that was necessary for the family which cultivated it. This maxim has now gone to swell the mass of exploded theories. The wine-grower of the South grows his wine and buys his corn. The land yields the products it is best fitted to yield, and so must man. This is the principle of division of labour.

With the development of civilisation, man's wants become more various, and his aptitudes more specialised. The consequence is, that he can produce more utilities than before; but these utilities are more limited in their nature; they are all of one kind. He now produces, not so much what he wants, as what others want. Hence it comes to pass that exchange becomes an ever more imperious necessity; for exchange consists in giving away what are to us superfluous utilities in order to obtain what are to us necessary utilities.

We purposely employ the word "utility" here instead of "thing" or "substance." When we get a musician to play for us, we are not exchanging our money for a certain amount of some substance; but we regard the agreeable sensation produced by his music as a utility, and we pay him for the sensation.

The whole mechanism of exchange is based on the variety of wants and aptitudes.

Every now and then we hear it said, "We must learn to be content. We must set a limit to our wants." How shall we limit them? It is right enough to say individually, "We must have no more wants than we can produce utilities to satisfy." But from another point of view, we must beware of these ethics of apathy. Under the guise of prudence, they tend to idleness. It is the stirring of new wants which impels man to strive, to develope, to augment his powers. It should be the aim of each of us to enlarge his life by multiplying and extending his activity; the development of our capacities keeps pace with that of our wants. The greater the extent and variety of both the one and the other, the more frequent must exchange become. Among primitive

F

peoples, it was confined to a few implements or other necessaries; in our more advanced civilisation it forms the principle and consequence of our every act.

The object of exchange is to bring the utilities possessed by each individual within reach of the wants of all the rest.

CHAPTER IX.

CIRCULATION.

MAN appropriates natural agents to his wants by subjecting matter to certain changes of condition. In the language of economy, these changes consist in the action of fixed capital upon circulating capital.

But these changes can only take place by means of exchange and transport. Industry consists in bringing together different kinds of circulating capital, and submitting them to the action of fixed capital. The metal-worker places ore from Spain and coal from England in a blast furnace. The metal thus obtained, it is the business of commerce to bring it in contact with the consumer, who turns it into nails, hammers, machines, and so on.

To all these various phenomena, the term circulation—a word far too restricted in its present use—should be freely applied.

Circulation is the series of phenomena by the aid of which circulating capital is transformed into fixed capital, or into fresh circulating capital.

I am aware that this definition, like most of those I have given, forms no part of the present vocabulary of economics. Coquelin's definition is very simple, and certainly does not err on the side of narrowness. According to him,[1] circulation is "the tendency to movement," a definition so wide that it embraces nothing. J. B. Say says, "It is the movement of money or commodities in passing from hand to hand." J. S. Mill says,[2] "The average number of purchases made by each piece (of money) in order to effect a given pecuniary amount of transactions."

M. Menier is the first economist who has at all grasped the importance of circulation.[3] This will be his title of honour in the history of economic science.

I shall myself ever owe him the deepest gratitude, since it was his vast practical experience which opened up to me new horizons which my theoretical studies would never have revealed to me. He showed me, by a thousand examples, how all economic questions are summed up in this one of circulation.

---

[1] *Dictionnaire d'Economie Politique.*
[2] *Principles of Political Economy,* p. 301, 7th edition.
[3] *Théorie et Application de l'Impôt sur le Capital,* Book iv., chap.

"What is my aim as a manufacturer?" he asks. "It is to transform my raw material as rapidly as possible into commodities, and my commodities again into fresh capital, at a profit.

"But is it not possible to determine the rate of this production, and to estimate the influence of rapidity of circulation on production generally?

"I have no hesitation in replying, Yes, it is possible; and it can be done in the simplest manner. A single illustration will serve the purpose. I disregard compound interest for the sake of simplicity.

"I start with a circulating capital of 100,000 francs (raw material), which is converted annually into circulating capital (commodities), and brings me in annually a net profit of 10,000 francs. At the end of ten years I have made 100,000 francs, thus doubling my original capital. I now work with a capital of 200,000 francs, making an annual profit of 20,000 francs; and at the end of another ten years I have a capital of 400,000 francs. From this I gain an annual profit of 40,000 francs, and in ten years more I have 800,000 francs.

"I have supposed this result obtained in thirty years, but if instead of thirty years, I had taken twenty, then at the end of thirty I should have had, not 800,000 francs, but 1,600,000 francs; and if instead of twenty years, I had taken only ten, it would have been 3,200,000 francs.

"Hence I conclude that *production advances in geometrical ratio to the rapidity of circulation.*"

Hence the production of a country depends on the rapidity of circulation. The better a nation utilises time and space, the more it produces.

CHAPTER X.

RÉSUMÉ.

It will be useful to sum up in a few words this analysis of the materials which constitute value.

In order to provide himself with utilities, man must triumph over three obstacles—over the inertia of matter, space, and time.

To obtain a utility possessed by another person, he must give that person an equivalent utility.

The various combinations by the aid of which these difficulties are overcome, so as to obtain, with a minimum of effort, in a minimum of time, a maximum of utility, form the constituent elements of value.

We will now proceed to examine the causes which increase or diminish value in relation to the various utilities.

BOOK III.

VALUE OF FIXED AND CIRCULATING CAPITAL.

CHAPTER I.

AN ECONOMIC CONTRADICTION.

"Since the wealth of a country consists in the value of the things it possesses, how comes it that a nation is rich in proportion as things are cheap?"

This point was raised by J. B. Say; and Proudhon, who cared far more for dialectical display than for the reality of things, took up the question and based on it his book, *Les Contradictions Economiques.*

He says:[1] "The value of a utility decreases as its production increases, and an unbroken run of success may bring the producer to poverty.

"Three years of plenty in certain provinces of Russia are a public calamity, just as some abundant vintages have been ruin to the vine-grower.

"From the relation of utility to exchange value, it results, that if, by malice or accident, exchange is rendered impossible to a producer, his full storehouses will profit him nothing.

"Utility is a condition precedent to exchange; but take away exchange, and the utility is null.

"The inevitable result of the multiplication of values is to depreciate them.

"There is thus a contradiction between the necessity of labour and its resutls.

[1] *Contradictions Economiques,* chap. ii.

"I challenge any serious economist to tell me, otherwise than by repeating or paraphrasing the question, how it comes that value diminishes as production increases.

"In technical language, value in use, and value in exchange, while necessary the one to the other, are always in inverse ratio."

"This," he adds, "is an inevitable opposition." So, the more people toil to become rich, the poorer they become! He gives his book the alternative title of *Philosophie de la Misère*.

It must be admitted that the question is not a purely captious one; it contains some truth, and economists have no more answered it as yet than mathematicians have solved the problem of Fermat.

In the first place, we must free this question from an incidental proposition which has nothing to do with it. Proudhon says: "Take away exchange, and utility is null." Robinson Crusoe disposes of this: "I cannot exchange my cavern, my gun, or my umbrella; but they are useful to me all the same."

But none the less, the problem awaits solution. M. H. Passy has attempted it, but without throwing any light on the subject. "Private wealth," says he,[1] "is in proportion to the value of the articles which compose it; but the public wealth, not being exchangeable, cannot be evaluated in any way; the more plentiful things are, the greater the wealth, and the less its relative value."

According to this argument, the richer a country is, the less it is worth. Every private person can say, "I am rich, for I have things of such and such a value, say x;" but when you add up the total of this individual wealth, which makes up the general wealth, it comes to zero! M. Passy has only emphasized the contradiction, instead of reconciling it.

Bastiat has attempted to settle the question by the aid of a brilliant and subtle theory.[2]

"There are two meanings, both of which may be legitimately assigned to the word *wealth*; namely, effective wealth, or the sum of the utilities which human labour, with the co-operation of nature, brings within reach of society; and relative wealth, which is the proportionate share of each in the general wealth, this proportion being determined by value.

"Every one has a share in the general wealth, equivalent to his own contribution to it."

Still, this is no solution. Bastiat attempts one in the next chapter, on property and community.

"Natural gifts, gratuitous materials, gratuitous forces—these form the common property of the community.

"But the human efforts applied to collecting these materials and

---

[1] *Dictionnaire d'Economie Politique*, Art. "Valeur."
[2] *Harmonies Economiques*, chap. v.

to directing these forces, which can be evaluated, exchanged, compensated, these efforts belong to the domain of private property.

"In other words, we do not stand in relation to one another as proprietors of the utility of things, but of their value; and value is the appreciation of reciprocal services.

"The ideas of proprietorship and of community are correlative to those of effort and of gratuitousness from which they spring.

"Whatever is gratuitous is common, for every one is admitted to the unconditional enjoyment of it.

"Whatever is the result of effort is appropriated, because the enjoyment is conditional on the taking some pains."

He shows that the co-operation of nature with man is gratuitous; the co-operation of man alone is onerous. Now human progress consists in relying more and more on the co-operation of nature, so that the co-operation obtained shall be more and more gratuitous.

"We gain in proportion as we succeed in sparing our own labour and capital, which are necessarily costly, and obtaining more and more of our products through the gratuitous services of nature.

"The wealth of man consists in the abundance of things which he possesses."

He concludes :—

1st. That utility tends to become more and more gratuitous and common, as it gradually emerges from the domain of individual ownership.

2nd. That value, on the contrary, which alone is capable of appropriation, and alone constitutes property in law and in fact, tends to diminish more and more, relatively to the utility to which it is attached.

There is a certain amount of truth in Bastiat's remarks, and we have ourselves observed that industrial progress consists in a gradually increasing appropriation of matter to our wants. But Bastiat, with his distinction between effective and relative wealth, far from replying to Say and Proudhon, falls into the same confusion as Adam Smith, Say, and Passy.

If wealth is in inverse ratio to value, why then do individuals estimate their fortune by its value, and why is a people rich in proportion to its possession of values?

If progress consists in increasing the number of gratuitous utilities at the expense of onerous ones, the wealthiest countries will be those whose value is the lowest.

How does a private person reckon the growth of his fortune? "I had property worth 100,000 francs; it is now worth 200,000 francs." Now what holds good with the individual cannot be false with regard to the nation; for the wealth of a nation is nothing but the sum total of the wealth of the sum total of the individuals who compose it.

We are again thrown back on the question, Is there any real opposition between value in use and value in exchange, or—to use the terms of our own definition—between utility and value?

The question was necessarily insoluble until we had determined with precision the respective parts played by fixed and circulating capital in production.

I have defined value as the relation of the utility possessed by one person to the wants of another person.

I have shown that effort is productive of utilities in proportion to the power of the tool.

The greater the power of my tool, or field, or factory, the greater is my value in relation to other people, for I have been able to appropriate more utilities, and can render them more services.

A waterfall, turning a paltry water-wheel, gives a force of ten horse-power; acting on a *turbine* (horizontal water-wheel), it gives a force of forty horse-power, it yields four times as much utility, and this utility again is exchanged for others, so that my waterfall is worth four times as much as before. If I employ this waterfall to grind corn, it follows that I can grind four times as much with the same effort. I can now charge only half what I did before for grinding, and at the same time make by it double what I made before, and consequently, both in relation to me and in relation to others, my waterfall is worth double what it was before.

Again, I have a field. This field was formerly distant from any road; it could not be supplied with the necessary manures, nor could its produce be brought within reach of those who wanted it. It yielded ten hectolitres, and the services of a horse and man were needed to bring this product to market. It now yields twenty hectolitres, the carriage of which to market needs no greater effort, if as much. I sell my grain at half the former price, and make the same profit as before. My field produces more utilities, and has a greater value, both for me and for others.

We have seen (page 57) how great has been the diminution in the consumption of coal for iron smelting, consequent on the improvements effected in the factories. Now the value of the factory must of course be increased, since it possesses a greater power of utility; while the utilities it supplies to consumers must fall in value, since they are more plentiful and cost less to produce. These examples will give us the solution of the problem put by Say and Proudhon.

It is the value of fixed capital which constitutes wealth, for its value expresses its power of utility. Now the power of utility of fixed capital is shown in the quantity of circulating capital produced by it. But the greater this production, the less laborious it is; and consequently, these utilities can be furnished at a lower price.

Therefore,—
The value of fixed capital is in direct ratio to the abundance of circulating capital; and the value of circulating capital is in inverse ratio to the power of fixed capital.

CHAPTER II.

THE MEASURE OF VALUE.

THE solution of this problem will give us the clue to some economic phenomena which have not yet been clearly explained.

A question much agitated in former days was that of the standard of value. It was equivalent to asking for a value to measure value by. It was simple nonsense. Value can only be measured by value, and all value is variable.

It is regulated by a single law—the law of supply and demand. Supply is my desire to dispose of the utilities I have, in exchange for utilities of another kind. Demand is my desire to obtain a utility, for which I am prepared to give another in exchange.

The value of a utility is in inverse ratio to the supply, and in direct ratio to the demand.

This law is the most indisputable in all economic science. Utopists curse it now and then. The Catheder Socialisten fight against it. Yet all their combinations, however ingenious, rest upon this. They attempt to falsify it for their own ends, but they never cease to invoke it. The cry of the Protectionists is simply a demand for the limitation of supply.

It needs no demonstration to prove that:

Value varies according to the urgency of the need, and the difficulty of procuring the utility.

Nevertheless, economists, instead of contenting themselves with the verification of this fact, have too often seen but one side of the question.

Adam Smith says that labour is the real measure of the exchangeable value of any commodity, and that the real price of a thing—that which it really costs the man who wishes to obtain it—is the labour and trouble he takes to get it. Perhaps so, but what will he sell it at? or rather, what utility can he obtain in the market in exchange for it? What purchasing power does it possess?

An epic is worth a great deal to its author, because it has cost him great pains to compose; but does that make it any the more valuable to others? You buy a fashionable bonnet of a fashionable milliner: does its value depend simply on the trouble of making it?

Stuart Mill says, the value of these tools, of these buildings, depends on the cost of production. Mr. Carey answers, that the value of existing capital is measured by the effort required to reproduce it, and not by the effort it cost in its production.

This is a double error. If you build a factory at a distance from the requisite supplies, and from any outlet for its produce, it may cost you dear enough, but it will be worth nothing; whereas a factory favourably situated in these respects, will be worth much more than its cost of production, or of reproduction either. The value of fixed capital is in proportion to the utilities it yields.

It is chimerical to look for a single source of value. Value is compound of complex elements, amongst which psychology plays an important part. Habit, routine, the pressure of a particular want, are so many causes of the variation of value. Desire is subjective; and value increases with rarity.

J. B. Say says that the utility of a thing determines the demand for it; and the expenses of production determine the extent of this demand. Stuart Mill says,[1] "Most things naturally exchange for one another in the ratio of their cost of production, or at what may be termed their cost value."

This holds good, to a great extent, of circulating capital in current use, though the price is modified by the rarity of the article, and by competition; but with regard to fixed capital, it is incorrect. The value of a particular hotel in a town does not depend on its cost price, but on its situation, on the development of the town, on fashion, etc.

The value of a utility is not to be measured by the amount of labour employed in producing it, but by the quantity of other utilities which it will fetch in exchange. Mdme. Patti may have improved her voice by labour; but if I expended a thousand times the labour on my voice that she has on hers, I should never succeed in exchanging the utility given by my voice for the hundred-thousandth part of the utilities which hers enables her to procure.

J. B. Say rightly says,[2] "The value of a thing is a positive quantity, but it is so only at a given instant. It is the nature of value to be constantly on the move, shifting from place to place. Nothing can fix it invariably, because it is founded on wants and on means of production which change with every moment."

Nevertheless, value has been treated as a substantial entity, although it is really nothing but a relation of utilities between themselves. Stuart Mill remarks very justly, "There cannot be a general rise of values. It is a contradiction in terms."[3]

A tool, being worn out, ceases to produce a certain utility. The value of the tool therefore falls; but the demand for the utility

---

[1] *Principles of Political Economy*, Book III., chap. vi., par. 1.
[2] *Cours d'Economie Politique*, vol. i., p. 70.
[3] *Principles of Political Economy*, Book II., chap. iv.

continues, and its value therefore rises. Thus it is with corn after a bad harvest.

A simultaneous rise or fall in the value of everything is impossible, because value is comparative. One species of capital rises or falls as compared with others.

We speak of "cheapness" and "dearness." A thing is "cheap" as compared with other things; it is "dear," as compared with its own price at a former time, or in other places, or as compared with the price of other utilities. Meat or land is said to be dearer now than formerly. Wine is dearer in Paris than in the Hérault, and Clos-vougeot is dearer than Piquette. Corn is cheap compared with truffles. There is no such thing as absolute cheapness or absolute dearness.

Everywhere we find, again and again, this play of fixed and circulating capital. Values, as we have said, are measured by values. If the proportion of circulating capital to fixed capital remained always the same, the value of the latter would neither increase nor diminish; but double the amount of circulating capital, the fixed capital remaining the same, and the latter will be proportionately more; that is, it will be necessary to double the circulating capital, in order to procure the same amount of fixed capital.

No doubt the relations between the different kinds of circulating capital are constantly varying, and so are the relations between the different kinds of fixed capital; but we shall show that the history of prices demonstrates the truth of the law formulated in the last chapter :—*The value of fixed capital is in direct ratio to the abundance of circulating capital, and the value of circulating capital is in inverse ratio to the power of fixed capital.*

J. B. Say says [1] that a house at 20,000 francs in Lower Brittany is worth more than one of 20,000 francs in Paris. If this were true, Lower Brittany would be richer than Paris. What he means to say, no doubt, is this: that the house in Lower Brittany is worth more relatively to surrounding objects. It can occupy more ground than the one in Paris, for ground is cheaper. It may be roomier, and have more light and air, for space, air, and sunshine are not as greedily appropriated in the country as in the large towns. But the house of the same price in Paris represents utilities of equal value, though of another kind; if it has less accommodation, it has a central situation, in the midst of a denser and more active population, etc.

Following out the same idea, Say adds, "An income of 10,000 francs in Brittany is much more considerable than the same income would be in Paris." If this were true, every one would leave Paris to go and live in Lower Brittany. What is really true is, that in

---

[1] *Traité d'Economie Politique*, Book I., chap. xxvii.

Lower Brittany, 10,000 francs will buy more potatoes, more buckwheat, cider, and fowls than in Paris; but many other utilities are far dearer there than in Paris, and thus Paris goes on attracting new inhabitants.

Adam Smith characterised the word price very correctly when he said it was the nominal value of things. A merchant must be able to estimate the relative value of his sales and purchases; he does so by the aid of money, an equivalent which serves him as a means of exchange. But as gold and silver are themselves utilities whose value is relative, price can never be absolute with respect to them.

As value is the relation of certain utilities between themselves, so price is the money valuation of this relation.

Prices, though fluctuating, are controlled by certain uniform influences. Davenant and King recorded, at the close of the seventeenth century, the curious proportions between dearth of production and rise in price, as shown in the accompanying diagram.

Or thus:—

Deficit as compared with mean consumption.	Rise as compared with mean price.
·1	·3
·2	·8
·3	·16
·4	·28
·5	·45

Porter[1] and Tooke[2] have accepted this statement.

M. de Molinari explains the cause of this difference. Every one must have noticed that it needs only a slight deficit in the harvest—that is to say, in the amount of corn in the market—to occasion a considerable

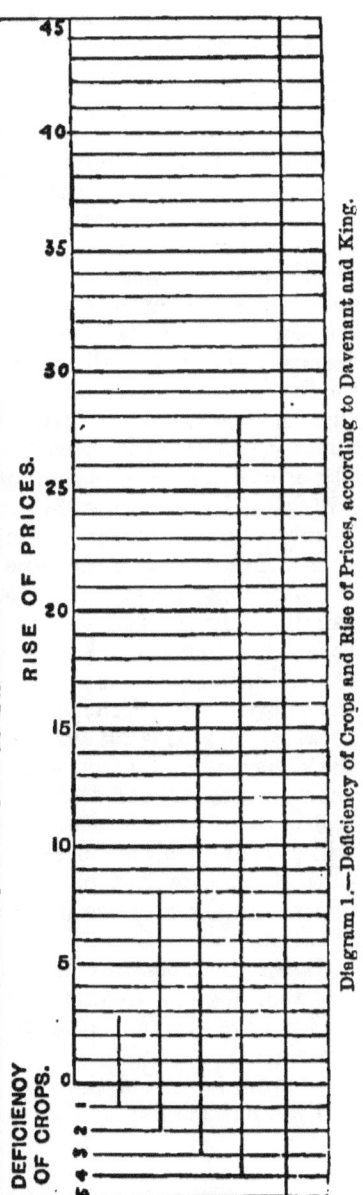

Diagram 1.—Deficiency of Crops and Rise of Prices, according to Davenant and King.

[1] *Progress of the Nation.*

[2] *History of Prices.*

rise in price. In 1847, when the deficiency did not exceed a quarter of the ordinary harvest, prices rose from twenty to forty and fifty francs in succession. While the supply fell in arithmetical progression, prices rose in geometrical progression. In the same way, only a slight increase in the harvest brings a considerable reduction of prices. From 1847 to 1849 the price of bread fell from fifty to ten or twelve francs, although the excess of the one year was not greater than the deficiency of the other.

The following circumstance, however, usually retards this geometrical progression :—

When a deficiency occurs in the production of an article, and its price rises in consequence, the demand for it falls. Suppose that in a town which usually consumes 100,000 hectolitres of corn at 20 francs, the supply falls short by 10,000 hectolitres. The price immediately mounts up to 24 francs, but less corn will be consumed at this price than at 20 francs. The demand will probably fall by about 5,000 or 6,000 hectolitres. The discrepancy between the supply of corn and the money offered in exchange decreasing, the price will fall till it becomes stationary at about 22 francs. So long as the supply of corn is steadily kept up, there will be no further variation. But if it does not, and if the stock is reduced by consumption to 80,000 and 60,000 hectolitres, and so on, the price will rise rapidly. On the other hand, the demand will continue to fall, firstly, because other and cheaper food will be substituted for it; and secondly, because the rising price will cease to come within reach of the poorest part of the population. But as every one will make the greatest sacrifices rather than die of hunger, the competition among the consumers of corn will still be very keen, and the discrepancy between the quantity of corn and the money offered in exchange will become more and more marked. The last thousand hectolitres will probably sell at an exorbitant price. Corn, and, in general, the absolute necessaries of life, are the things most susceptible of an enormous rise of price in consequence of a deficiency in the supply.

Hence:—

When the proportion between the quantities of two articles offered in exchange for one another varies in arithmetical progression, the proportions between the values of these two articles will vary in geometrical progression.[1]

It must be added that—

The applicability of this law is in inverse ratio to facility of transport.

---

[1] Molinari, *Questions de Politique et de Droit Public*, vol. i., p. 35.

CHAPTER III.

MONEY.

SOME of the Socialists and Communists of 1848 attributed all ills to money. Proudhon, who was not without some claim to an acquaintance with economic questions, wished to do away with it by means of his Bank of Exchange. He would have been an enthusiastic supporter of the English periodical, *The Exchange and Mart*, which serves as a medium for people who want to exchange a capital old horse for a snappish lap-dog. At public meetings in 1868 and 1869, we have heard the most furious anathemas launched against money. Even in England it appears that there are members of Parliament who share these prejudices, for Professor Stanley Jevons tells of one who remarked, not many years ago, "I am not surprised that the people are so poor, when there are so few shillings and sixpenny pieces, and when all the small coin in the kingdom would not pay the rates and taxes for one year."

This is only an expression of the notion that man can create wealth. We find it everywhere in economic science. Here it has the more scope, because most of the people who use money habitually neglect to consider its real function.

It has been supposed that money represented all other commodities, and that the total value of the money in a country must equal the total value of all the other property; and this notion is not yet so exploded as to make it unnecessary to refute it. A glance at Diagram 2 will be enough for the purpose.

According to M. Vacher, the wealth of France[1] may be reckoned at:—

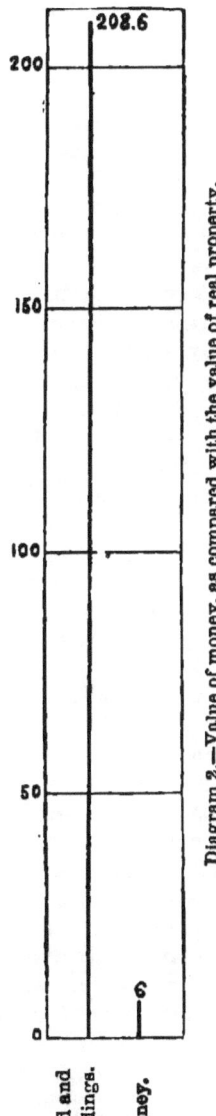

Diagram 2.—Value of money, as compared with the value of real property.

[1] *Journal de la Société de Statisque*, November, 1878. I shall adopt, throughout, the figures of Messrs. Vacher, de Foville, Stanley Jevons, Griffen, Newmarch, Sötbeer, Bertillon, etc., in addition to the official figures; but I leave the entire responsibility with their authors, lest I should be accused of grouping them for my own pur-

Land	fr. 156,600,000,000
Buildings on lease	15,600,000,000
Buildings	30,000,000,000
Property in mortmain	5,000,000,000
State Forests	1,400,000,000
	208,600,000,000
Coin	6,000,000,000

We see then that money in France represents something like three per cent. of the value of lands and houses alone. It is, therefore, but an infinitesimal part of the wealth of the country.

Man began with barter. But there was this inconvenience attaching to it, that of two men each might have things to exchange which the other did not want. They would have preferred some equivalent with which each could obtain what he did want. The next thing was to find this equivalent. In Athens, it was found in oxen; in Siberia and Canada, in furs; in Chinese Tartary, it was tea; in Scotland, nails; in the old English colonies of America, corn and tobacco; in North America and the West Indies, shells; in the Portuguese possessions at Angola, bits of straw; in Sumatra and Mexico, salt.

Europeans have largely employed whisky in their dealings with natives; and at the present time all the commerce of Africa is carried on by means of blue cotton goods manufactured in England, and known as guineas.

But the system had its inconveniences. An ox is a large piece of money, and it must have been sometimes difficult to get change for it; and besides, there are oxen and oxen. Then again, book-keeping must have had its difficulties. Among a hundred articles there are 4,950 possible exchanges, each article having to be valued in terms of every other article.

J. S. Mill draws attention to the confusion which would follow on the suppression of money as a medium of exchange. In the first place, we should have no common standard of value. It would be a daily perplexity to the housewife to reckon up her morning's purchases. And then, as Adam Smith says, money is an instrument of exchange serving to convey value.

Money must combine the following qualities: it must have a value of its own; it must be a commodity; it must be easily divisible; must be always identical with itself; must be durable. The value of money must be real. Nevertheless, among civilised peoples, where money is regarded as an instrument of circulation, it is rather

poses. Here, M. Vacher's figures relating to the value of property are too low, and those relating to money should also have been doubled. These figures have been disputed (Meunier, *Avenir Economique*, vol. ii.). But I am not here discussing questions of statistics; I am only attempting to show exact proportions.

what Lord Castlereagh called a sentiment of value, than value itself.

It is very useful to know what quantity of corn and what quantity of wax a pound of silver will buy. The commodity selected, as Professor Stanley Jevons has said,[1] becomes a *common denominator*, or *common measure of value*. Aristotle has pointed out very clearly the origin and character of money. He says, "Men invented among themselves, by way of exchange, something which they should mutually give and take, and which, being really valuable in itself, might easily be passed from hand to hand for the purposes of daily life, as iron or silver, or anything else of the same nature. This had at first a fixed standard simply according to its weight or size; but in process of time they put upon it a certain stamp, to save the trouble of weighing, and this stamp was affixed as a sign of its express value."[2]

Among recent definitions, we may give that of M. Michel Chevalier, completed by Stanley Jevons, which seems to us extremely accurate; "Pieces of money are ingots, the weight and purity of which are guaranteed by the integrity of the designs stamped on the surface of the metal." Or, more simply,—

Pieces of money are ingots of a certified weight and fineness.

But the value even of metallic money has long been a matter of faith.

Professor Stanley Jevons declares that in 1869, after an extended and searching inquiry, he was convinced that nearly half the half-sovereigns, and thirty-one and a half per cent. of the sovereigns were light weight.[3] French money is worse still. Its standard scarcely ever rises above the permitted minimum—a thing which ought to be quite exceptional.

In countries where the precious metals are found, and where money is regarded as a means of storing value, the standard is more rigidly maintained. In the East, silver coins are required to be of extreme purity, the standard being ·960,979, so that they may be the more easily stamped. The standard of silver coinage in the Latin Union is only ·835. Nevertheless, the law of Germinal, in the year XI. of the Republic, declares, in conformity with that of the 3rd Thermidor, in the year III., that five grammes of silver at a standard of ·9 shall constitute the monetary unit under the name of franc. Our money standard has thus, since the convention of 1866, become debased. But in ordinary life nobody cares about it. In monetary, as in all other economic questions, psychology plays a great part.

Here we have the explanation of Gresham's law: *The bad money*

---

[1] *Money*, 1877.
[2] *Politics*, Book I., chap. ix. (Bohn's Translation).
[3] *Money*, p. 112, 4th edition.

drives out the good, while the good money cannot drive out the bad. Why? Because most people pay no attention to the quality of money. It matters little to them whether a coin is a little the worse for wear or not. On the other hand, speculators in money put the new coins in the crucible, and circulate the bad. Hence it is that the State alone can withdraw bad coins from circulation.

We give here the current commercial equivalents of the metals in 1877.[1]

Gold	1		Tin	942
Platinum	3·5		Copper	1,696
Aluminium	7		Lead	6,360
Silver	16		Bar-iron	15,900
Nickel	71		Pig-iron	50,880

A glance at the above table will suffice to explain the ever-increasing use of gold as money, 6 grammes of gold serving for 100 grammes of silver, or 800 kilogrammes of iron. The economy of transport is obvious.

Gold has, besides, several other good qualities. It is ornamental; it is malleable; it has a high specific gravity; and it is not easily oxydised or dissolved. Mixed with a tenth part of copper, it becomes hard. Its point of fusion is not too high, and it does not evaporate at any known temperature. Old coins can be melted down at a very slight loss.

All these qualities, and especially the first, that of great value combined with small bulk, must insure its preponderance over silver. After beginning with leather, tin, copper, and silver, we have come to use gold coin almost exclusively. It is a logical advance which should not have escaped the attention of those alarmists who, like M. Michel Chevalier, in their panic at the discovery of the Californian diggings, urged on France the adoption of silver as the only standard.

Gold must in its turn disappear, at least to a great extent, because its employment is troublesome, and becomes less and less necessary. Paper is more portable than gold. The English Clearing House does business to the amount of £6,000,000,000 without a halfpenny.

The total value of the metals used as coin in England in 1876, was as follows:—

Gold money in circulation	£100,000,000
Bullion	15,000,000
Silver money	15,000,000
Bronze money	1,000,000
Total	£131,000,000

---

[1] At the present rate (1881), silver should be above 17.

The interest at 3¼ per cent. is £4,262,000

Loss of interest	£4,262,000
Wear and tear of coin	48,000
Expenses of coinage	42,000
Total	£4,352,000

It will be understood that the English are too good financiers not to endeavour to restrain this expenditure as much as possible.

Newmarch rightly says that gold is the change for the bank-note, as the bank-note is for the cheque, the cheque for the bill of exchange, and the bill of exchange for the transference of amounts from one account to another, and for current accounts.

The bank-note is daily losing importance in England; the use of the Clearing House tends to take its place, as it has taken the place of coin.

This is a consequence of the progress of circulation. The mechanism for the transmission of commercial movement has been successively lightened, till a couple of figures in a book have replaced the passing and repassing of bags of gold and silver.

It is in consequence of this movement that the countries which still maintain a double standard are doomed to undergo, within a given time, a considerable loss. It is true that Holland with her silver standard found an apparent increase in the number of her exports; but as they were paid for in a depreciated coinage, she lost the profits she expected to realise. She has since returned to the gold standard.

At the present time, the countries having a single standard comprise 140,000,000 inhabitants, while those having silver, paper, or a double standard, comprise 940,000,000. Among the latter are India and China; England, since 1816, has been amongst the former. This question of the standard is very simple. A standard of measurement is a fixed measure, to which all others can be referred; a standard of weight is in the same way an invariable weight; but since the money standard itself partakes of the value of money, it can only designate the form of money adopted as legal tender in any country, and having in that country a forced currency for all purposes.

In France we have adopted two forms of money—the franc, weighing five grammes of silver, at a standard of ·9, and the louis of twenty francs, at the rate of 155 to a kilogramme. Thus a fixed proportion of 15⅓ per cent. has been established between the two metals, based on the theory that one kilogramme of gold will be always able to fetch fifteen and a half of silver, neither more nor less.

Yet so far back as the seventeenth century, William Petty and Locke had shown the absurdity of taking, as the measure of commercial value, things between which there existed no invariable proportion, and had laid down that in every country there should be but one metal to serve as a standard of reckoning, as a legal tender, and as a measure of value.

Some governments—France amongst them—have not yet embraced this simple truth. We have even seen a publicist dedicating all his energies to securing the adoption of this conventional and fictitious proportion by all nations and for all time. M. Cernuschi might have found something better to do.

The nations composing the Latin Union, viz., France, Belgium, Greece, Italy, and Switzerland, have taken defensive measures by suspending the coinage of five-franc pieces. Practically, however, there is now but one standard—that of gold—since the possessor of silver bullion cannot have it coined.

At the same time, the five-franc piece continues to have a forced circulation for unlimited sums. It will soon be absolutely necessary to restrict this use to the making up of odd sums. Otherwise it is too plain what the situation must be; the French merchant, buying in England, must pay in gold; while the English merchant, buying in France, can pay in silver—that is, at a loss of ten to thirteen per cent. The gain to him is as clear as the loss to us. Hence the following result, attested by the condition of the vaults in the Bank of France.

				Gold.	Silver.
November, 1876				1,541,000,000	627,000,000 francs.
,,	1877			1,240,000,000	859,000,000 ,,
,,	1878			1,099,000,000	1,044,000,000 ,,
13 ,,	1879			803,000,000	1,207,000,000 ,,
11 ,,	1880			556,000,000	1,247,000,000 ,,

As this book is scientific, and not controversial, I will not pursue this point further than to show that gold and silver, like all other commodities, are not fixed measures, but expressions of variable relations. Money is a variable measure. In measuring other things, it measures also itself.

The following tables will show the part played by the precious metals since the discovery of America.

I take these figures from the work of Dr. Sötbeer of Göttingen, " Edelmetall, Produktion und Werthverhältniß zwischen Gold und Silber seits der Entdeckung Amerikas," published by Julius Perthes of Gotha.

The statistics of these matters are full of mistakes. Dr. Sötbeer has pointed out many of them. I shelter myself under his authority. No fewer than six or seven hundred elements enter into the composition of the following table. Dr. Sötbeer has endeavoured carefully to distinguish the exact value of each; but he has arrived at only an approximate result.

Average Annual Production throughout the World at Various Periods.

Periods.	Silver.	Gold.	Total Value in millions of francs.
	kilog.	kilog.	
1493–1520	47,000	5,800	30·7
1521–1544	90,200	7,160	45·2
1545–1560	311,600	8,510	99·7
1561–1580	299,500	6,840	91·0
1581–1600	418,900	7,380	120·0
1601–1620	422,900	8,520	124·9
1621–1640	393,600	8,300	117·5
1641–1660	366,300	8,770	113·0
1661–1680	337,000	9,260	108·1
1681–1700	341,900	10,765	114·5
1701–1720	355,600	12,820	124·7
1721–1740	431,200	19,080	163·5
1741–1760	533,145	24,610	205·7
1761–1780	652,740	20,705	219·1
1781–1800	879,060	17,790	259·9
1801–1810	894,150	17,778	263·2
1811–1820	540,770	11,445	161·6
1821–1830	460,560	14,216	153·0
1831–1840	596,450	20,289	205·0
1841–1850	780,415	54,759	366·6
1851–1855	886,115	197,515	888·2
1856–1860	904,990	206,058	922·2
1861–1865	1,101,150 [1]	198,207	893·4
1866–1870	1,339,085	191,900	970·5
1871–1875	1,969,425	170,675	1,038·3

(See Diagram 3, p. 84.)

Those who threaten us with an inundation of gold must see how small a quantity of it is distributed through the world compared with that of silver. M. Suss, a man of considerable weight in Austria, struck with this fact, has predicted the rapid exhaustion of gold. With equal appositeness, other economists have threatened our great grandchildren with the exhaustion of the coal supply.

If we assume all the gold and silver produced to have been coined,

---

[1] These figures are higher than those of the English Commission of Inquiry into the causes of the depreciation of silver. (See Mr. Goschen's report of 5th July, 1876.)

84 MONEY.

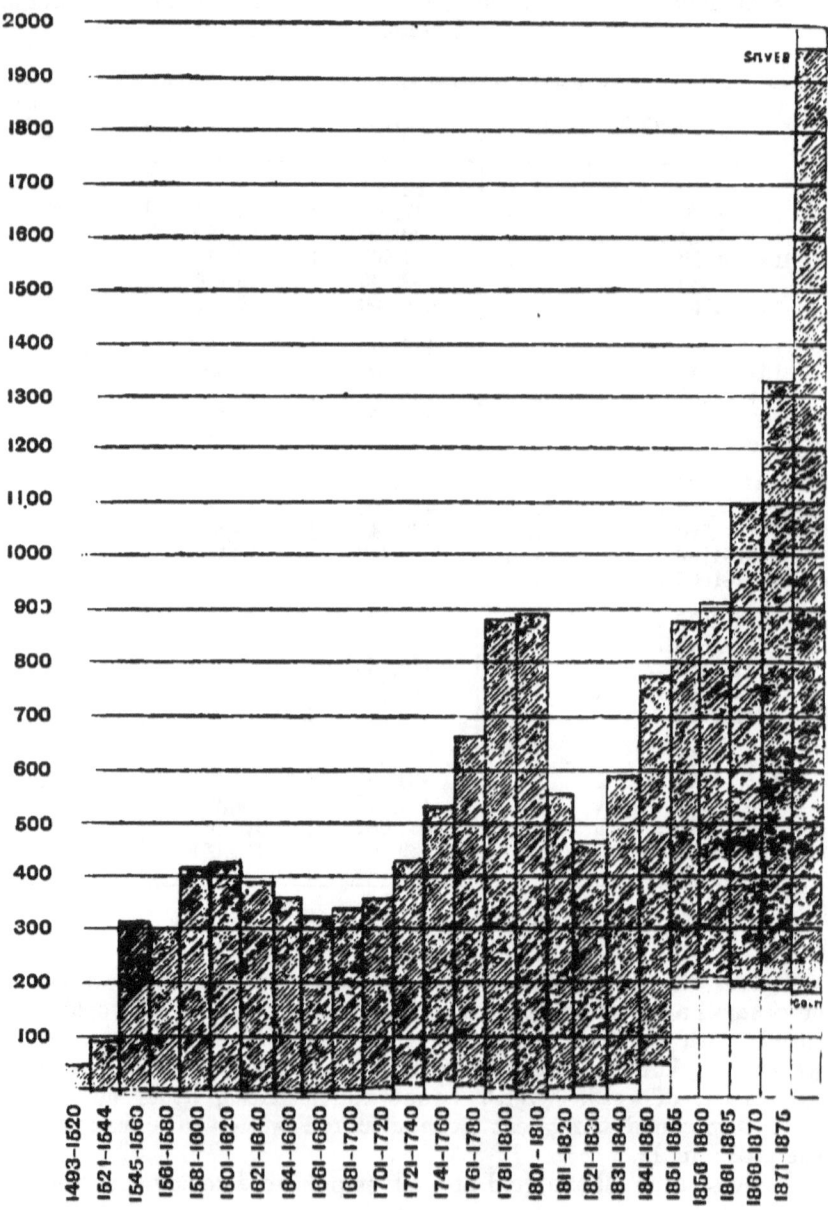

Diagram 3.—Annual Production of Silver and Gold, 1,000 kilogrammes to be taken as unity.

and the kilogramme of gold to be worth 2,790 marks, and that of silver to be worth 180, then we have the following proportions:—

Periods.	Silver.	Gold.
	Per cent.	Per cent.
1493–1520	34·3	65·7
1521–1544	44·9	55·1
1545–1560	70·3	29·7
1661–1680	70·1	29·9
1741–1760	58·3	41·7
1801–1810	76·4	23·6
1831–1840	65·5	34·5
1841–1850	47·9	52·1
1851–1855	22·4	77·6
1871–1875	42·7	57·3

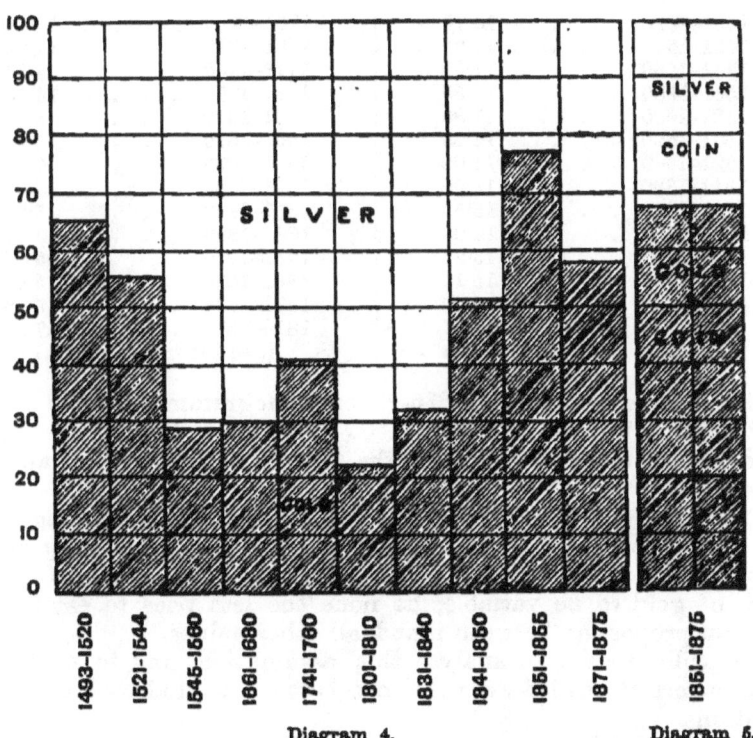

Diagram 4.   Diagram 5.

According to Dr. Sötbeer, the coinage between 1851 and 1875, *i.e.*, in a space of twenty-five years, in Great Britain, Austria, British India, the United States, France, Belgium, Italy, Germany,

Austro-Hungary, Russia, Norway and Sweden, and the Netherlands amounted to :—

Gold	. . . .	5,785,580 kilogrammes.
Silver	. . . .	42,098,340 ,,

Gold, then, constitutes 68·1 per cent. and silver 31·9 per cent. in value of the money coined. (See Diagram 5, p. 85).

Of this money, 1,029,000 kilogrammes of gold and 11,100,000 of silver was in existence already; thus the increase in silver was relatively less than the increase in gold, which was 46·2 per cent. Let the advocates of a double standard glance at the following figures :—

VARIATIONS IN THE PROPORTIONATE VALUE OF GOLD AND SILVER FROM 1501 TO 1878.

Periods.	Proportionate Value.	Periods.	Proportionate Value.
1501–1520	10·75	1751–1760	14·56
1521–1540	11·25	1761–1770	14·81
1541–1560	11·30	1771–1780	14·64
1561–1580	11·50	1781–1790	14·76
1581–1600	11·80	1791–1800	15·42
1601–1620	12·25	1801–1810	15·61
1621–1640	14·00	1811–1820	15·51
1641–1660	15·00	1821–1830	15·80
1661–1680	15·50	1831–1840	15·75
1681–1700	14·96	1841–1850	15·83
1701–1710	15·27	1851–1860	15·86
1711–1720	15·15	1861–1870	15·48
1721–1730	15·09	1871–1875	15·98
1731–1740	15·07	1876–1878	17·63
1741–1750	14·93	(See Diagram 6, p. 87.)	

It will be seen that in 1876-78 one kilogramme of gold would buy 17·63 of silver, while in 1500 it would only buy 10. It is needless to insist further on the constant fall in the value of silver.

Thus confronted with facts, one is compelled to acknowledge that the proportion between the values of gold and silver is variable. But stability is so necessary to man, that even while admitting the value of gold to be variable, he none the less tries to establish a uniform proportion between it and all other values.

We will proceed to analyse this assumption, and to show into what errors it has led even the men best acquainted with monetary questions.

We have got into a way of saying "Five grammes of silver at a standard of 0·9 is worth a franc," because the law of 7th Germinal, year XI. of the Republic, required this proportion of silver in the monetary unit which it called a franc.

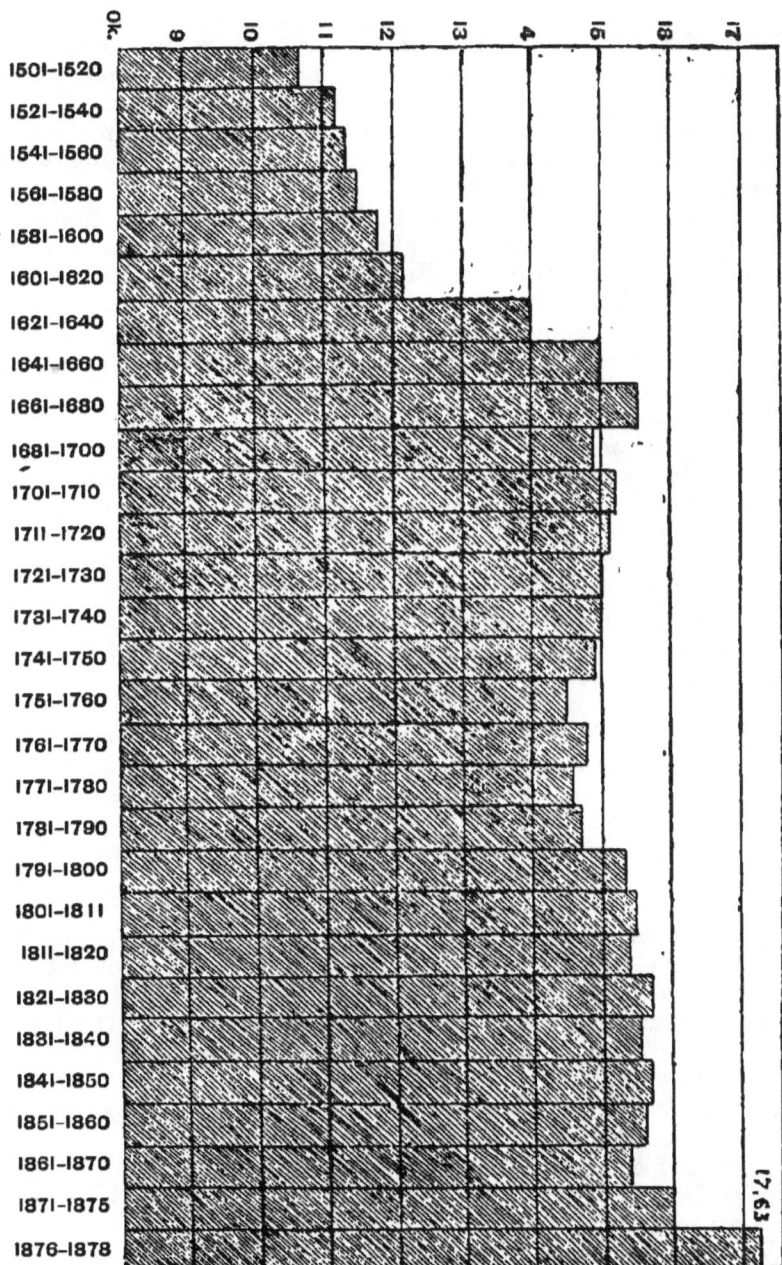

Diagram 6.—Proportionate Value of Gold and Silver.

J. B. Say has shown that this expression is incorrect. Five grammes of silver are worth five grammes of silver, just as five grammes of copper are worth five grammes of copper. The division into grammes does not impart a new quality to a metal.

Still, there is a certain amount of truth in the expression, which we will endeavour to disentangle.

In England, the cost of coinage is defrayed by the State. A sovereign is worth the same weight of bullion of the same fineness, neither more nor less.[1] In France, the cost of coinage at the bearer's expense is 6 fr. 70 c. per kilogramme of gold of 0·9 standard. The kilogramme represents 3,100 francs. Minting expenses deducted, it is worth 3,093 fr. 30 c.; and unless the Government should suspend the coinage, it cannot fall below this, for if the value of money were to fall below that of bullion, the owners of money would convert it into ingots.

The only variations in value arise from cost of transport and keeping, and from the demand for payment in cash. It is these variations which constitute the rates of exchange.

It is therefore correct to say that the kilogramme of gold is worth 3,100 francs, or, deducting cost of coinage, 3,093 fr. 30 c.; or that in England 123·27 grains of twenty-two carat gold are worth a sovereign. But how are we to express the value of francs or sovereigns? That is the question. To express the value of coin, we measure or weigh it, and we say it is worth twenty or thirty francs per hectolitre or per quintal. Clearly a greater or less amount of grammes of gold are needed to buy a given quantity of corn; and consequently the value of gold rises or falls as compared with that of corn.

Then people jump to the conclusion that gold has risen or fallen in value.

Yes; but compared with what? with corn? Yes, you say. But how do you know that corn has not gone up in value simply because the consumption has increased, because the means of transport have brought it within reach of the consumer, because agriculture cannot produce a sufficient quantity to satisfy the demand? The rise in corn may be quite independent of the value of gold; and the price of corn may indicate its value, not as compared with gold, but as compared with the other utilities for which money serves as a common denominator.

Diagram 7 compares the price of corn from 1861 to 1870 with its price from 1821 to 1830, long before the discovery of the great fields of gold.

We know that England and France are the two countries which have absorbed the most gold; it is, consequently, in these two

[1] If the coining is done through the Bank, one ounce of gold of standard fineness fetches £3 17s. 9d. instead of £3 17s. 10½d.

countries that the price of corn may be expected to have risen highest. But this is by no means the case. It has fallen 14 per cent. in England; it has risen only 17 per cent. in France; while in Austria and Hungary, where they are so short of gold that they are obliged to have recourse to paper money, it has gone up 131 to 142 per cent.

The price of corn, then, is not dependent on the abundance or scarcity of gold.

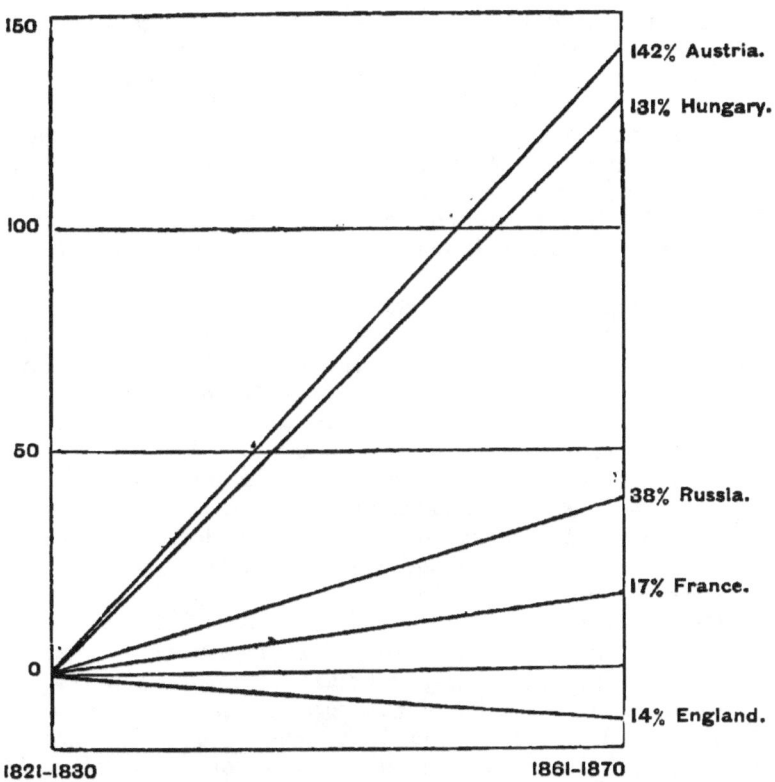

Diagram 7.—Price of Corn before and after the great Discoveries of Gold.

M. Levasseur says :[1] "To have a perfectly correct numerical expression, the term of comparison must consist, not of a single commodity, but of all." What, all? without exception? M. Levasseur certainly goes on to admit that the task is difficult, for he adds immediately, "If the price of all or nearly all commodities has

[1] *La Question de l'Or.*

risen one-tenth, we are not thence to conclude that all commodities have risen in value; for as value is nothing but a relation, a rise or fall of all values at once is nonsense; but we may conclude that the value of the precious metals—that is, the relation of one commodity to all the rest—has fallen in the same proportion."

In order to give this theory a semblance of truth, it would be necessary that all capital, both fixed and circulating, should experience a uniform rise. Has this ever happened? No doubt it may be said that in California, when the gold fever was at its height, and the miners who had rushed to the diggings under its influence were giving fifty francs for a bottle of wine, ten francs for a pound of sugar, and five for a pound of flour, the value of gold was very low, because gold was very plentiful, while all other commodities were scarce. But the soil, except just at the diggings, was equally valueless. How far, beyond the limits of its own contracted area, did this exceptional state of things make itself felt?

To return to the question; even admitting that a uniform rise in the price of all capital is possible, I deny that it proves a fall in the value of gold.

Let us imagine an island, the gold of which is limited to a certain unvarying quantity, sufficient for its requirements. Let us denote the rate of production and consumption in the island by the number 100, and the amount of its coin by the number 10.

Its population and consumption increase faster than its production. The price of meat and corn doubles. Are we to say that gold has fallen in value? According to M. Levasseur, Yes; according to the facts of the case, No. On the contrary, unless the islanders have had recourse to cheques and clearing-houses, gold will have gone up in value; and yet prices have risen.

It cannot be otherwise, unless we could suppose that the scarcity of gold might so paralyse business as to cause a fall in prices; and this would be impossible, for the use of paper money, or some other device, would assuredly supply in great measure the place of gold.

Again, when the quantity of the precious metals increases, does their value fall in proportion, and *vice versâ?* M. Levasseur declares that the only measure we can give of the value of these metals is their production. He ought at least to have added, "and their consumption."

According to Newmarch, in the decade 1865–75, all articles of commerce fell 27 per cent., while real property rose 49 per cent. (See Diagram 8, p. 91.)

PRODUCTION OF GOLD.

1861–1865. 206,058
1871–1875. 170,675

At least, 16 per cent.

ISSUE OF GOLD COIN AT THE LONDON MINT.
(Statistical Abstract.)

1856–1865	£52,788,000
1866–1875	47,278,000

Fall, 10 per cent. on the earlier period.

The total production of gold has fallen 16 per cent., and the issue of the London Mint has fallen 10 per cent. This being so, the price of fixed capital ought to have fallen, and that of gold to have

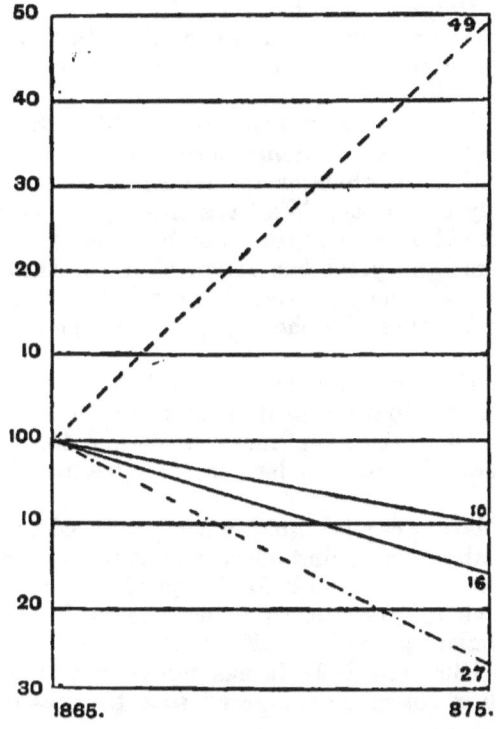

Diagram 8.—Rise and Fall of Gold in proportion to Fixed and Circulating Capital in England, 1864–1875. 49, increase in the value of fixed capital. 10, gold coin struck. 27, price of the chief commodities in London. 16, diminution in the production of gold.

risen; we ought, therefore, to have to record a fall in the value of fixed capital. On the contrary, there is a rise of 49 per cent.

"Quite so," some one will say; "but this rise results from there being still a surplus of gold, notwithstanding the diminished issue of coin, and the fall in the value of the metal." If this argument were true, it would still have to be explained why the fall in the price of circulating capital outruns the decrease of coinage. Does not the fall indicate a rise in the value of gold as compared with all circulating capital, raw material, and articles of commerce and of consumption?

Thus, the value of gold has fallen as compared with real property, and risen as compared with circulating capital; whence I am justified in concluding that the value of gold does not vary in proportion to its quantity, but in relation to the different kinds of capital, falling as compared with some, and rising as compared with others.

According to Diagram 7, it has risen 14 per cent. on the London market as compared with corn; and according to Diagram 8, it has fallen within ten years 49 per cent. as compared with the fixed capital of Great Britain.

Nevertheless, it would be an error to consider these proportions as strictly correct; for while money serves as the common denominator of all utilities, the changes in the value of these utilities do not depend solely on money. We have already observed that if corn is dear at a particular moment, it is not because money has fallen in value, but because the yield has fallen short of the consumption. In the same way, if a factory rises in value, it is not because gold has fallen, but because the factory produces more utilities than before.

At the same time, if I am asked—Is this fall in the value of gold to be attributed to a fall in its utility, and this rise in that of fixed capital to its producing more utilities? the answer cannot be doubtful. Yes, the gold is less useful; yes, the fixed capital is more useful.

Like all circulating capital, gold, when produced at a lower price, and in greater abundance, and more economically used, gradually sinks in value as compared with fixed capital. Still, at least within the decade above referred to, its value has sunk less than that of the bulk of circulating capital. We shall see elsewhere that in the period between 1850 and 1877 it has fallen in proportion only 10 per cent., which is not much compared with the steady rise of fixed capital.

There are, however, few historians and economists who do not speak of the value of gold as rising or falling absolutely. It is a singular instance of agreement among them. I will take, as an example, only the latest estimates. Professor Stanley Jevons declares that between 1780 and 1809 the value of gold fell 46 per cent.; from 1809 to 1849 it rose 14 per cent.; since 1849 it has fallen again 20 per cent. But the figures he gives in his table of prices since 1785 do not correspond with these oscillations.[1] According to M. de Foville, the fall in gold since the beginning of

[1] See *Journal of the Statistical Society* ("On the Variation of Prices"), vol. xxviii., 1865.

the century should have been 25 per cent. M. Roswag[1] asserts that it did not amount to 4 per cent. M. David, late Secretary to the Department of Commerce of the Swiss Federation, reckons it at $3\frac{1}{2}$ per cent. Lastly, Dr. Sötbeer asserts a fall in silver and a rise in gold.

Mr. Giffen says that gold has been rising in value for the last twenty years. Lord Beaconsfield, in a speech in the House of Lords, in 1878, on the agricultural crisis, said: "Gold rises in value daily, and its rise occasions the fall in prices." Mr. Patterson proved lately before the Statistical Society, that gold never ceased to fall in England and all over the world.[2]

It is a bad way of putting the question. No doubt gold has risen and does rise as compared with silver. But, compared with corn, it has risen in England and fallen in Austria; and, compared with houses and lands, it has fallen in England and France. In short, it has risen as compared with certain utilities which have become cheaper, while it has fallen as compared with other utilities which have become dearer.

Not long ago, I heard M. Gustave Hubbard, M. Gambetta's familiar on economic questions, at a dinner at the Progrès Social, speak, without contradiction, of the depreciation of metals as an incontrovertible fact. I could not help raising a timid protest, to the great indignation of all present—which shows that even economists sometimes mistake words for things. M. Hubbard said to me, "Look here; a louis of last century and a louis of this,—do you mean to say the value is the same?"

"That depends on what you want to buy."

"Well," he remonstrated, amid roars of laughter from everybody, "if you are going to put it like that!"

I am sorry for the laughers, but I do put it like that, and it cannot be put in any other way.

It is untrue to say, "The value of gold has risen or fallen," without specifying the utility with which you are comparing it.

Moreover, a glance at Diagram 8 and the following Diagrams will remind us that, for the reason given in Book II., gold is always falling in comparison with fixed capital.

The production of utilities by fixed capital is ever on the increase; and money also, which is circulating capital, increases in abundance, but its utility, instead of increasing, diminishes. By virtue of the law, according to which industrial progress consists in obtaining the highest possible inverse ratio between the consumption of circulating capital and the return yielded by fixed capital, man seeks to restrict the use of money by means of cheques, deposit banks, clearing-houses, and all the modern appliances for lending money.

---

[1] *Les Métaux Précieux*, 1875.
[2] *Journal of the Statistical Society*, March, 1880.

The law, then, which we have stated, holds good with regard to money:—

The value of fixed capital is in direct ratio to the abundance of circulating capital, and the value of circulating capital is in inverse ratio to the power of fixed capital.

Hence we may say—

Gold is a commodity.

The standard of money is a common denominator of values, and a medium of exchange.

The value of money is relative to the value of the utility for which it is exchanged.

The value of money is in inverse ratio to the utility of fixed capital.

CHAPTER IV.

RELATIVE VALUES OF FIXED AND CIRCULATING CAPITAL.[1]

I HAVE said that the value of fixed capital is in direct ratio to the abundance of circulating capital, and the value of circulating capital is in inverse ratio to the power of fixed capital.

The truth of this law has just been demonstrated with regard to money, and the same may now be done with regard to other capital. The demonstration will not take long. The facts speak for themselves.

AVERAGE PRICE OF A HECTARE OF LAND.

Year.	Francs.	Per cent.
1789	500	...
1815	700	40
1851	1,290	158
1862	1,850	290
1874	2,000	300

AVERAGE PRICE OF A HECTOLITRE OF GRAIN.

	Francs.	Per cent. on the prices of 1787–1809.
1787–1793	19·89	...
1800–1809	19·91	...
1820–1829	18·22	...
1830–1839	19·08	...
1840–1849	20·49	2·8
1850–1859	21·51	...
1856–1876	22·05	15·8

[1] This chapter was read at the meeting of the *Association pour l'Avancement des Sciences*, at Reims, 14th August, 1880. (See report and discussion in the *Temps* of 10th September, and in the *Economiste Français* of 18th September, 16th October, and 19th November, 1880.

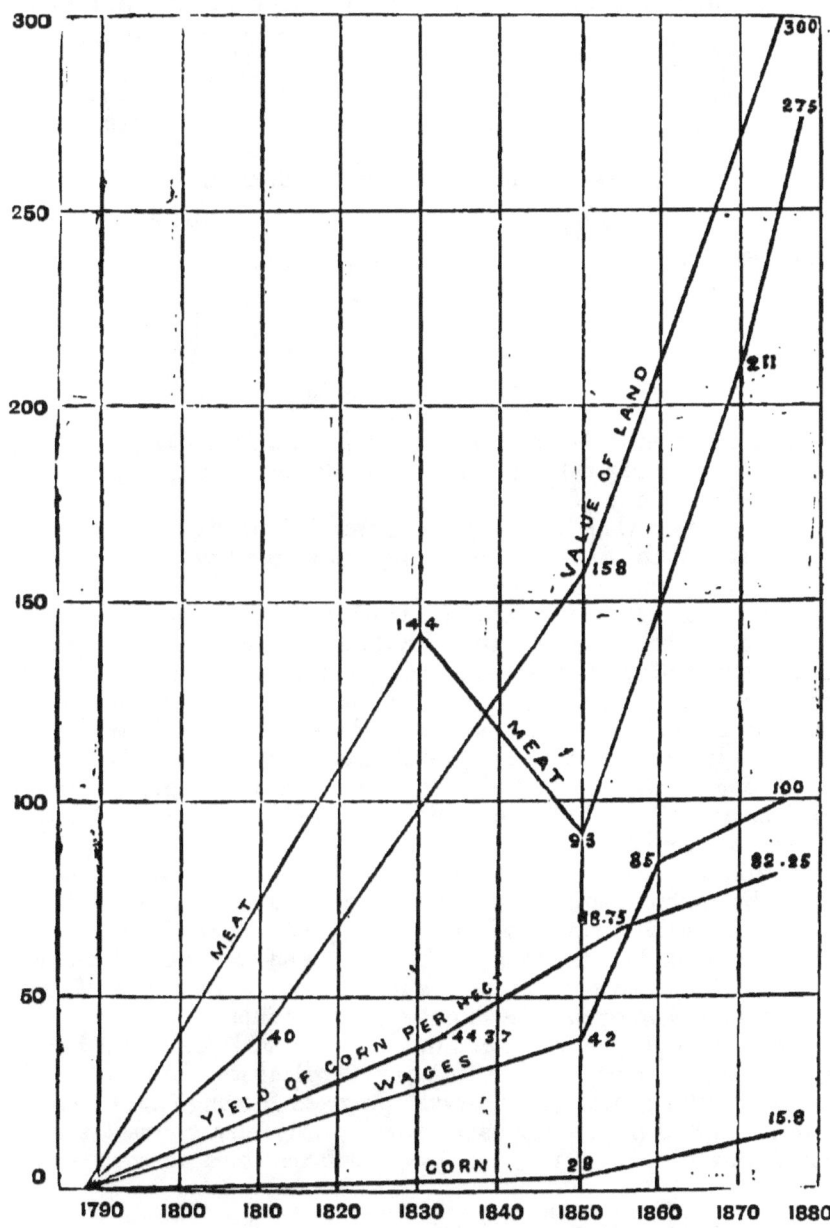

Diagram 9.—Price of Land and Agricultural Produce, 1787-1880 (after M. de Foville).

Average Wages of an Agricultural Labourer not Boarded.

	Francs.	Per cent.
1789	1· 0[1]	...
1850	1·42[2]	42
1862	1·85	85
1875	2· 0	100

Marché de Poissy et de Sceaux.

	Price of Beef per kil.	Per cent.		Price of Beer per kil.	Per cent
1780–1789	0f. 45c.[3]	...	1850	0f. 87c.	93
1810	0 97	...	1860	1 25	...
1820	0 96	...	1870	1 40	211
1830	1 05	144	1875	1 06	...
1840	1 11	...	1878	1 69	275[4]

(See Diagram 9, p. 95.)

Now we observe, between 1787 and 1875, an increase of 300 per cent. in the selling value of land, while the increase in the price of corn has been only 15·8 per cent.

We are told that the "land is in want of hands," and we hear complaints of the dearness of labour; yet wages have only risen 100 per cent.

The reason of the increased value of land is, that it is beginning to be turned to better account. No doubt the increase per hectolitre in the production of wheat has not exceeded 82 per cent., and this shows that the value of fixed capital does not rise iu a mere arithmetical proportion to the abundance of circulating capital. It rises not only in proportion to the greater quantity of utilities which the fixed capital has furnished, but yet more in proportion to the greater quantities of utilities which the fixed capital seems likely to be able to furnish.

Again, in estimating prices, not only must the increase of the yield be taken into account, but also the saving effected in the circulating capital employed in producing it. Thus the use of the drill has saved half the seed. Threshing machines have done away with an immense amount of manual labour. Facilities of communication have opened fresh outlets for produce.

Yet, although the value of land has risen 300 per cent., the rise is far below what it ought to be. Agriculture is perhaps the industry which has made least progress during the century. Chemistry and physiology have shown pretty clearly what are the conditions of cultivation, and have reduced them to very simple

---

[1] Paul Boiteau, *Etat de la France en* 1789, p. 509.
[2] Maurice Block, vol. ii., p. 39.
[3] Boiteau, *ubi sup.*
[4] Marché de la Villette (*Bull. de Statist. Municip.*).

formulœ; but so far they have been very little applied. The steam-engine, so widely employed in other industries, is here neglected. While three million horse-power is employed in manufactures, agriculture employs only twenty-five thousand. In short, it is impossible to instance all the utilities lost or neglected by man.

MM. Denayrouze and Ville calculate[1] that by means of irrigation and chemical manures it would be possible to increase the value of every one of the 33,000,000 hectares capable of such amelioration by 3,000 francs, at which rate the soil of France would gain an added value of a hundred milliards of francs.

The same phenomenon appears in England. I take the following figures from Mr. Caird[2]:—

INCREASE PER CENT. FROM 1771 TO 1850 AND 1878.

	1771	1850	Increase per cent.	1878	Increase per cent.
Rent of land	13s.	27s.	107	30s.	130
Production of corn, per acre . .	23 bus.	26½ bus.	15·22	28 bus.	22·7
Wages of agricultural labourers .	7s. 3d.	9s. 7d.	32·20	14s.	93·3
Price of bread, per lb.	1¼d.	1¼d.	16·60	1¼d.	...
Price of meat „	3d.	5d.	66·66	9d.	200

(See Diagram 10, p. 98.)

We know the difficulties which attend the transfer of landed property in England. It does not pass freely as in France; and for this reason Mr. Caird has estimated its rent rather than its value. But what does this steady rise in the rent of land mean, if not an enhanced production of utilities by the soil?

This rise is 36·7 per cent. greater than that in the wages of farm labourers. For the reasons we have already pointed out in the case of France, the increase in the production of corn is far less than the rise in rent. As to the price of bread, it is in 1878 exactly what it was in 1771! Its value, compared with the fixed capital, land, has fallen 130 per cent.; and, compared with the wages of farm labourers, 93 per cent.

It is true that meat alone has risen 200 per cent. in England and 275 per cent. in France, but this only proves a lack of production and an increase of consumption; it only proves that until the last few years man had not been able to overcome those hindrances of time and space which kept him from bringing his products within the reach of the consumers. The rise in price of this circulating capital proves but one thing—that it did not circulate enough.

[1] *La Richesse*, by L. Denayrouze (*Nouvelle Revue*, 1st March, 1879).
[2] *Landed Interest*, p. 157. 1878.

98 RELATIVE VALUES OF FIXED AND CIRCULATING CAPITAL.

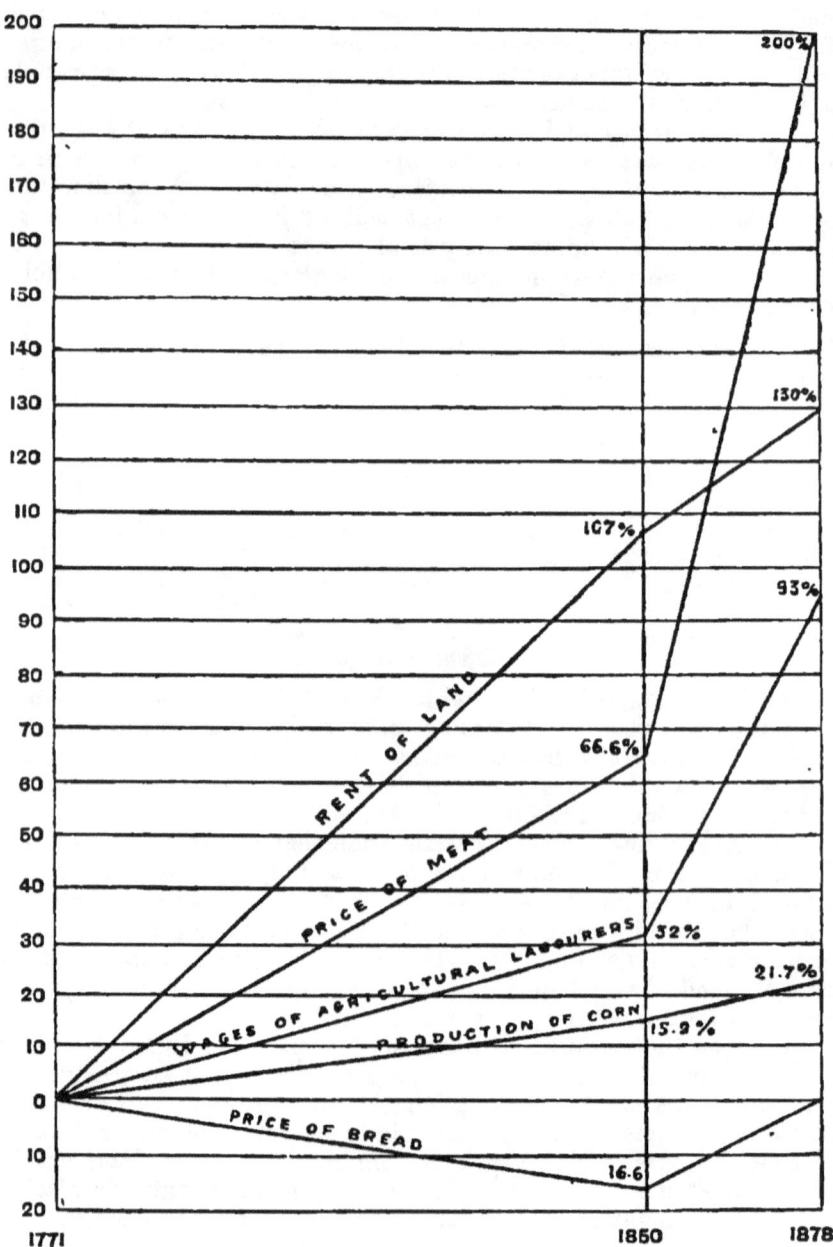

Diagram 10.—Price of Land, of Agricultural Products, and Rate of Agricultural Wages in England, 1771–1878.

From this rise in the price of meat, however, M. de Foville[1] has drawn a conclusion which seems to me incorrect. I reproduce his table, although I think it contains some inaccuracies; and in all these matters, accuracy is the main thing.

FROM 1820–1825 TO 1870–1875.

		Real rise per cent.	Real fall per cent.
Agriculture	Real property	187·5	...
	Animal food	142·5	...
	Food	...	2·5
	Native beverages	109	...
Importations of colonial produce.		...	36
Industries	Mineral products	...	51
	Textile fabrics	...	62·5
	Chemical products	...	59
	Various products	...	25

(See Diagram 11, p. 100.)

M. de Foville infers a downward tendency in the price of agricultural produce, and an upward tendency in that of manufactured products.

It would have been better for the consistency of M. de Foville's theory if he had not himself admitted that the price of "food" (by which, I take it, he means cereals, potatoes, and other agricultural produce) has fallen 2·5 per cent.

He has been much less struck by the fall in these than by the rise in animal food and in native beverages.

I have already shown one cause of the rise in meat; I will now point out another, which applies equally to native beverages.

There is a constant interchange going on between agricultural and industrial production. All the men employed in industrial production consume agricultural produce. Now industrial production has increased in much greater proportion than agricultural; and the consumption has not only become greater, but it has changed its character. The consumption of meat has almost tripled; production has been unable to keep pace with it, and the means of transport have been insufficient to bring it from abroad. The consumption of native beverages has tripled, and no other country has been in a position to make up to France the insufficiency of her own vintages. They have hardly yet learnt how to make wine in Spain.

[1] *Des Moyens de Transport*, p. 226. M. de Foville thinks that the purchasing power of money has fallen 25 per cent. since 1825. He therefore subtracts this from his estimate, and gives what he calls the real rise or fall. We have pointed out in the last chapter the error of this estimate. The amounts given ought, therefore, to be raised 25 per cent.

100 RELATIVE VALUES OF FIXED AND CIRCULATING CAPITAL.

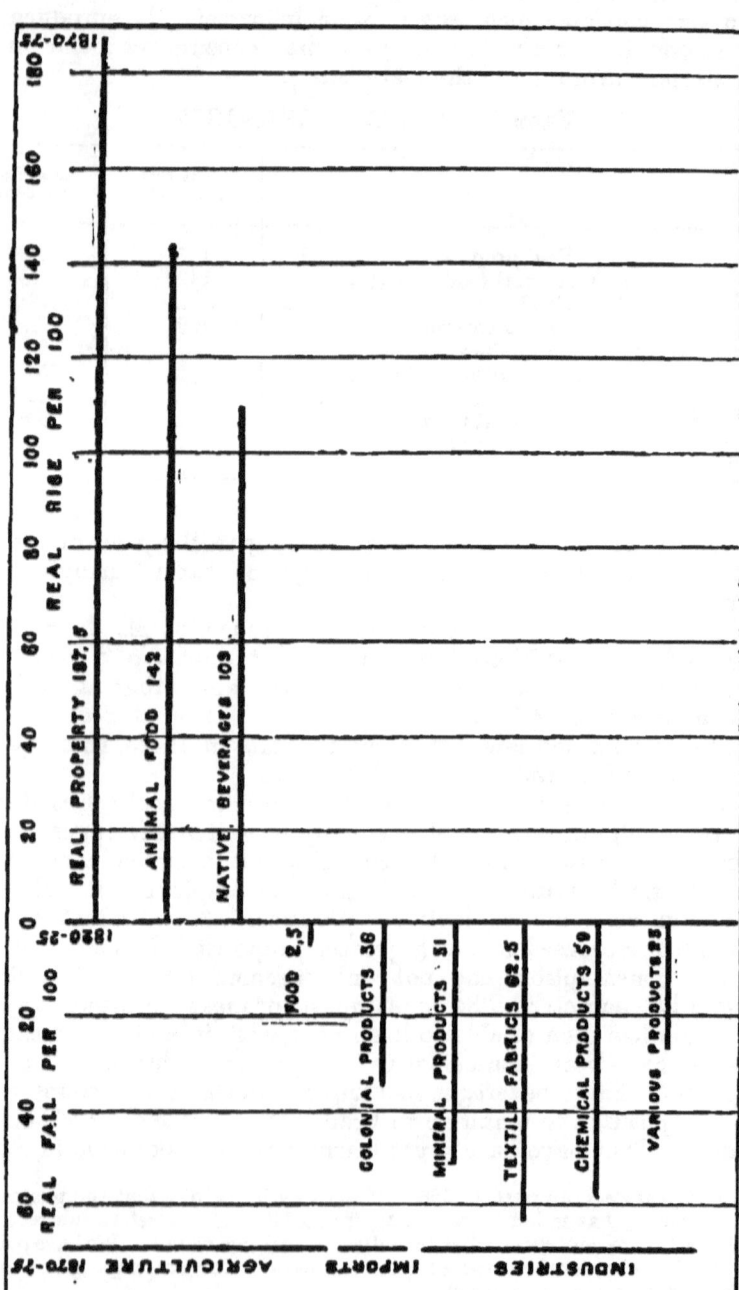

Diagram 11.—Rise and Fall in Real Property and various Products, from 1820-1825 to 1870-1875 (after M. de Foville).

These are the causes of the high price of meat and native beverages. In order not to anticipate, we will not here speak of the means of transport, which, by increasing the means of international intercourse, have multiplied the consumption of French wine, and stimulated the exportation of cattle.

Why has not the price of wheat gone up in the same proportion, seeing its consumption has steadily increased, driving out all inferior grains before it? Because wheat can be imported, in almost any quantity, from Odessa, from the mouth of the Danube, and from the United States.

M. de Foville's theory is not correct; and in attempting to prove it, he has only succeeded in establishing ours. Diagram 11 shows that while landed property (the most fixed of all fixed capital) has gone up 187 per cent., corn, tissues, colonial produce, mineral and chemical produce, and every other kind of circulating capital, meat and wines alone excepted, have fallen in the interval between 1825 and 1875.

Nor is this phenomenon peculiar to France; it presents itself under the same forms in England.

COMPARATIVE VALUES OF FIXED CAPITAL IN THE UNITED KINGDOM IN 1865 AND 1875.

(*From the Journal of the Statistical Society*, March, 1878, p. 12.)

FIXED CAPITAL.	Millions Sterling. 1865	Millions Sterling. 1875	Difference.	Per Cent.
Land	1,864	2,007	143	8
Houses	1,031	1,420	389	38
Mines	19	56	37	195
Iron Works	7	29	22	314
Railways	414	655	241	58
Canals	18	20	2	11
Gas Works	37	53	16	43
Quarries	2	4	2	100
	3,392	4,244	852	25

I have been obliged to deal with only a short period, because it is only during this period that we have reliable statistics as to the value of fixed capital. Here we see the value of land augmenting only 8 per cent., while that of houses goes up 38 per cent., that of factories 195 per cent., that of iron-works more than 300 per cent., and that of railways, which are not in England the property of the State, 58 per cent. Within the same period, the value of raw cottons and tissues has fallen 164 per cent., and that of silks 46 per cent., while corn has gone up only 5 per cent. (See Diagram 12, p. 102.)

RELATIVE VALUES OF FIXED AND CIRCULATING CAPITAL.

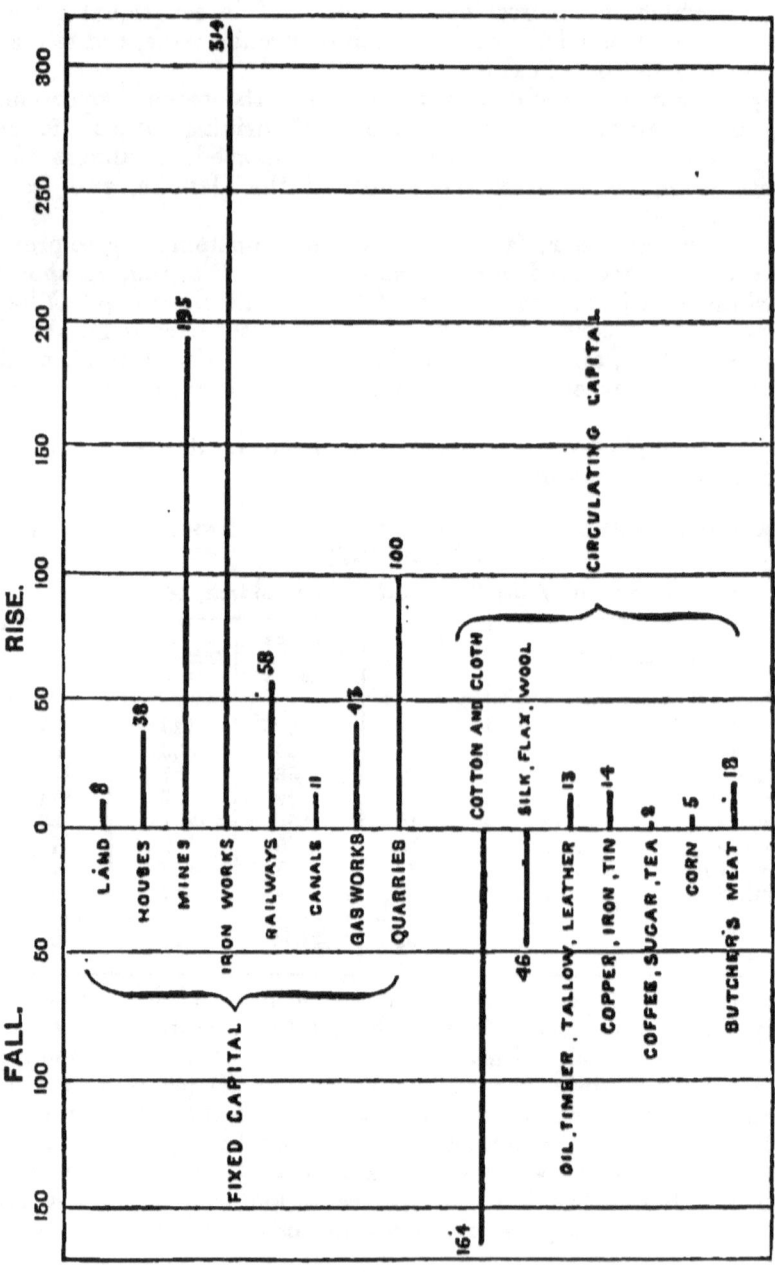

Diagram 12.—The amounts of Fixed Capital are taken from Mr. Giffen's tables; the amounts of Circulating Capital are from Mr. Newmarch's table G, which gives only the percentage (*Statistical Society's Journal*, 1878, p. 259).

Bk. iii. Ch. iv.] RELATIVE VALUES OF FIXED AND CIRCULATING CAPITAL. 103

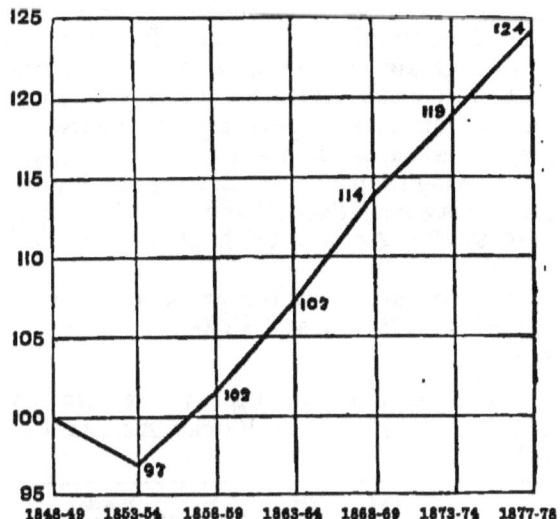

Diagram 13.—Value of Land at different Periods, taking 1848–1849 as 100 (after Mr. Charles Turner, Report of August 7, 1879).

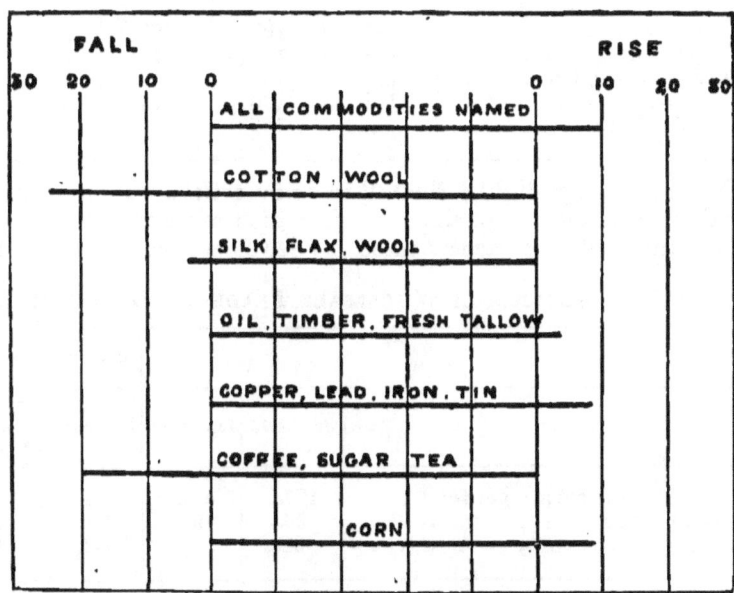

Diagram 14.—Increase or Diminution of Prices in the two Periods 1831–1845 and 1870–1877, taking Prices for the Period 1846–50 as 100.

It is plain, therefore, that in France and England fixed capital has acquired a much greater value than circulating capital.

I do not wish to weary the reader by multiplying instances; but, to avoid the accusation of manipulating our figures, let us take different periods, and examine the results.

We take the following proportions, showing the increase in value of land in England between 1848–49 and 1877–78, from Mr. Chas. Turner's report of the 7th August, 1879, on the Income Tax. (See Diagram 13, p. 103.)

Now look at the comparison of the prices of circulating capital during the two periods 1831–45 and 1870–77. We have the following figures:—

PROPORTIONATE RISE OR FALL IN PRICES FOR THE TWO PERIODS 1831–1845 AND 1870–1877, TAKING PRICES FOR THE PERIOD 1846–1850 AS 100.[1]

	After Jevons. 1831 to 1845.	1846 to 1850.	After Newmarch. 1870 to 1877.	Fall.	Rise.
1. All commodities named	115	100	125	...	10
2. Cotton wool	151	100	127	24	...
3. Silk, flax, wool	130	100	127	3	...
4. Oil, timber, fresh tallow, tin	115	100	120	...	5
5. Copper, lead, iron, tin	108	100	117	...	9
6. Coffee, sugar, tea	135	100	115	20	..
7. Corn	106	100	97	...	9
8. Butcher's meat	...	100	143	...	...

The rise is very slight; the fall in some articles much more considerable; and, on comparing periods which are closer together, we find the fall still more accentuated. (See Diagram 14, p. 103.)

PRICE OF CHIEF ARTICLES OF WHOLESALE TRADE IN 1873 AND IN 1879.[2]

Articles.	Jan. 1873.	Jan. 1879.	Difference	Diminution in 1879. Per Cent. compared with 1873.
Rolled iron (Scotch), per ton	127s.	43s.	84s.	66
Coal, per ton	30s.	19s.	11s.	37
Copper	91l.	57l.	34l.	37

[1] *Commercial History and Review* of 1878 (*Supplement to the Economist*, March, 1879, p. 53).
[2] *The Fall of Prices in England*, Robert Giffen (*Journal of the Statistical Society*, 1879, p. 66).

[Bk. iii. Ch. iv.] RELATIVE VALUES OF FIXED AND CIRCULATING CAPITAL. 105

PRICE OF CHIEF ARTICLES OF WHOLESALE TRADE (continued).

Articles.	Jan. 1873.	Jan. 1870.	Difference.	Per Cent. compared with 1873.
			DIMINUTION in 1879.	
Tin	142l.	61l.	81l.	57
Wheat, per quarter . . .	55s. 11d.	39s. 7d.	16s. 4d.	29
Flour, per sack	47s. 6d.	37s.	10s. 6d.	22
Beef, inferior, per stone . .	3s. 10d.	2s. 10d.	1s.	26
,, First quality	5s. 3d.	4s. 9d.	6d.	10
Cotton, per pound	10d.	5⅜d.	4⅝d.	46
Wool, per bale	23l.	13l.	10l.	43
Sugar, per quintal	21s. 6d.	16s.	5s. 6d.	26
Coffee	80s.	65s.	15s.	19
Pepper, per pound	7d.	4¼d.	2¾d.	39
Foreign saltpetre, per quintal	29s.	19s.	10s.	34

(See Diagram 15.)

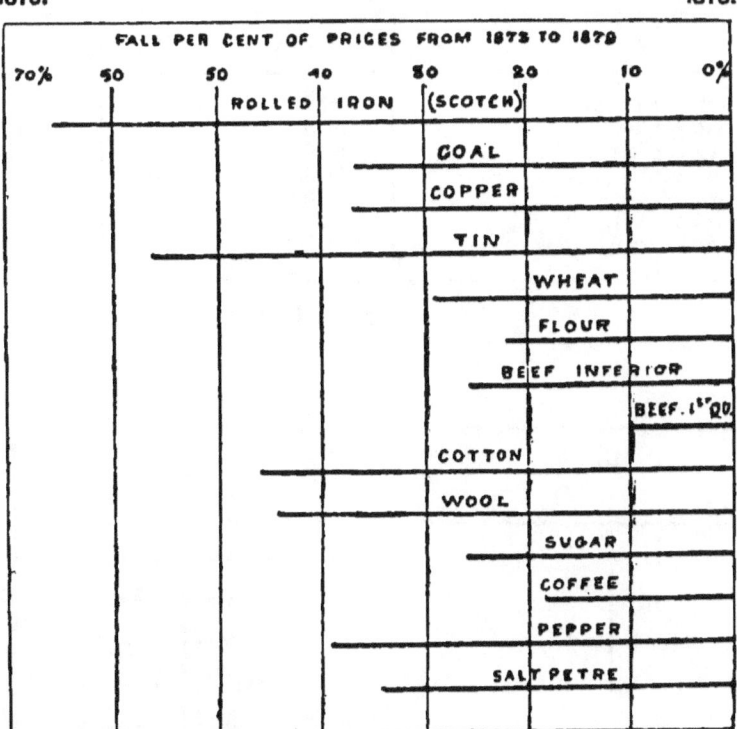

Diagram 15.—Fall per Cent. of Prices of Chief Articles of Wholesale Trade from 1873 to 1879.

RELATIVE VALUES OF FIXED AND CIRCULATING CAPITAL.

Consult the *British Trade Journal*, especially the number for the 1st of June, 1880, which contains special tables of prices from 1871 to 1880, and you will find throughout, beneath superficial fluctuations, a steady downward tendency in the price of circulating capital. Crises are spoken of as accidental phenomena; but they are a permanent phenomenon, rising in importance as the power of production becomes greater, and capital accumulates more and more rapidly. Manufacturers and agriculturists will have to make up their minds to look these conditions in the face.

Prohibitive tariffs will not check this phenomenon. The prices in the New York market are a proof of this.

PRICE OF COMMODITIES ACCORDING TO THE REPORT OF THE NEW YORK CHAMBER OF COMMERCE.

	Years.		
	1825–1829.	1873–1877.	Per cent.
Beef, per pound	$9·12	$9·80	+ 7·4
Coal, per ton	10·90	4·80	− 127
Cotton, per pound	12·40	14 60	+ 17
Iron, per ton	87·70	62·00	− 41
Leather	21·20	27·40	+ 29
Wheat	1·11	1·33	+ 19
For all commodities	...	...	− 42

(See Diagram 16.)

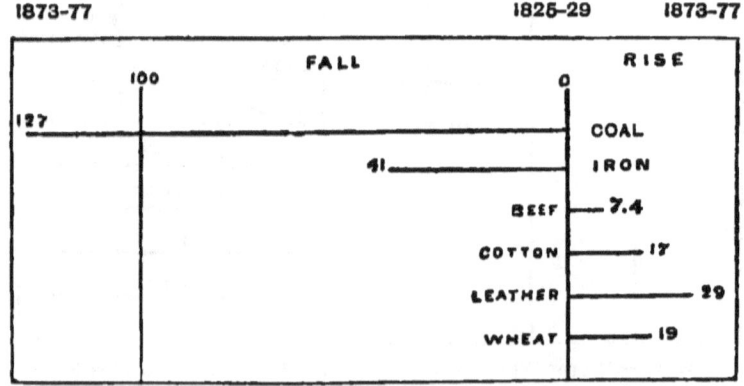

Diagram 16.—Rise and Fall of Circulating Capital at New York.

Yet everywhere, in France as in England, the price of circulating capital ought to have increased, since the consumption has considerably augmented. I take the following amounts from M. de Foville[1]:—

COMPARATIVE IMPORTANCE OF INDIVIDUAL CONSUMPTION IN FRANCE, IN 1820 AND IN 1870.

	VALUE OF AMOUNTS CONSUMED PER HEAD.					
	In 1820 at price for 1870.	In 1820, at price for 1870.		In 1870, at price for 1820.		In 1870 at price for 1820.
	fr.	fr.		fr.		fr.
1. Vegetable food .	47·05	63·55	20%	56·36	63%	77·12
2. Animal food .	24·35	45·52	37%	33·57	157%	62·64
3. Native beverages	12·30	23· 0	83%	22·60	226%	40·10
4. Various articles .	8·22	5·17	196%	24·61	88%	15·61
Food, total . .	91·96	137·24	49%	137·64	112%	195·47

(See Diagram 17, p. 108).

Now let us look at it from the other side. Go to Mexico, to the West Indies, where you will, wherever agriculture and manufactures are in a backward state, you will be met by the same condition of things,—circulating capital for the most part dear, and fixed capital (the soil included) for the most part valueless; a fact which confirms the law we have formulated as to the relations between the values of fixed and circulating capital, and which, at the same time, solves for us the apparent economical contradiction pointed out by J. B. Say, and commented upon by Proudhon: "Since the wealth of a country consists in the value of the things it possesses, how comes it that the nation is rich in proportion as the things are cheap?"[2]

It is clear, from what we have just seen, that this is a confusion of words; things can only be measured by things, and values by values; there cannot be a general rise or a general fall throughout a country; and, consequently, it is absurd to say that a nation is richest where prices are lowest. We must say, "the prices of certain things." But what things? We go back to the laws formulated in the last book; industrial progress consists in continually augmenting the utilities contained in fixed capital, and in economising the consumption of circulating capital in the form of raw material, while increasing the production of circulating capital in the form of products, the result of which is, that the value of circulating capital goes down, and that of fixed capital goes up.

[1] *Moyens de Transport*, p. 336.   [2] See page 68.

108 RELATIVE VALUES OF FIXED AND CIRCULATING CAPITAL.

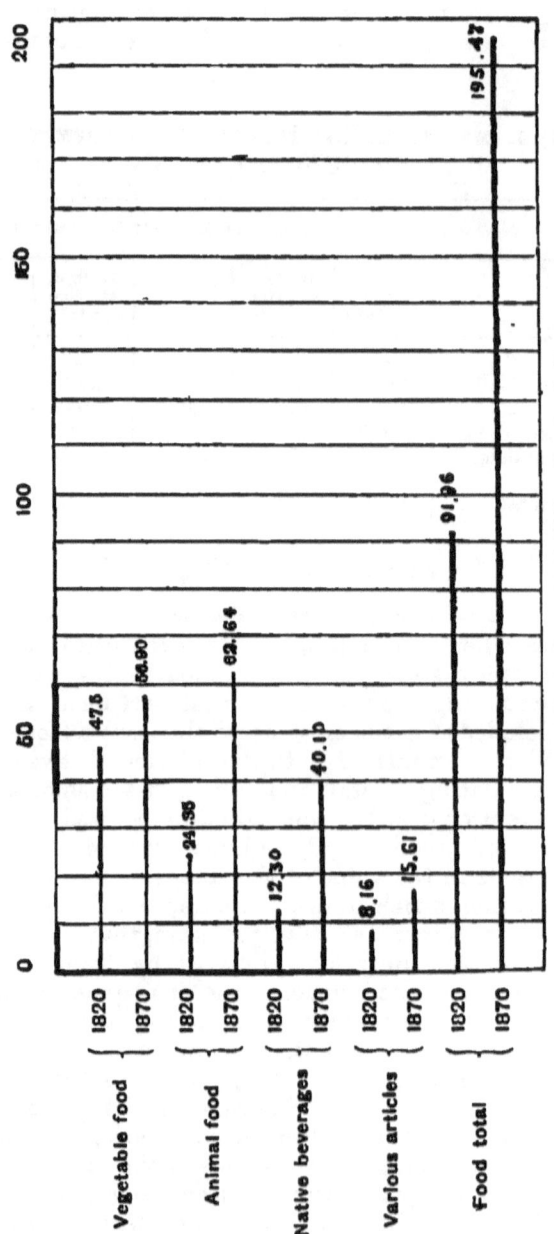

Diagram 17.—Individual Consumption in France.

Hence we obtain the following solution of the problem propounded by J. B. Say:—

The wealth of a nation is in direct ratio to the value of its fixed capital, and in inverse ratio to the value of its circulating capital.[1]

CHAPTER V.

THE RELATION OF SPACE TO THE VALUE OF CAPITAL.

I HAVE said that space is an economic factor, the importance of which we are only just beginning to recognise.

I have shown[2] how man, by the expenditure of a limited quantity of circulating capital in the construction of a road, a railroad, or a canal, succeeds in diminishing indefinitely the consumption of circulating capital in the transport of necessary articles.

A few figures will show the proportionate advantage.

By the most favourable calculation a man can carry thirty kilogrammes, and travel 30 kilomètres in a day; and supposing him to

---

[1] I put forward this formula at the Congress of the *Association pour l'Avancement des Sciences*, in August, 1880. It was discussed in the *Economiste Français;* M. Leroy-Beaulieu admits that it is at bottom sound; but a new theory can never be accepted at once in its integrity. Some little protest against it is absolutely necessary. M. Leroy-Beaulieu says: "It might well happen that the rent of land in the Old World might fall by one-third, or even by half, through the competition of new countries, without any retrogression of society or even impoverishment of the nation." I cannot agree with this view of M. Leroy-Beaulieu, and the land-owners will certainly think that he makes up his mind a little too easily to the diminution in the value of land. Would they have the same purchasing power the day after this diminution had taken place, as they had the day before? The event would be but the complete confirmation of my theory. The value of land would sink, because the new countries could produce corn, meat, etc., more cheaply than the old. There would thus be a fall in the value of circulating capital; at the same time, there would be a rise in the value of fixed capital out there. If this movement produced a fall in the value of fixed capital in the Old World, it would prove that the owners of that capital either were not able, or did not know how, to put it to a fresh use, which would enable them to combat the competition from abroad. In that case they would be ruined, and it is impossible to suppose that the wealth of the nation would not suffer in consequence.

M. Leroy-Beaulieu adds: "It is a misuse of words to say that the wealth of a nation is in inverse ratio to its circulating capital; we must at least interpose the correction 'in inverse ratio to the value of the units composing its circulating capital.'" My method of demonstrating this point will, I think, be enough to dispel any ambiguity. It was the price of the units, and not of the mass of the circulating capital of a country, that I compared.

The December number of the *Journal des Economistes* also contains some remarks on this question by M. Clément. It appears that M. Clément did not quite hear what was said. He will find, on reading this chapter, that his criticisms bear upon misapprehensions of this kind, and not upon any theory or statement of mine.

[2] Book II., chap. i.

spend three francs a day, the cost of transport will come to 3 fr. 33 cents. per ton per kilomètre.

A muleteer can drive two mules, each carrying 75 kilogrammes and doing 30 kilomètres a day. The cost of transport will now be calculated thus:—

Expenses of man	3 fr. 0 c. per day.
Ditto of two mules	3 fr. 50 c. ,,
Wear and tear of man and beast . .	1 fr. 0 c. ,,
Total . . .	7 fr. 50 c. per day.

Reckoning three hundred days in the year—that is, 3,150 kilometric tons for the two mules—the average rate comes to 87 centimes per kilometric ton.

The camel is thought a cheap means of conveyance; let us see what it costs. Fifteen merchants join together to go through the Soudan, and choose a guide; total—sixteen men. Each merchant needs three camels to carry his merchandise, and a fourth to carry his provisions and baggage; total—sixty camels. The camel can carry 400 kilogrammes 40 kilomètres a day, and can keep this up, if necessary, more than a month. His keep costs little, but the animal himself has a certain value; the period of gestation is twelve months, and the rearing is a long process.

The cost of transport by camel comes to:—

One man	2 fr. 50 c. per day.
Four camels	4 fr. 0 c. ,,
Wear and tear	2 fr. 50 c. ,,
Total . . .	9 fr. per day = 3,285 fr. per annum.

The caravan does two journeys a year, backwards and forwards, a total distance of perhaps 6,000 kilometres. The average load per camel being 400 kilogrammes, the total amount of transport effected by each merchant per annum will be 7,680 kilometric tons. The cost per kilometric ton has come down to 42 centimes.

At the inquiry made in 1861, M. Eugène Flachat reckoned the price of the kilometric ton transported by road at 20 centimes. M. Jacqmin, in a pamphlet on the scheme of the large carrying agencies for the period 1834–46, calculates the cost by *roulage accéléré* at 43 to $45\frac{1}{2}$ centimes per kilometric ton, and by *roulage ordinaire* at 23 to 28 centimes. The average would, therefore, be 35 centimes per kilometric ton.

The kilometric tariff on railways in 1835 was as follows:—

Merchandise per Ton, ordinary goods service (petite vitesse).

Coal	8 cent.	1st class . . .	12 cent.
2nd class . . .	14 ,,	3rd class . . .	16 ,,

The present tariff is :—

Merchandise.

Fast goods service (*grande vitesse*) . . . . 36 cent.
Ordinary goods service { 1st class . 16 cent. 2nd class . 14 cent.
(*petite vitesse*). { 3rd ,, . 10 ,, 4th ,, 8, 5, 4 ,,

The average charge, therefore, by ordinary goods service, is barely half that by waggon.

We are always complaining, and with reason, of the railway charges, and yet the cost per ton, not including incidental expenses, hardly comes up to an average of 6 centimes; and when we compare this charge with the average price of waggon carriage, as given by M. Jacqmin, we find that a saving of 76 per cent. has been effected.

But the toll[1] is higher than the carriage, as the following tariff of the fourth class shows,—

	Toll.	Carriage.	Total.
	fr.	fr.	fr.
From 9 to 100 kilog. at a maximum of 5 fr. . .	0·05	0·03	0·08
From 101 to 300 kilog. at a maximum of 12 fr. .	0·03	0·02	0·05
Above 300 kilog.	0·035	0·015	0·04

If the tolls were abolished on the railways, as they are already on roads and canals, the carriage would fall to two centimes. We should then have the following proportion,—

Per Kilometric Ton.
Porter . . . . Fr. 3·33
Mules . . . . 0·87
Waggon . . . . 0·25
Rail, 1835 . . . . 0·12
Ditto, 1879 . . . . 0·06
Ditto, without Toll . . . . . . 0·02

The annual trade of France from 1876 to 1878, was, in round numbers,—

Kilometric Tons.
Railways . . . . Fr. 8,000,000,000
Internal Navigation 2,000,000,000
Coasting Trade 1,000,000,000
Roads and Streets 8,000,000,000

This total of nearly twenty milliards of kilometric tons divided by the total number of the population of France, gives an average of 540 kilometric tons a year to each person, that is nearly one

---

[1] French railway tariffs comprise a double charge, first for the use of the road (*péage*), and secondly for the expense of carriage (*transport*).

and a half kilometric tons a day. These figures are exclusive of the great maritime trade, which is also counted by milliards of kilometric tons.

A man of the stone age could by no manner of means have effected the daily carriage of one and a half kilometric tons; and Robinson Crusoe, though possessed of some of the resources of civilisation, would have been equally at a loss.

"To move is to produce," says J. S. Mill. He could not have said a truer thing. The whole of industry consists in the bringing together of raw materials.

In 1838, Arago, who then opposed the introduction of railways, said, "It is not to be supposed that a couple of parallel iron rods can change the face of Gascony." Nevertheless the couple of iron rods were introduced, and the face of Gascony was changed, because these iron rods made it possible to transport the timber it produced.

There are millions of acres lying valueless in Africa, America, Asia, Australia, simply for want of being brought into communication with the centres of consumption. Let this be done by means of railways and canals, and these lands will forthwith acquire a considerable value, because they will have found an outlet for their produce.

The Americans know this so well, that the bankers of New York, who get up the railways, and the investors who take shares in them, look for their profit, not to the dividends of the railway, but to the enhanced value of the prairies of Iowa, the corn-lands of Illinois, the forests of Michigan, the coal and iron-works of Pennsylvania, and the emporiums of Chicago and Buffalo.

The value of fixed capital is proportionate to the power of the means of transport.

Wherever a railway penetrates into a remote part of the country, you will hear quiet people who live there complain, "Railways raise the price of everything." So they do, so far as the products of the locality itself are concerned; the railway creates a new outlet for them, and thus gives them an increased value; but, at the same time, it introduces circulating capital at a cheaper rate than was possible with the old modes of conveyance. It therefore brings about a rise in the price of circulating capital produced within the district, and a fall in the price of circulating capital brought in from outside. Thus it levels prices.

Not only so, but it also brings within reach of the fixed capital of the regions it traverses the raw material which is wanting to them—chalk, phosphates, coal, and so forth. It thus enables their fixed capital to produce what it could not produce before. It gives it a greater power of utility.

Formerly, Paris obtained its fruit and vegetable supply entirely from the land in its own neighbourhood; and the difference in the cost of transport gave these lands a marked advantage over more distant places. Now-a-days, the railway supplies Paris with corn from Marseilles, artichokes and asparagus from Algeria, cauliflowers, salad, and potatoes from Roscoff, strawberries from Bordeaux, peaches from Provence, melons from Cavaillon, and so on. Formerly, the radius of the milk-supply did not exceed twenty-five kilomètres; it now exceeds a hundred.

Hence has resulted a fall in the value of land in the environs of Paris, and a rise in the value of more distant land. This fall is however only relative and transitory. It is simply the consequence of the tendency of improved means of communication to level prices.

The carriage by road of a hectolitre of wheat (75 kilogrammes) costs two centimes per kilomètre, or two francs for twenty-five leagues. Hence arose monstrous inequalities in distribution, according as the harvest was scanty here and abundant there. Now the railway tariffs for corn vary from three to seven centimes per ton. One ton of corn contains more than thirteen hectolitres. It ensues that the inequalities in the price of corn in different districts tend more and more to decrease.

We give here the maximum inequalities recorded by the Ministry of Agriculture and Commerce for the nine following districts;—North-west, North, North-east, West, Central, East, South-west, South, South-east,—

	fr. c.		fr. c.
1859	4 61	1874	2 71
1865	3 65	1875	3 55
1870	2 86	1876	2 53
1871	2 54	1877	3 01
1872	2 94	1878	1 74
1873	2 0	(See Diagram 18.)	

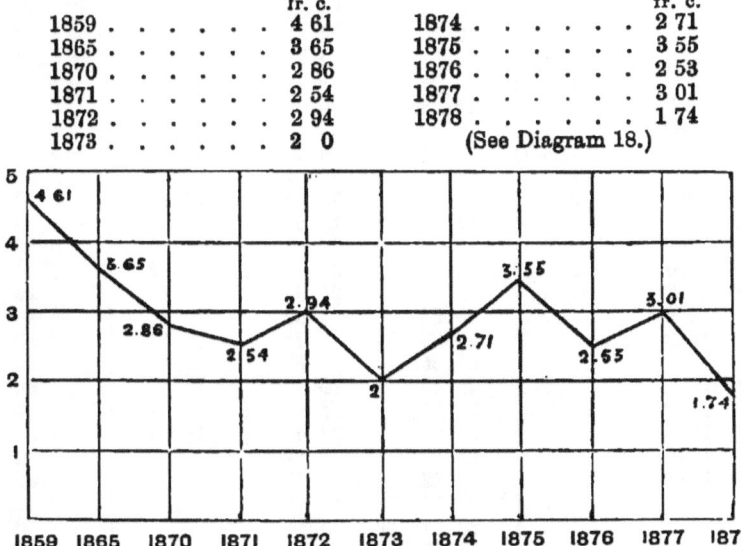

Diagram 18.—Maximum Inequalities in the Price of Corn among the nine Districts of France.

114 THE RELATION OF SPACE TO THE VALUE OF CAPITAL.

The same phenomena are observed in comparing different countries, as the following table shows,—

PRICE OF CORN PER HECTOLITRE.

Year	France.	New York.	Odessa.	Maximum Inequality.
	fr. c.	fr. c.	fr. c.	fr. c.
1835	15 25	18 45	9 37	9 08
1836	17 32	25 79	8 43	17 36
1837	18 53	30 76	8 28	22 48
1838	19 51	25 50	9 45	16 05
1839	22 14	22 04	10 88	11 16
1840	21 84	15 44	11 78	10 06
1841	18 54	17 13	11 83	6 71
1842	19 55	16 02	11 09	8 46
1843	20 46	14 12	9 49	10 97
1844	19 75	13 35	9 87	9 88
1845	19 75	15 26	10 78	8 97
1846	24 0	15 36	12 59	11 46
1847	29 01	20 30	14 90	14 11
1848	16 65	17 66	12 0	5 66
1849	15 37	17 0	11 80	5 20
1850	14 32	17 22	11 55	5 67
1851	14 48	14 24	9 10	5 38
1852	17 23	14 74	11 30	5 93
1853	22 39	23 20	11 76	11 44
1854	28 82	30 09	...	1 27
1855	29 32	34 85	...	5 53
1856	30 75	24 49	22 58	8 17
1857	24 37	21 92	19 53	4 84
1858	16 75	18 75	14 78	3 97
1859	16 74	20 0	14 02	5 98
1860	20 24	21 15	16 15	5 0
1861	24 25	20 20	14 31	9 94
1862	23 24	17 11	11 66	11 58
1863	19 78	15 53	13 26	6 52
1864	17 58	12 53	12 75	5 05
1865	16 41	17 20	13 60	3 60
1866	19 61	25 52	18 08	7 44
1867	26 19	23 05	18 70	7 49
1868	26 64	21 69	20 40	6 24
1869	20 33	15 21	16 15	5 12
1870	20 56	15 27	15 30	5 29
1871	25 65	19 28	17 85	7 80
1872	23 15	21 30	16 32	6 83
1873	25 62	23 69	19 0	1 93
1874	25 11	23 41	...	1 70
1875	19 32	17 73	...	1 59
1876	20 59	18 42	...	2 17
1877	23 44	20 85	...	2 59
1878	23 0	...	...	...

(See Diagram 19, p. 115.)

Bk. III. Ch. v.] THE RELATION OF SPACE TO THE VALUE OF CAPITAL 115

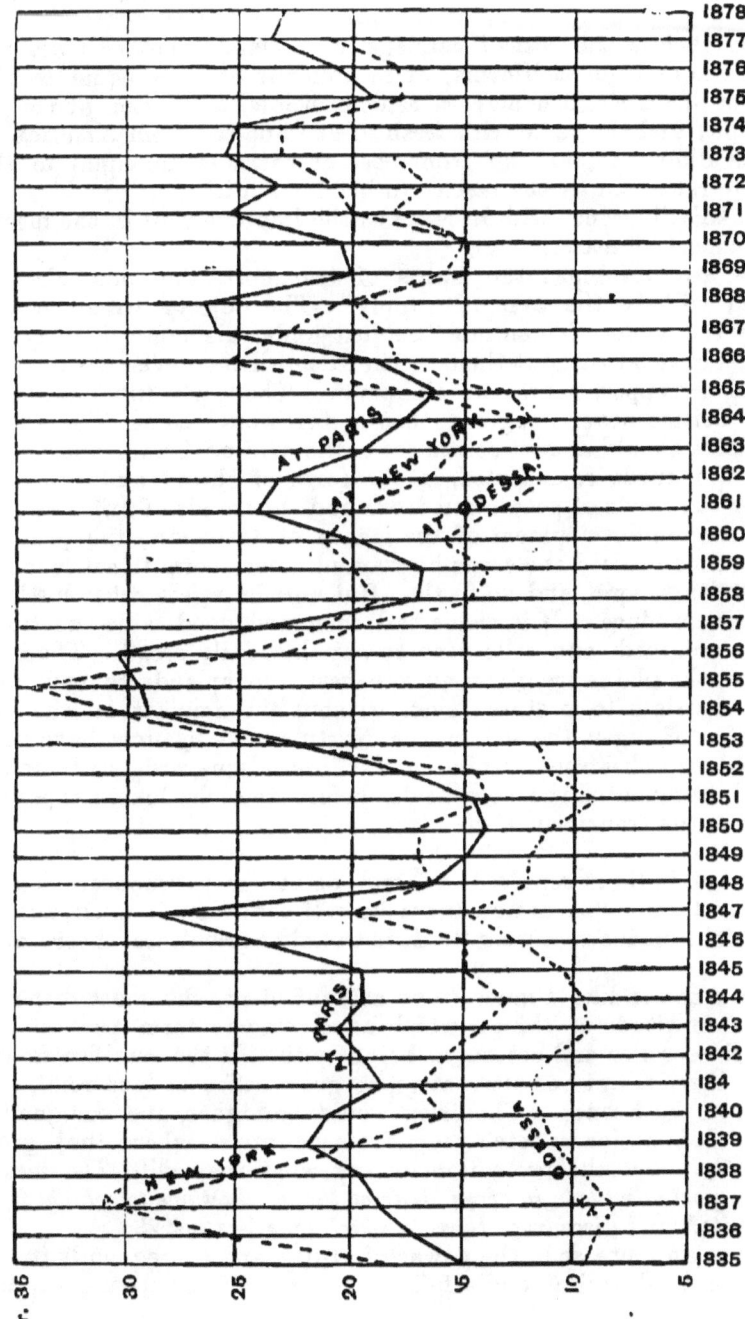

Diagram 19.—Average Price of Corn per Hectolitre in France, at New York, and at Odessa, 1835–1878.

Nevertheless, the cost of carriage to England, whether from the Black Sea or from California, of an amount of corn equal to the produce of an English acre, is seldom below, and often above 40 shillings; and the same with fresh meat imported from America.

This difference, arising from cost of carriage, is equal to the average rent paid by the farmer to his landlord.[1]

But this difference will decrease as the improvement in the means of transport increases.

The less developed the means of transport, the more circumscribed will be the area of supply. The objects which are to satisfy the wants of man must be just under his hand; if they are not, he must do without them. The Armoricans never dreamed of obtaining pepper, sugar, or cinnamon. The early inhabitants of Great Britain never imagined that a day would come when their coal-fields should attract cotton from the United States and India, to be afterwards re-exported, in the form of thread and calico, to supply the needs of people hundreds and thousands of miles away.

Before the development of the means of transport, the prudent husbandman raised the crops he wanted most; corn to eat, wine to drink, flax to spin, and so forth. But now he raises what his land will best produce. If it yields bad corn and good wine, he turns it into vineyard, and sells wine to buy his daily bread. Thus, in France, the plains are given up to wheat, the uplands to oats, and other districts to pasture; even without the imposts on the importation of sugar, the soil of the North would by now have been covered with beetroot; while in the South vineyards had almost entirely supplanted the corn-fields, before the phylloxera appeared to check the transformation.

Yet prejudice, repulsed at one point, only reappears under another form. "A nation must be self-sufficing; it must not be dependent on the foreigner." It is the old agricultural theory over again.

For a nation like France to be self-sufficient, she must dispense with a multitude of things which have come to form part of her daily life—coffee and cotton to begin with. If the sacrifice is too great, there is but one alternative, to grow coffee at Montreuil, and cotton in the Beauce. The price would be higher, and the quality poor. It is easier to fetch them from countries where they grow naturally. Let the protectionists say what they will, *The means of transport stimulate in every district the productions to which it is best suited, and discourage those to which it is less suited.*

Hence an increase in the power of utility, and consequently in the value, of fixed capital, and a fall in the price of circulating capital,

---

[1] Caird, *Landed Interest*, 1878.

since it is produced or obtained at less cost. We may therefore say,—

The means of transport, by giving to circulating capital a higher value where it is produced, and a lower where it is consumed, tend to equalise its price.

Since the means of transport at once bring raw material and carry away produce, they give to fixed capital a greater power of utility.

The equality in price of all capital of the same kind, and the value of fixed capital, are in proportion to the power of the means of transport.

CHAPTER VI.

THE RELATION OF TIME TO THE VALUE OF CAPITAL.—PRICE OF CREDIT.

THE Convention, adopting the idea of Turgot, incorporated with the law this declaration,—" Money is a commodity the price of which depends entirely on agreement, and varies, like that of all other commodities, with the relation of demand and supply."

But so keen is prejudice, that this decree had to be rescinded by that of the 2nd Prairial.

Even now, although the system of maxima (*i.e.* of fixing by law the maximum price of commodities), is condemned as absurd in the case of other commodities, it is still accepted as correct with regard to money.

But here again there is a confusion of ideas. We think of ourselves as borrowing money, because it is under the form of money that loans are effected. But they might be effected just as well under the form of bank-notes, cheques, or mere exchange of signatures. When you borrow money, even supposing it to be in good hard cash, you do not go and lock it up in a safe; you change it into something else, you pay your debts, you provide yourself with fixed or circulating capital. When we speak of the price of money, we are guilty in fact of a gross blunder, arising from that want of observation which constantly makes us take the sign for the thing signified. It was intelligible enough at a time when money was carefully hoarded. But it is disgraceful, at this time of day, to find such expressions still in use, not only in common parlance, but in legal phraseology.

If the rate of interest represented the price of the metal, it ought to be highest in England, where there is so little in circulation; whereas it is in England that it is at the lowest.

Mr. Tooke says, that every modification in the amount of coin in circulation produces a temporary effect on the rate of interest. He confounds the rate of interest with the rate of exchange. If the amount of coin in circulation is insufficient for the necessities of trade, the rate of exchange will rise; but not the rate of interest.

But I shall be told that there are two milliards of money (francs) lying idle in the vaults of the Bank of France, and that under these circumstances the rate of interest must fall.

Yes; but how comes all this money to be lying there? Because the people who received it in exchange for their commodities have found no opportunity of converting it into fresh commodities, or fresh capital; they are encumbered with it, as a grocer would be encumbered with a quantity of sugar that he could not dispose of. The grocer lowers the price of the sugar in order to make it sell. The holders of the two milliards of francs will lend at a lower rate, and will give a higher price for securities.

"But then," you say, "the converse should hold good; if the precious metals became scarce, interest will rise."

No; not if circulating capital is abundant, and does not readily find employment. Yes; if the scarcity of the precious metals is the sign of so brisk a demand for circulating capital, that it finds easy and remunerative employment.

It should never be forgotten, that even if money has an intrinsic value, it does not become a utility to its possessor until he uses it. It becomes a utility to him the moment it leaves his hands to be converted into some other utility.

We have said that the rate of interest represents the price of time, just as the cost of transport represents that of space. The rate of interest is governed by the laws which rule all other utilities.

Where circulating capital is scarce, or where there is not the organisation necessary for easily and safely utilising time, there the rate of interest is high.

The Visigothic law authorised interest at $12\frac{1}{2}$ per cent. on loans of money and 50 per cent. on loans of merchandise. In France and Italy in the thirteenth century the Jew and Lombard money-lenders charged on an average 20 per cent. In the Rhine provinces during the fourteenth century, 50 to 60 per cent. was not unusual. Now, on the contrary, the rate of interest is constantly diminishing. We may here call attention to M. Leroy-Beaulieu's mistake in connexion with this subject. He says,[1] "The persistent fall in the rate of interest increases the nominal value of all investments, whether in movable property or in lands and buildings. Within the last year, Rentes have gone up from 9 to 10 per cent.; all real property in towns, notably in Paris, has gone up in at least equal, sometimes greater proportion; and, the agricultural crisis notwithstanding, it has been the same over the greater part of the country."

[1] *Economiste Français*, Sept. 20, 1879. See also March 22, 1879.

Between 1872 and 1879, French 3 per cents. have gone up from 51 or 52 to 82, an increase in value of more than 50 per cent., or 7 per cent. per annum, without reckoning interest. It must therefore, at the very lowest, amount to 10 per cent. per annum; and, capital not being exhausted, it will still go up. So that M. Leroy-Beaulieu is not exaggerating when he calculates the gain at 13 per cent.

This upward movement never ceases. In 1880, the 5 per cents. rose above 120 francs. M. Leroy-Beaulieu was right as to the facts, but he failed to explain them. The laws we have already formulated explain them easily enough.

What do movable values for the most part represent? Fixed capital, mines, forges, railways, etc. The value of this capital steadily increases. Movable values are simply fractional titles to this property. Nothing is more natural than that they also should go up in value. Circulating capital, becoming too abundant, falls in value. It seeks to transform itself as quickly as possible into fixed capital. Now, as we have already laid down,[1] *a money-claim represents a co-proprietorship in fixed capital;* a mortgage is a share of the title to the property. The creditor becomes part-proprietor. Every advance on mortgage, every bond, is a mode of converting circulating into fixed capital. The Funds themselves are a mortgage on the entire property of France, guaranteed by the whole of her fixed capital. The fund-holders are joint proprietors of the national estate.

It follows from this, that the rise in price of movable values,—shares, bonds, and Rentes,—is simply one form of the enhanced value of fixed capital.

The fall in the rate of interest is a proof of the abundance of circulating capital. Here again we see the operation of the law we have formulated.

In the absence of any frightful destruction of capital by war, this state of things will assuredly continue; a standing warning to those capitalists and financiers who, after having denied the fact, and foretold a reaction, are now obliged to acknowledge its reality without understanding its cause.

But it may be objected that in England, during the last century, the legal interest in Queen Anne's time was only 5 per cent., that under the Walpole ministry Consols reached 107, and that under George III. interest fell to 3 per cent. It was during the eighteenth century that interest reached the lowest rate in Europe. From the end of that century it continued to rise until 1872; and only since then has it been falling.

I put the objection roughly, with some overstatement of the facts. But even so, taking them for the moment as correct, so far from contradicting my theory, it only confirms it.

[1] See page 53.

Since the close of last century, an immense amount of capital has been consumed in war; and by this means the accumulation and consequent depreciation of circulating capital, and the accompanying rise in the value of fixed capital, have been retarded. The same result has followed the creation of railways and other great public works, which have consumed tens of millions of money; they may in time become productive, but they are not so to begin with. The advance made is very considerable; and this has helped to retard the accumulation of circulating capital with its attendant phenomena. The loans to American and Asiatic States have similarly consumed an enormous mass of capital, which has for the most part been miserably squandered. We are now, however, beginning to recoup the capital advanced on the great works, almost all of which, as railways, canals, ports, etc., have moreover increased the rapidity of circulation. This has also been facilitated by the extension of telegraphs, by improved banking arrangements, and the like. Now, the quicker the circulation, the more rapidly does circulating capital become fixed. Hence an accelerated rise of movable values, and an accelerated fall of interest.

If there had been no wars, interest would long ago have fallen to 1 per cent.

In some countries, in new colonies for instance, the rate is still high, because there is a lack of circulating capital. In Australia, so late as 1850, a loan could only be effected at 15 to 20 per cent., however good the security. The rate has gone down a good deal since then. Between the different States of the Union, the rate of interest varies greatly, from 5 per cent. in New York, to 10 in Illinois, and 15 or 20 in Nebraska (this was in 1878).[1]

We may be sure that the same phenomena will arise here which we have observed with reference to the means of transport, viz., the levelling of prices. The time is not far off when colossal fortunes will no longer be made on 'Change, because the enormous fluctuations through which they were realised will, to the general advantage, cease to be possible.

We may therefore conclude that :—

The price of credit is in inverse ratio to the abundance and rate of circulation of circulating capital.

The tables published in 1878 by Mr. Inglis Palgrave in the *Banker's Magazine*, relating to the rate of discount in the great European banks, confirm this theory.[2]

Taking the year 1860 as a centre, we shall see that on only two occasions before that time did the rate of discount of the Bank of

---

[1] *L'Agriculture aux Etats-Unis*, a report by H. T. Mot, to the Société des Agriculteurs de France, p. 16.

[2] They have been reproduced in the *Bulletin de Statistique du Ministère des Finances*, July, 1878.

England fall to 2 per cent., viz., in 1851 and 1853; and in 1853, it only remained at that level for six days. Since 1860, on the contrary, it has fallen to 2 per cent. in seven different years—1862, 1867, 1868, 1871, 1875, 1876, 1877. During the two latter years it remained at this level 425 days, that is to say, considerably more than half the time; and during 1867 and 1868 no less than 483 days,—sixteen months out of the twenty-four.

During the period 1844–77, the mean rate of discount of the Bank of France was considerably higher than that of the Bank of England. The most usual rate was 4 per cent., and next to that 5 per cent. A commercial house might discount its bills at the Bank of England for 3 or $2\frac{1}{2}$ per cent., and at the Bank of France at 4 per cent., during the same number of days. The Bank of England rate was at 3 per cent. for 2682 days, and that of the Bank of France for 1518 days; the Bank of England remained at 2 per cent. for 1391 days; the Bank of France for only 270 days.

The average rates of discount for the three banks of England, France, and Germany, are as follows:—

Bank of England.	Bank of France.	Bank of Germany.
£3 16s. 3d.	£4 0s. 6d.	£4 8s. 7d.

that is, the English bank-rate of discount is less than the French by 5·5 per cent.,[1] and less than the German by 16·1 per cent.

Thus the lowest rate of discount lasted only half the time in France that it did in England, but still nearly one-eighth of the whole period; but at Berlin it never once fell to 3 per cent., and remained at $3\frac{1}{2}$ per cent. for only 54 days.

There is this much in common between the French rate and the German,—that 4 per cent. is the usual rate, and next to that 5 per cent.

We give the figures:—

Bank of France, 1844 to 1877:

    Discount at 4 per cent. during 4,399 days.
             "   5   "   1,935 "

                Total . . . 6,334 "

Bank of Germany, 1844 to 1879:

    Discount at 4 per cent. during 7,576 days.
             "   5   "   2,393 "

                Total . . . 9,969 "

---

[1] *The Economist*, Nov. 13, 1880.

Bank of England, 1844 to 1879:

<pre>
Discount at 4 per cent. during 1,293 days.
     "   5   "   "   1,106 "
                    Total . . . 2,399 "
</pre>

It is not the abundance of the precious metals which occasions this rate of discount, for we find :[1]—

	Cash.	In Bank.	In Circulation.	Per Head.
United Kingdom	£120,000,000	£32,000,000	£80,000,000	55s.
France	310,000,000	90,000,000	220,000,000	120
Germany	123,000,000	27,000,005	96,000,000	45

But Great Britain and her Colonies represent one-third of the banking power of the world.

	Banking Power.	Per Head.
Great Britain	£780,000,000	£23
France	340,000,000	9
Germany	280,000,000	7
The World	2,600,000,000	8

We see therefore that the low rate of interest or discount does not depend on the abundance of the precious metals, but on the organisation of credit, which admits of a greater economy of circulating capital, combined with a more rapid circulation.

While some Utopists were actually trying by main force to do away with the price of credit, the price was falling of itself by the mere force of circumstances.

But you cannot satisfy everybody.

According to some, gratuitousness of credit is the supreme good; according to Adam Smith, MacCulloch, Roscher, and Stuart Mill, it is the last and utmost ill. They have predicted that the extinction of interest will produce stagnation of wages, a want of initiative, and a stationary economic condition.

These fears are indeed chimerical. Capital must always seek investment; for if it is not utilised, production will cease, and the capital itself will soon be exhausted.

Gratuitousness of credit can never be more than relative. Stagnation will have no place in the civilisation of the future.

---

[1] *Progress of the World*, by M. G. Mulhall, 1880, pp. 31, 37. The figures relating to France are too low. They ought to be almost double. But this only strengthens the argument.

BOOK IV.

THE VALUE OF MAN.

CHAPTER I.

POPULATION.

MALTHUS has become a sort of scapegoat, on whose head we lay the responsibility for all the ills that flesh is heir to. He starts with the fact that when several products have each of them a power of reproduction equal to that of the producer, a more or less rapid geometrical progression necessarily ensues. The only question is, "Has every man a generating power equal to that of his father before him?" The answer seems to him to be in the affirmative. The increase of population will therefore be in geometrical progression.

But while a man may beget two or four children, who for the first fifteen or twenty years will consume without producing, he counts meanwhile for only one in the work of production. Hence it arises that the advance of production must always be a generation behind that of population.

Malthus formulates the law to which his name has been given in the following terms:[1] "Population, when unchecked, goes on doubling itself every twenty-five years, or increases in geometrical ratio. . . . The means of subsistence, under circumstances the most favourable to human industry, could not possibly be made to increase faster than in arithmetical ratio. . . . Taking the whole earth . . . and supposing the present population equal to a thousand millions, the human species would increase as the numbers 1, 2, 4, 8, 16, 32, 64, 128, 256, and subsistence as 1, 2, 3,

[1] *Principle of Population*, pp. 4, 6. 8th edition.

4, 5, 6, 7, 8, 9. In two centuries the population would be to the means of subsistence as 256 to 9; in three centuries, as 4096 to 13; and in two thousand years the difference would be almost incalculable."

This is reckoning after Perrette's fashion. She upsets her milk-pail, and her reckoning breaks down; but it would have been none the more correct if the milk-pail had not been upset.

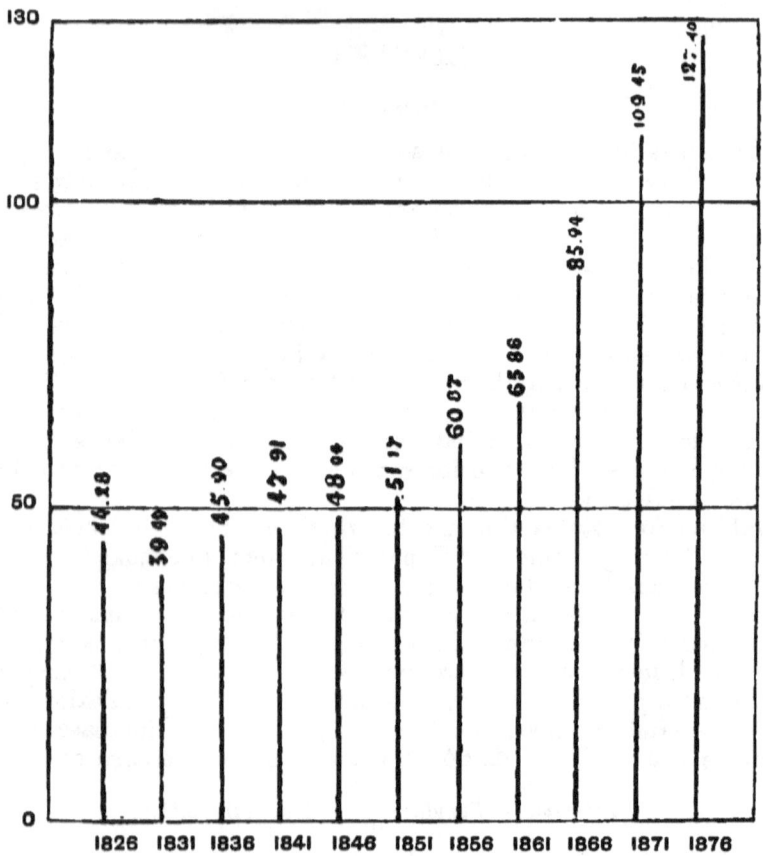

Diagram 20.—Proportion between the Capital Value of Recorded Successions to Property, and the Population of France.

We have to take into account the obstacles which hinder the rigorous application of this estimate. Malthus, who clearly saw and analysed them, divides them into two sorts—destructive and preventive checks.

Another little point, which quite escaped Malthus, but which must enter into our calculations, is the increasing industrial capacity of man. The son has no more children than the father had, but by the help of the steam-engine he can multiply his power of production tenfold.[1]

For the last century, facts have been giving the lie to the law of Malthus, and showing that *à priori* laws are worth just as little in

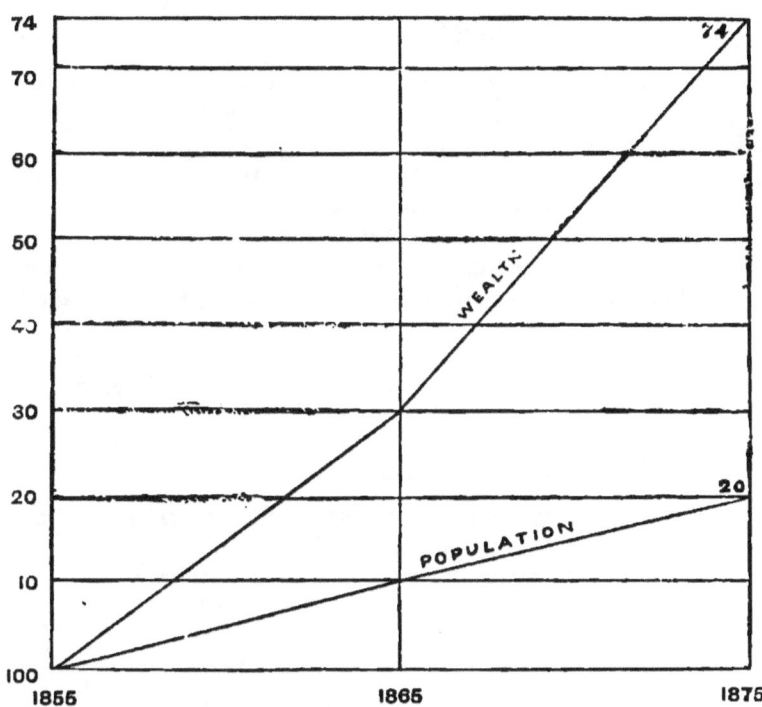

Diagram 21.—Proportionate Increase of Wealth and Population in the United Kingdom.

economic science as anywhere else. Look at France. A glance at the following table is enough to show that wealth increases there at a very different rate from population.[2]

[1] See Book II.
[2] This computation of wealth, though not rigorously exact, is a sufficient indication, and it extends over a considerable period. (See Vacher, *Evaluation de la Fortune de la France.—Journal de Statistique*, Nov., 1878.) It is too low, for it does not take account of the under-estimate of personal property given in probate duty returns.

Proportion between the Capital Value of Recorded Successions to Property, and the Population of France, 1826–1876.

Date of Census.	Number of Population.	Capital Value of Successions reported.	Proportion per Head.
1826	30,461,937	Fr. 1,337,359,808	Fr. 44·28
1831	32,569,223	1,286,271,015	39·49
1836	33,540,912	1,539,738,388	45·90
1841	34,230,178	1,640,409,974	47·91
1846	35,400,486	1,700,821,890	48·04
1851	35,783,170	1,831,372,639	51·17
1856	36,039,364	2,193,957,117	60·87
1861	37,386,313	2,462,868,220	65·86
1866	38,067,004	3,271,841,682	85·94
1872	36,102,921	3,951,245,604	109·45
1876	36,905,788	4,701,768,569	127·40

(See Diagram 20, p. 124.)

But it will be said that in France the population increases slowly. This is true; but in England it increases rapidly, and the result is:

United Kingdom.

	Wealth, per cent.	Population, per cent.
1855–1865	30	10
1865–1875	44	10

(See Diagram 21, p. 125.)

Population and Wealth of the United States in each Decade (1790 to 1870).

Year	Population.	Wealth.	Increase. Population per Cent.	Increase. Wealth per Cent.	Average Wealth per Head.
		(Estimated.)			
		$			$
1790	3,929,827	750,000,000	...	...	187·00
1800	5,305,937	1,072,000,000	35·02	43·00	202·13
1810	7,239,814	1,500,000,000	36·43	39·00	207·20
1820	9,638,191	1,882,000,000	33·13	25·40	195·00
1830	12,866,020	2,653,000,000	33·49	41·00	206·00
		(Official.)			
1840	17,069,453	3,764,000,000	32·67	41·70	220·00
1850	23,191,876	7,135,780,000	35·87	89·60	307·67
1860	31,500,000	16,159,000,000	35·59	126·42	510·00
1870	38,558,000	30,069,000,000	22·00	86·13	776·96

(After Mr. Giffen. See Diagram 22, p. 127.)

These facts show that the law of Malthus might be reversed, and that we might say, "Population increases in arithmetical, and wealth in geometrical proportion."

Malthus adds, that population increases with the means of subsistence, and is limited by them. At first sight nothing could appear more just, and yet the foregoing facts have shown that the means of subsistence may increase much faster than the population.

Again, Malthus forgets to say what he understands by the means of subsistence. It is clear that the words do not mean the same to an Englishman that they do to a Neapolitan; and even a Neapolitan would find it hard to resign himself to the worms, the larvæ, and the tiny shell-fish which make up the ordinary means of subsistence of a native of Tierra del Fuego or Australia.

Strangely enough, M. Ach. Guillard, the foster-father of the *Démographie*, has adopted this proposition of Malthus, giving it the name of "the general equation of subsistence." "The average population is proportionate to the available means of subsistence. Given the loaf, the man is born; withdraw the loaf, and the man disappears."

Dr. Bertillon has somewhat generalised M. Guillard's law. He formulates it thus: "In a healthy country, inhabited by a given race at a given stage of mental development, the population, and consequently

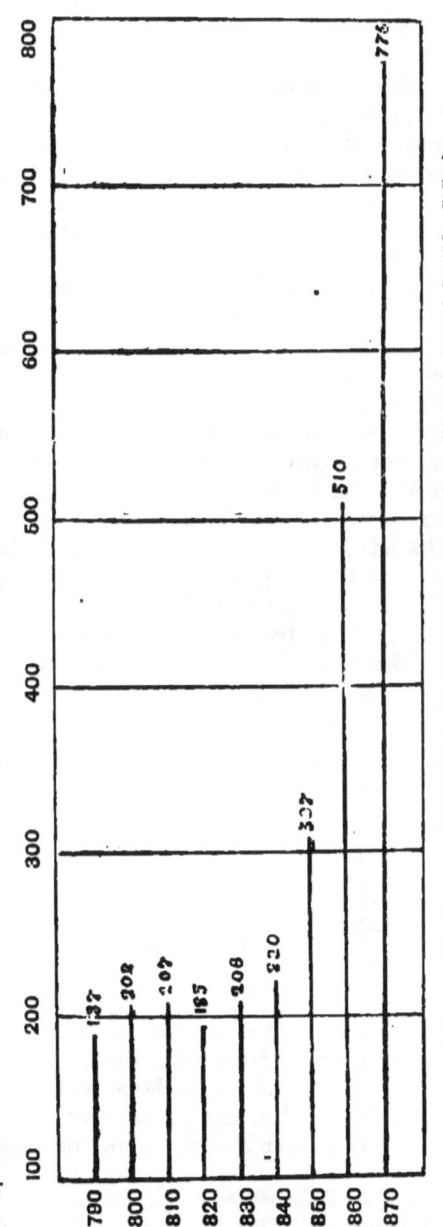

Diagram 22.—Average of Wealth in the United States in each Decade, 1790–1870 (after Mr. Giffen).

the number of births, tends to be proportionate to the quantity of productive labour of which that race at that stage of development is most easily susceptible." [1]

I shall content myself with remarking that there are very populous countries which have men, but which have not bread. If the proposition of Malthus and of M. Achille Guillard were true, India and Ireland would have been deserted long ago, in spite of the rice and the potatoes which there take the place of bread [2]; for in India and Ireland the means of subsistence, different as they are from ours, are far from being always proportionate to the increase of population. If this law were correct, France would be much more populous than it is, and Ireland much less so.

We see from Mr. Burgoyne's report, published in 1838, that the population of Ireland had almost doubled in half a century, while two-fifths of the men were without work, their agriculture being intermittent, and their industries nil. They eat nothing but an easily grown and not very nourishing potato. Milk is scarce. Neither bread nor meat is to be had; the only luxury is whisky. Nevertheless, the children marry almost before they are grown up, and multiply this misery. In the famine of 1847, after having exhausted their potatoes, they killed their pigs, and were next reduced to living on offal, and then on grass.

The population of Ireland in 1840 was 8,155,000; from 1846 to 1875 it has steadily decreased; in 1878 it was only 5,350,950—a net loss of 2,804,571, or thirty-five per cent. Yet the births have not ceased to exceed the deaths. The Registrar General's returns,[3] which in Ireland only go back to the beginning of 1864, record:

Year.	Births.	Deaths.	Percentage.
1864 . .	740,275	495,531	45
1868 . .	786,858	480,622	63
1870 . .	792,787	515,319	53
1875 . .	850,607	546,453	55
1877 . .	887,055	500,348	77

Since, then, the births in Ireland are always in excess of the deaths, whence comes the deficit?

From emigration. Here we have a check to the increase of population within any given area, which will exist until every square yard of the earth's surface has its inhabitant.

[1] *Réforme Economique*, p. 41, 1875.
[2] See the *Economist* for Nov. 13, 1880, *The Overpeopling of India*, according to Dr. Hunter, the Director-General of Indian Statistics.
[3] *Financial Reform Almanack* for 1879, p. 121.

Malthus indeed speaks of it, but does not regard it as serious. He says,[1] "Population invariably increases when the means of subsistence increase, unless prevented by powerful and obvious checks; these checks, and the checks which keep the population down to the level of the means of subsistence, are moral restraint, vice, and misery."

This law, modified by an "unless," lacks precision; and, besides, this enumeration of the checks to population is by no means exhaustive.

The soil of the United States supports to-day well-nigh as many millions of white men as it formerly supported thousands of red men. Schoolcraft reckons that every hunter who lives by the produce of the chase needs seventy-eight square miles for his maintenance. Oldfield assigns fifty square miles to the support of every Australian aborigine, and Admiral Fitzroy gives sixty-eight to the Patagonian. This obstacle to the population of a country would seem to confirm the law of Malthus; but it was not the one which Malthus had in his mind.

According to him, all creatures are reproduced in geometrical ratio, but they are mown down by want and the failure of the means of subsistence, and thus the equilibrium is restored. This obstacle is in reality less repressive than preventive. The fecundity of domestic animals is greater than that of wild ones, and why? Because their nourishment is more regular and more abundant, and requires less expenditure of force.[2] The same holds good of man in his savage state. Insufficiency of nourishment is common; he is often reduced to feed on wild fruit, insects, larvæ, worms, and even balls of earth. He devours all these without freeing them of their innutritious parts. Their value as food is small, and they cost much, not only to find, but also to masticate and digest. They would seem insufficient food even to an Irishman. In hunting and fishing, the savage has to undergo muscular exertion, not indeed long continued, but extremely severe while it lasts. His clothing and shelter is scanty. The drain on his energies is therefore considerable, and the reproductive capacity of the race is still more restricted by the fact that the woman undergoes even more fatigue and hardship than the man.

So much for the preventive check. There is also the repressive check. The individual, under such conditions, cannot live long. In some countries he runs the risk of being killed by wild beasts; and he moreover aids in his own destruction by fighting, whether in single combat, in family feud, or in tribal war.

In our own civilisation, on the other hand, the means of subsist-

---

[1] *Principle of Population*, p. 261, 8th edition.
[2] See Herbert Spencer, *Biology*, part VI., *The Laws of Multiplication.*

ence (as is shown in diagrams 20 and 21) greatly exceed the population; and man is more prolific, because he has better nourishment with less outlay of force.

What are the obstacles which impede the increase of population in geometrical ratio?

Wherever man restricts his idea of what is essential to him to such objects as he can procure without effort, he acquires a high degree of fecundity.

Such were the Tahitians, who were compelled to have recourse to such practices as infanticide for limiting their population. Such are the Boers of South Africa; such were the French of Lower Canada, easy-going people, devoid of enterprise, living in a country where land and the means of subsistence were easily procurable.[1] Their Anglo-Saxon neighbours—restless, eager, active, not easily satisfied—were far less prolific. We may observe the same thing amongst our European populations; and here we are met by two considerations of different kinds, the one moral, the other physiological.

Malthus points to moral restraint as one of the checks to population. I need not concern myself with the form which it assumes. The fact is, that there are in our civilisation a great number of persons who choose to limit, and who do limit, the number of their offspring. But the causes which influence them do not come within the domain of economics.

The beggar has many children, because he cares little about their fate. They can always be beggars, as their parents were before them. The origin of the word *prolétariat* itself points to this fact.

In the same way, very wealthy people can afford to have many children, because they have no anxiety about their future. And in countries where the custom of primogeniture exists, as in England, and where the father does not trouble himself about providing for his sons or dowering his daughters, large families are of constant occurrence.

These facts show that the number of births depends, amongst other things, on the ease with which the parents can give their children a position equal to their own.

At the present moment, France is Malthusian in practice, though not in doctrine. The virtue of frugality has been preached to the Frenchman, and the *bourgeois* has put this virtue in practice. He has laboured only to be able the sooner to rest. The man who is honoured has long been the man who "does nothing." In order to attain this dignity, the *bourgeois* lived scantily, and sought in economy a security for the future. Stinginess was the *bourgeois*

---

[1] Johnston, quoted by Herbert Spencer, *Biology*, vol. ii., *Laws of Multiplication*. See Letourneau, *Sociology*.

virtue. Logically enough, he stinted himself in children as in everything else.

Little by little, the peasant proprietors and large farmers perceived and adopted the *bourgeois* system. They began with scraping together a few crowns to buy a morsel of land. Then, foreseeing the partition of this land, and dreading its attendant expenses, which would have swallowed up at a single gulp all the fruits of their toil, they effected a further saving—in children, and contemptuously left it to the poorest classes to burden themselves with large families. We give the proof of this assertion.

Dr. Bertillon has divided France into three groups.[1] The first comprises thirty departments, in which more than one-fourth of the peasantry—about 285 out of every 1,000 inhabitants—are proprietors; the last comprises twenty-one departments, where less than one-fifth of the peasants are proprietors, or an average of 177 per 1,000; while thirty-one departments, where the peasant-proprietors number about 240 per 1,000, form an intermediate group.

MOVEMENT OF POPULATION ACCORDING TO THE NUMBER OF PEASANT PROPRIETORS PER 1000 IN EACH GROUP (1862).

Groups of Departments having—	Number of Peasant Proprietors per 1000 Inhabitants.	Marriages.	Births.	Deaths.	Number of Departments in each Group.
Most proprietors	285	25·3	24·78	23·23	30
Medium number	240	25·6	25·7	23·0	31
Fewest proprietors	177	25·87	28·1	23·2	21
Average . .	240	25·6	26	23·1	82

(See Diagram 23, p. 132.)

From this form of economy on the part of the *bourgeois* and the peasant there results a falling off in the number of births.

The increase of population is at the present time slower in France than anywhere else. For every 100 persons in England and France respectively in 1801, there were in 1876 or 1878, in England 212 persons, in France only 142.

[1] These figures have been taken from a remarkable work, entitled *Démographie de la France*, and published in the *Dictionnaire Encyclopédique des Sciences Médicales*.

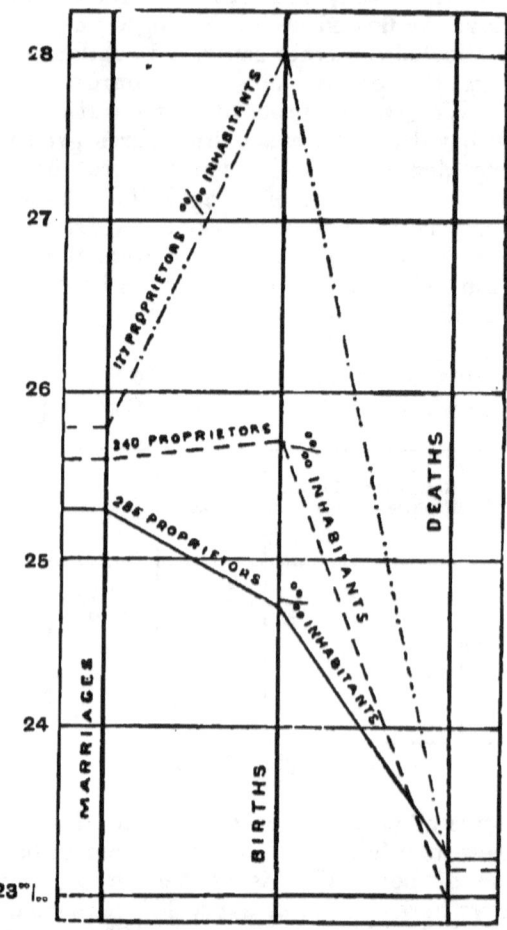

Diagram 23.—Increase of Population according to the Number of Peasant Proprietors per 1000 Inhabitants in each Group.

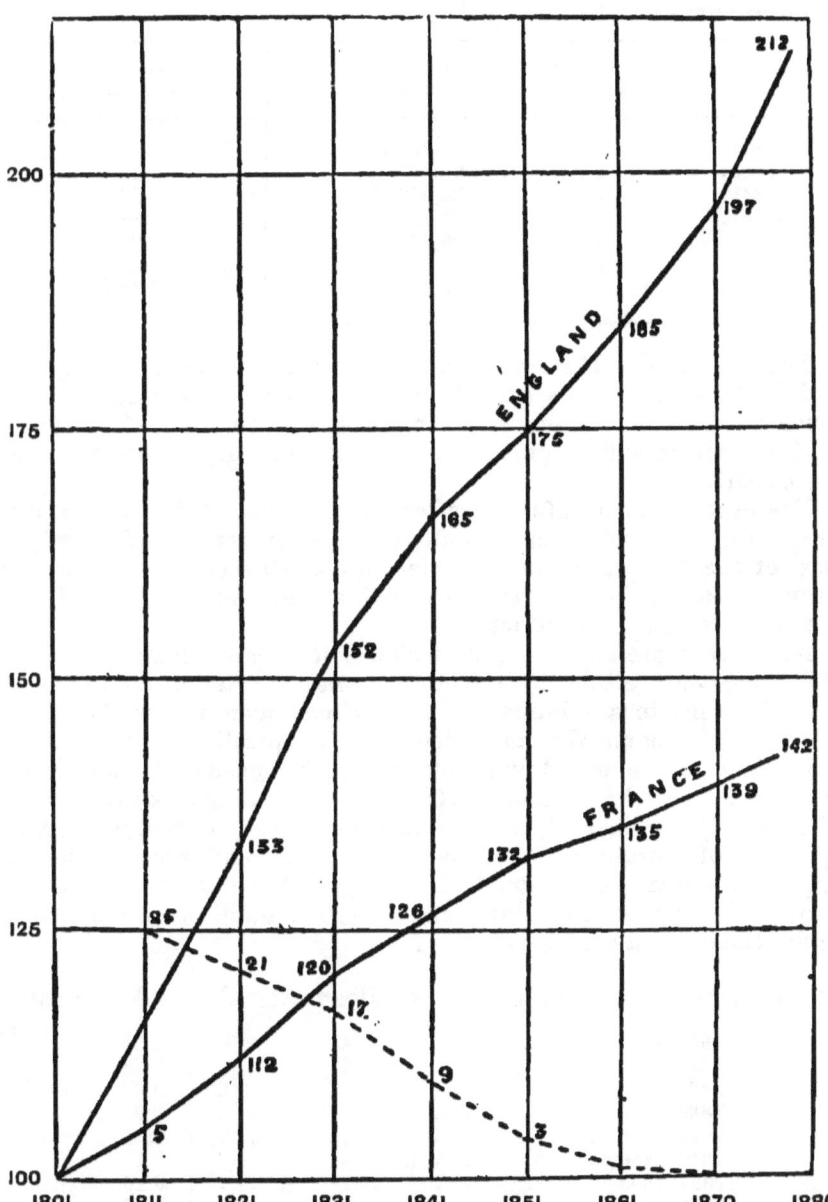

Diagram 24.—Increase per cent. of Population in France and England, irrespective of additions of territory. - - - - - - Decreasing Birth-rate in France.

	Population of the British Isles.	Increase per 1,000 Inhabitants.
1801	15,996,400	
1821	21,272,187	330
1831	24,392,485	525
1841	27,289,404	656
1851	29,571,644	750
1871	31,628,400	975
1878	33,985,000	1,126

The birth-rate in France is eighty per cent. lower than in England and Prussia. Does this arise from a plethora of inhabitants? Is there no room on French soil for one Frenchman more? On the contrary, the specific population of France is scanty, compared with her extent.

The necessaries of life are, after all, relative. With the peasant-proprietor, the one thing needful is his property. With a whole class of the *bourgeoisie*, it is a place under Government. And for France, taken in her entirety, it is not a daily ration of bread, but a certain amount of comfort.

Now there are two ways in which this comfort may be gained and preserved; either by redoubling one's efforts, or by reducing one's burdens to a minimum. Most Frenchmen prefer the latter course. We blame the imprudence of the spendthrift who brings children into the world without having the means of maintaining them in it; but the prudence which refuses to undertake the duties of paternity for fear of the burdens which they entail, is a grave symptom of moral inertia. The spring of life and energy must be broken in a man who, instead of acting, makes it his aim to avoid action. Looked at from this point of view, the following table must excite the deepest concern:[1]—

NUMBER OF LEGITIMATE CHILDREN (BORN ALIVE) PER MARRIAGE.

1800–1815	3·93
1816–1830	3·73
1831–1835	3·48
1836–1840	3·25
1841–1845	3·21
1846–1850	3·11
1851–1855	3·10
1856–1860	3·03
1861–1865	3·08

(See Diagram 25, p. 135.)

---

[1] *Economiste Français,* March 13, 1880; *Question de la Population en France,* by M. Paul Leroy-Beaulieu.

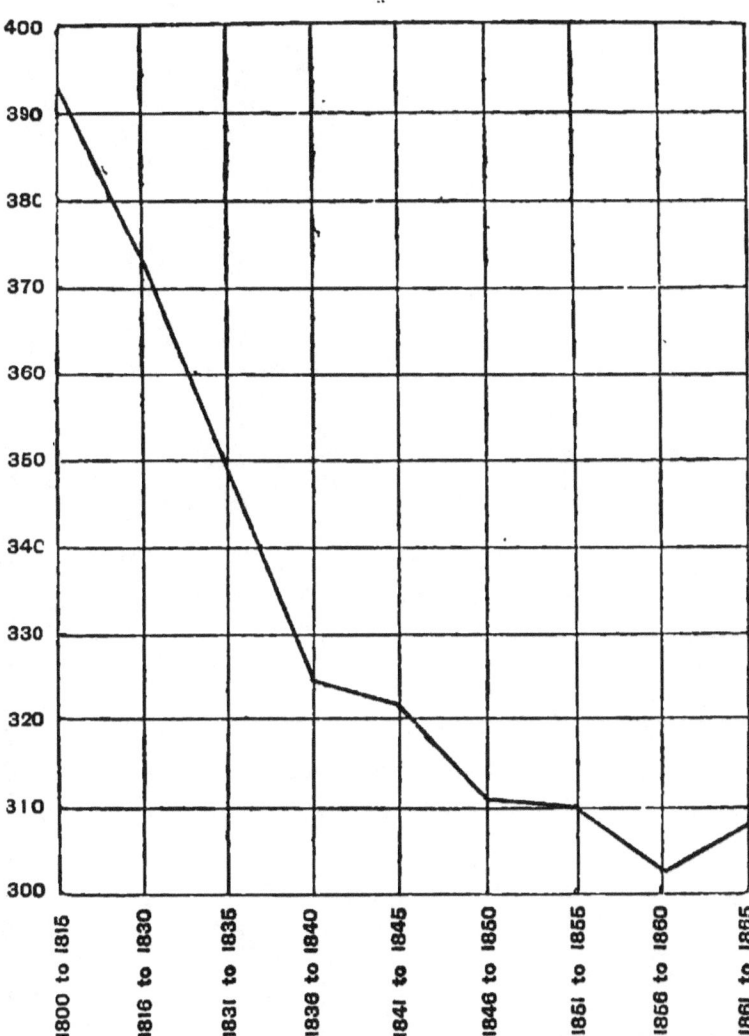

Diagram 25.—Number of Legitimate Children (born alive) per Hundred Marriages during various periods.

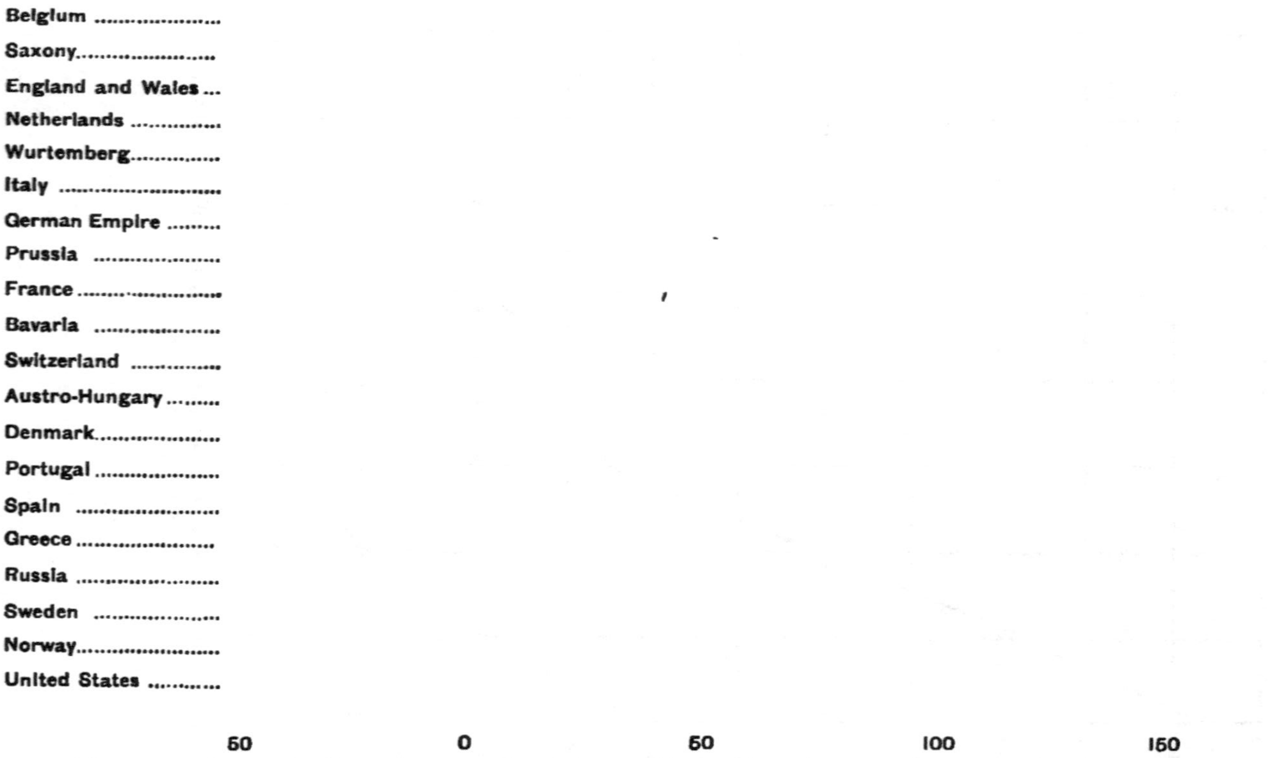

POPULATION.

Belgium
Saxony
England and Wales
Netherlands
Wurtemberg
Italy
German Empire
Prussia
France
Bavaria
Switzerland
Austro-Hungary
Denmark
Portugal
Spain
Greece
Russia
Sweden
Norway
United States

−50   0   50   100   150

Diagram 26.—Comparative Recent Increase of Population, and Number of Inhabitants per Square Kilomètre (after Dr. Bertillon).

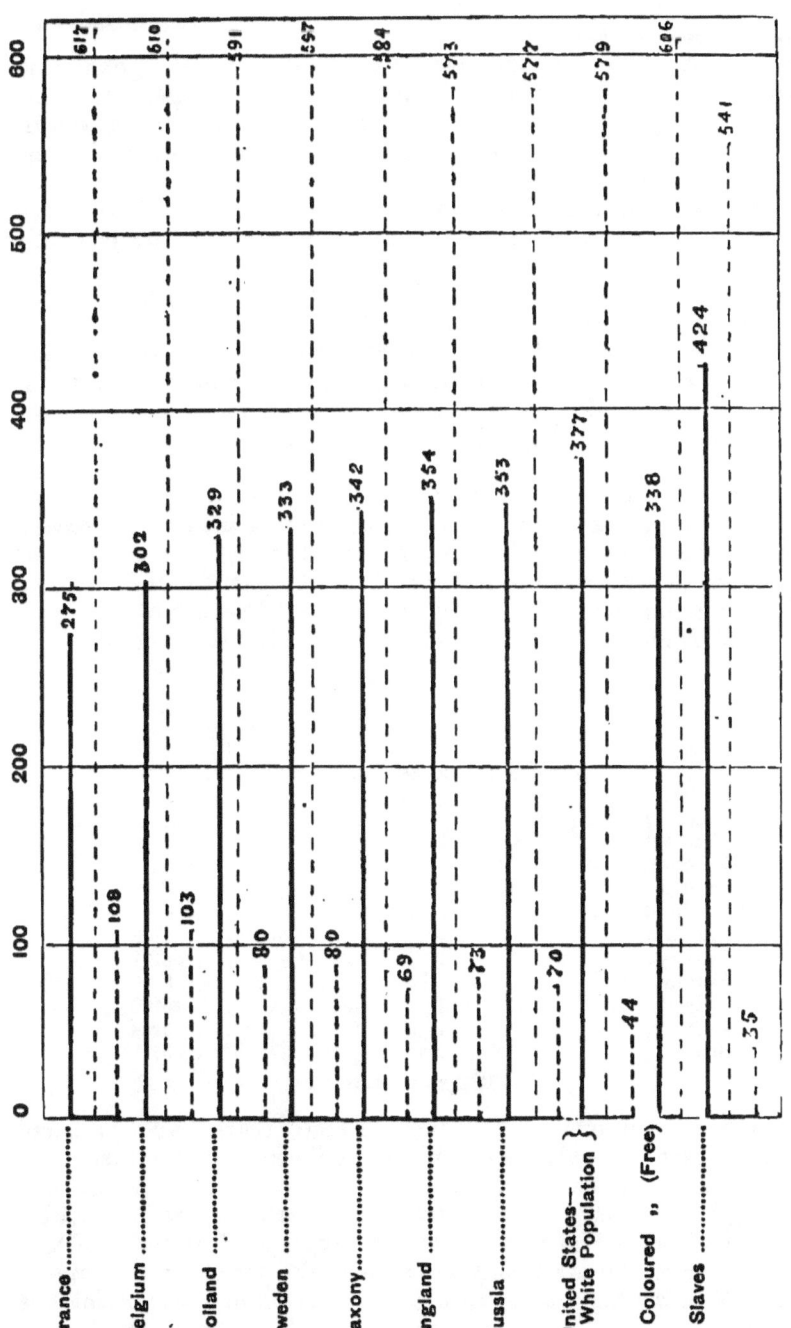

Diagram 27.—Population of Various Countries Grouped according to Age.

Let us cast a glance at Diagram 27, which shows the population of various States ranged in three groups according to age; viz., from birth to fifteen years, from fifteen to sixty, and from sixty onwards. Out of every thousand in France, there are but 275 living of the first group, while there are 617 of the second, and 108 of the third.

In England the proportion is very different. The first group gives us 354 per thousand, the second only 573, and the last only 73.

But to understand all that is implied in the above figures, we must turn to those relating to the slaves in the United States before the Emancipation. The first group is 424 per thousand—a number exceeding that of the corresponding group in the other countries; the second is 541, and the third only 35. If the birth-rate is high, the waste is enormous. They die early; the age of sixty is seldom passed.

In France the birth-rate is low, and the mortality between fifteen and thirty high; so that while France ranks fifth as to general mortality, she ranks second as to the mortality between fifteen and thirty years, her death-rate being 8·63 per thousand, while that of the Scandinavian countries is only from 5·8 to 6·7, that of Prussia 7, and that of England, with her vast and fatal industries, and of Spain, with her imperfect civilisation, only 8·2.

SURVIVAL TO THE AGE OF TWENTY.

(*Réforme Economique*, Fo. V., p. 57.)

	Proportion per 100 inhabitants.
Norway	72·6
Denmark	71·3
Sweden	69·8
England	64·4
Belgium	64·2
France	62·9
Netherlands	61·6
Prussia	58·6
Italy	53·4
Spain	51·1

(See Diagram 28, p. 139.)

The loss is enormous, for the man is already reared, and prepared to take his part in production, and in the increase of the race. He dies, and all this capital is gone!

This high mortality ought to attract our attention, for it undoubtedly springs from our absurd system of education, from our military service, and from the parsimony with which the young man's parents have provided for his wants, in order to leave him a larger fortune at their death.

This period over, the death-rate is very low; life is long; and to this state of things there attaches a certain inconvenience, since, after sixty years of age, a man cannot, as a general rule, be regarded any longer as an instrument of production, and becomes, therefore, a dead weight on the active portion of the population.

Arguing from analogy, we may apply to France the biological principle, that in general superior organisms live longer than inferior organisms.

We will go further, and apply another principle,—that among animals a species produces many young ones of which it takes no care at all, and a few of which it takes a great deal of care.

The French nation has few children; but of such as it has, it takes an amount of care, inadequate certainly, but yet superior to that of other races, at least as to its results. This population cares

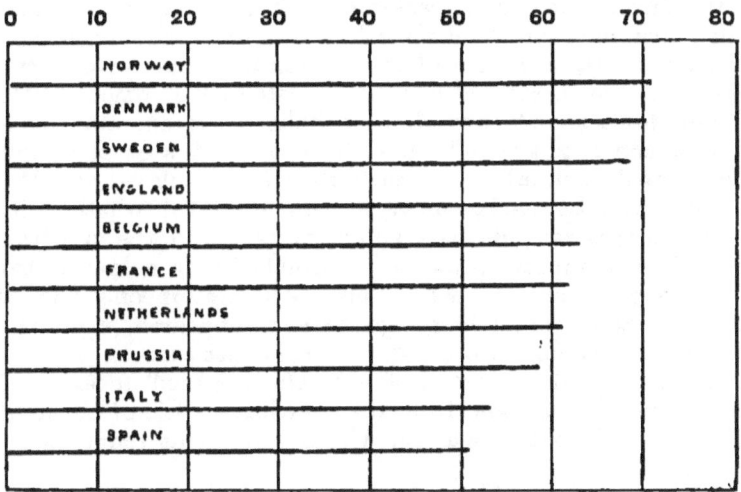

Diagram 28.—Survival to the Age of Twenty.

too much for its conservation, and too little for its renewal. The old are too many, and the young are too few; and the old bring in the government of the old,—old ideas, old things, the negation of all progress.

On the other hand, it may be said, the English population increases fast enough. What becomes of the surplus? They emigrate from Great Britain to the United States or Australia. In the thirty-nine years between 1837 and 1876, 8,000,000 persons emigrated—that is, on an average, 22,800 a year. Each emigrant would be worth about £175 to his adopted country; that is, £175 would represent the value, out there, of his rearing, education, and skill, and of the stock of money, clothes, etc., which he would bring with him. England has, therefore, contributed an annual average of £4,000,000[1] to the progress of America and Australia. And then, when a colony has become powerful, like the United States, she separates herself from the mother country, and closes her frontiers against her. In the meantime, the moment she is strong enough, she raises her customs tariffs, like Australia and Canada, so as to exclude English produce. England has, therefore, all the trouble and none of the profit. She only succeeds in raising up a host of competitors. Would not England have been better off if all these millions had been spent within her own borders?

The question is a complex one, and there is much to be said on both sides. But has this emigration been so altogether unproductive to England? Is it nothing to her to have her people settled all over the face of the earth, speaking the English language, retaining English manners and traditions? No doubt, had her population been less dense, the contest for existence would have been less intense; but that is stagnation; it is arrested development. "Every child you don't have," says M. de la Palisse, "is one man the less." And that man might have been a Papin, a Watt, a Stephenson!

Men crowd each other, but still they help each other. Plant a grain of wheat by itself, and it is very doubtful whether it will produce a single ear; but sow an entire field, and the multitude of stalks will be a mutual protection. Solidarity is a law of nature, even among organisms which are perfectly unconscious of it. Without it they would long ago have disappeared, even if they could ever have come into being. So it is with man.

I do not here take account of physiological hindrances resulting from various diseases, and from the over-heated life of our artificial civilisation; I do but note a fact with a view to its economic consequences.

The increase of population forces progress on every people which has not, like the Hindoo, given itself up to passive resignation. Beneath this pressure the contest for existence becomes more eager; man makes greater efforts; he develops his powers and his capacity for utilities. If we cannot say that all densely populated nations are strong, we can at least say that no nation with a sparse and stagnant population has ever been strong. So necessary is this density, that we everywhere see a movement towards the towns, where the population is closest.

The greatest prudence is needed in putting in practice the moral restraint advocated by Malthus. The exaggerated application of this principle threatens little by little to destroy the French population. If this should extend to the other races which form the front rank of civilisation, they will run the risk of some day being sup-

---

[1] *The Economist Commercial Review* of 1878, p. 5. *The Economist* says *forty* millions; but this is clearly a mistake.

planted by the less civilised peoples. Whole nations will share the fate which has already befallen the enfeebled and degenerate descendants of our aristocracy and wealthy *bourgeoisie*.

We see in France the fruits of a depressing form of political economy. In the early stages of civilisation, selection is stimulated by the strength of the man, and by the beauty, or at least the energy, of the woman. In our own, selection is determined by social position, by dowry, by title, regardless of physical disqualifications, hereditary or acquired. In England, every young man has learnt to count on himself, and every girl to count on herself; they unite to carry on together the contest for existence; there is real selection, the woman valuing the energy of the man, and the man the devotion of the woman.

Nevertheless, in this prolific country of England, certain distinguished men, advanced thinkers, founded in 1877 the *Malthusian League*, with Dr. Drysdale as its President. We give some paragraphs from the programme of this Society, which will explain its objects.

4. "The preventive measures consist in the limitation of children by abstinence from marriage, or by prudence after marriage.

5. "The prolonged abstinence from marriage which Malthus preached is the source of many diseases and sexual vices; early unions, on the contrary, tend to ensure sexual purity, domestic comfort, social happiness, and individual health; but it is a grave offence for men and women to bring into the world more children than they can suitably lodge, feed, clothe, and educate.

6. "Over-population is the most fruitful source of pauperism, ignorance, crime, and disease."

We can hardly give a flat contradiction to this statement, and say that it is right that men and women should bring into the world more children than they can suitably house, feed, clothe, and educate; but what do we mean by "suitably"? The question admits of the most various answers.

The Malthusian League puts the question again in another form; the restriction of population would have "an immense and almost immediate result in the diminution of the offer of labour, and the consequent rise of wages." This second view of the subject deserves careful examination, for it raises the question—What are the laws which regulate the value of man?

142   PROFESSIONS AND OCCUPATIONS.

CHAPTER II.

PROFESSIONS AND OCCUPATIONS.

WE are every day hearing the complaint that hands are wanted for agriculture. The phrase has become quite hackneyed. As far back as 1848, Ledru Rollin, in a speech on the right of labour, spoke of the depopulation of the country districts, and of the necessity of sending the workmen of the towns back to agriculture. In saying so, he certainly betrayed some ingratitude to those to whom we owe the Revolution, and put a somewhat strange interpretation on freedom of labour.

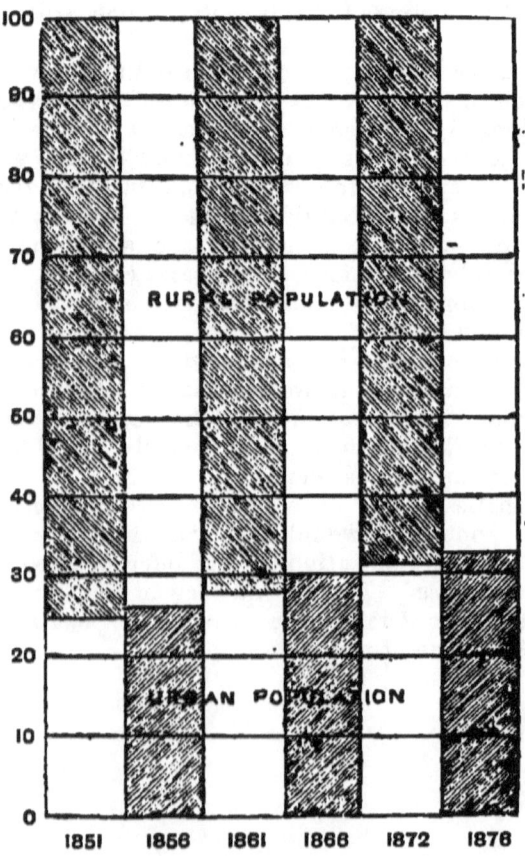

Diagram 29.—Proportion between Urban and Rural Population in France.

It is not in France only, but in England and everywhere else, that the rural population has an undoubted tendency to migrate towards the towns, and that agriculture thus tends to merge in manufacture.

Distribution Per Cent.

(Statistique de la France, vol. v., 1876, p. 24.)

Population.	Year.					
	1851.	1856.	1861.	1866.	1872.	1876.
Urban . . .	25·52	27·31	28·86	30·46	31·12	32·44
Rural . . .	74·48	72·69	71·14	69·54	68·88	67·56

(See Diagram 29, p. 142.)

Mr. Max Wirth has recorded the same facts in England.[1]

This movement is in accordance with the law we have stated—the tendency of an agricultural civilisation to develop into a manufacturing civilisation.

Under the present system of agriculture, the use of machinery being limited, man's capacity for production is feeble, and the wages

[1] In manufacturing countries, the manufacturing and the agricultural classes each form one continuous wave, moving, however, in opposite directions, the former steadily increasing and the latter steadily diminishing. The agricultural population of Saxony in 1849 was 32 per cent. of the whole; in 1861 it had fallen to 21 per cent., while the manufacturing population had in the same time risen from 51 to 56 per cent. In Great Britain this movement goes on jointly with the increase of the population and of exports and imports; that is to say, with the production of wealth. (*Lois du Travail*, p. 45.)

Year.	Imports.	Exports.	Total.	Population.	Population.		
					Agricultural.	Industrial.	Other Occupations.
	£	£	£		%	%	%
1811	26,510,186	32,890,712	59,400,898	12,596,803	35·0	44·0	21·0
1821	30,792,760	36,659,630	67,452,390	14,391,631	33·0	46·0	21·0
1831	49,713,889	37,164,372	86,878,261	16,539,318	30·0	48·0	22·0
1841	64,377,962	51,534,623	116,012,585	18,720,394	28·8	49·6	21·6
1851	110,484,997	74,488,722	184,933,719	20,959,477	26·2	51·0	22·8
1861	217,485,024	159,632,498	377,117,522	23,128,518	21·5	58·1	20·4

(See Diagram 30, p. 144.)

144 PROFESSIONS AND OCCUPATIONS.

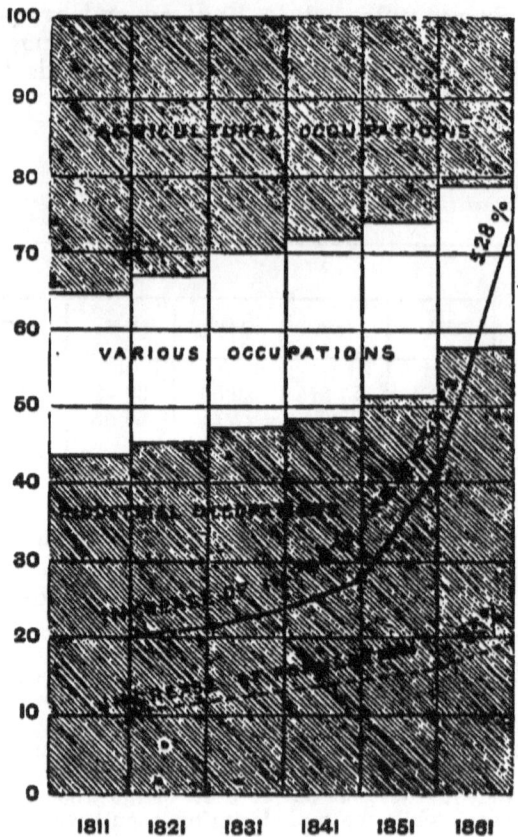

Diagram 30.—Movement of Industrial and Rural Populations in England, relatively to General Population.

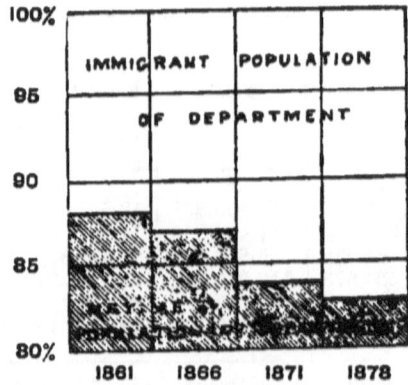

Diagram 31.—Proportion of Immigrant Population to Average Population in a Department.

of the agriculturist will, therefore, necessarily be lower than those of the artisan. Man now knows that he is not bound to the soil like a plant. The railway runs near him, and he knows that he can go where he finds himself the most valued. This increasing disposition to migrate is shown by the following figures:—

In 1861, the number of Frenchmen who remained in or had returned to their own department was 88·24 per cent. of the inhabitants; in 1866 it was only 87·45. Immediately after the war it fell to 84·97, and it is now only 83·74. This steady reduction in the stationary population shows how the displacement of populations grows year by year. (See Diagram 31, p. 144.)

Nevertheless, the agricultural population of France remains considerable, as the following tables show:—

		Number of Inhabitants.	Percentage.
Agriculture.	1st. Proprietors and peasants farming their own land	10,620,886	56·00
	2nd. Farmers, husbandmen, and *métayers*	5,708,132	30·09
	3rd. Various agricultural occupations (wine-growers, wood-cutters, gardeners, market-gardeners, &c.)	2,639,587	13·91
		18,968,605	100·00
Industries.	Manufactures	3,133,807	33·79
	Trades	6,140,670	66·21
		9,274,537	100·00
Commerce and transport		8,837,223	100·00
Liberal Professions.	Gendarmerie and Police	130,769	8·54
	Religion	229,667	15·00
	Public Service	567,541	37·06
	Education	222,641	14·54
	Law	148,905	9·72
	Medicine	141,830	9·26
	Science and Art	90,052	5·88
		1,531,405	100·00
Persons living exclusively on their own means.	Proprietors and fund-holders	1,957,037	90·94
	State pensioners	194,850	9·06
		2,151,888	100·00

(See Diagram 32, p. 146.)

146 PROFESSIONS AND OCCUPATIONS.

Occupation.	Number of inhabitants.	Percentage.
Agriculture	18,968,605	53·04
Industries	9,274,537	25·93
Commerce and transport	3,837,223	10·73
Liberal professions	1,531,405	4·28
Persons living exclusively on their incomes (proprietors, fund-holders, and pensioners)	2,151,888	6·02
	35,763,658	100·00
Unclassed population (beggars, vagabonds, and occupations unknown)	281,740	
	36,045,398	

(See Diagram 33.)

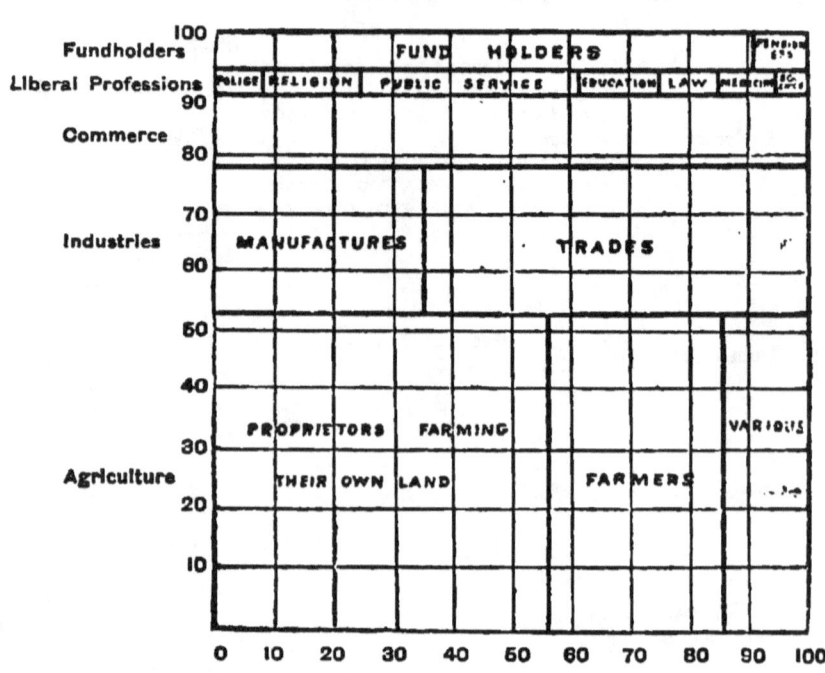

Diagram 32.—Proportionate Distribution of each Group of Occupations.

Diagram 33.—Proportion of Persons employed in each Occupation.

It is not every one in a country who labours at all. Some labour and produce for others; others enjoy the fruits of those labours.

Before giving the proportions of the active and inactive classes in France, I must make the reservation that a certain number of persons classed as active might more properly be classed as burdensome. Rats are active, but their activity is destructive. So it is with the activity of certain social parasites.

Dr. Bertillon gives these numbers as follows:—

It is computed that in 1866, out of every ten thousand of the entire population, the number of persons engaged in the so-called liberal professions (including the families and dependants) was:—

Persons living by professions connected with those scientific, literary, and artistic works which are the glory of our country, 16 to 17;

Persons living by professions concerned with the health of men and domestic animals, 36 to 37;

Persons living by professions connected with the maintenance of justice and equity between man and man, 46 to 47;

Persons living by professions connected with the education of our children, with the transmission of the inheritance of knowledge left us by our ancestors, 53;

Persons living by professions connected with the exercise of the various forms of worship, 62;

Persons living by the carrying on of public business, 108;

Lastly, persons living by the protection of the public peace at home and abroad, and of public and private wealth, 171.

I may mention in addition at the same period:—

Persons living by the hire of property in the country, 190;

Persons living by the hire of property in towns, 61 to 62;

Persons living by the loan of money to the State or to others, 196;

Persons living on Government pensions or on other means public or private, 39.[1]

Many of these professions appear at first sight useful and productive, while a closer scrutiny would show that there are magistrates, charged with the production of public safety, who have never produced anything but the public danger which results from contempt for the law, induced by the baseness of the judge.

Bertillon, *Dictionnaire Encyclopédique des Sciences Médicales*, Art. FRANCE.

RELATIVE NUMBER OF THE ACTIVE AND INACTIVE POPULATION OF FRANCE.

Occupations.	Active Population.				Inactive Population.		Total Population.	
	Employers.	Employés.	Workmen.	Day Labourers.	Families.	Servants.	Active.	Inactive.
Agriculture	3,906,381	136,628	967,267	1,626,174	11,006,901	1,325,254	6,636,450	12,332,155
Industries	1,125,680	192,686	2,600,864	549,717	4,584,398	221,192	4,468,947	4,805,590
Commerce and Transport	784,101	318,095	254,420	219,281	2,007,178	254,148	1,575,897	2,261,326
Liberal Professions	523,256	114,124	1,209	28,241	686,437	178,138	666,830	864,575
Private Means	943,617	10,135	...	81,200	755,985	360,951	1,034,952	1,116,936
Total Population (exclusive of soldiers, sailors, and others reckoned separately)	7,283,035	771,668	3,823,760	2,504,613	19,040,899	2,339,683	14,383,076	21,380,582

(*Statistique de la France*, p. L.) (See Diagram 34, p. 150.)

PROFESSIONS AND OCCUPATIONS.

PROPORTIONAL DISTRIBUTION.

Occupations.	Active Population. Percentage.				Inactive Population. Percentage.		Total Percentage.	
	Employers.	Employés.	Workmen.	Day Labourers.	Families.	Servants.	Active.	Inactive.
Agriculture	58·36	2·06	14·58	24·50	89·26	10·74	34·99	65·01
Industries	25·19	4·31	58·20	12·30	95·39	4·61	48·18	41·82
Commerce and Transport	49·75	20·19	16·14	13·92	88·76	11·24	41·07	58·93
Liberal Professions	78·47	17·11	0·18	4·24	79·40	20·60	43·54	56·45
Private Means	91·18	0·97	...	7·85	67·6	32·31	48·10	51·90
Averages	50·63	5·37	26·59	17·41	89·06	10·94	40·22	59·78
		49·37			100		100	
	100							

(*Statistique de la France*, p. li.).

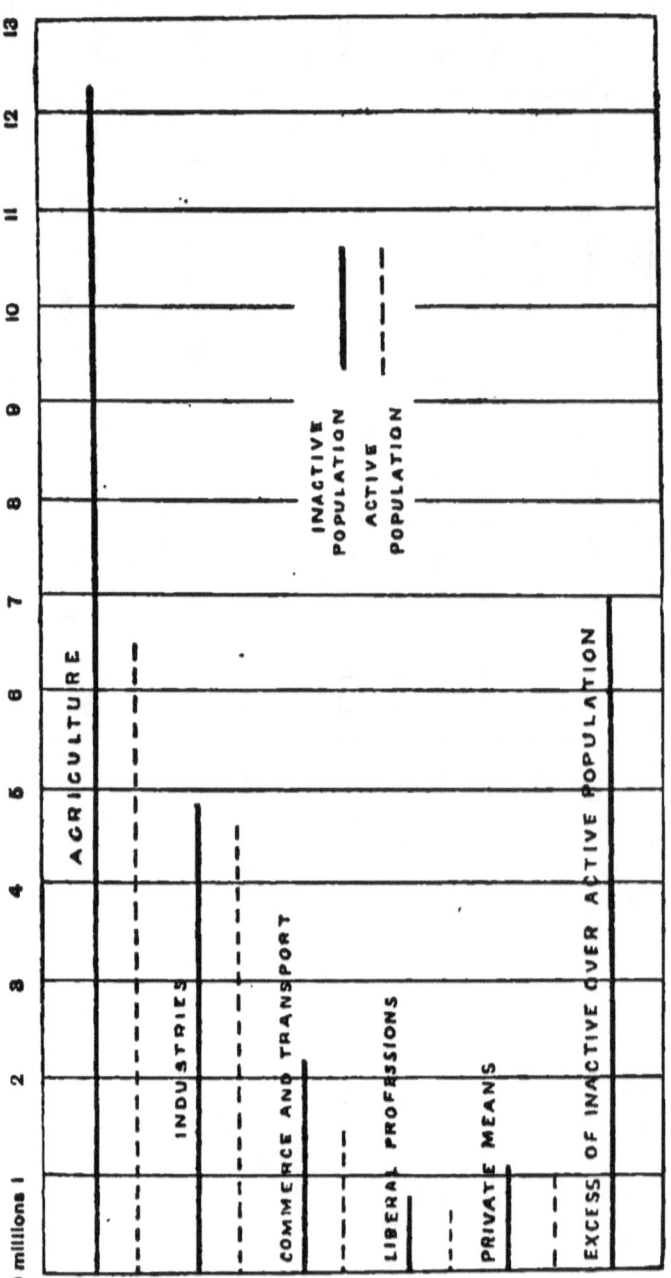

Diagram 34.—Relative Number of the Active and Inactive Population of France.

CHAPTER III.

THE VALUE OF MAN.

MAN, as we have said, appropriates utilities either by his own efforts or by exchange.

The personal effort of man is called labour. It is the employment of his mental or bodily forces in the transformation of the forces of nature into utilities.

Man can act directly; but if he is alone he acts feebly. Left to his own resources, we have seen that Robinson Crusoe attained with difficulty to the lowest possible standard of comfort; and yet Robinson Crusoe had at his disposal the means and methods of a highly developed civilisation.

Hence results a perpetual exchange of the utilities possessed by each individual.

Now each individual possesses a certain number of utilities; and the greater their number, the greater his power of acquiring others by purchase.

Man can be the owner of two kinds of utilities; the one, which is commonly called capital, external to himself,—an inert mass of soil, machines, coal, stock-in-trade—things by themselves useless; the other, consisting of things incorporated in himself, his intellectual faculties, the knowledge he has acquired, his natural aptitudes and personal attributes.

He can exchange these utilities for others. We speak of the relations of capital and labour, and we make of them two hostile entities. In reality, there can be no relations except between utilities of different kinds.

I am a workman, I have learned a trade, I can make locks. I am possessor of the utility known as a lock. Whoever wishes to have locks will have to apply to me. But who will he be? The possessor of some other utilities, personal or impersonal. He will exchange some of his utilities for mine. Suppose he is a professor; he will exchange his utility, knowledge, for my utility, locks. But perhaps I do not want his utility, knowledge? Others, however, do want it; and thus his utility, knowledge, realised under the form of fees, will give him the power to purchase my utility, locks.

But this professor does not, perhaps, consume immediately all the utilities which he has received in exchange for those he has given. He lets them lie unproductive in his chest, or else he transforms them into land, mines, railways, or some other form of fixed capital. I, the locksmith, consume at once the utilities I receive in exchange for those I have given. Consequently I have at my disposal only my personal utilities, while the professor has added to his personal utilities a number of impersonal utilities. His purchasing power is therefore greater than before; and the difference between his purchasing power and mine is also greater than before. But if it has been gain to him, has it been loss to me? By no means; for if his purchasing power has become greater, he can purchase more locks; my locks will therefore go up in value, and the power of my utilities will be increased.

When people oppose the terms capital and labour, they misuse the words. It is simply an exchange of personal and impersonal utilities.

Man is a fixed capital, capable of producing utilities, just like a field, a machine, or any other implement. His superiority as an implement lies in his being able to improve himself; and the more he is improved the more capable he is of producing utilities, and consequently the greater his value. The more a steam-engine can do, and the less circulating capital it consumes in doing it, the better engine it is.[1] The same rule applies to man. He too consumes fuel in the form of bread, meat, and wine. If he produces half as much again with the same amount of fuel, his power of utility will be doubled and his value proportionately increased.

Now, in what way is his power of production capable of augmentation? It is augmented by knowledge, which has shown him easier and quicker methods of subjecting matter to changes of condition and of place; and by the use of the steam-engine, which substitutes its own force for that of his muscles. His capacity for utility increases in proportion to the power of the tool he uses. Now what does his power of utility represent? It represents his value.

We may say then,—
The value of man is in proportion to the power of his implements.

For want of observing this fact, many people have authoritatively declared that machinery must destroy labour and lower wages. Such was Sismondi's prophecy, and it has been often repeated since, although the increase in the demand for labour and the amount of wages has repeatedly demonstrated its falsity. In 1760 Arkwright took out his first patent for the spinning jenny. At that time there were in England 5,200 spinners using the spinning wheel, and 2,700 weavers, in all 7,900 persons engaged in the production of woven materials.[2] Combinations were formed against his machine, and against that of Hargraves, and he was obliged to take out several patents in succession. The steam-engine of Watt, which was to bring Arkwright's loom into general use, was not invented till 1774, and it was not till 1775 or 1777 that steam cotton mills began to spread through the United Kingdom.

In 1787, a Parliamentary inquiry showed that the number of

---

[1] See Book II.
[2] Michel Chevalier, *Cours d'Economie Politique*, vol. i. p. 354.

work-people had mounted up to 320,000, an increase of 4,400 per cent. Since then machines have been improved and the same amount of work has needed fewer hands to do it; yet the number of workmen has gone on steadily increasing.

Mr. Baines, in his *Statistical Documents*, states that in 1833 there were in the United Kingdom 237,000 work-people employed in spinning and weaving cotton by machinery, and 250,000 hand weavers, in all, 487,000 persons employed exclusively in the spinning and weaving of cotton stuffs. By reckoning the workmen employed in subsidiary industries, such as calico-printing, he makes it up to 800,000 workmen.

If we add to these the thousands of persons employed in the trades to which the existence of these work-people gives rise, we come to the conclusion that the machinery, which, when first introduced, was to have been the ruin of 7,900 spinners, was in 1833 providing two million persons with the means of subsistence. Since that time like causes have produced like results. The number of persons now living by the cotton industry cannot be less than 2,500,000.

J. B. Say explained the causes of this phenomenon. Suppose 300,000 francs are employed in a manufacture, one-third in raw material, and two-thirds in wages. The manufacturer finds a machine which saves one-third. Will he let the 100,000 francs thus saved lie idle? No. He will lower the price of his produce in proportion, which will proportionately increase the consumption, and the increased consumption will require the extension of his works, or, if he does not put the money into his business, he will put it in a bank, or lay it out in investments, and the capital thus set free for use will stimulate to fresh enterprises, which in their turn will demand increased human effort. The more abundant circulating capital becomes, the more eager are its possessors to find it employment and to convert it into fixed capital.[1] They cannot do so without the aid of human effort. Whether they found a factory, or build a house, or invest in a railway, still they are demanding human effort. And the greater the demand the higher the price.

Furthermore, the value of the circulating capital produced by man diminishes in proportion to its abundance.

The value of man, as of all fixed capital, is in direct ratio to the abundance of circulating capital.

This law is demonstrated by the following figures, which show the increase of wages in France during the nineteenth century:—

---

[1] See Book II.

Average Daily Wages of Builders' Workmen Employed on Charitable Institutions.

(After M. de Foville, *Economiste Français*, 5th Feb., 1876.)

	1824–33.	1834–43.	1844–53.	1854.	1855.
	fr.	fr.	fr.	fr.	fr.
Masons	2·00	2·07	2·15	2·26	2·34
Carpenters	2·15	2·21	2·32	2·44	2·52
Joiners	2·16	2·22	2·30	2·41	2·49
Locksmiths	2·26	2·32	2·42	2·55	2·64

Average Daily Wages in the Building Trade in the Chief Departmental Towns, Paris not Included.

(After M. Foville, *ubi sup.*)

	1853.	1857.	1871.	1872.
	fr.	fr.	fr.	fr.
50 % Masons	2·07	2·40	3·06	3·07
50 % Carpenters	2·20	2·53	3·34	3·43
47 % Joiners	2·02	2·31	2·85	2·98
39 % Locksmiths	2·16	2·44	3·02	3·01

Average Daily Wages of Workmen in the Building Trade in Paris.

	1805.	1810.	1853.	1866.	1875.	Increase.
	fr.	fr.	fr.	fr.	fr.	%
Navvies	2·25	2·25	3· 0	4· 0	4· 0	77
Stone masons	3·35	3·50	5· 0	5·50	5·50	69
Bricklayers	3·25	4· 0	5·25	6· 0	6·25	92
Masons	3·25	3·25	4·25	5·25	5·50	69
Rough wallers	2·50	2·50	3· 0	4·25	5· 0	100
Labourers	1·70	1·90	2·50	3·35	3·50	105
Carpenters	3· 0	3·25	5· 0	6· 0	6· 0	100
Joiners	3·50	3·25	4· 0	4·50	5· 0	42
Smiths	5· 0	5· 0	5· 0	6·50	7· 0	40
Fitters	3·75	4· 0	4·25	4·60	5·25	40
Glaziers	3· 0	...	3·75	5· 0	5 25	75
Plumbers	4·25	..	4· 0	5·50	6· 0	41
Slaters	5· 0	...	5· 0	6· 0	6· 0	20
Painters	4·25	...	4· 0	5· 0	6·· 0	41
Locksmiths	...	...	4· 0	5· 0	5· 0	

We give the seventeen departments in which, according to M. de Foville, the wages for field-work had in 1862 risen the least.[1]

[1] *L'Economiste Français*, January 8, 1876.

Average Daily Wages.

Department.	1849–53.	1855.	1862.	Increase from 1849–53 to 1862.
	fr.	fr.	fr.	%
Côtes-du-Nord	0·80	0·90	1·14	42·5
Finistère	0·86	0·91	1·14	32·5
Morbihan	0·82	0·94	1·18	43·9
Haute-Garonne	1·03	1·08	1·21	17·5
Ille-et-Vilaine	0·97	1·03	1·29	33·0
Ariège	1·05	1·18	1·35	28·6
Tarn	1·15	1·22	1·37	19·1
Haute-Vienne	1·14	1·25	1·37	20·2
Tarn-et-Garonne	1·06	1·26	1·40	32·1
Gers	1·12	1·26	1·43	27·7
Landes	1·20	1·37	1·44	20·0
Basses-Pyrénées	1·10	1·17	1·44	30·9
Indre	1·26	1·55	1·48	17·4
Mayenne	1·14	1·20	1·50	31·6
Hautes-Pyrénées	1·10	1·12	1·50	36·4
Manche	1·21	1·33	1·53	26·4
Pas-de-Calais	1·08	1·30	1·53	41·7

The following are the twenty departments where the wages of field-labour were highest in the same year.

Average Daily Wages.

Department.	1849–53.	1855.	1862.	Increase from 1849–53 to 1862.
	fr.	fr.	fr.	%
Seine	2· 0	2·38	3·10	55·0
Seine-et-Oise	1·80	2·17	2·66	47·7
Seine-et-Marne	1·90	2·23	2·56	34·7
Bouches-du-Rhône	1·97	2·16	2·50	26·9
Rhône	1·92	2·20	2·50	30·2
Jura	1·75	1·92	2·50	42·8
Eure	1·69	1·87	2·37	40·2
Var	1·65	1·92	2·35	42·4
Aube	1·67	1·83	2·33	39·5
Marne	1·72	1·90	2·30	33·7
Yonne	1·65	1·74	2·26	37·0
Haute-Marne	1·66	1·92	2·22	33·7
Charente-Inférieure	1·72	1·91	2·22	29·0
Vaucluse	2·04	2·30	2·20	7·84
Doubs	1·63	1·85	2·17	33·1
Gironde	1·52	1·75	2·16	42·1
Ardennes	1·75	1·84	2·16	23·4
Oise	1·54	1·77	2·15	39·6
Lot-et-Garonne	1·47	1·78	2·13	44·9
Hérault	1·52	1·76	2·12	39·5

Average Daily Wages of Women in Paris.

Trades.	In 1844.[1]	In 1853.[2]	In 1860.[3]	In 1872.	Increase.
	fr.	fr.	fr.	fr.	%
Shirt hands	0·90	1·50	1·75	2· 0	122
Staymakers	1· 0	1·50	2· 0	2· 0	100
Dressmakers	1·25	1·75	2· 0	2· 0	60
Embroiderers	1·50	2· 0	2· 0	3· 0	100
Lacemakers	1·50	2·30	2·50	3· 0	100
Closers	1·50	2·50	2· 0	3· 0	100
Artifcl. Flower makers	1·50	2·50	2·25	3· 0	100
Laundresses	2· 0	2·50	2·50	3· 0	50
Trouser makers[4]	1·75	2·50	2·75	4· 0	128
Average	1·43	2·12	2·20	2·78	94

Average Daily Wages of Women in the Chief Towns of Departments.[5]

Trades.	In 1853.	In 1872.	Increase Per Cent.
	fr.	fr.	
Milliners	1·12	1·37	22
Shirt hands	0·90	1·38	53
Embroiderers	0·98	1·38	41
Staymakers	0·97	1·46	51
Dressmakers	1·08	1·49	38
Trouser makers	1·05	1·50	43
Closers	1· 0	1·52	52
Laundresses	1·25	1·53	22
Waistcoat makers	0·95	1·57	65
Lace makers	1·08	1·66	54
Artificial Flower makers	1·33	1·78	34

In the following tables we give the daily wages of workmen, boarders and non-boarders, in the chief departmental towns, Paris excepted, according to the *Statistique Annuelle de la France*, vols. vi. and vii.[6]

[1] Figures quoted by M. Louis Blanc in his *Organisation du Travail*. They may be a little within the truth.
[2] Statistics published by the ministry of Agriculture and Commerce.
[3] Statistics of Parisian industries in 1860, according to the inquiry made by the Chamber of Commerce.
[4] *L'Economiste Français*. March 15, 1876, *Variations des Prix en France*, de Foville.
[5] According to M. de Foville (*Economiste Français*, January 8, 1876).
[6] Published by the Ministry of Agriculture and Commerce.

THE VALUE OF MAN.

DAILY WAGES OF BOARDED WORKMEN.

Year.	Ordinary Rate.	Maximum.	Minimum.	Increase.	
	fr.	fr.	fr.	Per Cent.	Absolute.
1853	0·96	1·23	0·74	...	...
1871	1·40	1·82	1·10	46	0·44
1876	1·49	1·93	1·18	55	0·53
1877	1·51	1·93	1·21	57	0·55

DAILY WAGES OF NON-BOARDED WORKMEN.

Year.	Ordinary Rate.	Maximum.	Minimum.	Increase.	
	fr.	fr.	fr.	Per Cent.	Absolute.
1853	1·89	2·36	1·53	...	...
1871	2·65	3·36	2·19	40	0·76
1876	2·86	3·64	2·34	51	0·97
1877	2·87	3·64	2·37	52	0·98

Taken altogether, the average rate of wages has increased 53 per cent. in twenty-three years, or 2·3 per cent. per annum.

USUAL SALARY OF WOMEN (NOT BOARDED) IN THE CHIEF DEPARTMENTAL TOWNS, PARIS EXCEPTED.

Trades.	Average Ordinary Wages.				Increase.					
					Absolute.			Per Cent.		
	1853.	1871.	1876.	1877.	1871.	1876.	1877.	1871.	1876.	1877.
	fr.	fr.	fr.	fr.	fr.	fr.	fr.			
Laundresses . .	1·25	1·50	1·65	1·65	0·25	0·40	0·40	20	32	32
Embroiderers . .	0·98	1·45	1·61	1·64	0·47	0·63	0·66	48	64	67
Staymakers . .	0·97	1·42	1·55	1·55	0·45	0·58	0·56	46	60	58
Dressmakers . .	1·08	1·42	1·56	1·57	0·34	0·48	0·49	32	44	45
Trouser makers .	1·05	1·45	1·53	1·57	0·40	0·48	0·52	38	46	50
Lacemakers . .	1·08	1·71	1·76	1·78	0·63	0·68	0·70	58	63	65
Artificial Flower makers . .	1·33	1·70	1·85	1·98	0·37	0·52	0·65	11	40	49
Waistcoat makers	0·95	1·51	1·0	1·61	0·56	0·67	0·66	59	70	69
Shirt hands . .	0·90	1·29	1·42	1·41	0·31	0·52	0·51	32	58	57
Milliners . . .	1·12	1·40	1·66	1·45	0·28	0·54	0·33	25	48	39
Closers	1·0	1·46	1·63	1·65	0·46	0·63	0·65	46	63	65
Total average .	1·07	1·48	1·62	1·62	0·41	0·55	0·55	38	51	51

The first thing that strikes one in this table, is that the average wages of women hardly exceed half those of men; nevertheless, they have participated in almost equal proportion in the general rise which has taken place between 1853 and 1877.

PARISIAN INDUSTRIES—USUAL WAGES OF WOMEN.

Trades.	Average Ordinary Wages.[1]			Increase.			
				Absolute.		Per Cent.	
	1853. fr.	1871. fr.	1877. fr.	1871. fr.	1877. fr.	1871.	1877.[2]
Laundresses	2·50	3· 0	3· 0	0·50	0·50	20	20
Embroiderers	2· 0	3· 0	3· 0	1· 0	1· 0	50	50
Staymakers	1·50	2· 0	2· 0	0·50	0·50	33	33
Dressmakers	1·75	2· 0	2· 0	0·25	0·25	14	14
Trouser makers (women)	2·50	4· 0	4· 0	1·50	1·50	60	60
Lacemakers	2·30	3· 0	3· 0	0·70	0·70	30	30
Artificial Flower makers	2·50	3· 0	3· 0	0·50	0·50	20	20
Shirt hands	1·50	2· 0	2· 0	0·50	0·50	33	33
Closers (women)	2·50	3· 0	3· 0	0·50	0·50	20	20
Total average	2·12	2·78	2·78	0·66	0·66	31	31

We see that in Paris women's wages are double what they are in the country; but their tendency to rise seems feebler.

The highest wages, both in Paris and in the departments, are those of jewellers and ornamental sculptors. And why? Because these are trades which require natural gifts and a long apprenticeship; consequently the man who is master of one of them has a greater power of utility, and therefore a greater value, than an unskilled workman. Accordingly the wages of these trades have gone up 75 per cent. in Paris, while the unskilled workman's have risen only 53 per cent. If there are some trades in which wages have increased more rapidly than in that of jewellery, it is because there is a growing tendency among the working classes to select those trades which have a refined and artistic side. The supply of labour in these trades accordingly becomes greater, and they are more easily recruited.

The average increase of wages has been greater in the country than in Paris, though Paris wages are still in advance of country wages by one-third or even half. It will be easily understood how such an advantage attracts all the more able workmen to Paris, and how this very supply of labour has checked the continued rise in

---

[1] *Statistique de la France*, p. xlvi.
[2] The wages have not varied from 1876 to 1877.

wages. On the other hand, this influx has reacted on the principal country towns. In order to retain skilful workmen, it has been found necessary to raise their wages.

This rise of wages has taken place in England as well as in France. You may have seen in London groups of beggars of both sexes, clothed in rags through which the bare shivering skin peeps here and there, with their boots full of holes, and with a look of hopeless resignation on their wan dejected faces; and you have perhaps thought that here was the last degree of misery short of death itself. Yet they are positively well off, compared with their forefathers.

Sixty years ago, the number of paupers in London was 106,000.[1]

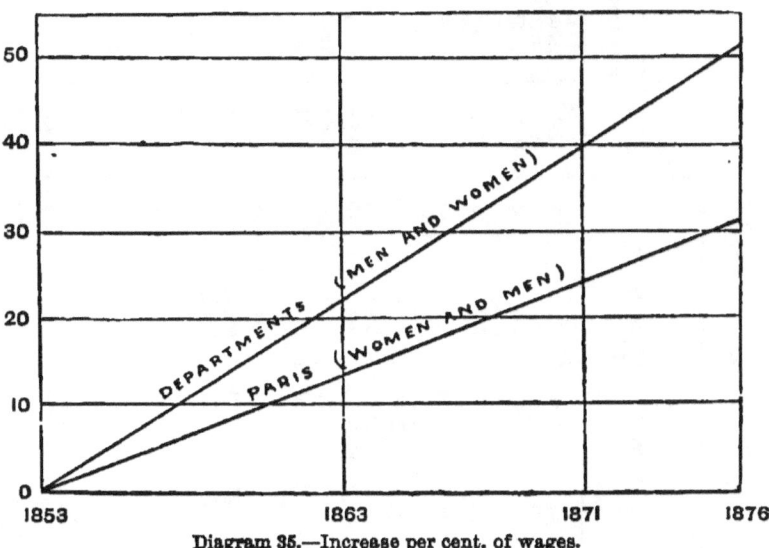

Diagram 35.—Increase per cent. of wages.

In 1875 it was less, although the population had tripled. But the cost of maintaining 100,000 paupers in London is now five times what it was in 1815. Whence comes this difference? Almost all commodities, including bread, sugar, and tea, are cheaper now than they were then. Paupers do not fix their manner of life for themselves, it is fixed for them by others, and it must be inferior to that of the worst-paid workmen.

The difference arises from the fact that the idea of what is indispensably necessary, even for paupers, has risen of late years. We know too that in England, when wages have gone up considerably, they fall again on any depression of trade. There is then, no doubt, a certain amount of suffering; but it is nothing to be compared with

[1] Danson, *Lectures*, p. 42.

Wages of Handicrafts in the Chief Departmental Towns.

Workmen not Boarded.

Trades.	Ordinary Average Wages.			Increase.					
				Absolute.			Per Cent.		
	1853. fr.	1871. fr.	1876. fr.	1877. fr.	1871. fr.	1876. fr.	1877. fr.	1871.	1876.	1877.
Jewellers and Goldsmiths	2·74	3·58	3·97	4·04	0·84	1·23	1·30	31	45	47
Butchers	1·73	2·58	2·74	2·84	0·85	1·01	1·11	49	58	64
Bakers	1·90	2·92	3·39	3·31	1·02	1·49	1·41	54	78	74
Brewers	2·20	2·83	3·24	3·33	0·63	1·04	1·13	29	47	51
Brickmakers	1·88	2·58	2·85	2·80	0·70	0·97	0·92	37	52	49
Quarrymen	2·02	2·80	2·91	3·06	0·78	0·89	1·04	39	44	51
Coachbuilders	2·21	3·16	3·42	3·48	0·95	1·21	1·27	43	55	57
Hatters	2·12	3·0	3·21	3·20	0·88	1·09	1·08	41	51	51
Coal-heavers	1·83	2·71	2·52	2·56	0·88	0·69	0·73	48	38	40
Pork-butchers	1·79	2·63	2·71	2·87	0·84	0·92	1·08	47	51	60
Carpenters	2·20	3·34	3·65	3·74	1·14	1·45	1·54	52	66	70
Wheelwrights	2·06	2·94	3·18	3·23	0·88	1·12	1·17	43	54	57
Braziers	2·21	3·03	3·15	3·31	0·82	0·94	1·10	37	42	50
Sockmakers	1·80	2·34	2·39	2·46	0·54	0·59	0·66	30	33	37
Ropemakers	1·76	2·36	2·56	2·63	0·60	0·80	0·87	34	45	49
Shoemakers	1·68	2·50	2·70	2·76	0·82	1·02	1·08	49	61	64
Cutlers	1·80	2·61	2·73	2·83	0·81	0·93	1·03	45	52	57
Slaters	2·16	3·19	3·56	3·57	1·03	1·40	1·41	48	65	65
Cabinet makers	2·20	2·98	3·30	3·36	0·78	1·10	1·16	35	50	53
Tinsmiths and Lampsellers	2·04	2·86	3·08	3·08	0·82	1·04	1·04	40	51	51
Smiths	2·42	3·22	3·51	3·51	0·80	1·09	1·09	33	45	45
Watchmakers	2·43	3·43	3·86	3·86	1·0	1·43	1·43	41	59	59
Printers	2·40	3·26	3·92	3·45	0·86	1·52	1·05	36	63	44

Bk. iv. Ch. iii.] THE VALUE OF MAN. 161

Gardeners	1·78	2·47	2·65	2·70	0·69	0·87	0·92	39	49	52
Masons	2·07	3·06	3·24	3·28	0·99	1·17	1·21	48	56	58
Farriers	1·94	2·79	2·96	3·02	0·85	1·02	1·08	44	53	56
Joiners	2·02	2·86	3·13	3·20	0·84	1·11	1·18	41	55	58
Pastrycooks	1·97	2·31	2·81	2·60	0·34	0·84	0·63	17	43	32
House painters	2·20	3·16	3·32	3·39	0·96	1·12	1·19	44	51	54
Hairdressers	1·35	2·17	2·42	2·30	0·82	1·07	0·95	61	79	70
Plumbers	2·25	3·14	3·27	3·32	0·89	1·02	1·07	40	44	47
Stove-makers	2·27	3·23	3·35	3·41	0·96	1·08	1·14	42	47	50
Potters	1·95	2·65	2·72	2·67	0·70	0·77	0·72	36	39	37
Bookbinders	1·92	2·51	2·81	2·82	0·59	0·89	0·90	31	46	47
Pit-sawyers	2·01	3·31	3·33	3·29	1·30	1·32	1·28	65	66	64
Sculptors	3·42	4·80	4·93	4·81	1·38	1·51	1·39	40	44	41
Saddlers	2·14	2·87	3·05	3·11	0·73	0·91	0·97	34	42	45
Locksmiths	2·16	3·02	3·25	3·28	0·86	1·19	1·12	40	55	52
Tailors	1·96	2·84	3·15	3·03	0·88	1·19	1·07	45	61	54
Stonemasons	2·39	3·48	3·74	3·64	1·09	1·35	1·25	46	56	52
Tanners	2·01	2·76	3·08	3·01	0·75	1·07	1·0	37	53	50
Upholsterers	2·39	3·30	3·54	3·53	0·91	1·15	1·14	38	48	48
Dyers	1·91	2·65	2·85	2·85	0·74	0·96	0·94	39	50	49
Navvies	1·57	2·40	2·65	2·67	0·83	1·08	1·10	53	69	70
Weavers	1·43	1·94	2·50	2·33	0·51	1·07	0·90	36	75	63
Coopers	1·98	2·70	2·96	3·02	0·77	0·98	1·04	39	49	52
Turners in wood	1·94	2·77	2·98	3·01	0·76	1·04	1·07	39	54	55
Turners in metal	2·52	3·45	3·72	3·74	0·95	1·20	1·22	38	48	48
Basket-makers	1·80	2·53	2·75	2·74	0·73	0·95	0·94	41	53	52
Nightmen	2·0	3·07	3·08	3·07	1·07	1·08	1·07	53	54	53
Glaziers	2·06	2·89	2·99	3·05	0·83	0·93	0·99	40	45	48
Average	2·06	2·90	3·12	3·14	0·84	1·06	1·08	41	51	52

The wages which have gone up most must have been those of sculptors, who earned 3 fr. 42 c. in 1853 and 4 fr. 80 c. in 1871: they earned up to 4 fr. 95 c. in 1876. Some of the most skilful workmen in this trade received as much as 4 fr. 70 c. in 1853 and 6 fr. 50 c in 1871. Next to them come the jewellers and goldsmiths, whose wages were 2 fr. 74 c. in 1853 and 3 fr. 58 c. in 1871, the watchmakers, the carpenters, the stone-masons, and the workers in metals.

M

Wages of Handicrafts in Paris.

Workmen not Boarded.

Trades.	Average Ordinary Wages.				Increase.					
					Absolute.			Per Cent.		
	1863. fr.	1871. fr.	1876. fr.	1877. fr.	1871. fr.	1876. fr.	1877. fr.	1871.	1876.	1877.
Jewellers and Goldsmiths	4·25	6·0	6·50	6·50	1·75	2·25	2·25	41	53	53
Butchers	4·50	6·60	6·0	6·0	1·60	1·50	1·50	32	33	33
Bakers	5·0	4·25	6·65	6·65	0·50	1·65	1·65	13	33	33
Brewers	3·75	3·30	4·25	4·25	0·30	0·50	0·50	10	13	13
Brickmakers	3·0	4·0	3·30	3·30	1·0	0·30	0·30	30	10	10
Quarrymen	3·0	5·50	4·0	4·50	1·50	1·0	1·50	37	30	50
Coachbuilders	4·0	6·50	5·50	5·50	2·50	1·50	1·50	62	37	37
Hatters	4·0	6·50	6·50	6·50	1·0	2·50	2·50	20	62	62
Coal-heavers	3·0	...	4·0	5·50	1·0	1·0	2·50	...	33	75
Carpenters	5·0	...	6·0	6·0	1·0	1·0	1·0	25	20	20
Wheelwrights	4·0	5·50	5·50	5·0	1·0	1·0	1·0	22	25	25
Braziers	4·50	5·50	5·50	5·50	1·0	1·0	1·0	22	22	22
Sockmakers	1·75	2·0	2·25	2·25	0·25	0·50	0·50	14	29	29
Ropemakers	3·0	4·0	4·0	4·0	1·0	1·0	1·0	33	33	33
Shoemakers	3·0	3·50	3·60	3·60	0·50	0·60	0·60	17	20	20
Cutlers	4·0	5·0	5·50	5·50	1·0	1·50	1·50	25	37	37
Slaters	5·0	6·0	6·0	6·30	1·0	1·0	1·50	20	33	30
Cabinet makers	3·50	5·0	5·0	6·0	1·50	1·50	2·50	43	20	71
Tinsmiths and lampsellers	3·50	4·0	4·0	4·0	0·50	0·50	0·50	14	14	14
Smiths	5·0	6·50	6·50	6·50	1·50	1·50	1·50	30	30	30
Watchmakers	4·50	5·0	5·0	6·0	0·50	0·50	1·50	11	11	33
Printers	5·0	6·0	6·0	6·0	1·0	1·0	1·0	20	20	20
Gardeners	2·50	4·50	3·75	3·75	2·0	1·25	1·25	80	50	50
Masons	4·25	5·0	5·0	5·0	0·75	0·75	0·75	17	17	17

THE VALUE OF MAN.

Farriers	3·65	5· 0	5· 0	5· 0	1·35	1·35	1·35	37	37	37
Joiners	3·50	5· 0	5· 0	6· 0	1·50	1·50	2·50	43	43	71
House painters . .	4· 0	6· 0	6· 0	6·25	2· 0	2· 0	2·25	50	50	56
Hairdressers . . .	2· 0	3· 0	3· 0	3· 0	1· 0	1· 0	1· 0	50	50	50
Plumbers	4· 0	5· 0	6· 0	6· 0	2· 0	2· 0	2· 0	25	50	50
Chimney-curers . .	4· 0	5·50	5·35	5·35	1·50	1·35	1·35	37	34	34
Potters	4· 0	3·85	3·85	3·85	0·35	0·35	0·35	10	10	10
Bookbinders . . .	3·50	5·50	5·50	5·50	2· 0	2· 0	2· 0	57	57	57
Pit-sawyers . . .	3·50	5· 0	5· 0	5·85	1·50	1·50	2·35	43	43	67
Sculptors	3·50	7· 0	7· 0	7· 0	3· 0	3· 0	3· 0	75	75	75
Saddlers	4· 0	4·50	4·50	4·50	0·50	0·50	0·50	12	12	12
Locksmiths . . .	4· 0	4·50	4·50	4·50	0·50	0·50	0·50	12	12	12
Tailors	4· 0	5· 0	5· 0	6·50	1· 0	2· 0	2· 0	67	67	67
Stonemasons . . .	5· 0	6· 0	6· 0	6· 0	1· 0	1· 0	1·50	20	20	30
Tanners	3·75	5· 0	5· 0	5· 0	1·25	1·25	1·25	33	33	33
Upholsterers . . .	4· 0	5· 0	5· 0	5· 0	1· 0	1· 0	1· 0	25	25	25
Dyers	3·50	5· 0	4·50	4·50	1·50	1· 0	1· 0	43	29	29
Navvies	3· 0	4· 0	4· 0	4·50	1· 0	1· 0	1·50	33	33	50
Weavers	3· 0	4· 0	4· 0	4· 0	1· 0	1· 0	1· 0	33	33	33
Coopers	4·25	5·60	5· 0	5· 0	1·35	0·75	0·75	32	18	18
Turners in wood .	4· 0	5· 0	5· 0	5· 0	1· 0	1· 0	1· 0	25	25	25
Turners in metal .	5· 0	6· 0	6· 0	6· 0	1· 0	1· 0	1· 0	20	20	20
Basket-makers . .	3·75	4·50	4·50	4·50	0·25	0·75	0·75	7	20	20
Nightmen	4·50	5· 0	5· 0	5· 0	0·50	0·50	0·50	11	11	11
Glaziers	3·75	5·50	5·50	6· 0	1·75	1·75	2·35	47	46	63
Average . . .	3·81	4·99	5· 0	5·18	1·17	1·19	1·37	31	31	36

Although information respecting the wages of workmen in Paris is abundant, the extreme subdivision of labour renders it difficult to obtain average results. *The Statistical Department* has endeavoured to arrive at these results by combining the figures supplied by the Chamber of Commerce with information received from the Prefecture of Police. In the preceding table, as also in the following, the wages of workmen not boarded by their masters are alone treated of. The proportionate rise is perceptibly less in Paris than in the departments. The greatest rise is in the hat trade. In many of the various trades connected with clothing and furniture wages have increased barely more than 10 per cent. These official figures seem to us rather within than beyond the truth.

what formerly existed. There was a very severe crisis in England in 1878; but, according to the Board of Trade reports, there was no decrease in the expenditure of the wage-earning classes.[1] The importation of food has not fallen off, and its increased cheapness has made up for the fall in wages. The importation of animal food has increased, especially that of bacon, which is largely consumed by the labouring classes; while the slight falling off in imported vegetables is balanced by the increase of the home supply. The crisis was felt more severely by the classes just above the working classes; the consumption of wine decreased, while that of spirits was scarcely affected at all.

This spending power of the working classes, which was much better maintained in 1878 than in preceding crises, checked the fall of manufactures.

According to Professor Leone Levi, the average wage (obtained by dividing the sum total of the earnings by the number of the workers), is as follows:—

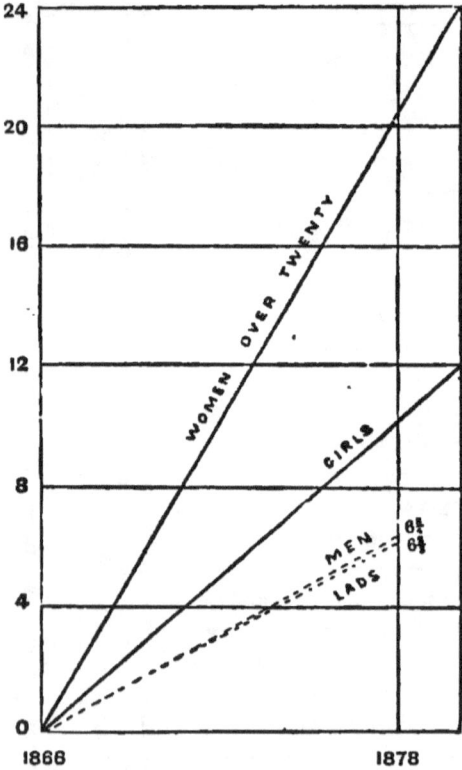

Diagram 36.—Increase of Wages: Women and Girls, Men and Lads (Levi).

	Men.		Women.	
Year.	Below 20, per week.	20 and upwards, per week.	Below 20, per week.	20 and upwards, per week.
1866	7s. 6d.	19s. 6d.	8s. 0d.	11s. 0d.
1878	8 0	21 9	9 0	13 8
Increase, per 100	6⅔	6¾	12	24

[1] *The Economist*, 25th March, 1876, p. 358.

In the same way, we observe a rise of wages in Alsace. We take the figures from a work by M. Charles Grad,[1] who quotes from an inquiry made by the Société Industrielle of Mulhouse.

WAGES IN THE SPINNING TRADE AT MULHOUSE, FROM 1835 TO 1880.

	1835.	1845.	1855.	1865.	1880.	Per cent.
	fr.	fr.	fr.	fr.	fr.	
Overlookers	2 91	3 50	4 37	4 58	6 25	115
Enginemen	1 88	2 30	3 17	2 88	3 50	86
Oilers and Greasers	1 50	1 80	1 58	2 50	3 10	107
Strap-makers	1 50	1 83	2 42	2 50	4 0	160
Scutch-hands (women)	0 96	1 04	1 06	1 33	1 70	77
Card-menders	1 33	1 42	2 83	2 22	2 70	103
Card-cleaners	...	...	1 79	1 96	2 35	?
Women Carders	0 87	1 0	1 01	1 31	1 60	81
Throstlers	1 50	1 50	1 59	1 78	2 40	60
Mule Spinners	1 75	2 60	3 75	4 12	...	143
Self-acting Mule Spinners	...	...	2 50	3 52	4 25	143
Piecers	0 65	0 75	1 25	1 42	2 30	256
Doffers (children)	...	...	0 92	1 08	1 60	?

(See Diagram 37, p. 166.)

In a silk-ribbon factory at Guebwiller, the increase during the interval 1848–80 was from 15 to 77 per cent.,[2] thus:—

	In 1848.	In 1880.
	fr. fr.	fr. fr.
Weavers (men)	2 0 to 3 30	2 10 to 4 25
„ (women)	... ...	2 0 „ 3 80
„ (children apprentices)	... ...	1 20 „ 2 25
Warpers (women)	1 50 „ 2 50	1 90 „ 3 0
Fluters (women)	0 50 „ 0 80	1 25 „ 2 55
Finishers-off (women)	0 40 „ 0 70	0 66 „ 1 60
Winders (women)	0 75 „ 1 50	1 50 „ 2 35
Folders	1 0 „ 1 25	1 70 „ 3 05
Dyers	1 50 „ 2 50	... ...
Overlookers	2 0 „ 4 50	... ...

(See Diagram 38, p. 167.)

In the same interval, wages have gone up 44 per cent. in the tanneries of Strasburg; they have risen 25 per cent. in fifty years

---

[1] *Economiste Français*, 16th Oct., 1880, p. 474; *Les Salaires dans l'Industrie Manufacturière*, by Charles Grad.
[2] Id. ubi sup.

166 THE VALUE OF MAN.

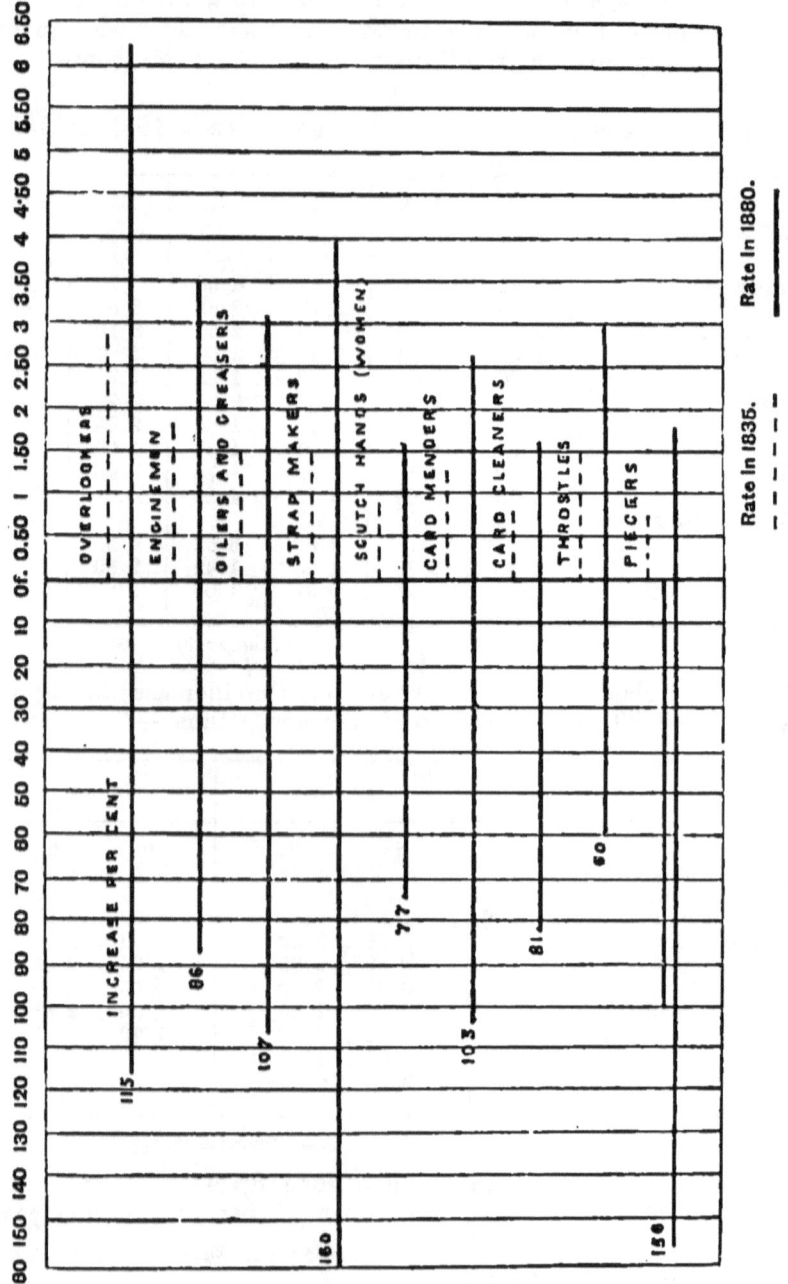

Diagram 37.—Wages at Mulhouse in 1835 and in 1880.

in the glass works of Wildenstein, and 36 per cent. since 1854 in the two great machine shops of Mulhouse and Grafenstaden. Among metal-workers, the price of a day's labour varied as follows between 1854 and 1878:—

	1854.	1865.	1878.	Per cent.
	fr.	fr.	fr.	
Smiths and Founders	4 23	4 60	5 18	20
Planers and Assistants	2 57	3 06	3 70	44
Turners and Drillers	3 28	4 28	4 60	40
Fitters and Moulders	3 30	2 51	4 30	30
Modellers and Joiners	2 44	2 86	4 10	68
Braziers	2 50	3 44	4 40	76
General average	2 80	3 08	3 80	36

(See Diagram 39, p. 168.)

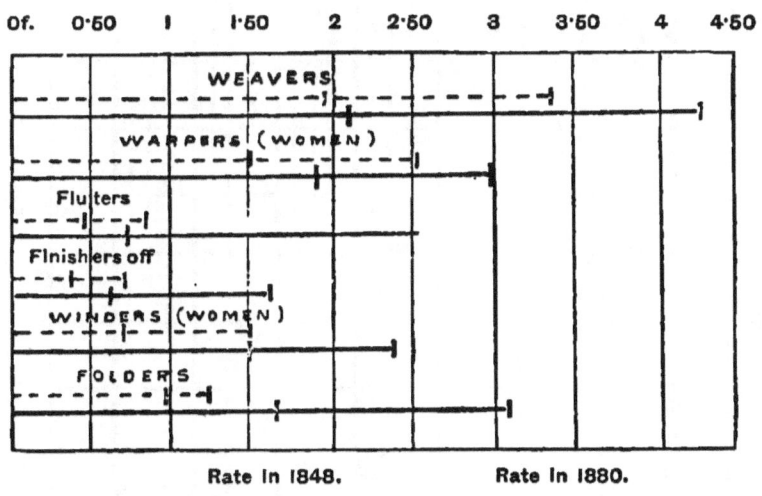

Diagram 38.—Wages of Workpeople at a Silk-ribbon Factory at Guebwiller in 1848 and 1880.

M. Charles Grad draws attention to the fact that in the textile, as in the metallurgic industries, it is the lower class of workmen whose wages have risen the most in the last half-century. The explanation is this, that the level of capacity of the working classes is higher than it was, and consequently, men have been more easily recruited for the more difficult and better paid work. This is one of the causes which have checked a further increase in the wages of this class of men. In the less difficult crafts, the demand for labour is steadily growing, and this labour is applied to better and better

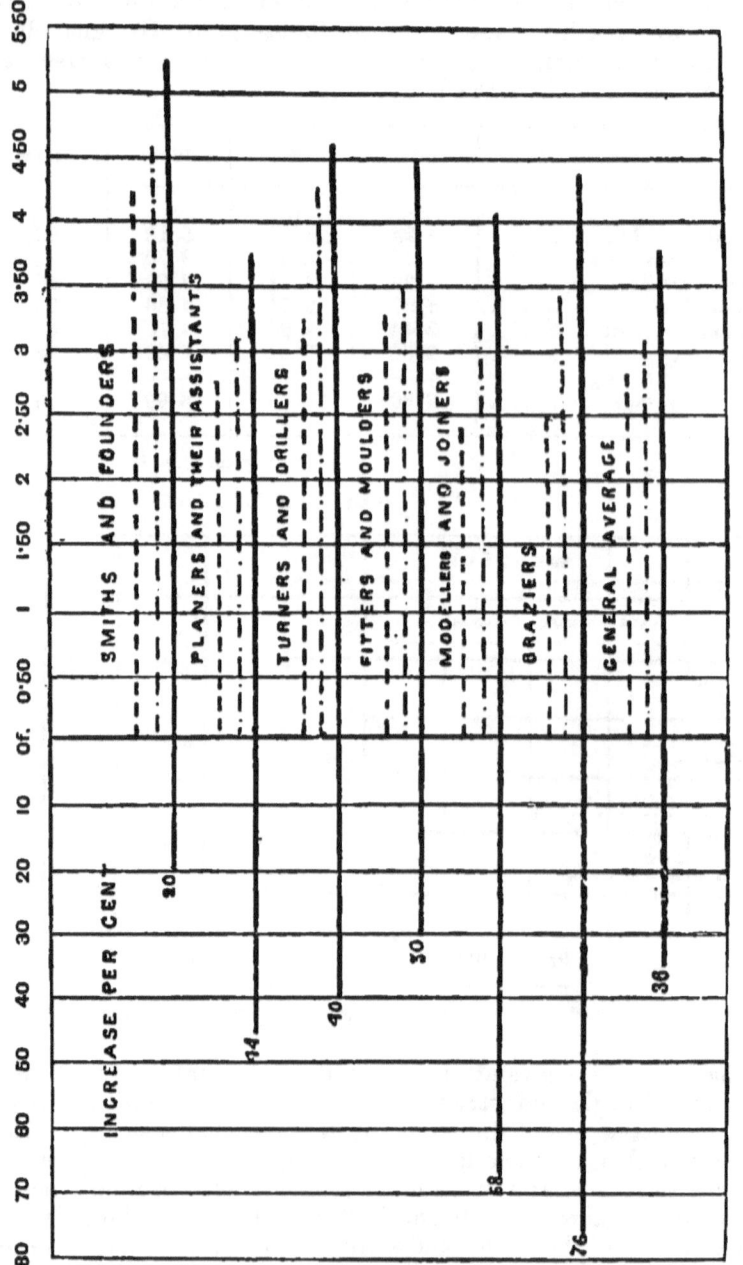

Diagram 39.—Wages of Workmen in Metals at Mulhouse and Grafenstaden in 1854, 1865, and 1878.

advantage, owing to the better implements employed. So that first the labourer's wages are raised, and secondly, he is put in a position to maintain this rise

The remarkable rise in the wages of women which we have observed in England is due to similar causes. Men have abandoned the trades in which they competed with women, because better channels have opened out for their activities. The demand for women's labour has become more and more considerable. The

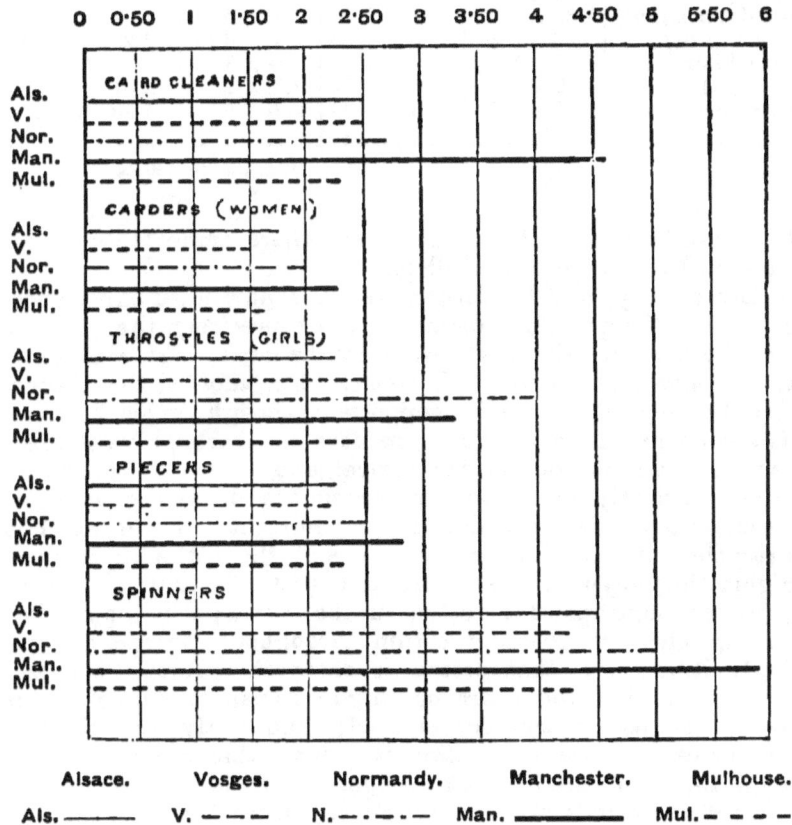

Diagram 40.—Wages in Manufacturing Industries, by Charles Grad (*Economiste Français*, 17 September, 1880, p. 353).

first luxury of a household which has obtained a competency is a servant. The increase in the demand for women's work is one of the most characteristic signs of the progress of public wealth.

On comparing the wages paid in the different cotton-spinning districts, we find the following variations :—

	Alsace.	Vosges.	Normandy.	Manchester.	Mulhouse.
	fr. fr.	fr. fr.	fr. fr.	fr.	fr.
Scutch hands (men)	2 0 to 3 0	2 0 to 3 25	2 0 to 2 25	2 80	1 70
,, (women)	1 50 ,, 1 75	1 75 ,, 2 0	1 80 ,, 2 0	...	...
Machine hands	2 30 ,, 3 75	3 25 ,, 3 75	3 50 ,, 4 0	...	...
Card-cleaners	2 0 ,, 2 50	2 25 ,, 2 50	1 50 ,, 2 76	4 60	2 35
,, (girls)	1 20 ,, 1 75	1 40 ,, 1 50	1 50 ,, 2 0	2 30	1 60
Combers (girls)	1 40 ,, 2 0	...	...	...	...
Drawing-frames (girls)	1 30 ,, 2 0	1 75 ,, 2 25	2 20 ,, 2 50	3 0	...
Throstlers (girls)	1 20 ,, 2 25	1 80 ,, 2 50	2 0 ,, 4 0	3 23	2 40
Wasters (children)	1 0 ,, 1 50	0 90 ,, 1 25	1 0 ,, 1 75	...	1 60
Piecers (men)	1 50 ,, 2 25	1 25 ,, 2 25	1 50 ,, 2 50	2 81	2 30
Spinners (men)	3 50 ,, 4 50	3 75 ,, 4 20	4 0 ,, 5 0	5 90	4 25

(See Diagram 40, p. 169.)

Wages are highest in the two towns where trade is the most prosperous, Manchester and Mulhouse.

Mr. Brassey says that his father, with his unrivalled experience, observed that the price of labour, or, more precisely, the quotient obtained by dividing the day's work by the day's wage, was much about the same everywhere. M. Siemens has adopted this theory, and Mr. Brassey, jun., likewise supports it, though in his book on *Foreign Work and English Wages,* he does not thoroughly establish it. At first sight it appears paradoxical, and I have not tested its accuracy sufficiently to be able to pronounce decisively upon it. The results above given certainly go to confirm it. I will take but one example. In Manchester the wages of the cotton operatives are higher than anywhere else; but Manchester is near Liverpool, the greatest emporium for cotton in the world; it is the market which regulates the prices of cotton throughout Europe, and accordingly it is there that cotton is cheapest. Tariffs between Liverpool and Manchester are not high; transport is quick; coal is cheap; the best machinery is used; and lastly, the English operative's capacity for production is greater than anybody else's. Although his wages are higher than those of any of his competitors, they do not necessarily tax production any more heavily than the much lower ones of his Norman rival.

The value of wages is not exactly measured by their amount in money. An equal sum will procure more food, better lodgings, and more comforts in one place than it will in another. To this must be added sundry institutions which are now appended to the majority of industrial establishments—workmens' dwellings, savings banks, retiring pensions, co-operative societies, and last, but not least, schools!

THE VALUE OF MAN.

By comparing the rates of wages in the three following countries, we shall find the laws we have laid down again confirmed:—

WEEKLY WAGES.

Trades.	Wages.	Price of Bread.	Price of Meat.
NEW YORK.	*Francs.*	*Francs per lb.*	*Francs per lb.*
Bricklayers	60 to 75	0·22½	Beef.
Masons	60 ,, 90		0·40 to 0·80
Carpenters and Joiners	45 ,, 60		Veal.
Painters	50 ,, 80		0·40 to 1·20
Plasterers	50 ,, 75		
Plumbers	60 ,, 90		Mutton.
Smiths	50 ,, 70		0·45 to 0·80
Cabinet-makers	40 ,, 60		
Strap and harness-makers	60 ,, 75		Pork.
Bakers	30 ,, 40		0·80 to 1·0
Butchers	40 ,, 60		
Tailors	50 ,, 90		
Shoe-makers	60 ,, 90		
ENGLAND.			
Bricklayers	40·60	0·20 to 0·25.	Beef.
Masons	40·80		0·50 to 0·70
Carpenters and Joiners	41·25		Mutton.
Painters	36·25		0·60 to 0·80
Plasterers	40·50		
Plumbers	38·75		Pork.
Smiths	40·60		0·50 to 0·60
Cabinet-makers	38·50		
Strap and harness-makers	34· 0		
Bakers	32·25		
Butchers	36·15		
Tailors	25 to 36·50		
Shoe-makers	36·75		
BELGIUM.			
Bricklayers	30· 0	0·20 to 0·25	Beef.
Masons	30· 0		0·80 to 1·0
Carpenters and Joiners	27· 0		Veal.
Painters	21·10		0·80 to 1·0
Plasterers	27· 0		
Plumbers	30· 0		Mutton.
Smiths	22· 0		0·80 to 1·0
Cabinet-makers	24· 0		
Strap and harness-makers	24· 0		Pork.
Bakers	24· 0		0·80 to 1·0
Butchers	...		
Tailors	...		
Shoemakers	...		

The following table shows that the fluctuations in the wages of iron-workers have formed but a very small item in the wide fluctuations which the price of iron has undergone within the last eleven years:—

	Average Price per Ton.	Wages of Puddlers.
	£ s. d.	s. d.
1868	6 11 3	8 0
1873	11 8 4	13 3
1874	10 18 11	11 6
1875	7 10 4	8 3
1877	6 17 1	8 3
1878	6 7 4	7 6
1879	5 18 7	7 0

(See Diagram 41, p. 173.)

In the same way, Diagram 42,—showing the elements which, at various times, have gone to make up the cost price of a ton of iron,—proves that variations in the rate of wages have, up to the present time, had but little influence on the price of commodities.

Wages are higher in England than in Belgium, and higher in the United States than in either; and why? Because in the United States the supply of labour is less, while their machinery is extremely perfect, their available fixed capital abundant, and, thanks to their system of credit, circulating capital circulates with a rapidity of which we are here only beginning to form an idea.

There is a subjective political economy easier to understand than the objective form. "The law of wages" is a phrase which is constantly appearing in pamphlets and at public meetings. The real "law of wages" is what I have just stated, but that is not what they mean.

Some people have a habit of crediting their opponents with ideas they never entertained, or of putting their ideas in an absolute form which they never gave them. Having once presented these ideas, they treat them as genuine, and deduce from them all sorts of consequences. The more startling and absurd these consequences are, the better they are satisfied. Their work might have been more useful if they had first verified their premisses; but then their theory would have vanished in the process, and they would have lost the benefit of it. Now, for men like Proudhon and Lassalle, truth is the second thing, and a brilliant and startling theory the first. They have found in Social Economy a last refuge for the scholastic method.

Lassalle says, "According to Ricardo, the average of wages is fixed by the absolute necessaries of life."

In the first place, Ricardo says no such thing, at least in no such absolute form. Here are his own words: "The natural price of

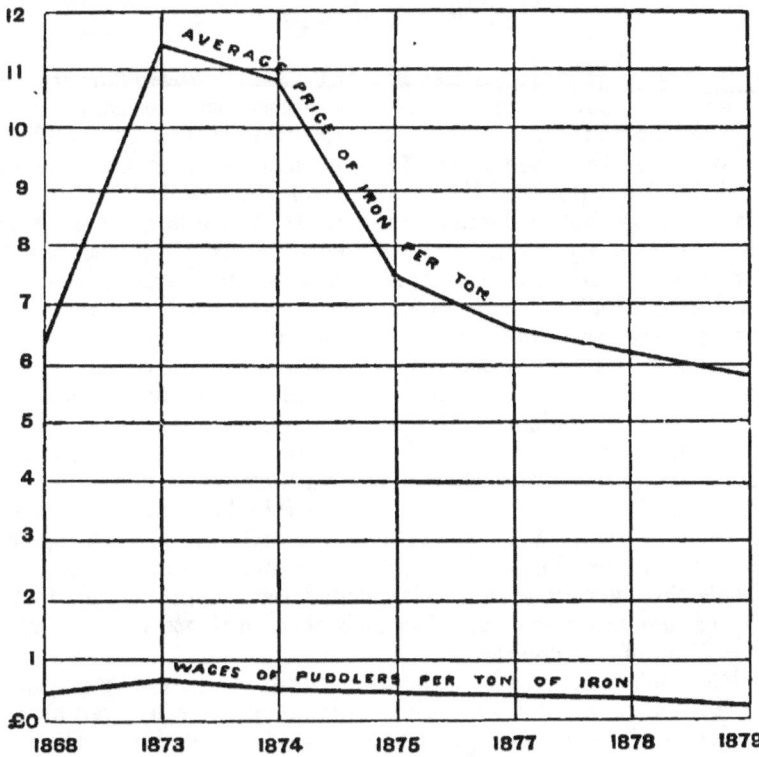

Diagram 41.—Fluctuations in the Price of Iron and in the Wages of Ironworkers.

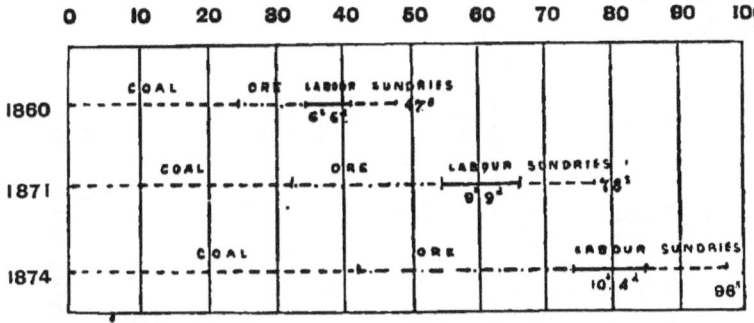

Diagram 42.—Cost Price of a Ton of Iron in England (the figures from Brassey's *Foreign Work and English Wages*, p. 316).

labour is that price which is necessary to enable the labourers, one with another, to subsist and to perpetuate their race, without either increase or diminution. . . . The natural price of labour, therefore, depends on the price of the food, necessaries, and conveniences required for the support of the labourer and his family."[1]

This is somewhat different from what Lassalle puts into his mouth; but, even so, Ricardo himself admits that his proposition is not accurate, for he adds:[2] "It is not to be understood that the natural price of labour, estimated even in food and necessaries, is absolutely fixed and constant. It varies at different times in the same country, and very materially differs in different countries. It essentially depends on the habits and customs of the people. An English labourer would consider his wages under their natural rate if they enabled him to purchase no other food than potatoes, and to live in no better habitation than a mud cabin."

This proposition of Ricardo is as false as the law of Malthus from which it is derived (though Malthus refuted it). In basing his theory of profits on the fall of wages, he commits a manifest error, for if this theory were true, profits would rise in proportion to the poverty of the labourers, and the richest manufacturers would be found in the poorest countries.

For Ricardo's theory to be true, three conditions must be granted:—that the fixed capital to which human effort is applied should always retain the same degree of power; that raw material and products should experience neither rise nor fall; and that exchange and credit should be subject always and everywhere to the same conditions.

The following table[3] proves that *the proportion of the price of food to the rate of wages is in inverse ratio to the industrial development of a country.*

Countries.	Average weekly Rate of Wages.	Price of the Week's Food.	Deduction for Food.
	s.	*s.*	Per cent.
United States	48	10	21
Great Britain	33	11	33
France	20	8	40
Belgium	22	10	45
Germany	18	9	50
Italy	13	8	64
Spain	15	10	67

[1] *Principles of Political Economy*, p. 85, 2nd edition.
[2] *Ibid.*, p. 90.
[3] *Progress of the World*, by Michael G. Mulhall, p. 56.

Yet we are daily seeing Ricardo's error repeating itself. M. Jacqmin, manager of the Chemin de Fer de l'Est, declares that the expense of a train depends solely on the rate of wages; and that if wages were doubled, the receipts remaining the same, the cost price of a train would likewise be doubled.

And has the price of coal, of iron, of machinery, of making and maintaining the permanent way, nothing to do with the cost of a train? Does the system of management adopted by a great company make no difference to the working expenses? Does it make no difference whether the train goes full or empty?

The price of labour, like that of all other commodities, obeys the law of demand and supply. If the demand for labour is greater than the supply, the price rises; if the supply exceeds the demand, it falls. If the supply becomes so great as to reduce the price to zero, the workman does not work, he begs.

The workmen, or rather those who profess to speak in their name, have inherited a prejudice shared by Adam Smith, Ricardo, and Sismondi.[1] They will not allow that any labour is productive which is not immediately embodied in some material form. Consequently they do not recognise as earnings the remuneration received by persons of whose work they perceive no direct and palpable product.

According to this doctrine, the physician does not work. Still, no one will deny that when he produces health, his labour is embodied in an appreciable object having a certain value; the healthy man's power of production is superior to that of the sick man, and he is, therefore, worth more. By the same reasoning, the judge and the advocate do no work; yet the judgment of the one, following on the pleading of the other, may have strictly material results; in civil cases it is converted into a sum of money given or received; in criminal cases, into the imprisonment or liberation of one or more persons.

Led by this prejudice, the working man pays little regard to administrative capacity. Yet its effects are material enough; the men who organise railway companies, construct and open new lines, and manage the traffic upon them, furnish distinct and undeniable products. These objectors would deny to administrative ability any claim to remuneration; and yet there is no other element of production of equal value with this, inventive ability excepted.

No one can admire the inventor more warmly than I do. In him we have a man who takes one of Nature's forces, hitherto unutilised by man, be it steam, sunlight, or electricity, and he enlists it in the service of humanity. By utilising this force, he substitutes for human effort the labour of a natural agent. There is no greater

---

[1] See Sismondi, *Political Economy, and the Economy of Government*, Book I.

or more useful work. What would the nineteenth century be without Watt, Fulton, Stephenson, or Morse? It will be said that if these men had never lived, others would have produced the same inventions; but this is bad reasoning. How long would it have been before others produced them? These men were the first comers; is the time they saved of no account? Inventive capacity, doubtless, will develop more and more with the growth of objective instruction, but it is not yet become so common as to have but an ordinary value. Indeed, it has the greatest value of all; and no inventor has ever been rewarded in anything like proportion to the wealth he has produced. Watt and Stephenson may have made thousands, but what are those thousands to the wealth which the steam-engine and the railway have conferred upon humanity?[1]

The greatest inventor is he who has the greatest appetite for utilities.

The principle of the company which centres around Mr. Edison is easily understood:—" Produce, invent, and we will give you a large share of the profits. We shall still be gainers, since without you we should not have these inventions at all." The very people who have such a horror of inventors, are always working at some problem which nothing but an invention can solve. Everybody has some time or other expressed a desire which could only be satisfied by an invention.

An invention is completed; so far, so good; but it has to be set working. Here comes in the need of administrative ability. Very complex elements enter into its composition—initiative, energy, perseverance, the instinct of order, the power of control, and the art of co-ordinating interests. These are qualities rarely united in one individual.

How many inventions have been long held back for want of the men fitted to put them into operation! What millions of money wasted for want of intelligence in employing them! At this moment, there is available capital in England, in France, in Belgium, in Holland, in Switzerland, in the United States—the whole world is there to fertilise—and yet to what miserable uses the money is often applied, all for want of administrative capacity in its possessors! And this incapacity is nowhere more marked than in the administration of national affairs. Look at the statesmen who have succeeded each other at the head of the nations for centuries past! By the harm they have done, and by the good they have not done, we may estimate the value of administrative capacity.

Administrative capacity must then receive remuneration, and large remuneration, in virtue of its rareness and of its production

---

[1] See *L'Inventeur*, by Yves Guyot, 1866.

of utilities. Capitalists are already ceasing to grudge it this remuneration, and they will grudge it less and less. The Utopists in vain strive to contest its legitimacy for the sake of their mollusc equality; it exists by the force of things.

And I say this not only of private enterprises, but also of public affairs. It is a most mistaken and a most uneconomical calculation, for a democracy to starve those who are charged with the management of the interests of the community. The consequence will be that practical men will seek profit and security by devoting their energies to their own affairs, and leave the greater risks and doubtful advantages of public life either to wealthy incapables, or to intriguers, or to charlatans, or to enthusiasts. Enthusiasts, indeed, are exceptional; powerful, remarkable, and useful as they may be, they are always a little quixotic; and to make such men the pillars of the State would be an imprudence if not a blunder. As to the others, they would be capable of bringing the country to ruin "with a light heart."

The physical labour of man tends to disappear, and is being advantageously replaced by the intellectual labour of man and the physical labour of the machine. Instead of acting, man directs action. It may be said that the share of intellectual labour in production is in proportion to the power of fixed capital.

When the labourer shows his horny palm, and says, "We are the workers, and we alone," he deceives himself. We may hope that his sons will not have these horny palms, the sad, though honourable, tokens of manual labour; but they will be none the less workers, exerting themselves to obtain a definite product.

Conclusion:—

Man is a form of fixed capital, subject to the law which defines the relative values of fixed and circulating capital.

The value of man is in proportion to the power of his implements. His value augments in proportion to the abundance of circulating capital and the power of fixed capital.

The relation of the price of food to the rate of wages is in inverse ratio to the industrial development of the country.

CHAPTER IV.

THE ORGANISATION OF HUMAN INDUSTRY.

WE have defined human labour[1] as the effort necessary for the appropriation of utilities.

We shall also show that the value of man is in proportion to the power of his tools and to the abundance of circulating capital.[2]

---

[1] See Book I., chap. iv., p. 56.   [2] See the foregoing chapter.

We have now two questions to examine. First, as to the present organisation of co-operation in productive labour; and secondly, as to the probable changes it may have to undergo.

There are some pretended reformers with an antiquated ideal who wish to revive the trade-guilds—reminiscences of the Roman guilds—which were formed in the Middle Ages and which lasted till the Revolution.[1] They have never reflected on the vices inherent in these guilds, which the perusal of the foregoing chapter will have enabled our readers to perceive at a glance.

We have seen that the most perfect form of association is that which best distinguishes between interests and individuals, and specifies most clearly the common interests which it brings together.

Now the guilds of arts and trades were modelled on the social organisation in the midst of which they grew up. Each guild formed a little feudal State, ruled by the masters, who aimed, and aimed successfully, at making themselves an hereditary caste, and enforcing on every one not of their own order a host of almost impossible conditions as the price of entering it. Each master became a petty baron, to whom the workman was no better than a serf.

Under the pretext of protection, the master exercised the most absolute despotism over the apprentice and the journeyman. The unfortunate who aspired to the freedom of his craft, had first to serve a long apprenticeship to one master. Nor was it every one who could become an apprentice. At Lyons certain conditions of birth were imposed. All professions were closed to the married man. The masters made the rules, and in every guild they squeezed the very last farthing of profit out of the young workman. The apprenticeship lasted four years for ropemakers, seven years for wire-drawers, seven for shoemakers, eight for shield-smiths, nine for belt-makers, ten for glass-cutters, and twelve for chaplet-makers. The apprentice had to pay besides on an average twenty silver sous a year. If he could not pay it in money, he had to make it up by an extended time of service. This was the minimum charge. The master might charge more if he liked, but not less. "More money and more service may he take if he be able."

Handed over powerless to his master, subject to all his requirements and all his caprices, the apprentice had no appeal. If, driven by want and ill-usage, he ran away, no one might offer him asylum. Like a serf, he could be treated as an article of commerce, and sold by one master to another. Unless he was the son of a master, his troubles did not end with his apprenticeship. He became an

---

[1] See *L'Inventeur*, by Yves Guyot.

assistant. The number of assistants a master could have was limited, like the number of apprentices. The assistant's time was his master's, from sunrise to sunset. He was engaged by the month or year; and however brutal the master might be, the journeyman could not break the engagement.

How was he to become a master? In some guilds, even marrying a master's daughter was not enough. In others, less close, he had to give a year to executing a sample of his work, which was to be approved by jurors chosen from among the masters. The masters, always anxious to restrict their number, naturally condemned his work, unless the poor workman softened their severity by means of "gifts and feasts." In addition to these voluntary expenses, there were official and compulsory expenses. For a master clothier in the seventeenth century, the cost of a banquet was 3,240 livres. The freedom of the guild itself was bought; for a locksmith, joiner, or wheelwright it came to 1,200 or 1,500 livres, and in some other guilds to 4,000 or 5,000 livres. The journeyman whose resources were not equal to these charges was doomed to perpetual servitude without hope of change. If he attempted to set up on his own account, he was pursued and hunted down like a wild beast.

Turgot, in the preamble to the edict of 1776, abolishing guilds, freedoms, and wardenships, says,—"In almost all the towns the exercise of the different arts is centred in the hands of a small number of masters, who form a community by themselves, and who alone, to the exclusion of the other citizens, may make or sell the articles of their particular trade, so that those of our subjects who through choice or necessity adopt a trade or craft cannot carry it on without having first obtained the freedom thereof, which freedom can only be obtained by undergoing a trial as tedious and injurious as it is unnecessary, and by paying numerous dues and exactions, whereby a portion of the funds needed by them for entering upon their business, or even for mere subsistence, is spent in absolute waste. Those who cannot sustain these losses are reduced to a precarious existence under the control of the masters, and thus languish in poverty," and so on.

Turgot declares that "the right to labour is common property, the first and most indefeasible of all rights."

This edict was of a character too revolutionary to be acceptable in a society founded essentially on privilege. The guilds were re-established the same year; but they were finally suppressed in 1789, and the more or less interested and ignorant attempts since made to restore them have been in vain. Their restoration would be too retrograde a step. They are contrary to the law of the development of association, for they confuse individuals with interests, persons with things. They absorb human individuality. They are a species of conventual establishment, less and less likely to find a place in our modern civilisation. The stronger the individuality, the more vehemently it must protest against any such absorption.

CHAPTER V.

THE PRIVILEGES OF MASTERS.

BUT the Revolution knew not how to distinguish the Corporation and the Association. In destroying one abuse, it created another. Hence the law of 14-17 June, 1791. Chapelier, in his report, says innocently, "All citizens must be allowed to assemble; but citizens of certain professions must not be allowed to assemble in support of their alleged common interests." The law declared:—

"Art. 1. The abolition of every kind of corporation of citizens of the same trade being one of the fundamental principles of the French Constitution, their virtual re-establishment, under any form or pretext whatsoever, is strictly forbidden.

"Art. 2. Citizens of the same trade or profession, contractors, shop-keepers, the workmen and journeymen of any craft whatsoever, shall not, when met together, nominate presidents, secretaries, or syndics, keep registers, pass decrees or resolutions, or make rules in support of their alleged common interests."

This was but a doctrinal error, springing from a confusion of ideas; but later on, in a time of reaction, it became the avowed object of the Legislature, not to guarantee the individual liberty of all, but to confirm the masters in their privileges.

The law of Germinal, year XI of the Republic, contained this formidable article:—

"Art. 7. Every coalition on the part of workmen for the purpose of discontinuing work in certain shops, for raising the price of labour, . . . six months' imprisonment."

The advantage which this article conferred on the masters appeared so scandalous, that the compilers of the Penal Code felt it necessary to soften it, at least in form, by substituting the following expressions:—

"Art. 414. Every coalition among those who have work done. . . .

"Art. 415. Every coalition on the part of workmen to occasion a stoppage of work."

As a matter of fact, Art. 414 could have none but an ironical application, while Art. 415, notwithstanding the addition of the verb 'occasion' (*faire*), was applied with a roughness which made this refinement of expression wholly superfluous. Moreover, in spite of the law of 1864, it is still enforced. The spirit which inspired these laws survives, not only in our magistracy, but in governmental and official circles.

The same spirit of privilege is stamped on other regulations. By Art. 1781 of the *Code Napoléon*, which was not repealed until 1868, the master's evidence, in case of disputes with his workmen, is to be received on his bare word. By the decree of the 17th Dec. 1803, the workman's service-book (*livret*) was assimilated to the passport, and its retention by the master was made compulsory; the master might note in it all the advances made by him to the workman, and return it only when they had been repaid him in the form of work done; at the same time, he could dismiss the workman at pleasure, and any future employer would be responsible for debts still due to him, deducting one-fifth from the workman's daily wages for the payment of them. On every change of situation, the workman must have his *livret* inspected by the police commissioner; and journeymen butchers and bakers had to deposit their books in his hands. Amongst other vexatious regulations, the registry-offices were in most cases managed by the prefecture of police, and invested with a monopoly. The old guilds had been practically restored for the benefit of the prefecture of police.[1] These rules were indeed a little relaxed under the Government of July; the law of 1854, while it retained the *livret* system, forbade all comment, favourable or unfavourable. The date of entry was put down, and the book returned to its owner. Indeed, in spite of the law, many workmen never used it at all.

Some very sincere and earnest democrats declaim against the demand for privileges on the part of the workmen as unreasonable, and contrary to the principle of equality. But who taught the workman to misunderstand the principle of equality and claim caste privileges for his own class? First, the nobility and gentry of the past; next, the *bourgeoisie* of the present.

M. Persil, Procureur-général of the Court of Paris in 1833, confessed with much simplicity the inequality under which the workmen laboured. "It would be risking everything if we were to let the workmen realise their own position as compared with the classes above them, and feel that they are men like the others, and entitled to the same enjoyments."

Observe, that M. Persil does not ask that the existing order of things should be changed, but only that the workmen should not be permitted to realise it.

Unfortunately, the facts were so patent, that working-men found out for themselves that they had not exactly the same rights and advantages as their masters; it was easy for them to compare their

---

[1] See Levasseur. *Histoire des Classes Ouvrières depuis* 1789.

own poverty with their masters' luxury; they knew well enough that it was they, and not the masters, who were subjected to the *livret* system; they were quite aware of the provisions of Art. 1781 of the *Code Napoléon*, and that laws which already pressed hard upon them were aggravated by the police regulations; they knew that the masters alone could combine, and that in the contests between the two classes the judges belonged by ties of birth, marriage, and relationship to the masters' class. The explosion of 1848 revealed that they knew all this, and more besides, in spite of the silence in which M. Persil would fain have buried these questions.

Then the Persils were much surprised. "What!" said they, "the workmen not content? We never let them know that they had any right to be discontented! They are clearly in the wrong! And now they want the tables turned. Hitherto all the privileges have been ours; now they want all the privileges to be theirs. What madness!"

Their madness was brought home to them by the cannon-ball, by the state of siege, by wholesale transportation, and other convincing arguments. But they were not satisfied; and there was some reason for their dissatisfaction.

CHAPTER VI.

THE RIGHT TO LABOUR, AND THE ORGANISATION OF LABOUR.

THE *bourgeois* electorate had what Buckle calls the Protective spirit, which might more correctly be called the mendicant spirit. For the beggar is a person who claims a favour, an alms, a privilege, now by entreaties, now by threats.

It was this spirit which inspired the Socialist doctrines of 1848, doctrines which appear in all the theories and discussions of that time. The refutations of their opponents fell harmless, because they could always be shown to be contradictory. What were the Protectionists to answer, when M. Louis Blanc, attacking free competition at home, said to them, "But, gentlemen, if competition is a good thing, why do you ask to be protected against it? My system is not my own; I have adopted yours."

The Protectionists say, "Cotton, iron, coal, are necessary industries; the making of musical instruments constitutes part of the national property. Insure us against foreign competitors, who make all these things better and cheaper than we."

For the last sixty years they have gone on repeating these lamentations, and they repeat them now. M. Louis Blanc interposed, "You are secured from competition, and you keep the profit to yourselves. We, in our turn, are going to secure the profits of the monopoly of production to the workman. You can invoke no economic principle against this proposal, your principles are the same as ours; you can only protest in the name of your own interests, and confess that you want to keep your monopoly to yourselves. Well, we want to take it from you, and give it to the workman."

So put, the argument is unanswerable.

Unluckily, M. Louis Blanc was too ignorant of even the simplest notions of economy to force his adversaries on the horns of this dilemma.

He entangled himself in contradictions as complicated as a skein of thread that a kitten has been playing with, and then declared that if he aimed at securing the monopoly of production to the State, he did so in the name of liberty! He spins off such aphorisms as this: "As long as competition exists, liberty is impossible," and then proceeds to "organise labour" on paper. "The Government should be regarded as the supreme regulator of production, and invested with large powers for the accomplishment of its duties. It must avail itself of competition for the purpose of destroying competition. It must raise a loan to be applied to the creation of *ateliers sociaux* (co-operative workshops) in the more important branches of national industry."

It never occurs to M. Louis Blanc to doubt that this loan will be taken up by the capitalists it is designed to ruin; he agrees, however, to pay them interest for their money, but not to allow them the smallest participation in the profits.

The State will, of course, possess all the virtues; it will never speculate; it will prefer to buy dear, when, by choosing its time, it might buy cheap. The price of its products will be fixed by clockwork, irrespective of demand and supply. It is to regulate the industries, not to take them over. Private manufacturers may exist alongside those of the State; but M. Louis Blanc himself adds, "In every important industry, the co-operative workshops must compete with private enterprise, and the struggle will not last long."[1]

Whatever advantage the workman in M. Louis Blanc's national workshops may enjoy as a producer, he loses as a consumer. Like the simplest disciple of Pouyer Quertier, M. Louis Blanc is averse to cheapness. The co-operative workshops must, to use a favourite expression of the Protectionists, take care to maintain prices at "a remunerative rate."

The following is M. Louis Blanc's formula for measuring work and wages. "Duty in proportion to strength and capacity, rights in proportion to needs;" but he does not tell us by whom or by what standard these needs and capacities are to be measured.

[1] *Organisation du Travail*, p. 88, 4th edition.

The basis of the co-operative workshop is to be "the substitution of the point of honour for the motive of self-interest, and consequently, the immediate or proximate equalising of wages, till society attains the ideal towards which it should strive—to produce according to its strength, and to consume according to its needs."

Against that frightful egoism which might find its way into the national workshops, as everywhere else, M. Louis Blanc has an infallible remedy. "Let a post be set up in every workshop with this inscription: 'Where brothers associate for work, every idler is a thief.'"

Although it was the aim of M. Louis Blanc's system to equalise wages, the application of that system began with a monstrous inequality. He admitted that the inclusion of the entire production of France within his organisation was not the work of a day; he therefore received into his co-operative workshops only certain privileged persons. If private industry attempted to compete, it must lower its wages. He could not increase the comfort of the few without diminishing that of the many.

M. Louis Blanc is the sworn foe of capital, yet he says, "The secret of doing better than your neighbour is to have more capital than he." Indeed? Does not history show that the great owners of capital have often made a destructive use of it, and that the rich man often fails where the skilful and persevering man succeeds?

M. Louis Blanc's economic theories are irrefragable because they are intangible. When you come to look at them, you find they have nothing in them. You are astounded that they should ever have deluded even the most ignorant. Yet his recent speeches give us reason to believe that he held to these theories to the last. We cannot but regret that, with his high position in politics, and the consideration in which he was held, he never introduced a bill into the Chamber of Deputies for organising one or more co-operative workshops. The fabrication of tobacco and matches, for instance, might have been handed over to them by way of a beginning.

"*La foi qui n'agit point, est-ce une foi sincère?*"[1]

Alas! the *Organisation du Travail* will remain an eloquent witness to the economic aberrations which agitated France from 1840 to 1850, the traces of which we see even now from time to time, not only at workmen's meetings, but in the Chambers themselves.

In 1848, the workmen demanded the right to labour (*droit au travail*). This expression has acquired, in the imagination of many good *bourgeois*, an almost Satanic character. And yet, where did the workman get it, if not from the electoral classes of the Restoration

[1] Racine.

and of the Government of July, who have never ceased to ask for and to uphold prohibitive tariffs in the name of national labour? In the disgraceful discussions which have taken place within the last few years in the Chamber of Deputies and the Senate upon the Customs tariffs, what did the representatives of the cotton and metal industries urge and insist upon, if not the right of labour?

In the original draft of the Constitution of 1848, Article 7 was framed thus:—

Art. 7.—"The right of labour is the right which every man has to live by his labour. It is the duty of Society, through the channels of production and other means at its command, hereafter to be organised, to provide work for such able-bodied men as cannot find it for themselves."

This Article was modified as follows:—"It is the duty of society by fraternal assistance to protect the lives of necessitous citizens, either by finding them work as far as possible, or by providing for those who are incapacitated for work and who have no families to support them."

The wording of these two forms shows the theologico-metaphysical character which, at that time, distinguished such discussions. Society was regarded as an entity having means and powers of its own, derived from nobody knows where. People could not see that it was nothing but the whole body of citizens. One must read the speeches made at the time, in order to form a conception of the haziness which enveloped the whole subject. Men of political intellect quite perceived the impossibility of arriving at any practical result. M. Ledru-Rollin, who maintained the necessity of including in the Constitution an acknowledgment of the right of labour, twice made the remark, at which we smile to-day, but which seems then to have surprised no one: "When you have admitted the right of labour, you are not obliged to have it in operation the very next day." The plain meaning of the right of labour is this: "Find me work, and give me wages enough to keep me and my family." "Wages enough!" But what are "wages enough?" Where do insufficient wages begin? Will you be content with potatoes, like the Irishman? And what work? Will you, who are a goldsmith, be content with unskilled labour? Certainly not. Then society must turn goldsmith in order to employ you, and go on producing always and all the same, regardless of the law of demand and supply.

But, to go on producing, society must have capital, and where is it to come from? A loan, says M. Louis Blanc. That is to say, so much capital is to be withdrawn from circulation; and if this capital is not used to as good purpose as it otherwise would have been, it is a dead loss to society. This involves a reduced power of purchasing labour. In order to create work, society will have helped to diminish the demand for it!

I have just touched on these economic aberrations by the way. Like their originator, they have gone the way of all flesh, and the offshoots they have left have little of the vigour of the parent stem.

Mr. Holyoake sums up in a single sentence the whole history of the Socialist doctrines of 1848 : "The Socialist State promises you a right, and, when you ask for it, gives you a bullet."

Napoleon III., in his prison at Ham, had amused himself with a Platonic Socialism ; when it came to putting it in practice, he simply played into the hands of intriguers and jobbers. Of the measures in favour of the workmen he accepted only two—in 1864, the law on combinations, and in 1868 the repeal of Article 1781. But he was a relentless persecutor of the workman—witness the bloody episodes of the strikes of Aubin and the Ricamarie ; and he demoralised them by sending into their midst police-spies, commissioned to intoxicate them with false notions in order to frighten the *bourgeoisie* with the apparition of the spectre of the Revolution.[1]

CHAPTER VII.

EXCEPTIONAL CONDITIONS OF LABOUR.

WE often hear Socialist speakers and writers declaim against the law of demand and supply. They might as well declaim against the rotation of the earth.

And yet there is some truth in these declamations, though they cannot upset the law of demand and supply. The workman may fairly complain that it is always being twisted to his disadvantage. Thus, in a certain arrondissement in Paris, one person in every seven or eight is in receipt of public relief. A man who ekes out his wages with the public alms can afford to work at a lower price than one who has only his own resources to reckon on. This is what the English poor-rate has come to. Invented in the fourteenth century, and systematised in the sixteenth, it has made pauperism a profession, maintained at the cost of those who labour. In attempting to succour the distressed, the State has created distress by depreciating the price of labour.

In the case of women, the operation of the law of demand and supply is checked by prostitution. Certain workwomen look for their living, not only to the day's work, but to the night's debauch ; the master naturally makes his calculations accordingly, and says to himself, "I know that my workwomen cannot live on the wages

---

[1] We have lately seen similar commotions produced by the same means and for the same ends. The chief editor of Mdlle. Louise Michel's journal, *La Révolution Sociale*, was a secret agent of the Prefecture of Police.

I give them without other means. I can get them at the price, and I take them." I wish this economic argument could sink into the minds of all young women; it would go further with them than all those arguments from religion which, so far, have only resulted in the state of things we see around us.

We have soldiers who work in the towns, and policemen off duty, who are shoemakers, tailors, and watchmakers. In charitable institutions, like Bicêtre, the pensioners carry on small trades; convict labour in France is let out to contractors.[1] The convents, under the plea of caring for the orphan, keep a number of young girls at forced labour up to one-and-twenty, bringing them up economically on the Word of God. Exempt from licences, and subsidised by gifts and legacies, they are able to defy the law of demand and supply. The Protestants—from purely philanthropic motives, I admit—have opened workrooms for girls, but they compete with free labour. Deaf mutes have been humanely taught to print; but they print for certain houses in Paris, and thus cheapen free labour.

The Protectionists all cry out that native labour will be ruined, if products similar to its own are imported freely into France. They have sent working-class delegates before the Customs Commission. Strange to say, these delegates never pointed out that, if the protection of native industry demanded by the cotton spinners, by the coal and mining companies, and so forth, is to be effectual, it ought to be supplemented by protection against the imported labour of Belgians, Germans, Piedmontese, etc. This is a necessary consequence of the protective system. If you protect products, without protecting the workman who produces them, you give protection to capital only, since you do not hinder the importation of foreign labour. The American workman is as logical in demanding the expulsion of the Chinese as the English workman would be illogical if he demanded similar protection, and as the French workman is illogical when he demands protective duties on cotton yarn and submits to the competition of Belgian workmen. Had this argument ever been advanced in the Chamber of Deputies, it would have been interesting to hear the answer given by the champions of "native labour."

These traditions of the mendicant spirit have not yet completely disappeared; and they have been exhibited in England, the country of all others where they have the least foundation.

But for every prejudice with which the workman has been reproached we can find a *bourgeois* origin.

In the year XI. of the Republic, Regnault de Saint Jean d'Angély proposed to fix a minimum number of working hours; and on the

---

[1] In England it is confined to naval and military works.

26th September, 1806, a police regulation appeared fixing the hours of work and the meal times of the building trade in Paris. The workmen now wish to fix a maximum—turn and turn about. The English workmen's agitation, first for nine and then for eight hours a day, is well remembered. The hours of work for women and children are settled by law.

Man certainly is no mere machine, intended to turn out such and such a product incessantly and automatically until it is itself worn out. Nothing can be more just than Macaulay's observations on the usefulness of the English Sunday:—

"That day is not lost. While industry is suspended, while the plough lies in the furrow, while the Exchange is silent, while no smoke ascends from the factory, a process is going on quite as important to the wealth of nations, quite as important as any process which is performed on more busy days. Then, the machine of machines, the machine compared with which all the contrivances of the Watts and the Arkwrights are worthless, is repairing and winding up, so that he returns to his labours on the Monday with clearer intellect, with livelier spirits, with renewed corporal vigour. Never will I believe that what makes a population stronger, and healthier, and wiser, and better, can ultimately make it poorer."[1]

Lassalle's axiom, "Production is in inverse ratio to labour," leads to a slightly absurd conclusion; but it is none the less true that too continuous labour exhausts, and that the intensity of the effort is in inverse ratio to its duration. It is a question of mechanics. A week consists of 168 hours. Ten hours' work a day for 6 days leaves 108 hours. Allow 9 hours a day for eating, sleeping, and going to and from work, and you have 45 hours left for family intercourse, friendly gatherings, reading, study, and personal concerns. Is that too much? I think not.

But that is not the question. The question is, whether the law is to determine the hours of labour. A law of the 14th September, 1848, reduced them to twelve hours in mills and factories. Subsequent decrees have modified it by a host of exceptions. Workshops employing fewer than ten hands were exempted from its operation at a time when such workshops formed nine-tenths of the whole number. This regulation has practically fallen into disuse. In 1880 a bill was brought into the Chamber of Deputies for reducing the hours of labour to ten, not only in factories but also in workshops. The Working Men's Congress of Havre gave the measure its energetic support. Nevertheless, if this law ever came to be applied, it would very soon raise a clamour of protests. What would become of the small manufacturers of Paris, who now and again break into such furious activity? Are they to do a fixed

---

[1] Speech on the Factory Acts.

amount of work all the year round, the same in the dead season as in the busy season? And what about this perpetual interference of the police in the workshops? Between public health and humanity, we are getting back to the regulations of Colbert.

I quoted just now a passage from Macaulay relating to the Sunday's rest; was there ever a more unpopular law in France than that of 1814, which enforced it? It has never really been observed.

In 1859 a London Workmen's Association began the nine hours' movement. In 1861 the employers, to put a stop to it, introduced payment by the hour instead of by the day. At the present time the hours of labour are, in fact, only $56\frac{1}{2}$ per week, and yet certain trades unions demand the interference of the law. Not so; let the labourers by all means be free to combine to fix their wages and conditions of labour; nothing can be more reasonable. But if the State is to interfere with the hours of labour, there is no reason why it should not interfere with the rate of wages. It is but two sides of the same question.

To be really advantageous to the workman, the measure must be framed thus: "Work shall be reduced to nine hours a day; wages shall not be reduced."

"But you admit that the law should protect children?" They are not able to protect themselves. They may be shamefully overworked by their parents and by masters, who abhor negro slavery, but do not extend their philanthropy to white children. English legislation with regard to the labour of children, of young people of both sexes between fourteen and sixteen years of age, and of women, has been codified in the Factory and Workshop Act, 1878. With the labour of men above eighteen the law does not interfere. The first five days of the week give ten or ten and a half hours' work a day, Saturday only six and a half. But the English legislature has clearly seen how difficult of application such regulations are, and has accordingly not imposed uniform rules in all cases; in some industries, the hours can be extended to fourteen for forty-eight days in the year, and in others for double that time. Protective measures of this kind are often carried to great lengths. In France, the application of the law relating to children's labour bristles with difficulties. In Paris, the half-time schools have not been attended with anything like the success expected from them, and yet there is probably not another city in the world where the treatment of apprentices is so paternal.

In Germany, the number of children employed in manufacturies has steadily decreased; and from many industries they have been entirely excluded. It may be questioned whether such exclusion is always an advantage, either to industry or to the children themselves.[1]

See *Economiste Français*, Nov. 15, 1879.

One of the questions mooted at the first public meetings held after the passing of the law of 1868, was that of the employment of women. The men demanded its prohibition by law. In subsequent working-men's congresses, they have taken care not to go quite so far. The women who took part in these meetings, far from demanding such favours, wished to have a greater number of callings thrown open to them. At the same time, in that restrictive spirit which we have such difficulty in getting rid of, they wished night-work for women prohibited. They did not see that this must inevitably exclude them from certain occupations. If night-work is forbidden in the factories, why not in the markets; and why should not the market women be obliged to bring their vegetables in the morning? It would be only putting people's lunch a little later. Men must replace women in folding the newspapers. A strange way of opening up fresh avenues for women's labour!

This restrictive tendency may lead us rather a long way. The Commune issued a decree forbidding bakers to work at night. Rochefort parodied it with "Lamp-lighters may only work by day." If we try to regulate the conditions of labour by law, we soon reach the *reductio ad absurdum*.

Liberty of contract between the employer and the employed, and the independence of the contracting parties: this is all that should be guaranteed by the law.

In past times the law intervened in favour of the employer, giving him the power to impose his will and his wages, acknowledging a value in his affirmation which it refused to those of the workmen, and giving a sanction to his combinations; and in thus taking sides it was wrong. If it were now to side with the workman, granting him monopolies, and creating a minimum limit of wages and a maximum limit of work, it would be wrong again. It would fulfil the well-known description of a military movement, "the same thing over again, only just the opposite." It would be creating a privilege as before; it would be imposing a forced contract, instead of allowing a free one.

Some legislative modifications are required from a legal point of view. With regard to accidents, for instance, Article 1382 of the *Code Civil* lays down that, "Any act whatsoever of one person by which another is injured, obliges the person who has caused the injury to make it good."

"Art. 1383. Every one is responsible for the injury he has caused, not only by his act, but also by his negligence or imprudence."

A workman is killed by a fall from the scaffold, or crushed by a heavy piece of masonry; as the law stands, he has no claim to compensation, unless he can prove that the accident happened through the master's fault.

In some trades, such as carpentering, engineering, mining, the day's work is a struggle in which the workman daily risks his life; in others, such as those which employ injurious chemicals, there is not even a struggle; the workman is condemned to certain death within a limited time. The sanitary regulations of the Hygienic Councils have been of no use at all. As to the masters, they are not only excessively careless, but sometimes show the most incomprehensible obstinacy. It was not until after several strikes that the workmen in foundries succeeded in compelling the masters to substitute the use of fecula for that of coal dust.

When a miner is killed by fire-damp, of course the fire-damp is to blame. If the accident had been on a large scale, public opinion would have been roused, and a subscription raised. But the miner was killed just the same; and nobody takes any notice. There is some advantage in being killed in company. *Væ soli!*

This demonstration is not a solution. Most companies have established funds for pensions and temporary assistance. But in any case, they take care that they themselves are not responsible. An engineman passes his life among machinery; he has to oil it whilst in motion; one day, in a moment of forgetfulness, he is caught by it, and either killed or frightfully mutilated. So much the worse for him. All his own fault. He should have taken better care. If the master is generous, he may do something for him or his family; if not, they are cast on the streets, and reduced to beggary.

Clearly, this state of things is not fair. If a soldier is wounded in battle, no one asks whether he has been imprudent; he gets his pension. It ought to be the same on the field of industry. The workman who is killed or wounded at his work must be regarded as a victim to professional duty.

A bill for remedying this injustice was brought into the Chamber of Deputies by M. Martin Nadaud in 1880; and a somewhat similar bill is under the consideration of the English Parliament. Both of these we heartily approve.

Contractors and all who employ workmen in dangerous trades will insure themselves against possible accidents, and we shall be spared the melancholy spectacle of maimed and crippled creatures who have no resource but public charity. Charity is very much a matter of chance; and for these chances we ought to substitute certainties.

So also in the two or three classes of unwholesome trades, the masters should be held answerable for the sickness and mortality among their men.

CHAPTER VIII.

THE LABOUR MARKET.

We now proceed to the question of the relations between labour and capital, endeavouring to divest it of all those prejudices on both sides which tend to obscure it;—with the certainty of thereby offending both parties.

It is useless, not to say disingenuous, to try to persuade master and workman that their interests are identical. It is the employer's interest to buy as cheap as possible. It is the workman's interest to sell as dear as possible. That is the plain truth.

Is there no agreement, then, between these opposing interests? There must necessarily be some sort of agreement, as in any other case of exchange. But the conditions of exchange may be favourable to one of the parties and unfavourable to the other, or they may be disastrous to both. We have therefore to examine whether the present organisation of the labour market is a rational application of the laws of economic science.

Some employers are shocked at the idea of regarding labour as a commodity. "What," they say, "are our workpeople no longer to be subject to us? Why, they are our children, our family!" Some fathers, however, do not treat their children particularly well; and, at any rate, men do not want to be treated like children.

The workmen, for their part, also exclaim against the idea. "It is a desperate theory for us," they say. "Labour is not like a commodity, and wages are not like a contract, for the workman is not a free seller. The capitalist is always free to employ labour, and the workman is always forced to sell it. The value of labour is completely destroyed unless it is sold on the instant. Unlike real commodities, labour is a form of capital which is not susceptible of accumulation, nor even of saving." It remains to be proved, however, that all real commodities are capable of accumulation and saving. Nobody will dispute that strawberries and fresh eggs are commodities. Can they be saved or accumulated?

The value of labour is utterly destroyed, unless it is sold at once; it is just the same with the value of all motive power.

It is assumed that the capitalist is always free to employ labour, and the labourer always forced to sell it. True, the capitalist is free not to employ labour, but on condition of not employing his capital. The owners of a coal-mine are not bound to employ labourers; but in a year's time their mine will be flooded, and the galleries sunk in; their capital will make no return, and if they have engagements which they cannot meet, they will become bankrupt. Still, it is true they can afford to wait some time, whilst the workman must feed himself and his family every day. In this respect the dealer in labour is at a disadvantage in comparison with the dealer in capital. But, in any other transaction, is not the need of one of the contracting parties always more urgent than that of the other? If the seller's need is the more urgent, the price falls; if the buyer's is the more urgent, the price rises. Now, for a long time past, the wages of labour have steadily gone up. It is clear, therefore, that the buyer's need has been the more urgent.

It is in England that the most practical, persevering, comprehensive, and successful efforts have been made for the regulation of the labour market. It is therefore to England that we shall first turn our attention.

At their first appearance, the Trades Unions were looked on as mysterious, violent, and bloody conspiracies. It was a war between labour and capital. Capital had all sorts of privileges secured to it by law. Labour was not in a position to dispute its terms. The law of demand and supply was infringed, as it is infringed wherever the monopolist can impose his own terms on the other contracting party. In Edward the Sixth's time, a workman convicted of taking part in a conspiracy for raising wages, had his ears cropped. Such treatment called for reprisals. In 1813, the Luddites declared war against machinery. By way of teaching them to amend their lives, nine-and-twenty of them were hanged in York alone. Their associates continued for some years to ravage the country about Nottingham. Symptoms of the same kind appeared all over England. The workmen knew well enough that the laws oppressed them. They did not clearly see the cause of their sufferings, nor the way to remedy them.

It is one of the great difficulties of social diseases, that the patient has to make his own diagnosis and his own prescription. The task is difficult, and the doctor is generally wrong. He poisons the wound in trying to cure it. In England, perhaps neither masters nor men knew exactly what wanted doing; and the workmen blamed the new machinery, when they ought to have been claiming for labour the right to make its own terms with capital. As it was necessary to concede something, and impossible to allow the destruction of machinery, the workmen were gradually allowed freedom of combination. The thing was done reluctantly and badly. In 1824, the restrictive labour laws were abolished, but they were re-enacted the next year, and never definitely repealed until 1839. There still remained amongst the litter of old English laws provisions against associations for influencing the course of labour. Trades Unions, local and general, were founded nevertheless. They had the double character of societies for mutual assistance and for mutual defence. Little was known of them until after the inquiry of 1868, consequent on the crimes committed in Manchester and Sheffield in 1866. When a Sheffield saw-grinder named Broadhead boasted before the commission of having been the instigator of murder and incendiarism, there was a general scare. The *Times*, in a moment of panic, proposed that the masters should make a clean sweep of all the Unionists in their employ. But the English quickly recovered their coolness. It was utterly impossible to suppress these associations; it was felt that workmen ought to have the right to combine for the defence and furtherance of their own interests; and, so far from being proscribed, they were not only left unmolested, but their existence was legally recognised.

The Trades Unions registered in 1877 have a revenue of £254,565, an accumulated capital of £374,989, and comprise 260,222 members.[1] They are but the minority of English workmen; yet their power is incontestable; it proves, not indeed that their organisation is a good one, but that they have an organisation. What use do they make of it?

The charges brought against them may be summed up as follows: They put into a common fund contributions intended for insurance in case of death or sickness, and those intended for strikes and trade purposes, and then apply the fund chiefly to the latter class of purposes. They are almost all subject to a despotic directing committee. They would gladly oppose the use of machinery; and since they cannot destroy existing machinery, they do their best to prevent the introduction of improvements. The report of the Society of Ironfounders for 1879 asserted that there was only one remedy against machinery—to work shorter time and produce less. They prohibit piece-work; and in some trades, such as brickmaking, the workman is bound not to work too hard. Houses in Manchester are said to have gone up 35 per cent. in consequence of the brickmakers' rules, the workmen, of course, paying their share of the increase, like any other tenants. They demand equal wages for all workmen, notwithstanding differences of skill. Like the guilds of the Middle Ages, they try to restrict the number of apprentices; under pretence of emancipating the workman, they hold him in the closest bondage, obliging him to conform to their rules, and depriving him of the first of all liberties, the right to labour, by forbidding him to labour except under stated conditions, and requiring him to leave his employment whenever the committee orders a strike. The pessimists go very near to attributing to the Trades Unions the industrial crisis which lately prevailed in England. People must always have a scape-goat.

---

[1] See Brassey, *Foreign Work and English Wages*, and Bevan, *Manufacturing Industry*.

Happily, there are persons in England who keep a cool head, and go to the bottom of things. These men say :—

"Trades Unions, make what exertions they may, will not alter the law of demand and supply, any more than they will stop the rotation of the earth. The age of Joshuas is past. They will never prevent the fall of wages when there are no outlets for industry; while the eagerness of manufacturers to extend their business on the least appearance of an opening must of itself stimulate a demand for labour which will result in a rise of wages without the interference of Trades Unions. If the Trades Unions were to raise the wages in a given trade higher than that trade could support, it would die out. The demand for labour would decline in consequence, and wages would fall. The recent labours of Professor Leone Levi have shown that the wages of non-unionist workmen have within the last ten years undergone a greater increase than those of the members of the most powerful Unions between 1866 and 1878. Women's wages have gone up 24 per cent., and those of men generally $6\frac{3}{4}$ per cent.[1] The powerlessness of Trades Unions to hinder the fall of wages during a crisis is pointed out in the Report of the Durham Miners' Association. 'In 1874 our income was £47,004, and our expenditure £23,613; so that for this one year our income exceeded our expenditure by £23,390. But in 1875, 1876, and 1877 there was a relative diminution of receipts and an increase of expenditure. Income in 1877, £33,290; expenditure, £60,513; difference, £27,223. Every one must see that this state of things cannot last long.' It is only when the supply of labour is scarce that the workmen can dictate their own terms to the masters. During the American war wages doubled and tripled. They subsequently declined, but still remained from 50 to 75 per cent. higher than during the previous twenty-five years. There needed no Trades Unions to produce this result. Workmen in the building trade find it easier than others to force a rise in wages, because their industry is limited to fixed localities, and has nothing to fear from foreign competition. Thus, in the United States, masons and brickmakers have made from 11s. 3d. to 15s. a day. In 1873 they even reached 18s. 10d. a day. These conditions are to a great extent independent of Trades Unions. The strikes of masons in London and of joiners in Manchester in 1877 were failures. The masters have answered the workmen's unions by powerful associations among themselves, which give them a power of resistance equal to that of the strongest Trades Unions. To the strike they oppose the lock-out. They insert in their agreements a clause for relieving them, in case of strikes, from the obligation of fulfilling their contracts by the appointed time. As to the exclusive

---

[1] See Book IV., chap. iii., Diagram 36, p. 164.

spirit of the Trades Unions, they are no doubt wrong in forbidding piece-work, in demanding equality of wages, in trying to put down freedom of labour among their members, in opposing machinery, and in getting up strikes; but they have abandoned the wild theories formerly professed at Ghent and Lyons. In 1877, the president of the Trades Union Congress at Bristol denounced in the most energetic terms the outrages which had taken place against manufacturers in Manchester. The following was the programme for 1879 of the Parliamentary Committee of the associated Trades Unions:—

1st. Amelioration of the law respecting accidents, so that workmen and their families may be indemnified in case of death or injury due to the negligence of the employer;

2nd. Reforms in the administration of justice: (*a*) Summary jurisdiction of magistrates, with right of appeal and trial by jury, and diminution of useless imprisonments; (*b*) Appointment of free referees;

3rd. Codification of the criminal law;

4th. Reform of the jury law;

5th. Extension of the Act of 1875 respecting employers and workmen to ships whilst in British waters;

6th. Increase of the number of inspectors of factories and workshops;

7th. Reform of the patent law;

8th. Abolition of imprisonment for debt;

9th. Certificates of competence for engine-drivers.

Certainly we have nothing here but what is practical and admissible.

In conclusion, Trades Unions may do good service by collecting information as to the condition and future prospects of labour. Such information will be a guide to the workman in his negotiations with his employers. He will then understand that it is his interest that capital, that "sensitive and volatile element of production,"[1] should not emigrate abroad, for if it does, the purchasing power of his labour must disappear. He will therefore not drive it away by his exorbitant demands. On the other hand, the capitalist will see that the workman must be paid as highly as the conditions of production will permit."

We have given the pros and the cons, let us now turn our attention to the strikes which, according to Mr. Bevan, have taken place in England within the decade 1870-79 inclusive.

[1] Brassey.

LOCALITIES AND TRADES AFFECTED.

Trades.	Towns.	Weeks.	Date.
Carpenters and Joiners	Heywood	28	1872
	Wolverhampton	27	1877
	Manchester	52	1877
	Dunfermline	40	1878
	Hartlepool	34	1878
	Shields	34	1878
Tailors	Merthyr	27	1874
	Blaenafon	47	1875
	Aberdeen	57	1875
	Bradford	20	1878
Dock Labourers	Shields	23	1873
Miners	South Wales	21	1875
	Burnley	26	1876
	Dronfield	36	1877
	Pembrokeshire	28	1876
	Kinneil	26	1878
	Church Lane	36	1878
	Manvers Main	26	1878
Ironworkers	Wishaw	20	1873
	Middlesborough	29	1873
	Parkgate	22	1875
	Aberdare	26	1879
	Bradford	36	1879
Shipwrights	Glasgow	20	1870
	Dumbarton	28	1876
	Runcorn	26	1876
	Glasgow	23	1877
Glass-workers	Sunderland	26	1876
	Glasgow	33	1876
	Alloa	56	1878
Masons	London	33	1877
	Newcastle	24	1878
	Kirkcaldy	36	1878
	Wigan	30	1879
	Barnsley	31	1879
Spring-makers	Sheffield	28	1875
Tinmen	Edinburgh	33	1879
Engine-drivers	Newcastle	21	1871
	Ashton	22	1879
	Belfast	26	1879
Railway Employés	Taff Vale	25	1876
Workmen in Tobacco Factories	Newcastle	24	1879
Plumbers	Nottingham	38	1878
	Darlington	37	1876
Compositors	Dublin	31	1878

Number of Strikes.

Year	Strikes
1870	30
1871	98
1872	343
1873	365
1874	286
1875	245
1876	229
1877	180
1878	268
1879 (1st December)	308
	2,352

Duration of Strikes

Year	Weeks
1870	68
1871	279
1872	988
1873	1,093
1874	812
1875	684
1876	952
1877	759
1878	1,621
1879	1,774
	9,027

Or 54,162 working days (*Journal of the Statistical Society*, March, 1880, p. 46).

The following have been the results, so far as the writer has been able to ascertain, which attended these various strikes:—

	Number of Strikes.	Lost.	Won.	Compromised.	Explanations.	Result unknown.
1870	30	1	8	2	11	19
1871	98	5	10	11	26	72
1872	343	6	8	8	22	321
1873	365	...	...	...	...	365
1874	286	...	...	...	...	286
1875	245	23	17	9	49	196
1876	229	24	15	16	55	174
1877	180	15	7	10	32	148
1878	268	43	3	15	61	207
1879	308	72	3	20	95	213
Total	2,352	189	71	91	351	2,001

When production increases, the number of strikes increases with it; during a crisis they fall off; as soon as the crisis is over they begin again. These figures show that the workmen in their strikes observe the law of demand and supply of labour; when the demand is weak, they submit; when it is strong, their pretensions rise with it.

Some strikes, however, are entered upon without hope of success; they have been provoked by some injustice, against which the workmen wish to protest. Such strikes are the most heroic, and surely the most legitimate.

Out of these 2,352 strikes, 314 have been due to the colliers, 187 to the carpenters, 151 to the masons, 127 to the iron-workers, 120 to the cotton-operatives, 100 to the ship-builders, and 96 to the engineers and fitters.

Within these ten years, strikes have occurred in only 111 trades, and Mr. Bevan remarks that it is "encouraging to have to record how few trades have struck compared with those that have not."

Mr. Bevan has calculated the loss of wages resulting from 110 strikes. Reckoning five working days to the week, and estimating the daily loss per man at four shillings, he makes a total of £4,468,950. The strike among the ship-builders on the Clyde in 1877 alone cost £300,000; the strike of the Durham miners in 1879 cost £240,000. These sums are not included in the total given above. If 112 strikes give a loss of more than five millions, what must the loss on the remaining 2240 amount to? And what of the indirect losses through depreciation of house-property in the districts liable to great strikes, through unpaid rents, through the accumulation of debt on the head of the workman, causing heavy losses to the tradesmen who have given him credit, and through sickness and physical deterioration and the sufferings of the wives and children? Sometimes a strike absolutely destroys the industry in the place where it has broken out. This was the case with the dockyards at Millwall.[1] Work migrated elsewhere. A slight reduction of wages for a short time might have saved an industry. A few months later, a reduction of 20 per cent. is necessary, and even that comes too late.

At the same time, it is only fair, in speaking of the waste and ruin produced by strikes, to draw attention to a very just remark of Mr. Howell's, the Parliamentary Secretary of the Trades Unions. If 10 or 20 per cent. of the workmen engage in a contest on behalf of the whole trade, the rest of the men will share in the benefit, and the loss should therefore be calculated on the whole number. If two hundred out of a thousand men in a district go on strike and obtain an increase of wages for the remaining eight hundred, and thus prevent future strikes, the advantage is obvious.

---

[1] This fact is disputed by Mr. Brassey.

The result of the discussion at the meeting of the Statistical Society has been to show that nowhere else is the workman as well off as in England, and that his condition has improved since the strikes.

We must take into account the limited time which the workmen have had in which to organise themselves. It is only for the last dozen years that the unions have had a legal existence. And yet we expect them to be quite perfect, to commit no errors, to be carried away by no passions, and to weigh with the most perfect accuracy the conflicting interests of themselves and their employers. But are we so perfect, we, who exact so much? Does no shade of prejudice overcloud our intellect? Have we overcome that vanity which leads us to look on ourselves as superior beings, and impels us to resist, not only because it is our interest, but because we are childishly ashamed to give way?

The strike is a mode of warfare, bringing with it all the destructive consequences of war, ruin of capital, deterioration of machinery, distress to the workman; but it is after all only an application of the law of demand and supply.

The Trades-unionists would be surprised if we told them "You are buying up the market. It was hardly worth while holding up the monopolists to execration, if you were going to take their place and carry on the business." Yet what do they do? They monopolise labour, they warehouse it, they prohibit its sale by retail. To strike, is to create a scarcity of labour.

Labour becomes too abundant, its price falls too low, its possessors restrict their offers, just like a merchant withholding his commodities from sale until prices have risen. But he cannot wait beyond a certain time without the prospect of ruin. It is the same with the workmen and with their employers; both have to come to an agreement, measured by their respective powers of resistance, and always regulated by the law of demand and supply.

I am simply writing a treatise on Economic Science; and my object in going into these details is only to draw from them certain principles. With regard to the strikes in France, there is only one point to detain us. They have no organisation; there are no Trades-unions to support them. Yet we labour under such a weight of ignorance in matters of economy, that, no sooner does a strike occur, than we imagine it a riot; and all the powers of the State, the administration, the magistracy, the police, the gendarmerie, the army, are enlisted against it. The painful reminiscences of Aubin and the Ricamarie are still in men's minds. If M. Gambetta protested against the presence of troops at Creusot in 1870, he did not protest against their presence at Anzin in 1878, and at Roubaix in 1880. When the workmen refuse to work under conditions which do not suit them, we call it insurrection. The law of 1864, on combinations, is a hostile law, full of traps and pitfalls into which the strikers must needs fall whenever the Government pleases. M. Emile Ollivier pompously announced in his report, "Absolute freedom of combination to all classes; and a rigorous repression of violence and fraud." The maxim is just; but where does liberty of *combination* end and liberty of *association* begin?[1] The strike is the only object for which the law allows workmen to act in concert; and then in what a fashion! A combination at St. Etienne, having nominated a committee of sixteen members, was convicted of having formed an association of more than twenty persons, and condemned under Art. 291 and the law of 1834. This law is still in force.

If syndicates are now established, it is by virtue of a tolerance capricious and uncertain, as tolerance always is. There are not only many magistrates, but many politicians, who entertain pretty much the same ideas as to strikes and workmen's associations as those to which M. Lepelletier gave utterance in his speech, made in 1867 as Public Prosecutor, against the operative tailors of Paris. "The strike is a conflagration, disastrous and terrifying, but transient; that is extinguished already. The Association is the hearth from which fresh flames may burst to-morrow; that must be extinguished too."

We for our part, on the contrary, demand liberty of association for the workman as for all other citizens; it is a right; and it has been practically useful in England. For the solution of all those irritating questions which arise between employers and workmen we can show that it is indispensable.

Practical men, and economists who do not mistake recrimination and declamation for argument, think that the true means of avoiding strikes is the formation of great associations of workmen and employers. Mr. T. Wood Bunning has shown[2] that they will reduce the friction which arises where men are debating their respective interests; that the delegates of both parties, acting on behalf of their respective constituents, would insure to the arrangements decided upon the stability indispensable to great industrial enterprises. Mr. Brassey, too, shows how useful these associations might become in diffusing information as to the value of labour and the industrial situation.

[1] The law of France distinguishes between *coalitions* (or combinations) and *associations*. The *coalition* is a temporary union of workmen for demanding higher wages or going on strike, and is permitted by a recent law passed in 1864; the *association* is permanent, and, under an old law unrepealed by the enactment of 1864, is illegal if its members exceed twenty in number. The French Chambers have had before them a proposal, which will probably shortly become law, for granting the French Trades Unions (*syndicats professionels*) a certain amount of freedom.

[2] *Journal of the Statistical Society*, March, 1880.

All these arguments will appear incontrovertible, except to people who pretend that the best way of coming to an agreement is to misunderstand each other.

It is by means of these associations, these Trades Unions, these syndical chambers, that the labour-market must be organised.

At the time of the joiners' strike in Manchester in 1877, joiners were being paid in Manchester $8\frac{1}{2}d$. an hour, in Liverpool $8\frac{1}{4}d$., at Bradford $8d$., at Lincoln $7\frac{3}{4}d$., at Lancaster $7d$., at Cambridge $6\frac{1}{2}d$., at Gloucester $6d$., at Winchester $5\frac{1}{2}d$., and at Frome $4\frac{3}{4}d$.

The labour being the same, and the differences in the conditions of existence very insignificant, this difference in wages proves that the labour-commodity has not yet been able to organise its outlets; for the prices of commodities, *e.g.* corn, tend to a level in proportion to the development of the means of transport, and the facility and rapidity of circulation.

Now, man remains the commodity least easy to transport; he is not always alone, he has a wife and children; he is held back by ties of family and friendship; by habit, by the dislike of uncertainty, by the inertia common to us all; and finally, by the want of information as to the state of trade in other places.

In 1850 M. Max Wirth founded the *Arbeitgeber* (Labour-exchange).[1] M. de Molinari attempted to realise the same idea in Belgium. Both enterprises were unsuccessful. Their failure does not, however, prove the idea a false one. It accords with all those historic laws which we have explained and verified. The separation of the man from the thing, of the personality of the man from the service he performs, and the definition and limitation of this service, are undeniable tokens of progress. The slave was an article of exchange; he belonged body and soul to his master, who could require everything from him, even his life. It was little better with the serf; and the journeyman of the ancient guild is still his master's liege man. To-day the workman gives nothing but his labour. He sells a fixed and clearly-specified product while he himself remains independent. He can think what he pleases, believe what he pleases; no one calls him to account for his life; he hands over to his employer a specified product at a fixed price, just as a merchant at Havre delivers to his correspondent in Paris a chest of coffee. The workman is a dealer in labour. In place of the exchange, he has the strike. It is a coarse expedient, with none of those conveniences which the exchange possesses. In place of brokers there are, in some trades, registry offices. Everywhere the labour commodity is sold retail.

In the Trades Unions we see the formation of a wholesale labour market. The committees of the Trades Unions are real brokers,

---

[1] See Max Wirth, *Les Lois du Travail*, pp. 210-213.

whose business it is to regulate the price of the commodity labour. When they enter into negotiations with the commodity capital, they do not deal with the commodity labour by retail, but wholesale.[1] It follows that they learn that labour must submit to the law of demand and supply, like every other commodity.

The miners of Newcastle organised a general committee, and admitted the principle of a sliding scale of wages.[2] It has since been adopted in other parts of England. The institution of this sliding scale has shown the workmen something of the difficulties with which colliery managers have to contend, and the causes of the differences between the price of coal at the pit's mouth and the price paid by the consumer. Out of the £1 5s. per ton paid by the London consumer, only 4s. 5d. reaches the colliery owner in Northumberland or Durham. The wages of miners in England rose between 1871 and 1873 to 6s. 6d. or even 8s. 0d. per day; a crisis supervened, and they fell to 2s. 0d. or 2s. 6d. The shock was severe, but it was borne more easily than it would have been if the miners had not been kept informed of the economic situation.

It is only by means of associations of this nature that questions like the following can be solved. A coal company has six pits close together; in one the coal is excellent, and easily obtained, and the pitmen can realise high wages; in the other five they cannot make as much. The only thing to be done is to strike an average.

It is the glory of Mr. Mundella to have established boards of arbitration, and to have introduced the habit of referring to them. It has been the prevention of many strikes.

The trade syndicates in France pursue objects similar to those of the Trades Unions in England. They date from 1861, and are the result of the information acquired by the workmen at the Exhibition. Their delegates, in a memorial dated the 2nd of February, 1868, and addressed to the Minister of Commerce, demanded:—

1st. Modifications in the *conseils des prud'hommes*.
2nd. The repeal of Article 1781 of the *Code Civil*.
3rd. The abolition of the *livret*.
4th. The right of public meeting.
5th. The establishment of syndical chambers of workmen similar to those of the masters.

The French delegation at Vienna demanded:—

1st. The institution of legal commissions to inquire into and decide upon differences between masters and workmen.
2nd. The introduction of a system of technical education more practical than that provided by the ordinary official course.

The Workmen's Congress, held at the Salle Franklin, Havre,

---

[1] *Journal of the Statistical Society*, March, 1880, p. 55.
[2] Mr. T. W. Bunning.

from the 14th to the 22nd December, 1880, voted the following resolutions, under the head of *Question du Salariat* :—

1st. Repeal of all laws restricting association. Absolute freedom of every open and public Association, with liberty to adopt such form as may be most convenient.

2nd. Recognition of syndical chambers as entitled to civil rights, and their admission to tender for public contracts.

3rd. Revision of the law relating to *prud'hommes;* their decisions to be rendered executory within three days.

4th. Abolition of registry offices, and substitution of the offices of the syndical chambers.

5th. Admission of syndical chambers to give evidence in Parliamentary inquiries.

6th. Limitation of the working day to ten hours at most.

7th. Abolition of the *livret.*

8th. An active supervision of work in workshops and factories by inspectors from the workmen's syndical chambers.

9th. Wages not to be reduced by fines or stoppages.

10th. Workshop regulations to be approved by the syndical chambers and *prud'hommes.*

11th. Masters to be forbidden by law to oblige their workmen to subscribe to relief funds belonging to their establishments.

12th. Labour in prisons to be abolished, and agricultural penitentiaries to be substituted; labour in convents to be suppressed, pending the suppression of the convents themselves.

13th. Abolition of the *octroi*, of indirect taxes, and of imposts on articles of consumption.

14th. Imposition of a single tax on fixed capital, based on a new valuation.

15th. Lastly, the Congress voted for the creation by the executive committee of a reserve fund for old age. A circular to be addressed to all the syndical chambers, requesting their opinion on this important subject.

Some points in this programme are open to exception, and some show the old exclusive mendicant spirit; others are admirable, and the revolutionary Collectivists have found scarcely anything more to ask for at present. Moreover, the Congress paid extraordinary attention to the question of instruction and apprenticeship.

The system of apprenticeship is almost everywhere unsatisfactory. The workmen all look on the apprentice as their servant. He goes the rounds, sweeps the shop, and picks up his knowledge of the trade hap-hazard, often amidst taunts and blows. Some workmen, far from helping him, regard him with an evil eye as a future competitor, who will bring down the price of labour and overstock their calling; and they would willingly rid themselves of him, in order to keep a monopoly of production. The syndical chambers, by demanding the establishment of technical schools, give evidence of a great moral improvement.

Lastly, these chambers proclaim freedom of labour. That is the great thing. The odious despotism of the old guild must not be revived under the form of trade associations. It has been this frightful spirit of class and caste which has petrified for so many centuries the Eastern civilisations of India, China, and Japan.

At the discussion on Mr. Bevan's work at the Statistical Society,[1] Mr. T. W. Bunning, the Secretary of the Northumberland and Durham Colliery Owners' Association, who, from his position, must be supposed to be a well-informed and experienced person, said, with a sagacity which is only too rare, "Men of all classes have very much the same passions, and we may fix a pretty equal percentage of reasonable and unreasonable people among them. They are all influenced by the same motive—personal interest; and this personal interest does not prevent strikes, because neither of the two parties can measure the interests of the other." In general, the masters think they do too much for their men, and the men think they do not do enough. Masters and men have the same prejudices; they cannot see that they are two contracting parties, buyer and seller.

Many workmen think the masters are monsters, who could pay higher wages if they pleased, and who do not raise them out of pure ill-will. This ignorance of economy, which is often shared by the masters, creates two kinds of prejudices. There springs up on the part of the workman a boon-begging spirit, which turns to hatred if it is not satisfied; and on the part of the employer, the habit of making himself master too literally. Both substitute the idea of favour for that of justice.

No doubt, from a moral point of view, we must admit that there are some excellent employers, who have done a great deal for their workpeople. They have turned to account their hereditary administrative capacity, and the experience they have gained in business, to provide institutions for their men, such as the men themselves could never have created or even imagined. They have given them an interest in the extension of their business. As far-seeing calculators, they have not chosen to sacrifice everything to the present opportunity, and make a profit out of the poverty of their workmen by taking advantage of all the fluctuations in the demand and supply of labour. And then, in moments of discouragement, they complain, "We do everything we can for them, and they give us no credit for it. They are an ungrateful lot."

But in the first place, the effort made is not collective, it is isolated; and secondly, it is the tendency of the workmen to see

[1] *Journal of the Statistical Society*, March, 1880.

but one thing—the difference between the gains of capital in a thriving industry, and the wages of their own labour; and they overlook the fact that if their wages were suddenly raised, in however slight a proportion, the gain would soon turn to loss. Besides, they do not consider the risk. They see the immense profits made at a given moment, but they cannot calculate the average profit, allowing for the fluctuation of prices. Sometimes they run up the cost price—"Raw materal, so much; my labour, so much"—and think they have made a very close calculation; but if the master's reckoning had been no closer, the works would long ago have been closed. The workmen's ingratitude is not ingratitude, but ignorance.

Employers and workmen must realise that it is their mutual interest to understand each other. Many have already done so. It is by common agreement that they must find the solution of the questions now pending between them.

The manufacturers complained in the year XI. of the Republic of the workmen's habit of violating their articles of apprenticeship and contracts for work. Such complaints are still heard from time to time; but are not the employers themselves chiefly to blame for it? They all say, "I mean to be master in my own house." Accordingly, they reserve their freedom; they will not bind themselves to long engagements. The consequence is, that the workmen for their part get into the habit of not considering themselves engaged, and when the fancy takes them, when they think the moment favourable for striking, they stop work, walk off, and leave their master in the lurch. The employer has his own contract with a third party. If his workmen all at once raise their price, his loss may be very serious. Suppose the stokers of one of the gas companies go on strike for a single day, a whole town is left in darkness. Or suppose the engine-drivers of a railway company refuse to work, they can suspend the traffic over a whole countryside.

In old times, the English workman could not leave his master at all; but there is not much chance of bringing back that state of things; and the employer is beginning to see that if he is to guard his own freedom of action, the men will take it into their own hands to guard theirs, and it is therefore his interest to make a solid contract. Accordingly, the more intelligent of the large manufacturers have recourse to various contrivances for attaching their workmen to their establishments, providing houses, alms-houses, and schools, giving bonuses and increased wages for long service, retiring pensions, and annual gratuities.[1] The railway companies give commissions to their agents.

---

[1] See for details, *Patrons et Ouvriers de Paris*, by A. Fougerousse.

The employers, who must have labour, are as much interested as the workmen in the solution of these questions. Most of them have not yet found this out, and yet they need but glance at the facts to be convinced of it.

As we have shown, capital increases much faster than population, at least in England, France, and the United States. This proportion tends to increase as fresh mechanical means of production are introduced. There will consequently be a want of hands, for the demand for labour will outrun the supply. The capitalist will then have to do his utmost to procure the most productive labour possible under the most favourable conditions possible. In another half century, if no war should in the meantime occasion one of those terrible destructions of capital which retard civilisation for years, the commodity labour will be scarcer than the commodity capital.

It may be said that there are still millions of hands at command, Are not the Chinese even now invading the United States? and after the Chinese, are there not the negroes? There is not much to fear for the supply of labour.

That is one side of the question. But people forget that the world is not troubled with a plethora of population; that only the smallest part of its natural forces is utilised; that it is but forty years ago that a great industrial revolution began to change the conditions of production. Now, the farther we go, the more must natural forces take the place of human; the less important is muscular strength, and the more important is intellectual power. The more advanced races will take the whole intellectual direction of production, leaving the more disagreeable employments, which will be daily decreasing in importance, to the less advanced races. But, thanks to the progressive applications of science, the productive power of human labour will go on increasing, and will augment, first the amount of capital, secondly, the purchasing power of capital, and thirdly, the supply of capital. And, since the value of labour is in proportion to the supply of capital, wages will continue to advance.

Employers have too long regarded the workmen as their debtors. Already the reduction in the rate of interest, the difficulty of finding profitable investments, and the losses to which their foreign ventures have exposed them, have shown them that, if they mean to go on producing, they must allow a larger share to the other contracting party. Their own interest compels them to see that solidarity is no empty word. Agriculturists are complaining of the want of hands. What is the meaning of this phrase? That the supply of capital is greater than the demand for work. It will be increasingly so in all industries. The egoists and idiots who wish to enjoy all the advantages of society, on condition of having them all to themselves, may like it little enough, but it is none the less a sign of progress. The employers of labour will have to make advances to it, to pay it attention, as the small tradesman makes advances to the customer; and these advances will take the form of co-operative associations, of participation of profits, of provision for the education of children, for the sick, and for old age.

This solidarity shows itself already in several joint enterprises in which the workman is a real partner. We cannot examine them in detail, but we may point out certain prejudices which tend to their disadvantage. For instance, the Trades Unions are averse to piece-work, and so, in theory, are some French workmen; mostly those who think that the workman should do as little work as possible, without considering that the less he produces, the less he can claim for his produce. To the honour of our country, we may say that only a very small minority prefer work by the day. With piece-work the workman feels himself free. He makes a bargain with his employer, who finds him in raw material, tools, and motive power. So long as he delivers the piece at a given time and under fixed conditions, he is independent. He works without supervision, and saves his dignity. Piece-work maintains the distinction between the man and the thing, the human individual and the utility he produces. It specifies the function of the man, who owes a fixed service in return for a fixed price. Piece-work is one of the progressive forms of the organisation of labour, and, in large undertakings, it begins to be substituted for other modes of labour wherever it can be applied.

At Creusot and at Terrenoire it has been observed that the workman engaged on piece-work does not work harder, but he works more intelligently. His work is said to be 75 per cent. better, and he earns 50 per cent. more. Both parties are gainers, the workman by 50 per cent., and the employer by 25 per cent.

At Cail's factory the workmen are engaged *à l'affûtage*, that is, at so much an hour for the work they do. Each one becomes a contractor, has his own implements, work-bench, steam, and share of accommodation.[1] It takes four workmen to fit an engine; suppose their united wages for the job to come to £32, they will be divided thus: first, each man will be paid so much per hour according to his ability; secondly, he will be paid according to the number of hours he has worked; thirdly, the balance of the £32 will be divided among the workmen in proportion to the wages they receive. There are no sub-contractors.

In the next case, we find little groups of men filling the place of sub-contractors. In the slate quarries of North Wales, three or four men form a co-partnery, and undertake to extract slates from the

---

[1] The workman finds the **small tools** himself, while steam and machinery are provided by the employer.

portion of the quarry assigned to them, at so much per thousand. These men form a third of the total number of workmen. The rest are employed by them. The quarry owners supply the more expensive implements, while the associated workmen find the powder and small tools.[1]

There are two kinds of labour: servile labour, enforced by chains and whipping; and free labour, stimulated by pride in one's work. It is needless to say which of the two is the more productive. Time-work is a relic of servile labour; piece-work is the highest expression of free labour. It is the beginning of association.

As a proof of the efforts made towards the common agreement of which we have been speaking, we must note the participation of workmen in the master's profits.[2]

A German economist, M. Victor Böhmert, head of the statistical department in Saxony, has gone into this subject in detail. He included in his inquiry 120 establishments in different countries, under different conditions, and representing different industries. The following are the conclusions he has come to:[3]—

1st. The participation in profits works well in almost all cases, and raises both the material and the moral condition of the men.

2nd. The system cannot, of course, be preached as a panacea for social maladies, or as a concession to absolute justice; it is simply a thoroughly understood system of wages, the adoption of which, in the majority of cases, and according to the nature of the employment, may become as profitable to those who find the work as to those who find the labour.

3rd. The idea of adopting this system is always fair and reasonable, but its application does not admit of a rigid adherence to one particular form or method. On the contrary, several different forms may be adopted concurrently, for the purpose of gradually improving the system of remuneration.

4th. The great variety of circumstance exhibited in the special reports by the various industries proves how much depends on places and persons, and shows that each case should be dealt with on its own merits and according to its peculiar circumstances. Each enterprise is a little world in itself, and demands a special development, as well as united action on the part of those concerned in it. It may be laid down as a principle, that participation in its highest form demands of each person concerned more effort as well as superior practical skill.

5th. In order to apply the system successfully, attention must be paid to the following conditions:—

[1] *Foreign Work and English Wages*, by T. Brassey, p. 242.
[2] *Bulletin de la Participation aux Bénéfices*, 2nd year (Librairie Chaix).
[3] An analysis of this report will be found in the *Journal des Economistes* for July, 1880.

(*a*) The participation must be so arranged as to establish a real and practical community of interests between masters and men.

(*b*) The question of wages is independent of that of profits. Wages can only depend on variations in the labour market, and not on the rate of profits.

(*c*) In making the general estimate, the industrial and commercial sides of the question must be kept apart, and there must be no mixing up of the separate questions of labour, capital, and the object of the enterprise.

(*d*) It is well, in apportioning shares of profits, to take into consideration the total remuneration received by each person interested, and even, in some cases, the time spent in the employ of the firm or company.

(*e*) As large a portion of the profits as possible should be divided, in order that the shares may not be so small as to be a matter of indifference to the men.

(*f*) As many of the men as possible should be made sharers in the profits; and their share should be made independent of the will of the master or of any fresh director.

(*g*) In every enterprise formed on this principle, an adequate reserve fund should be set aside; first, to meet extraordinary repairs of buildings or machinery; secondly, to make good possible losses.

(*h*) The shares should not, as a rule, be included in the general expenses, and they should bear interest; but it should be provided that at the expiration of a fixed term of service, or in domestic emergencies, or for buying a house, or during prolonged stagnation of trade, the men should have a right to receive the share of profits standing to their credit.

6th. It is the essential object of this system to invest each individual workman with a certain amount of capital, so that he may gradually and quietly pass from the position of a wage-earner to that of a capitalist, and have his modest share in the public property. The sooner this object is attained, the sooner will the prevailing hostility between masters and workmen be put a stop to. But it is for those who have proved the strongest in the struggle for existence to be the first to set about removing this hostility.

Some undertakings of this sort have failed. One instance quoted is that of Briggs' Colliery, where the men were admitted to a share of the profits, but only after a deduction of 10 per cent. for interest on capital, irrespective of the rate of profits realised; and, this being found too moderate, it was presently raised to 14 per cent. Under these circumstances, the workmen found the idea of participation somewhat illusory;* and they were perhaps not wholly wrong. The system was started in 1865, and abandoned in 1875.

When we hear of a failure, we must look into its causes; and when we hear of a success, we must ask whether it is of a nature to justify the general adoption of the system. Here lies the difficulty of questions of this kind. Take the case of the workmen engaged in the construction of a railway or a harbour, or piercing an isthmus like that of Suez or Panama. The works are mortgaged perhaps for millions of pounds sterling, they will take years to finish, and not till then can the contractors and capitalists know whether they are to gain or lose by them. In the meantime, the workmen must be lodged, clothed, and fed. In a case of this sort, they would hardly care for a share in profits which might turn out to be losses.

The wages system will never die out, because there are plenty of people who prefer the security of the present to the chances of the future.

In France there are many workmen who have a little capital; they get it from their parents, country people who have bought land, or as a dowry with their wives, or by their own saving. What do they do with it? Many of them know perfectly well that it is far more advantageous for them to remain plain workmen than to set up on their own account. They see for themselves that the management of capital is not the easy matter that people who have never had it imagine. They put their money in State or municipal loans. At Roubaix they join in dozens and half-dozens to buy lottery shares. If they have luck, they divide the prize in proportion to the amount contributed by each.

A wage-earner here is a share-holder there. It is the same with all of us who live by our work and are paid for it.

Accordingly, we must be on our guard against wishing to limit the combinations of capital and labour to one fixed form. The forms are as varied as the kinds of production. But we may safely affirm, without fear of deluding ourselves or others, that, by the force of things, some agreement of this kind will be brought about. Workmen will learn to read, write, and reckon, to think, and to speak; they will know how to fight for their own interests. Yesterday things were different; they had to submit to the will of a man who not only had the money, but knew how to use it to his own advantage, and who enjoyed all sorts of legal privileges. But to-morrow will not be like yesterday.

CHAPTER IX.

CO-OPERATION.

WE now come to the most important industrial transformation which has been attempted this century,—co-operation.

It is a good thing for the workman to have a capital outside himself in addition to his bodily forces. But how is he to get it? Prudent people say, "By saving."

But, as we have said before, saving is a depressing passion. It is all very well for a well-fed, well-clothed, well-housed man to tell other people to save—that is, to deny themselves. It is the doctrine of religious asceticism. Once started on this road, why not hold up to the workman's imitation the hermits of the Thebaid, or the fakirs of India? Does not privation weaken the most robust? Does not insufficient nourishment mean loss of force?

Englishmen have not the frugality which is so much admired in the French peasant. They seek the same end in other ways, and they find it in other ways; in ways which at first sight perhaps seem paradoxical—in co-operation, which is saving through spending. You buy what you want at the stores, at the current price; the difference between current price and cost price is profit; the profit is saved and becomes capital, and this capital may be used to found industrial establishments.

In 1826 the *Co-operative Magazine* said in so many words, "Mr. Owen never proposed that the rich should give of their riches to the poor; he claims that the poor shall be placed in a position to create new wealth for themselves."

Co-operation in England has run through three stages: the enthusiast stage, from 1821 to 1830; the socialist stage, from 1831 to 1844; and the practical stage, beginning in 1844 with the foundation of the celebrated association of the Rochdale Pioneers.

The story of this association is always being told, and it cannot be told too often. At the outset, twenty-four workmen contributed one pound each; in 1878, there were 10,187 members, the capital was £292,344; the amount turned over in the year, £300,000 at least, and the profits in 1878 alone, £52,694. No one was allowed to put more than £200 into the society.

In 1863, Mr. Abraham Greenwood, President of the Rochdale Pioneers, established in Manchester a "Limited Liability Wholesale Co-operative Society." It is an aggregation of smaller societies, each member of which subscribes only five shillings, so that a society of a hundred members has a hundred shares, a society of five hundred members five hundred shares, and so on. This society has now three factories, one at Leicester, which makes 300,000 pairs of shoes a year; another at Crumpsall, for biscuits, sweetmeats, and dry soap; and a third at Durham, for soap. It has butter warehouses in Ireland; it has a bank with deposits amounting to £6,000,000; in 1864 it had 18,337 shareholders, and in 1878 it had 300,000 shareholders, with a capital of £405,599, and effected sales to the amount of £2,739,581. Its profits had risen to £33,350.

Nevertheless, the regular development of co-operative societies has been surrounded with difficulties. They have had no legal existence. The managers could go off with the cash-box, and when the case came into court, they were acquitted.[1] Sometimes the society has grown too rich, and not knowing how to lay out its capital, it has obliged its members to withdraw it.[2]

The object is to organise productive associations. They may be organised on various principles. In some societies, as in that of the Manchester printers, all the capital is subscribed by the stores; there are no individual shares.

In Lancashire, the co-operative societies have become proprietors of a considerable number of joint-stock concerns; and although their success has not been altogether unchecked, the French Protectionists quote their returns to show what profits can be made.

The division of profits may be variously arranged. As a rule, they should be divided between the managers; the workmen who form the society, in proportion to their respective salaries; and the customers, in proportion to the value of their purchases.[3]

From Mr. Cowen's Parliamentary Report on Co-operative Societies in England, it appears that there were, in 1877, 12,000 of them in the United Kingdom.[4] In England alone, not including Scotland and Ireland, they had, at the end of 1878, a share capital of £5,347,199, a deposit capital of £692,478; their receipts during the year had been £18,460,758; and their net profits £1,565,497. They numbered 499,584 members.

The Report of the twelfth annual Congress of Co-operative Societies, held in 1880, gives the details of the operations of sixty-six societies for 1878 and 1879. The following are the totals :—

	Capital.	Sales.	Profits.
1878	£2,544,399	£8,871,247	£672,009
1879	2,581,501	8,030,160	683,491

These figures attest the formidable extent of the business operations of these societies; and it must not be forgotten that co-operation has only existed for forty years.

The success of co-operation has given rise to some illusions in France. Frenchmen, whose attention was attracted by the marvellous successes of the Rochdale Pioneers, saw only the thousands they had made, and overlooked their labours, their struggles, and even the very principles of their organisation. They thought there

---

[1] Holyoake, *History of Co-operation*, vol. ii., p. 114.
[2] *Ibid.*, vol. ii., p. 113.
[3] *Ibid.*, vol. ii., p. 122.
[4] *Ibid.*, vol. ii., p. 113.

was some magic in the word "co-operation;" they took it for a philosopher's stone which would turn everything to gold. But it is not the name that makes the gold, but the thing; you do not get what you want by gilding a word like an idol, and then invoking it, but by putting your own shoulder to the wheel. Unluckily, they expected a miracle; no miracle came, and unreflecting enthusiasm was followed by the apathy of discouragement.

Nevertheless, some co-operative societies have prospered. There is one at Roubaix, founded on the English model, for an unlimited period. Having saved by expenditure, it has made an arrangement with *Le Nord* Insurance Company, and buys houses for its members.[1] At Rheims, a co-operative society for buying articles of consumption has been in existence for thirteen years, and has now fifteen branches in the town, and is in a flourishing condition. At Puteaux, there is a similiar society which is doing well.

Insurance companies make considerable sacrifices by way of commission. Ever since 1865, M. Engel Dolfus has had the effects of all the workmen in the employ of the firm of Dolfus-Mieg insured. The insurance agent goes through the rooms, asking who will insure. Some accept, some decline. Those who accept gain very considerable advantages.

In France, co-operation is still feeling its way. But the time lost will soon be regained, if workmen will study economic facts instead of working themselves up with metaphysical declamation.

One of the obstacles to the success of co-operative movements, in England, as in France, has been the workmen's contempt for administrative capacity. They often choose the greatest talker instead of the best manager.[2] They often concern themselves with matters which have no bearing on the prosperity of the association. Then again, the workmen, not seeing the need of highly paid administrative skill, deprive themselves of the services of men really fitted to take the direction of their affairs. Mr. Brassey observed that the secretary of the Council of the important Trades Unions of Glasgow receives only £10 a year, and took it as indicating a profound ignorance of economic laws.

The following resolution was passed at the Congress of English Co-operative Societies held in 1877: "The Congress remains firmly convinced that co-operative societies should be based on the principle of reconciling the opposing interests of the capitalist, the workman, and the buyer, through the equitable division of profits among them."

I cannot close these remarks better than by quoting a few passages from the work of Mr. Holyoake, who for forty years has

---

[1] The *Temps* for July 23rd, 1880, gives the rules.
[2] *History of Co-operation*, vol. ii., p. 120.

been actively concerned in the English co-operative movement, and has had an important share in determining its leading features.

"Co-operation seeks the material means of growth. It husbands provisions for its members by creating stores, and supplies articles of utility by manufactures; it aims at the ownership of land and vessels; it builds; it engages in commerce and farming operations, with a view to the self-employment of its members; it provides for their education and self-government, that society may be self-sustained and self-controlled. Its means are capital and industry. The capital it saves by economy or hires, using it as an agent, and paying it its fair market value as such, and paying it no more. Its policy is to divide the entire profit made by thought, skill, and labour, equitably among those who produce it. This is what co-operation means, and the nature of the principles which will influence the future of industry."[1]

"Workmen have their affairs in their own hands now, and they will learn to clear their way, and to pay their way, as the middle-class have learned to do.[2]

"The instinct of co-operation is self-help. Only men of independent spirit are attracted by it.[3] . . . I have proved, as I have proceeded, what I said in the beginning, that it asks no aid from the State; it petitions for no gift from individuals; it disturbs no interests; it attacks nobody's fortune; it attempts no confiscation of existing gains; but stands apart, works apart, clears its own ground, gathers in its own harvest, distributes the golden grain equitably among all the husbandmen; and without needing favours or incurring obligations, it establishes the industrious classes among the possessors of the fruits of the earth."[4]

The future progress of co-operation will depend on the union and perseverance of those in whose hands the movement may be.

CHAPTER X.

CONCLUSION.

From this assemblage of facts, we may draw the following conclusions.

Production will take many and various forms which will change the conditions of labour. From this time forward, manufacturers on a small scale will obtain from those who deal in motive force a

---

[1] Holyoake, *History of Co-operation*, vol. ii., p. 443.
[2] *Ibid.*, vol. ii., p. 451.
[3] *Ibid.*, vol. ii., p. 453.
[4] *Ibid.*, vol. ii., p. 455.

share in the advantages enjoyed by manufacture on a large scale. The invention of small motors is everywhere a desideratum, and one of these days it will be realised. With improved means of transport, it will be less necessary for industry to congregate in the towns. The utilisation of hydraulic force, and the power of transporting force to a distance will change some of the existing conditions of the workshop.

But, however you may multiply theoretical combinations, you will find two characteristics of modern industry always the same; 1st, division of labour; 2nd, the constant predominance of industry on a large scale. Whether these characteristics recommend themselves to individual tastes or not, is not the question. They exist, and the workman had better not waste his time in complaining of them, but try to turn them to the best advantage. The State is powerless to put capital into the hands of the workmen. They can have it only by their own exertions, and by organisation of one sort or another. Their aim should be to establish an equitable interchange, instead of expecting everything from an equitable distribution. They should set themselves to strengthen all those associations which make it possible for them freely to discuss the price of their labour and to insure their future.

And, above all, we commend to their observation the law they have so often disregarded—that the form of association approaches perfection in proportion as it recognises the distinction between interests and persons.

Let them remember that all liberties are summed up in one—freedom of labour.

We must seek to realise—

1st. The organisation of the labour market through trades unions, trade syndicates, labour exchanges, and joint committees.

2nd. A better agreement between employers and employed; security guaranteed by the employer; and a more binding system of contract.

3rd. The establishment and development of co-operative societies.

BOOK V.

EXPERIMENTAL ECONOMICS.

In Book I. we defined the terms used to express the principal phenomena of economic science.

In Book II. we analysed the constituent elements of value.

In Book III. we showed the relations between fixed and circulating capital.

In Book IV. we considered man himself as an economic factor.

In Book V. we are to study the various systems he has invented to satisfy his economic requirements.

CHAPTER I.

LANDED PROPERTY.

LANDED property has, especially within the last century, been made the subject of the most passionate discussion. Like the physiocrats, the great majority of people in France are so accustomed to look on landed property as the only property, that they have got into the habit of omitting the adjective. Utopists and Conservatives, the *prolétariat* and the *bourgeoisie*, have, each in their turn, shown equal ignorance in accusing and defending it, in attributing to it all good and all evil. They have all started with Rousseau's declaration, " The man who first took it into his head to enclose a piece of land and to say, ' This is mine,' and who found other people simple enough to believe him, was the real founder of civil society."

To the Utopist, this enclosed ground was Eve's apple, the original sin from which all subsequent ills have sprung. The *bourgeois*, who thought of nothing but his houses and farms, did not dispute this theory of their origin, but contented himself with saying, "Eve's apple agrees with me very well, and I am going to keep it." Lamartine exclaims, " I know no man in France who reverences property as I do; I regard it as a divine principle, as the law of God, and not of man." [1] All disputes about property have turned on this question: Had the Adam of property the right to enclose his land? It is the characteristic of scholastic disputants to wrangle endlessly about hypotheses, until it occurs to some one to test the hypotheses themselves.

Rousseau's theory of property has generated Ricardo's theory of rent (1817). Ricardo imagined the first owner as taking the best land himself and leaving the worst to others. Here is what he says: [2]

"Suppose land,—No. 1, 2, 3,—to yield, with an equal employment of capital and labour, a net produce of 100, 90, and 80 quarters of corn. In a new country, where there is an abundance of fertile land compared with the population, and where therefore it is only necessary to cultivate No. 1, the whole net produce will belong to the cultivator, and will be the profits of the stock which he advances. As soon as population had so far increased as to make it necessary to cultivate No. 2, from which ninety quarters only can be obtained after supporting the labourers, rent would commence on No. 1; for either there must be two rates of profit on agricultural capital, or ten quarters, or the value of ten quarters, must be withdrawn from the produce of No. 1 for some other purpose. Whether the proprietor of the land or any other person cultivated No. 1, these ten quarters would equally constitute rent; for the cultivator of No. 2 would get the same result with his capital, whether he cultivated No. 1, paying ten quarters for rent, or continued to cultivate No. 2, paying no rent. In the same manner it might be shown, that when No. 3 is brought into cultivation, the rent of No. 2 must be ten quarters, or the value of ten quarters, whilst the rent of No. 1 would rise to twenty quarters; for the cultivator of No. 3 would have the same profits whether he paid twenty quarters for the rent of No. 1, ten quarters for the rent of No. 2, or cultivated No. 3 free of all rent."

Ricardo decides that "Rent is that portion of the produce of the earth which is paid to the landlord for the use of the original and indestructible powers of the soil." [3]

This theory is based on the theory of final causes. It presupposes that the earth was created for the use of man, and that consequently man had only to occupy it for it to bear him what he wanted.

Now, we find, on observing the facts, that fertile lands are fertile for themselves, and not for man; they are covered with trees, shrubs,

---

[1] Speech on the Preamble of the Constitution.
[2] *Principles of Political Economy*, chap. ii., p. 52, 2nd edition.
[3] *Ibid.*, p. 47.

or herbage; they are marshy, miasmatic, liable to inundation, the haunt of wild beasts and reptiles. Before man can avail himself of their fertility, he has first to free them from their natural products. This preliminary labour demands a vast outlay of strength, time, tools, and often of combined labour, and a considerable absorption of circulating capital. It is easy enough to say, "This land is mine." The difficulty lies in the occupying it.

A glance over the vast tracts of fertile land still unappropriated might have been enough to prove this truth; but people have preferred to carry on endless discussions on the theory of rent. The American economist, Mr. Carey, who had opportunities of observing the manner in which land is appropriated in a new country, was the first to assert that appropriation, instead of beginning with the most fertile, begins with the least fertile land.

Man, weak and isolated, requiring a prompt return for his labour, clears first the dry friable uplands, where there is no luxuriant vegetation to encounter. The first English colonists in America settled on the sterile soil of Massachusetts, and founded the colony of Plymouth. In New York State, Manhattan Island was first cleared; and in ascending the Hudson they kept always to the high lands, leaving the richest land, which requires most labour in clearing and draining, unoccupied to this day. The same phenomenon appears everywhere, in New Jersey, on the Delaware, in Georgia, Alabama, Florida, and along the banks of the Mississippi, millions of acres of which are covered with splendid trees. It is easier to fell the little pines on the hill-side than to get rid of this exuberant vegetation. The first colonist of Wisconsin planted himself on the highest land, known as the Great Rampart. It has passed into a proverb in the United States, that the damp prairies are the terror of the first emigrant, and make the fortune of the last. Thus it is that the poor lands of New England have enriched their owners, whilst the rich lands of Lower Virginia and North Carolina, of which the Dismal Swamp forms part, have not yet been brought under cultivation.

Humboldt records the same state of things in Mexico. The vegetation along the narrow plain which skirts the sea-border is magnificent but fatal. Accordingly, the Spaniards used this plain only as a stepping-stone to the upper regions, where the Indians preferred maintaining a laborious existence by agriculture to descending into the plains. All through Mexico and Peru, the advanced posts of civilisation are confined to the table-lands. It is the same in Costa Rica and Nicaragua. Quito is built high and dry on the hills, not down in the valley of the Orinoco. There is not a single town on the banks of the mighty Amazon.

Whence came the Aryan peoples? Tradition is not far wrong in making them descend from the mountains. When Egypt was at the height of her prosperity, the Delta was cultivated; but in her decadence the canals were allowed to overflow and the Delta was deserted.

In England, the Lincolnshire fens are the lands most recently brought under cultivation. They are also the most fertile. What was the largest town in Gaul at the time of the Roman conquest? Autun. Where did Vercingetorix concentrate all the efforts of the Gallic people? In the Morvan. It is in Auvergne, in the Cevennes, and in Brittany, in barren and mountainous countries, that we find the most traces of the Roman occupation. During the frightful distress of the 14th and 15th centuries, the Beauce relapsed into forest. Look at the fat pastures of Holland, won from the sea; and at our own rich polders, slowly and laboriously reclaimed!

Man appropriates the land he can cultivate, not the land he would prefer to cultivate.

Such an occupation of the land is very different from the imaginary process described by Rousseau. Moreover, private property is the most recent form of property.[1] No such thing existed in primitive times. The soil at first belonged to the horde that covered it. Then, going a step higher, it belonged to the family, the tribe, the Greek γένος, the Latin *gens*, the Celtic *clan*, the German *cognatio*. We find this system of collective property existing in China before the year 2205 B.C. It still exists in some outlying provinces. It is stamped on the traditions of all Oriental races.

The labours of Mommsen have shown that the agrarian commune was the primitive system of Italy. It still lingers in popular tradition as the golden age. It made way for the collective property of the family or *gens*. The intervention of the State in sales and bequests of land is explained by the idea that the transmission of land is a public interest, which cannot be subject to private caprice. Private property dates from Numa; and side by side with it existed the *ager publicus*, or common domain, which later on was monopolised by the patricians.

Among the Germans, hereditary property included only the house and the close surrounding it (*terra salica*). The common land was called the *mark*. Each family was entitled to the temporary enjoyment of a share in each of the divisions of the mark, but had no permanent or hereditary right over it. Individual ownership appears only in the *allod* of the Saxons after the Roman occupation. The copartnership of the family among the Germans is evidenced

---

[1] *De la Propriété et de ses Formes Primitives*, by M. Emile de Laveleye. *Ancient Law*, by Sir H. S. Maine. *Origin of Civilisation*, by Sir J. Lubbock, etc. (See Menier, *Avenir Economique*, vol. i., Book V.) M. Letourneau, in his *Sociologie*, pp. 284, 394, does not fully admit this law. He quotes instances of private ownership in Australia, in Tahiti, and among the Kabyles; but they do not really invalidate the law involved in the facts we are considering.

by—1st, the *faida*, or *venvelta;* 2nd, the obligation to pay the *wehrgeld*, or composition for military service; 3rd, the guardianship of the *munduald*, or chief of the family; and 4th, hereditary seisin. The whole family being proprietors, there was no succession, but continuity of possession.

Family communities, under the name of *sociétés taisibles* (tacit societies), existed till the end of the middle ages, and a few are even now to be found in the Nivernais, Auvergne, and the Bourbonnais.[1]

England was originally occupied by agrarian communities; but her social organisation became modified during the Anglo-Saxon period; and by the time of the Norman invasion the mark had become the manor. The feudal system gave to the lord the forests and pastures which had remained undivided amongst the villagers. The meadows were apportioned annually among the tenants. The arable land became private hereditary property. But all the customs of the early agrarian community were maintained. Every peasant had his lot in each field of the agricultural series; cultivation was co-operative.

In the Russian *mir* we find ourselves in actual contact with the earliest idea of property under patriarchal rule. "The patriarchal family," says M. de Laveleye, "is the basis of the *commune;* and the members of the *mir* are generally considered as descendants of a common ancestor. The ties of family have preserved among the Russians a power which they have lost elsewhere. The family is a sort of permanent corporation, under the almost absolute authority of a chief, called the elder. All goods are in common; house, garden, furniture, crops, are the common property of all the members of the family." Every one knows what has been the outcome of this organisation, maintained down to our own time by the despotism of the Czars. The Russian peasant is ignorance itself. His ill-used wife has to perform the hardest and most fatiguing labour. Russia, with her rich soil, has the feeblest agricultural production; she is two thousand years behindhand in her processes; the cultivator reaps only three or four times what he has sown. But since the emancipation of the serfs, the patriarchal system has shown a tendency to fall to pieces. "The feeling of individual independence undermines and destroys it." The young people obey the Elder no longer. The married son wants a home to himself, and each couple forms a separate household. Among the South Slavonian races, and also among the German Swiss, there are still family communities forming the basis of the land system; but these communities are scattered by the approach of a railway.

Now propose this system to the French peasant; say to the young

---

[1] See Dupin for an account of the *Communauté des Jault*, visited by him in 1840.

man about to marry, "You are to go on living with your parents, your brothers and sisters, your brothers-in-law and your sisters-in-law; and you can all help in cultivating the collective property." He will tell you fast enough, "We want our independence."

These facts are not in accordance with the statement of certain collectivists,[1] that "you may almost measure the degree of civilisation by the extent to which collective appropriation has taken place."

This being so, what becomes of Ricardo's theory of Rent? of Proudhon's assertion, that "property is robbery?" of the law of 1849, prohibiting under heavy penalties any discussion of the principles of property?

Property, then, has not always possessed the purely individual character with which Rousseau invested it. It began by being collective and undivided; and in proportion as civilisation has progressed and individuality has become stronger and more self-conscious, it has become individualised. There is no place for metaphysical questions as to the right of property, or for mutual recriminations. Landed property, like all other property, may assume various forms according to varying degrees of civilisation and social organisation, and according to the nature of the produce and the mode of working the soil.

The proprietor is not the privileged monster Ricardo makes him, nor the incarnation of evil he seems to be to the popular imagination. He is a man who, whether by accident of birth or circumstances or by his own exertions, finds himself in possession of fixed capital; this fixed capital, if well kept and cultivated, produces utilities in the shape of corn, potatoes, sheep, and oxen. These utilities the landlord exchanges for others; their value varies according to the law of demand and supply.

But the owner, instead of himself producing these utilities, may let this instrument of labour, this implement called land, to some one else. For the hire of this instrument he will receive a sum x, just as he would if he had lent money. The better the condition and the greater the power of utility of the implement, the greater will be the amount x.

According to Ricardo's theory, the first occupier of the most fertile land should, at the end of a certain time, have received an enormous rent.

But the facts have not confirmed his theory on this point. If the value of land as fixed capital has greatly risen, still it has risen much less than the value of much other fixed capital, such as mines and factories. And these mines, also, lie at the disposal of any one who will take them! The world still contains many millions of

---

[1] *La Revue Socialiste*, January, 1880.

tons of coal without an owner! It is only the other day that we began to work the coal-field of the Pas de Calais.

The owner of the soil, like every other possessor of fixed capital, has the advantage of possessing an instrument productive of utilities; but it is not enough to have this instrument, he must be able to use it. It is the difficulty of using it which has led to the custom of letting land. The owner sacrifices a part of the profit he might have derived directly from it, in favour of an indirect profit, smaller but surer. Why is it that even in France, where the land is so subdivided, farmers are found who prefer renting land to buying it with the money they now use in cultivating it? Because this land is prepared ready to their hand; because it is irrigated, drained, or planted; because it has available means of communication to bring them their raw material and ensure an outlet for their produce. For the rent he pays, the farmer might have acres of very fertile land in America. Out in the West, he might have four acres almost for nothing. He prefers to rent a few hectares near Paris, or in the Département du Nord. The value of land is not in proportion to its supposed natural fertility, but to the density of population, the abundance of circulating capital, and the facility of transport. It is not land, any more than any other natural agent, that is wanting, but the art of using it.

No doubt the possessors of the soil have often been privileged persons; and they are every day making efforts to preserve and even to increase their privileges. When the English landlords were fighting for the maintenance of the corn laws, what were they doing? They were insisting on the privilege of selling their own corn dearer than foreign corn, so as to profit by the difference, and to raise the value of their land. The French protectionists are claiming the same privilege when they levy a duty on meat and cry out for one on corn. They try to lay a tax on articles of consumption and to exempt themselves from its operation; and if they find themselves to a great extent mistaken, the mistake is due to their ignorance of the reflex action of economic laws.

These privileges, these extravagant claims, are anti-economic, and must be strenuously opposed. When the nomad tribe or family settles down, the destiny of man becomes fixed to the soil, like that of a vegetable. Under the feudal system, if there was no land without a lord, the lord was bound to the land. So, of course, was the serf. The titles, rights, and services of man were all bound up with the soil. It was thus difficult of transmission. The proprietor and his property tended to be indissolubly united. Traces of these notions still exist in our codes and customs; but they are gradually disappearing as we free ourselves from all the impediments which check our progress. The oyster sticks to the rock, shell and all, and never moves; the snail, if it moves at all, must drag its shell along with it. In some stages of civilisation, no doubt, it may have been a very good thing for man to be attached to his shell; but it has weighted him heavily in the race of life. Those who have gone the fastest and acquired the most are precisely those to whom the possession of the soil has been forbidden—the Jews. Paradoxical as it may seem, a similar cause has made the greatness and power of England.

The system of landed property in England is detestable, because it hinders the circulation of land. The following table gives a view of the distribution of landed property in the United Kingdom.[1]

	Number.	Per Cent.	Extent of Land.	Per Cent.
Proprietors of less than one acre each	852,438	72	Acres. 188,413	0·2
,, of from 1 to 100 acres	252,725	21	4,910,723	6·7
,, ,, 100 to 1000 acres	41,090	3·5	15,133,057	20
,, ,, 1000 acres and upwards	10,888	0·9	51,885,118	71
,, of land the acreage of which is uncertain	6,459	...	...	...
,, of land the rent of which is uncertain	124	...	2,570	...
	1,163,724		72,119,881	

This table, although it shows that out of 72,000,000 acres, 51,000,000 are divided among 10,000 proprietors, gives but an inadequate idea of the importance of the great landlords in England, for out of this number 977 persons possess 10,000 acres and upwards apiece. Thus 71 per cent. of the soil is in the hands of 90· per cent. of the total number of proprietors, while 72 per cent. of the proprietors possess only 0·2 per cent. of the soil among them.

Mr. Caird reckons that the entire arable land in the United Kingdom is held by 180,000 owners, and that only one per cent. of the soil is covered by properties of less than ten acres; and even this is almost exclusively building property.[2]

In England the land question is absorbing every one's attention, and the economists of the Cobden Club are not behindhand in demanding a radical modification of the laws.

I have already pointed out that this system of tying up the land has resulted in a diminution of its produce, its value, and consequently its rent. I have also said that this system of aristocratic

---

[1] *Financial Reform Almanack*, 1879, p. 17.
[2] Caird, *Landed Interest*.

privilege has contributed to make the greatness of England. And in this way:—

The English middle class, not being able to invest its savings in land, throws them into manufactures, or into ventures in foreign countries, and thus keeps them in circulation, instead of locking them up, like the French *bourgeois*, in small properties, a system which merely enables them just to scrape along, and gives them an ideal, not of active production, but of depressing economy. The following table shows how much people have been mistaken in thinking that there is no wealth outside landed property.

Schedule A.

GROSS REVENUE OF LAND AND FIXED PROPERTY.

Years.		
1848–49	£47,982,221	= 100
1853–54	46,772,256	= 97
1858–59	48,931,916	= 102
1863–64	51,390,046	= 107
1868–69	54,961,481	= 114
1873–74	57,402,720	= 119
1877–78	49,388,384	= 124

Schedule D.

PROFITS OF INDUSTRIES AND COMMERCE.

Years.		
1848–49	£80,929,700	= 100
1853–54	104,962,480	= 130
1858–59	106,547,938	= 132
1863–64	132,786,351	= 164
1868–69	165,526,682	= 204
1873–74	240,100,756	= 297
1877–78	250,635,707	= 309

Report of Mr. Charles Turner, Controller-General, 7th August, 1879, *The Economist*, March 13, 1880.

(See Diagram 43, p. 226.)

According to these tables, the returns from trade and manufactures are almost half as much again as those of real estate.

In France, the conditions of real property are just the converse of what they are in England. According to statistics published in 1868, the entire soil of France, exclusive of woods and forests, was divided in 1862 amongst 3,225,877 farms; and dividing the area of cultivated soil by this number, we have $10\frac{1}{2}$ hectares as the average extent of each farm. But the following table shows the real division:—

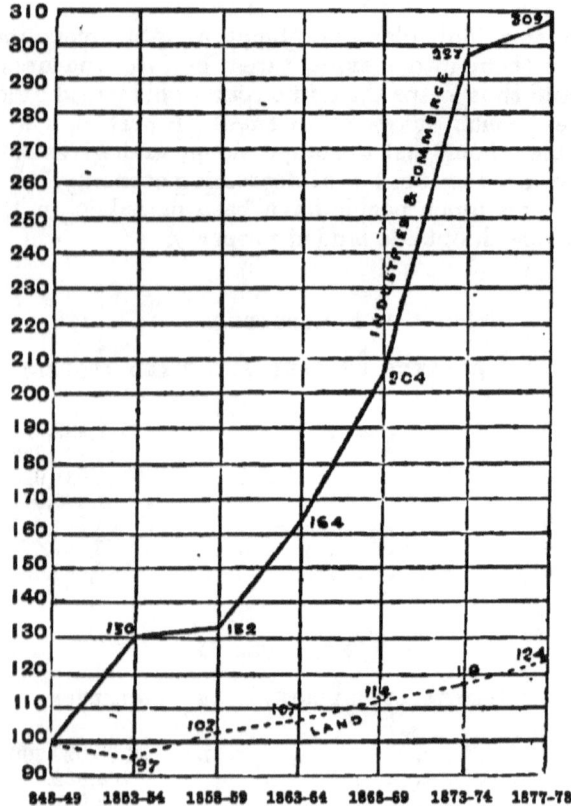

Diagram 43.—Increase per Cent. of the Profits of Industries and Commerce, compared with the Revenues of Land, in England.

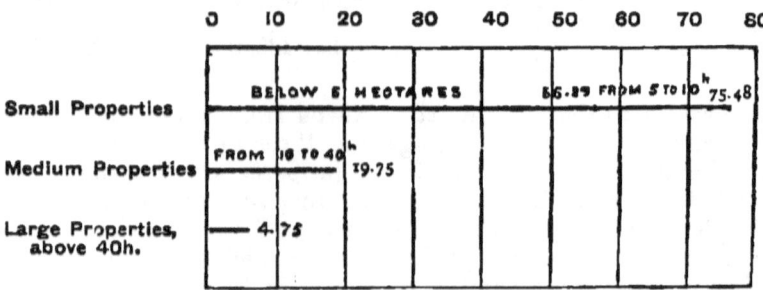

Diagram 44.—Distribution of Property in France.

LANDED PROPERTY.

	Number.	Percentage.
Small properties, of 5 hectares.	1,815,558	56·29
,, from 5 to 10 hectares	619,843	19·19
Total	2,435,401	75·48
Medium properties, from 10 to 40 hectares.	636,309	19·75
Large properties, above 40 hectares	154,167	4·75
	3,225,877	99·98

(See Diagram 44, p. 226.)

In 1876, the various agricultural employments numbered :—

		Per Cent.
1. Proprietors cultivating their own lands	10,620,886	56·0
2. Farmers, husbandmen, and metayers	5,708,132	30·09
3. Various agricultural occupations, wine-growers, wood-cutters, gardeners, market-gardeners, etc.	2,639,587	13·91
	18,968,605	100·0

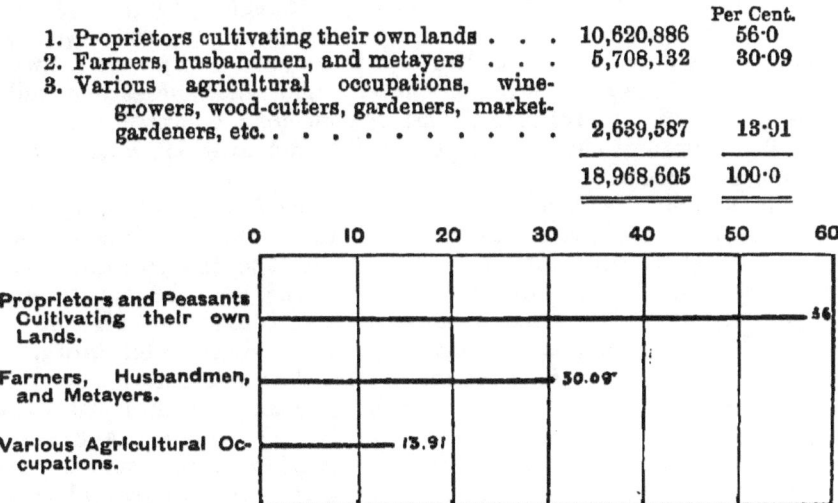

Diagram 45.—Agricultural Occupations.

This state of things emphasizes a fact long ago observed—the passion of the French peasant for the land. "The land is his mistress," says Michelet; and in order to possess her, he has made and is still making all the exertions possible to a man of narrow education.

This subdivision has had the advantage of inciting the peasant to work, and of giving him self-reliance. His bit of land makes him feel he is somebody, gives him solidity, and increases his powers of action and of resistance. But on the other hand, this subdivision keeps agriculture at the empirical stage. Our methods are those of our fathers—no machinery, no scientific processes, no engineers to reduce the productivity of the soil to a formula. At the same time, subdivision must give rise to association.

The peasant has long looked on machinery with suspicion; but he is beginning to see that there is some good in it. Drainage and irrigation are absolute necessities, and they cannot be done each on his own little plot; associations must inevitably be formed for the purpose. They have existed for centuries in the Vaucluse and the Bouches du Rhone. They will continue to multiply, and to consolidate isolated interests.

Moreover, the *bourgeois* proprietor is beginning to see that if the land which serves him as an investment has its advantages, it has also grave disadvantages for a man who looks for a return without troubling himself about it. The pride he took in treading his own soil is beginning to disappear. The railroads are making him a traveller, and breaking up his attachment to a particular spot. He finds personal property far more convenient than land, which involves draining and planting and legal proceedings; or houses, which he must look after and keep in repair, and with the tenants of which he cannot always keep on good terms. So he goes to the stockbroker instead of the notary, and takes shares in a railway or a mine, or buys into the *Rente Foncière*, a company based on the observation of this very psychological fact to which I have been drawing attention.

This tendency is so strong, that for the last few years it has somewhat checked the rise in the value of land. The small capitalist, who formerly farmed out his land, has sold it to the peasant. But the migration of the peasants to the towns, and the consequent scarcity of agricultural hands, must put a stop to the subdivision of the soil. The migrating peasant sells his share to his brothers, and seeks some other field for the capital thus obtained.

We may therefore predict a radical change within the next generation or two in the condition of landed property in France. Some legislative measures alone are wanting to facilitate it. In trying to find guarantees for landed property, we have really loaded it with burdens. We must learn to realise that land is just like any other utility, and make it just as easily transmissible. There is nothing utopian in this. The system has already been attended with complete success in Australia, and that under circumstances of the greatest difficulty.

The relations of property in a new country are complicated by the conflicting interests of stock-farming and agriculture. Everyone knows that the English law of conveyancing is a complete chaos. Mr. Torrens, a man of equal initiative and perseverance, has, by the Act known by his name, placed the law of real property on a perfectly simple basis. Its mechanism is briefly as follows. The Act is permissive; if a proprietor wishes to avail himself of it, he makes an application to the Registry Office, sending in with it his title deeds and a description and plan of the property. On the expiration of six months, during which any counter-claim may be put in, the Registry issues a certificate of title, in the form of a coupon bearing on it a small plan of the property with a list of all charges and mortgages on it. This certificate of title is transferable by simple endorsement; and if the title is afterwards disputed, the action must be brought against the Government. By this guarantee the proprietor's title is rendered unassailable.[1]

Since July 2, 1858, when it became law in South Australia, this Act has been successively adopted by Victoria, Queensland, and New South Wales.

The chief economic improvements yet to be introduced into our system of land tenure are these:—a greater security for land; the removal of all legal risks; the substitution of the registrar for the conveyancer; a system of registration paying its own costs, but not intended as a means of revenue; and the transmission of land by simple endorsement of the title-deed.

I know there are some people in France whose cry is for "the collective appropriation of the soil."[2] It is possible they may have some scheme drawn up ready for legislation, in which they define their meaning and explain how the thing is to be done; but if they have, they have so far kept it a secret. For my own part, I do not at present see how the collective appropriation of the soil is possible, except by means of syndicates and societies capable of improving the lands they possess. To occupy the land is not enough, it must be put to use; and in order to this, a large amount of circulating capital must be laid out in farm buildings, roads, drainage, irrigation, clearing, and manures, and in labour, whether human, animal, or mechanical.

As to any purely speculative questions with regard to the rights of property or persons, our previous observations have put them quite out of court.

Property is a necessary fact, for natural agents have no utility until they have been appropriated. So far, it is not land that has ever been wanting, but the power to utilise it.

Ricardo's theory of rent is based on a misstatement of facts. The least fertile, and not the most fertile lands are the first cultivated.

As civilisation advances, property becomes more and more individual and transferable.

---

[1] For further details see *Réforme Economique*, Sept. 15, 1877. Thanks to the courtesy of Mr. James Stansfeld, M.P., I have had access to some very rare Parliamentary papers bearing on this subject. I am now preparing a complete study of the scheme, with a view to its application in France.

[2] Declaration of the Congress at Marseilles, and of the Collectivist Congress at Havre.

CHAPTER II.

COMMERCE.

We have defined Exchange as the relation of utilities between themselves.[1]

We have said that its object is to bring the utilities possessed by one individual within reach of the wants of others.

The practice of exchange is called commerce. The word is compounded of *cum* and *merx;* to carry on commerce is to exchange. M. Charles Dunoyer did well to recall the derivation of the word, for it dissipates some false notions.

Trade has always been looked on as the domain of certain classes, who were long regarded with contempt. The Flaminian Law forbade the Roman patricians to trade. To evade this law, they traded through their slaves. In France, even at the present day, the civil population is, by virtue of this old prejudice, divided into traders and non-traders. The former are under a special jurisdiction, a special code, special burdens. No distinction could be more absurd. Are we not all trading every day of our lives, either as buyers or sellers? Are we not all dealers in something or other,—journalists, artists, labourers, land-owners,—selling our talents, our muscular strength, or the produce of our land?

Trade, then, is not an occupation confined to a few individuals, it is the constant occupation of the whole body of citizens in every country where civilisation is advanced enough for diversity of wants and division of labour.

Our needs are varied, and so are our capabilities. You have utilities of one sort, and I of another. Each of us wants some of the other's utilities. We exchange.

We find the same prejudice applied to trade, of which we have already spoken as applied to labour. Some people think that it is not productive of utility because it produces nothing new. True, but it places utilities within reach of the wants to be satisfied.

The trader is sometimes called a parasite. But he is the piston-rod of the engine. How would it work without him?

A Breton peasant has hens which lay him a dozen eggs. He does not want the eggs, and he does want other things. There is a great demand for eggs in Paris. If there were no traders to collect the eggs of a hundred such peasants, and send them to Paris, if there were no traders in Paris to buy them up and bring them within reach of the consumer, the Breton peasant must keep his eggs and the Parisian can have none to eat. It is very possible that the peasant sells his eggs too cheap, and that the Parisian buys them too dear; but this only shows that the organisation of com-

---

[1] Book II., chap. viii.

merce is defective, its machinery too complicated, and its friction too great. It does not show that commerce itself is useless.

The utility given is equal in value to the utility received; and hence some economists have argued that exchange produces no utility. They do not see that the utility I give is superfluous to me, and that the utility I receive is superfluous to the man who gives it me. A wine-grower produces several thousand gallons of wine. He cannot drink them all; if he cannot exchange them, he will produce only the hundred gallons or so necessary for his own consumption. Again, a manufacturer produces miles upon miles of cotton thread. He would never produce them if he could not exchange them. Every one makes, not what he wants, but what he can make best, and then exchanges it for what he wants.

Products are exchanged for products. The more a nation produces, the more outlets it opens to other nations. It is absurd to think you must ruin a country to make it buy your commodities. Once ruined, what has it left to buy them with? It is your interest that your neighbour should be rich. The trader's prosperity depends on the wealth of his customers.

Protectionist theories are now being once more dinned into our ears; they are set forth with the impudence of ignorance in our legislative assemblies, and they are so strong that even their opponents have to treat them with a certain respect.

"We must favour production," that is the cry. But why? Do we produce in order to produce? Are we to work for the sake of working, like the squirrel in his cage?

Cast your eyes over the world, what do we see? On the one hand, corn, cotton, cloth, iron, produced in great quantities; on the other hand, people who want all these things and have none of them — the producers anxious to sell, everybody else eager to buy, and yet the first selling less than they would like to sell, and the last buying less than they would be glad to buy. And then our profound financiers complain of "over-production!"

Is the world so gorged to repletion? Have we really more meat, and wine, and bread than we can find a use for? Is there no one in want of a shirt or a coat? Have we reached such a height of well-being that all wants are satisfied, and no fresh ones are forthcoming?

Far from it. In the first place, most men cannot satisfy their most primitive needs; and in the second place, men's needs are capable of indefinite expansion. It is absurd to speak of over-production except with reference to this or that particular place, where there is a lack of exchangeable products. The whole art of exchange lies in bringing together surplus products. To aid circulation, to open fresh outlets, to act as a channel of communication—this is the use of trade.

The effect of the opening up of new markets upon production has been well brought out by M. Courcelle-Seneuil.[1] In Adam Smith's pin factory, ten workmen turn out 48,000 pins a day. Now, supposing that there is not a sufficient demand for these 48,000 pins, it will be necessary to reduce the number of workmen, thereby reducing the division of labour, or else to shorten the hours of labour. In either case the labour will be less productive, and there will be a waste of force. If, on the other hand, there is a demand for 100,000 pins, instead of 48,000, there will be no corresponding increase in certain expenses, such as those of book-keeping; and thus there will be pure gain. Hence we may say,—

The cost of production is in inverse ratio to the extent of the market.

In the good old times, every kind of production formed the monopoly of some trade or guild. It was a privilege conceded by the king. When the discoveries of Columbus and the Portuguese opened up fresh fields to Europeans, every productive country, every object of consumption, became the exclusive monopoly of some company. From the 16th to the 18th century, the maritime trade of Europe was centred in the hands of about seventy privileged companies. At first these privileges may have had their use in stimulating enterprise; but later on, the companies, resting on their oars, gave themselves up to the one object of selling little and selling dear. Such is the necessary tendency of all similar organisations. It is the unavowed and perhaps unconscious aim of the modern protectionist.

The idea of free competition was unknown in France until the middle of the 18th century; and the honour of formulating it belongs to the physiocrats.

Competition involves activity, effort, conflict; but the apathetic cannot endure activity and effort; and in every contest the strong prevail, and the weak go to the wall. Yet in human history it has been the strong,—those who were first on the field,—who have demanded the suppression of competition, in order to banish all rivals from the territory they have acquired. The masters tried to forbid the journeyman the freedom of his craft. The existing companies try to prevent the consumer from buying cheap the articles they mean to sell dear. There never was a monopoly which was not to the advantage of the strong, and to the detriment of the weak.

The opponents of competition can have but one object—to secure the advantages they have acquired by birth or individual effort from being diminished by rivalry. They have no wish to improve their machinery or to produce better articles at a smaller cost;

---

[1] *Cours d'Economie Politique*, vol. i. p. 151.

they only want the *status quo*, but they want it all to themselves; they set their faces against all progress achieved from without.

Darwin speaks of the struggle for existence. It is the struggle for economic existence which has been the cause of all material progress. Competition rouses from the apathy of content, and unceasingly stimulates the effort to improve. It is the grand agent of evolution. Competition fixes the natural level of prices. The Protectionists raise endless discussions on cost price; but no one knows what it is, apart from competition.

There are not three manufacturers in ten whose articles have cost them precisely the same. Varying conditions make the cost price vary in almost every case. But it is fixed, so far as the purchaser is concerned, by competition; and the best managed factory gains more, and the worst managed factory gains less. The mean price, which represents the expenses and profits of the majority, is determined simply by the law of demand and supply, acting through competition.

Competition so enters into the very nature of things that whenever the Legislature has tried to put it down, its restrictions have been systematically evaded. Smuggling has never been looked on as a disgrace. Public opinion has held its own against authority.

The mercantile system, based on the theory of the balance of trade, dates in France from the time of Colbert; in England, from Cromwell; in Spain, from Philip II. Its aim was, to attract the precious metals into the country, and to prevent their going out of it. In spite of experience, it still forms a tenet of the protectionists.

Now, the following table shows that never has the importation of the precious metals been so great in France as since the conclusion of the treaty of commerce of 1860.

VALUE, EXPRESSED IN MILLIONS OF FRANCS.

	Imports.	Exports.	Excess of Imports over Exports.
1st decade, 1827–1836	1,809	697	1,112
2nd ,, 1837–1846	1,711	754	957
3rd ,, 1847–1856	3,563	2,244	1.389
4th ,, 1857–1866	6,877	5,025	1,852
5th ,, 1867–1876	6,479	3,007	3,472
Total	20,439	11,727	8,782
Average for the 50 years	409	235	176

Within this last period, the annual average movement of the precious metals has been,—

Imports	Fr. 647,000,000
Exports	300,000,000
Difference in favour of imports	Fr. 347,000,000

(See Diagram 46, p. 235.)

And it was during this period, which records an excess of three and a half milliards of import over export, that we paid the war indemnity of five milliards.

Then we hear of the American spectre, of the invasion of American corn, and the drainage of our gold. Truly the protectionists are somewhat given to metaphor. Here are the latest figures:—

	Imports.	Exports.
1877	Fr. 683,095,000	Fr. 141,194,000
1878	543,581,000	189,158,000
1879	332,016,000	424,351,000
1880	295,759,000	475,073,000

Thus, in the last two years, the custom-house returns attest an exportation of 899,000,000 francs and an importation of 627,000,000 francs, the difference being 272,000,000 francs. Now, during the last decade we had an excess of three and a half milliards of import; and during the last fifty years, an excess of 8,782,000,000! We see that it will be many years before the excess of our exports of the precious metals will occasion a serious monetary crisis.

But we owe this recent excess in imports, not to free trade, but to protection, which closes the United States against our products. But are the United States themselves the better for it? The ship which arrives at Havre from New York laden with corn, does but a bad stroke of business, if she gets nothing but a few bags of gold for her return cargo. What she wants is, not gold, but French products, on which her owners may make ten or twenty per cent., to the great advantage both of the French producer and of the American merchant and consumer. Exchange in money is but a make-shift. Even now, in debates on the customs, or in newspaper estimates,—even those which pass for reliable,—we constantly hear of the balance of trade; and when the total importation exceeds the total exportation, we are told that the balance of trade is against us. Yet, J. B. Say long ago [1] showed that in reality it is now just the reverse. And Bastiat has clenched the demonstration

---

[1] *Traité d'Economie Politique*, Book I., chap. xvii.

by a conclusive instance.[1] "A friend of mine, a merchant, having effected two transactions with very different results, I was curious to compare the way in which these results figured in his own books with that in which they figured in the custom-house returns.

"M. T. despatched a ship from Havre to the United States, laden with French commodities, principally what are called 'articles de Paris,' the declared value of which amounted to 200,000 francs. Arrived at New Orleans, it appears that the expenses incurred amounted to 10 per cent., and the various dues to 30 per cent. of the original value, which raised it to 280,000 francs. It realised a profit of 20 per cent., or 40,000 francs, and yielded a total of 320,000 francs, which the consignee converted into cotton. Charges for transport, insurance, commission, etc., on this cotton came to 10 per cent., so that on reaching Havre, the new cargo figured on the custom-house books at 352,000 francs. Lastly, M. T. sold the cargo for 422,400 francs, thus making a profit of 70,400 francs, or 20 per cent.

"Thus, there appeared in M. T.'s books, to the credit of the profit and loss account,—that is to say, as profit,—two items, one of 40,000 francs, and the other of 70,400 francs; and M. T. is quite sure that he is not deceived on this point.

"But how do the partisans of the balance of trade read the custom-house returns? They find that France has exported 200,000 francs and imported 352,000 francs, and conclude that she has squandered the profits of her past economies, that she has impoverished herself and is on the road to ruin, and that she has given away to the foreigner 152,000 francs of her own capital.

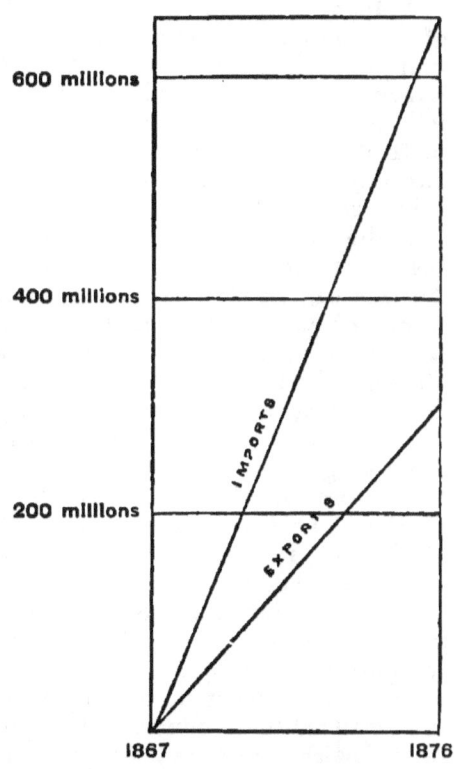

Diagram 46.—Average Annual Movement of the Precious Metals in France from 1867 to 1876.

"Some time after this, M. T. despatched another ship, also laden

[1] *Sophismes Economiques*, 1st series.

with 200,000 francs worth of the products of our national labour. But the unfortunate vessel foundered just outside the port; and all that remained for M. T. to do, was to enter the two following items on his books :

"'Sundries account owes to *x* 200,000 francs for the purchase of various articles despatched by the So and So.

"'Profit and Loss account owes to Sundries 200,000 francs for the total loss of cargo.'

"Meanwhile, the custom-house registers exports to the amount of 200,000 francs; and as there are no imports to register, it follows that the partisans of the balance of trade must see in this shipwreck a clear net profit to France of 200,000 francs. It also follows, according to this theory, that France has a very simple method at her disposal for perpetually doubling her capital; she has only to let her merchandise clear the customs, and then chuck it into the sea."

If the balance of trade is always to be in favour of this country, the French merchant must always lose by his foreign transactions. As this can hardly be the object he has in view, it is not to be wondered at if he does his best to turn the balance of trade against the country; and in this attempt he fortunately succeeds, despite all the efforts of the custom-house. Thus it is that in every European country, the imports exceed the exports, notwithstanding all that Governments can do to bring about the opposite result. According to the protectionist theory, the United Kingdom must be the poorest of all, for its imports for the years 1869-73, averaged £331,120,000; and its exports, £224,000,000; and in the year 1878 alone, its imports amounted to £328,000,000; and its exports to £192,000,000.

The protectionist idea of trade is all going out and nothing coming in; which is a violation of the very principle of exchange. Under the plea of encouraging home manufactures, they apply themselves very conscientiously to closing all outlets for them; for as produce is exchanged for produce, if foreign nations cannot sell their goods to us, neither are they likely to buy ours. England has boldly swept away all barriers without waiting for reciprocity. She has thrown open her gates to the enemy, to the great satisfaction of her own consumers—in other words, of her whole population; troubling herself very little at the excess of her imports over her exports.

Foreign Trade of the United Kingdom before and after the Reforms of Sir Robert Peel.

	Imports.	Exports.
1840	£62,000,000	£110,080,000
1850	152,320,000	115,800,000
Difference	£90,320,000	£5,720,000

Before and after the Treaty of Commerce with France.

	Imports.	Exports.
1860	£210,520,000	£164,520,000
1879	363,000,000	249,000,000
Difference	£152,480,000	£84,480,000

Reciprocity is one of those catch-words which are always springing up even among people who call themselves freetraders. The word is wrong in itself, for we do not exchange like products.

Moreover, it is our interest to be flooded with the products of other countries at a cheaper rate than we could produce them ourselves; and if other countries think fit to pay dear for our products, that is their own concern. We consume for ourselves, and it is our interest to buy cheap. Not only do the protectionists wish to keep foreign products out of their own country, they also ask for bounties to help them to inundate foreign countries with their goods; for their whole commercial policy is based on this precept, Do to others as you would *not* that they should do to you.

Every bounty on exportation is paid out of the pockets of the tax-payers, or at least of the consumers, of the country which pays it. And what for? To supply a foreign country at a cheaper rate than it could supply itself. It is simply making a present to your rivals.

At this moment, our sugar duties are levied in such a manner as to constitute a bounty on exportation,—with what result, we may learn from the following extract.[1] "This bounty may raise the price of beet-root; but the profit which will accrue from it to some Frenchmen will be paid by all. The whole nation is in fact doubly taxed. In the first place, the bounty, whether it cost £750,000 or only £360,000 a year, represents a very serious charge on all French

[1] Fawcett's *Free Trade and Protection.*

tax-payers. This tax, however, is only one part of their burden; for if the encouraging of this export raises sugar only a farthing per pound (and this is a very moderate estimate), the additional price which Frenchmen are compelled to pay is no less than £1,000,000 a year."

In England there is no tax on sugar, so that Englishmen can buy French sugar cheaper than their own. The English sugar-refiners grumbled, and demanded a tax on importation to neutralise our bounty; but public opinion found prompt expression in the *Times*. "The French are mad, with their export bounties. We are not going to match their folly with our own. Our refiners can take to some other industry; and our consumers, thanks to the sacrifices made by the French exchequer, will get their sugar cheap."

The cotton-manufacturers of Lille, with their coal on the spot, compete ruinously with those of Rouen, who have to fetch theirs by boat. Those in the Vosges have water-power at hand, but then their transport expenses are heavy; these three groups of cotton-spinners ought surely to be protected against each other. Nay more, the woollen trade may justly cry out against the competition of cotton clothing. Cotton is a foreign product; wool is a native product; why not be logical, and prohibit cotton?

The wood-fed iron-furnaces of Brittany have been forced to die out. If they had only had a good proscriptive tariff, prohibiting the importation into the province of coal-worked iron, they might have gone on to this day.

The protectionists may say, "We never talked any such nonsense." But the fact that they are demanding protection against Alsace and Lorraine, which were French provinces only yesterday, shows what they are capable of. Their logical ideal is, to confine the nation to their own factories. Notwithstanding the relations between the value of circulating and of fixed capital, they say, " If you want to make money, you must have high prices. Therefore, the prices of the circulating capital we produce must be artificially raised, and then we shall grow rich."

They forget that they themselves, as consumers, prefer to buy in the cheapest market. They forget another thing—that a factory can afford to reduce its profits almost indefinitely, so long as it can indefinitely multiply its products.

How could they overlook the simple fact, that, while manufactured articles have almost all fallen in value, manufactures themselves have risen? Can they not see that the masses are now the great consumers? When things are cheap, everybody buys; and everybody can afford to buy more than anybody.

But if prices are raised, consumption is checked, and production with it. Production being checked, all who were engaged in it are obliged to limit their consumption; and every fresh diminution in consumption re-acts on production. Ruin, misery, stagnation; this is what the protectionists are conscientiously and in all simplicity fighting for.

If their theory were true, it should be applied, not only to foreign produce, but to internal trade. The system must be re-established between province and province, and that even more strictly than before. Each commune ought to be self-sufficing. It should be protected against the competition of its neighbours.

On the same theory, the more difficulty we have in obtaining necessaries, the richer we are. We cannot too much admire the efforts people make to become poorer, with the idea of becoming richer. There is really no irony more cruel than that of the protectionist system; and, unfortunately, it does not confine itself to words. Its true followers belong to two classes,—the dupers and the duped. The dupes are ignoramuses, who find in this chimera the satisfaction of their need of something absurd to believe in. The subjective power of the human mind extends to everything must have its superstitions in economics, as in religion.

Commerce consists in bringing together the wants of man and the utilised forces of nature.

With subdivision of labour, individual labour grows more effective, outlets multiply, and the exchange of products becomes more necessary.

Every obstacle to freedom of trade hinders the fall of circulating capital, and, consequently, the rise of fixed capital.

The system of protection is therefore the best fitted to ruin a country.

CHAPTER III.

COMMERCIAL CRISES.

In Economy, as in all other social phenomena, psychological facts play an important part. It is because they have not been sufficiently taken into account that we have had so many erroneous explanations of commercial crises.

M. Juglar has written an interesting work on the subject. He enumerates, with some surprise, as the precursors of all commercial crises, the following symptoms: great prosperity; enterprises and speculations of all descriptions; a rise in the price of land and houses, in the demand for labour, and in wages; a fall of interest; a credulous public; and a taste for commercial gambling.

Of these facts Stuart Mill gives the following explanation. The accumulation of capital is limited by the rate of the profits it yields; if it becomes too plentiful, investors seek enterprises which offer larger profits. Then we have a break-neck race in speculation,

This explanation is an application of the law of Malthus to capital. Capital, being too abundant, risks and destroys itself, and this destruction restores equilibrium. Crises, on this theory, are a necessary evil; they are a natural check on the indefinite expansion of capital. Since there are no more wants in the world to be satisfied, since the entire population of the globe has reached the extreme limit of its powers of consumption, and no one any longer says, " I should like to be rich," it follows that there must be now and then a destruction of capital. The crisis clears the ground, and enterprise begins afresh.

Very able financiers concur in this view of the question. M. G. de Laveleye[1] says that there is nothing left to do in England, France, or Belgium. There are no new railways to make, no new canals to open. The great public works are completed. It is the same in Holland and Italy, and even in Spain, whose traditional indolence is now fully justified. In Germany, the means of production and transport are already too great, and clearly out of proportion to the possible requirements of the country. Asia, Africa, America, Oceania, have all reached their maximum production and consumption. Humanity has nothing to do but fold its arms.

And yet production goes on,—and production is ruin. There are too many producers and too few consumers. The glut of 1877 was not a momentary difficulty; it is a permanent and ever intensifying crisis.

Such is the theory of an eminent financier. Nor is it his own invention merely; many economists have broached it; and those who do not adopt precisely the same formula find complicated explanations, which all come to the same thing, and reinforce the protectionist cry of " over-production."

But then comes the question—Is every one comfortably fed and clothed and lodged? Is every member of the human family satisfied and content? Is nobody hungry any more, all the world over? You say,—

"The supposition is absurd; every one knows the contrary."

" Then the accepted explanation of commercial crises is equally absurd ? "

" Yes."

The true explanation of commercial crises has been given by Mr. Bonamy Price.[2] It agrees exactly with our view of the part played by fixed and circulating capital in production.

Why is production excessive? Because there is a falling off in the means of purchase.

And whence comes this falling off?

[1] *Du Caractère de la Crise Economique Actuelle.* Brussels, 1879.
[2] *Contemporary Review,* May, 1879.

It must be remembered that the power of purchasing lies in the possession of commodities, that money is simply a medium for the exchange of these commodities, and that the buyer can only procure the money by first selling his own commodities.

Every purchase made with money implies a previous sale of commodities in order to obtain this money; so that every purchase is only one-half of a transaction. A hatter sells a hat for a guinea, and with the guinea buys a pair of shoes; the hat is exchanged for shoes. It is the hat that has bought the shoes. Wholesale transactions clearly show that all purchasing power resides ultimately in commodities.

Whence then comes commercial depression? Surely from a want of commodities to exchange. Hence it is that trade becomes stagnant, factories work half time or not at all; the money-market is disturbed; banks and great commercial houses fail. It is all because there is a lack of commodities to buy with.

But how comes it that buyers and consumers have lost their purchasing power? Why have they fewer commodities to exchange? It is the consequence of a general fact, itself due to several possible causes. There has been an excess of consumption, more has been consumed and destroyed than has been replaced. It is this that has done the mischief, that has brought about a diminution of the stock of commodities to be exchanged, and so has reduced the consumers,—that is to say the purchasers,—to poverty.

Crises, therefore, do not spring from over-production, but from over-consumption.

But what is over-consumption? Are not all things made to be consumed? Yes. All products are consumed and destroyed, some very quickly, as food, coal, and such-like things; others very slowly, like machinery, buildings, ships, and fixed capital generally.

But here comes into play a distinction which explains the nature and essence of over-consumption. All articles of consumption divide themselves naturally into two classes, 1st, those which minister to production, and 2nd, those which minister to luxury and enjoyment. The difference between the two classes is this,—circulating capital applied to articles of the first class is consumed indeed, but it is reproduced by means of those articles, as the food and clothing of farm labourers, the manure put into the soil, and the wear and tear of ploughs are reproduced in the resulting harvest; circulating capital expended on luxuries,—say on hounds and whippers-in,—disappears and leaves nothing behind. We know that capital is the sum total of everything necessary to the production of wealth; and it is clear that if the capital thus destroyed is fully restored in the products realised, the productive power of the nation will remain intact, its wealth will be undiminished, its sales and purchases will go on as before, and there will be no sign of commercial depression. The prosperity of the country is untouched, because it has the same quantity of commodities to exchange. Now let us look at the other side of the question. Suppose that a portion of the capital destroyed is not replaced in products. The necessary consequence will be that, the producing power having fallen, there will be a real diminution of wealth. The country will now be poorer, because it has less to exchange. The reason is plain. The capital which was destroyed has been only in part restored; and this is true over-consumption.

It is said that bad harvests produce commercial crises; and this is true. But why? Because a bad harvest represents an excess of consumption. All the expenses of cultivation have been incurred, labourers and their families have had to be maintained, horses to be fed, carts and ploughs and raw material to be bought and used—is not all this consumption? A good harvest will replace all this consumption, and more than replace it; it yields a profit, and this profit is an increase of purchasing power. But, if the harvest is bad, then the things consumed in cultivation are not replaced by new products. There is a real destruction of capital. The purchasing power of the cultivator is diminished.

Now, look at the late crisis. There have been great famines in India and China, those important customers of England, and their purchases in Yorkshire and Lancashire have accordingly diminished; England herself has suffered from a series of bad harvests, and her agriculturists have had less power of purchasing manufactured articles. In France we see the same thing, as a consequence of bad harvests and vintages.

Adam Smith says that the main trade of every civilised nation is that which is carried on between town and country. In his time this was correct. It will become less and less so as machinery is more and more used in agriculture. At the same time, the agricultural population of France is, as we have seen, even now considerably in excess of the urban population. A bad harvest reduces their purchasing power; the manufacturers whose ploughs or whose stuffs they should have bought cannot get customers for their wares. They in their turn find their purchasing power diminished.

This loss may be represented by the following figure.

AGRICULTURE.

The purchasing power of the agriculturists is thus diminished 50 per cent.

But the manufacturer also has made advances of fixed capital reckoned to produce 100. The agriculturist can buy only 50.

INDUSTRY.

50 per cent of the power of this fixed capital is therefore wasted; and in this way the purchasing power of the industrial classes, both masters and men, is diminished in the same proportion, and they in their turn consume less of the produce of others.

Every one knows that water stands at the same level in vessels which communicate with one another. So here, a general fall proves the solidarity of all interests.

Nor is this all. When the harvest is bad, the consumer pays dearer for his corn and meat and wine. Even if his resources remained the same, their purchasing power is weakened. Thus the industrial production of the entire country is crippled.

The protectionists, whose ideal it is that the country should always pay famine prices for its corn and meat, apply themselves in all sincerity to ensuring a permanent crisis.[1]

War, again, represents a formidable excess of consumption, its operation being nothing but destructive. It withdraws a great number of men from productive labour—men who must be fed and clothed all the same, while they bring in no return for their consumption. It disturbs industry; it destroys roads, railways, and other appliances of industrial activity. All this is over-consumption. We are taxed now-a-days for the maintenance of vast armaments, not to create wealth, but to destroy it; the utilities they consume are for ever deprived of all purchasing power.

But to return. We have said that the eve of a crisis is invariably signalised by all the appearances of prosperity; industries multiply, railways are made, and great public works undertaken; capital is squandered in foolish investments. The economists and the public become alarmed, and we are warned against over-production. But it is really over-consumption.

You undertake great works; but the formation of fixed capital is itself over-consumption, for it represents an excess of consumption over production for a certain period, the difference being represented by the diminution of purchasing power during that time.

[1] See M. Menier's speech on free-trade in the Chamber of Deputies, Feb. 19th, 1880.

The work undertaken, the engine, factory, or other instrument of production, whatever it may be, will no doubt, in course of time, make up this loss, but gradually. The support of the workmen who build a ship is a temporary loss of wealth. They must consume food, and this does not at once bring in an increase of purchasing power.

Now, suppose the canal or harbour to have been made; in all this fixed capital there lies locked up a large amount of circulating capital. There results a temporary diminution of purchasing power. This phenomenon was remarked by Mr. Hyndmann, in that article on the bankruptcy of India which created such a sensation in England about the end of 1878. He pointed to the famine then devastating India, and cutting down her inhabitants by hundreds of thousands. What! cried the public, are there no railways, no irrigation works? Why have they not prevented this catastrophe? Not only have they not prevented it, they are partly responsible for it. They have been constructed by means of loans and taxes which have absorbed the whole circulating capital of the Indian population. Then comes the famine. The iron road brings down to starving Madras and Bombay the grain of the Punjaub and the North-west Provinces. But the purchasing power is gone; the people have not the means to buy the grain when it arrives, and they die of hunger.

In the same way Mr. Bonamy Price, in the article we have already referred to, explains the crisis in the United States. "We are now," he says, "in a position to perceive the magnitude of the blunder of which the American people were guilty, in constructing this most mischievous quantity of fixed capital in the form of railways. They acted precisely like a land-owner who had an estate of £10,000 a year, and spent £20,000 on drainage. It could not be made out of savings, for they did not exist; and at the end of the very first year he must sell a portion of the estate to pay for the cost of his draining. In other words, his capital, his estate, his means of making income whereon to live, was reduced. The drainage was an excellent operation, but for him it was ruinous. So it was with America. Few things, in the long run, enrich a nation like railways; but so gigantic an over-consumption, not out of savings, but out of capital, brought her poverty, commercial depression, and much misery. The new railways have been reckoned at some 30,000 miles, at an estimated cost of £10,000 a mile; they destroyed three hundred million of pounds worth, not of money, but of corn, clothing, coals, iron, and other substances. The connection between such over-consumption and commercial depression is here only too visibly that of parent and child.

"But the disastrous consequences were far from ending here. The over-consumption did not content itself with the wealth used up in working the railways and the materials of which they were composed. It sent other waves of destruction rolling over the land. The demand for coal, iron, engines, and materials kindled prodigious excitement in the factories and the shops; labourers were called for on every side; wages rose rapidly; profits shared the upward movement; luxurious spending overflowed; prices advanced all round; the recklessness of a prosperous time bubbled over; and this subsidiary over-consumption immensely enlarged the waste of the national capital set in motion by the expenditure on the railways themselves. Onward still pressed the gale; foreign nations were carried away by its force. They poured their goods into America, so overpowering was the attraction of high prices. They supplied materials for the railways, and luxuries for their constructors. Their own prices rose in turn; their business burst into unwonted activity; profits and wages were enlarged; and the vicious cycle repeated itself in many countries of Europe. Over-consumption advanced with greater strides; the tide of prosperity rose ever higher; and the destruction of wealth marched at greater speed."

Fixed capital is an implement of permanent value; but it repays not all at once, but little by little, after long use. Consequently, the formation of fixed capital implies a temporary destruction of capital, an excess of consumption, a decrease of purchasing power.

Take a railway, for instance. It has cost in wages and maintenance of labourers, and in materials of all sorts, say ten thousand pounds per mile. This £10,000 is for the time withdrawn from circulation. No doubt it will eventually be more than repaid, but it is a question of time. We see this going on in the United States. A crisis raged there for two or three years; by that time the capital consumed had been replaced, and the crisis came to an end.

Another point: fixed capital cannot be utilised if there is no available circulating capital. Ships and railways are useless if there are no commodities for them to convey; a factory cannot be worked unless there are consumers ready to buy its products. If, then, circulating capital has been so far exhausted as to take a long time replacing, fixed capital must meanwhile remain unproductive, and the crisis is so much the longer and more severe.

The simplest observation shows that the crisis of 1876–79 was due to no other cause. We have just seen how it was brought about in the United States. In Germany, it was owing to the frightful consumption of capital in fortresses and armaments, in which the Government has, by the help of the war indemnity, been able to indulge itself.

England, for her part, has been supplying circulating capital to the United States, Turkey, Egypt, and her own colonies. Some of these have become insolvent, and the others will take long to regain their purchasing power. Hence a crisis.

And this is only one side of the question. In economic matters there is always a reflex action to be taken into account. The English manufacturers, for instance, furnish India, Australia, and America with rails, engines, iron bridges, etc. The demand being considerable, they augment their means of production, and add the consumption of their own circulating capital to that of their customers. When purchasers fall off, they have no longer the circulating capital to employ their fixed capital. Thus, in 1873–4 the number of blast furnaces in England rose from 876 to 959. In 1878 only about half that number were at work.

All over-production is really over-consumption. The over-producer is one who begins by consuming, in wages and raw material, a sum which he afterwards fails to recover.

Superficial observers have seen only the last stage, and overlooked the first; and so they fall into the mistake of fancying, in full nineteenth century, that there is an excess of production, when, out of the thirteen hundred millions who people the globe, not one million perhaps are in a position freely to satisfy their wants.

Over-production may exist in particular industries, but it cannot exist in all at once. When all industries suffer simultaneously, it is from a very different cause, as we have already shown.

But the human mind is sluggish. The capitalist is seldom a man of initiative. The manufacturer, who is, is mostly guided in the choice of his product and in the method of producing it, not by thorough scientific observation, but by chance and personal inclination.

Man is an imitator. Certain manufacturers succeed, and immediately other manufacturers and other capitalists say, "Let us manufacture the same thing." They hardly think to inquire whether the manufacturers first in the field are not equal to satisfying the whole demand. This instinctive movement has the good effect of provoking competition, of stimulating innovations, and of cheapening the market; but these improvements are not effected without difficulty; and often the production of a particular thing is out of all proportion to its utility. Then the struggle for existence does its work. The weak disappear, the strong survive; and the former, not unnaturally, complain of over-production.[1]

Economic science, like all other sciences, has its commonplaces. Economists are accustomed to say that " Capital applies itself to the most profitable branches of trade, and rapidly abandons the less profitable." "Rapidly?" No, not quite. It does, no doubt, abandon them perforce after a long and often cruel struggle, but not till then.

Capitalists are like sheep; they must do as the rest do. Each takes his capital where every one else takes theirs, and then he is astonished at the congestion of capital.

[1] See, with regard to the psychological aspect of crises, the *Spectator*, for the 28th of December, 1878, p. 1628

Notwithstanding all the marvels which have been accomplished this century, we cannot conceal from ourselves that the industrial and commercial classes are largely creatures of routine. But if they cannot keep pace with changing wants and new economic conditions, they must take the consequences.

We have said that exchange is one form of division of labour; but our means of communication, much as they may have improved during the last half-century, are still far from perfect. Thus it happens that A manufactures an article which B may want. But in order that A may sell his article, it is not enough that B wants it. A must be able to find B.

Now, A may make a good many articles in the belief that somewhere or other there are Bs who want them. Jerome Paturot made millions of night-caps on the ground that there are millions of people in the world unprovided with them. But if Jerome Paturot's night-caps do not fall into the hands of those who use them, and if he cannot persuade those who do not use them that they are absolutely indispensable, he will simply have been guilty of over-production.

But if Jerome Paturot cannot make good the consumption which this production has entailed, he will fail, and his failure will make itself felt on all sides. It is a waste and destruction of capital. It is over-consumption.

Those persons—and there are a good many of them—who attach some mysterious power to money, say that money is the cause of crises.

"The determining cause of all these crises," says M. Emile de Laveleye,[1] "lies in the drain on the precious metals." This phrase just expresses the notion which has given the name of "money market" to the mechanism for the interchange of capital. The drain on the precious metals is an effect and not a cause. There is a demand for money; why? Because there are payments to be made, and the debtor has not commodities sufficient to pay with; or because the seller is in want of money, and insists on being paid in coin.

We have seen of what secondary importance money is in business transactions in ordinary times; but it is a vehicle, an intermediary. Now, foreign countries, or certain parts of the country, may have absorbed great quantities of money. India and Russia, for instance, having no use for English products, such as iron, machinery, or textile fabrics, require payment in gold for their cotton and their corn. Usually, this demand for gold is a symptom of distress in the country which makes it. It prefers it to manufactured articles, because it needs it for its internal consumption. If it is not to be

---

[1] *Le Marché Monétaire et ses Crises*, p. 193.

had in the country from which it is demanded, then there is first obstruction, and then stoppage, just as it would be if there were much traffic and a want of vehicles.

It has been said that crises arise from the excessive issue of bank notes. This was Sir Robert Peel's opinion. Mr. Tooke has proved by facts that in all cases of a rise or fall in prices, that rise or fall has preceded, and therefore cannot have been caused by, the increase or diminution in the issue of notes.[1]

Here, again, the effect has been taken for the cause. Paper obtains credit only when it is quite certain that it can be reduced to money. Here the psychological question recurs. Those who ask for the money do not want to keep it, they only want to have it for a moment in order to exchange it for other products. The absence of money is of importance only so far as it shows that there is a difficulty in procuring it, and that this difficulty arises from an interruption in the exchange of products which might have procured the money, or have rendered it unnecessary to have recourse to money at all.

The assignats, which occasioned such a fearful crisis, represented excellent value, viz., land; but it was fixed capital, not readily transformable into circulating capital, which was what every one was wanting at the moment. But metal money may be abundant during a violent commercial crisis. It is the story of the miser dying of hunger in the midst of his gold. The crisis of 1857 occurred eight years after the immense discoveries of gold in California. It had nothing to do with an absence of gold; but the Crimean War had produced over-consumption, a bad harvest had aggravated this over-consumption, there was not circulating capital enough to carry on production, and there were therefore no products to exchange.

Bagehot advises the banks to lend as much money as possible during times of panic. Panic arises from the idea that you have no money. You must show that you have. Once produce this conviction, and the drain of gold will stop of itself as soon as the sums it was intended to pay are paid; and the natural interchange of products again begins to work.

The merchants,—who, to a certain extent, understand these things, —have sometimes faced them with surprising heroism.

In 1797 the Bank of England suspended cash payments; in 1811 the Government gave forced currency to its notes, and this regulation lasted down to 1822. Following the example set them by their fathers under analogous circumstances in 1745, the merchants, bankers, manufacturers, and ship-owners of London immediately called a meeting, in which it was decided that they would in no

[1] *History of Prices.*

case refuse to receive bank-notes in payment of sums due to them, and that they would do their utmost to effect their own payments in the same manner. It is for scientific history to render homage to these nameless heroes.

Even crises have had their apologists. A correspondent in *The Times* of the 11th of January, 1879, congratulated the United States on the crisis they were then undergoing. Up to 1875 all expenditure, both public and private, had been recklessly increased. Then came the crisis, and every one reduced his expenditure within proper limits. "Retrenchment" was the order of the day in public business; sinecures were abolished; unnecessary public works were abandoned. The expenses of New York State had amounted in 1874 to £3,500,000; in 1878 they were reduced to £1,500,000, out of which £115,000 were put aside to pay off the debt.

There is some truth in the idea that sorrow has its uses. We do not begin to take care of ourselves till we find ourselves thoroughly ill. But sometimes it is then too late.

Even statesmen are constantly encouraging the destruction of capital. They fancy that prodigality promotes trade. Fêtes, balls, the building of palaces—all this is good for trade. The construction of the fortifications round Paris was good for trade. They do not see that they are creating a waste of circulating capital which is never reproduced; and which, thus consumed, loses all purchasing power. They will say next that war affords a good outlet; so it does, in a sense, and so does a sieve. The capital thus swallowed up can create no further demand for labour. Man himself, therefore, falls in value; wealth decreases; and a crisis follows, more or less intense, more or less prolonged, but always, and in any case, disastrous.

Hence: *Commercial and financial crises are produced, not by over-production, but by over-consumption.*

CHAPTER IV.

BANKS.

I HAVE said that credit is analogous to transport.[1] The one tends to annihilate time, and the other to annihilate space. But the language of Economy is still far from exact, inasmuch as it has given to the word "credit" an unforeseen extension of meaning, not only setting aside its etymology,—which would not much signify,—but including under the term a range of functions not strictly of the same nature.

Thus, the institutions which deal with credit may carry on operations of a very varied character.

[1] Book II., chap. vii.

They may take upon themselves the charge of the precious metals, bonds, and securities, or guarantee a certain standard of coin. These are simply measures of security.

Or they may undertake the more economical transfer of bullion. Here they touch upon the domain of transport, since the object is to surmount the obstacle of distance.

Or, lastly, they may make it their business to discount bills, to make advances, and to defray loans; and here their object is to economise time.

All the institutions which carry on all or any of these operations are included under the name of *Banks*.

Adam Smith[1] has admirably described the functions of banks during the seventeenth century, in small States such as Hamburg or Genoa. They had nothing to do with discounting, nor with the custody of money, nor even with saving the transport of money. They concerned themselves only to procure good money.

In order to understand this, we must imagine a little State enjoying a great trade, like Genoa, Hamburg, or Amsterdam. It receives from the neighbouring States all sorts of worn and clipped money to such an extent that, at Amsterdam, the current coin was depreciated 9 per cent. As soon as a good coin appeared, it was melted down and exported; and the consequence was, that as good money was not always to be had for paying bills of exchange, the value of such bills fluctuated in a manner very injurious to the interests of commerce. " In order to remedy these inconveniences, a bank was established in 1609, under the guarantee of the city This bank received both foreign coin and the light and worn coin of the country, at its real intrinsic value in the good standard money of the country, deducting only so much as was necessary for defraying the expense of coinage and the other necessary expense of management. For the value which remained after this small deduction was made, it gave a credit in its books. This credit was called bank money, which, as it represented money exactly according to the standard of the mint, was always of the same real value, and intrinsically worth more than current money. . . . The money of such banks (*i.e.* Venice, Genoa, Amsterdam, Hamburgh, and Nuremberg,) being better than the common currency of the country, necessarily bore an agio, which was greater or smaller according as the currency was supposed to be more or less degraded below the standard of the State. The agio of the Bank of Hamburgh, for example, which is said to be commonly about 14 per cent., is the supposed difference between the good standard money of the State and the clipped, worn, and diminished currency poured into it from all the neighbouring States."

---

[1] *Wealth of Nations*, Book IV., chap. iii.

To this very important function of creating a good coinage was added next that of the custody of money. The bank guaranteed the money entrusted to it against fire, thieves, and other accidents. Then came another question—the saving of time and space. It was no longer necessary to count or carry the money; a simple transfer on the books was enough.

The Bank of Amsterdam did not lend out the smallest part of the moneys deposited with it. For every florin for which it gave credit on its books it paid the value of a florin in money or bullion. Existing, as it did, for the public service, and not for its own profit, it was placed under the care of the four burgomasters. Such was one form of the primitive bank.

The Italian banks were financial companies for lending money to the Governments of their respective cities. It was not till later on that they undertook commercial banking operations.

The need of security led to the formation of deposit banks. The English merchants used to place their money in the Tower of London, until Charles I., without consulting them, seized £200,000 under pretence of a loan. The merchants withdrew the rest, and adopted the custom of placing it with the goldsmiths, a custom still maintained in Liverpool. It is this need of security which now leads to enormous sums being deposited in the Banks of England and France.

If a bank of issue allows interest on deposits, it must find employment for them.

In order to economise the transport of money or commodities, antiquity itself invented the bill of exchange. It was known in Athens, and at Rome. It was in constant use in the fourteenth century. One of the most important parts of a banker's business is that which deals with bills of exchange.

The late Professor Stanley Jevons recounts the expedients used as substitutes for metal money:—[1]

1. The replacement of standard money by representative money.
2. The intervention of book-credit.
3. The cheque and clearing system.
4. The use of foreign bills of exchange.
5. The international clearing system.

The list is not in chronological order, for the bill of exchange preceded the cheque. The London and Westminster Bank, the first deposit bank that issued cheques, dates from 1834. The cheque has only been used in France since 1865, and is hardly yet acclimatised.

Yet the idea is very simple. Two people have business relations, sometimes buying, sometimes selling. They see that it is a waste

---

[1] *Money*, p. 190.

of labour to be constantly sending money to and fro between th(
It is only necessary to pay the difference, if there is any.

Now, since merchants are in the habit of depositing their mo)
in common centres, a simple transfer on the books is all that
required. The cheque is an order to transfer. The bit of pa
that A gives to B means that the sum which has so far stood
the credit of A shall henceforth stand to the credit of B.

In England a system of compensation was established betw
the banks before the use of cheques was introduced. The Cleari
house was established in 1775, to avoid the carriage of money, s
to save the rounds of the bank clerks. Twenty-six banks, acting
their own initiative, and without legal intervention, formed a priv
association, meeting in a common room. In 1810 the associa
banks were forty in number; they are now only twelve, but
tremely powerful. They effect a daily settlement on paper amount
to £20,000,000. This represents a weight in gold money of
tons, and in silver money of 2,500 tons. Not a single shill
passes; all differences are settled by drafts on the Bank of Engla

Here is a real bank of exchange, which Proudhon would h
done well to study, instead of dreaming of one of his own.

In 1858 Sir John Lubbock and Mr. W. Gillett organise(
clearing-house system for the provinces. This system is v
simply explained by Professor Stanley Jevons, in the follow
diagram :—

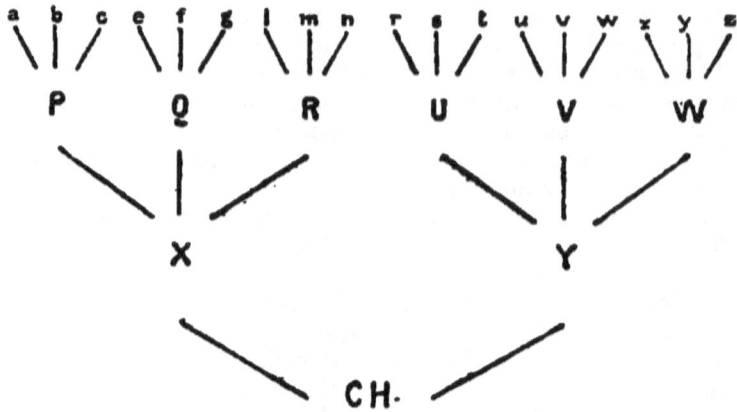

Diagram 47.—The Provincial Clearing-house System.

Every country bank has a current account with some bank
London; and all the London banks settle their mutual transacti
daily through the Clearing-house. It follows that a payment

¹ *Money*, chap. xxi.

e effected between persons in different parts of the country, *viâ* London. In Diagram 47 let P, Q, R, be country banks, having a London agent X; and let U, V, W, be other country banks, having London agent Y. If P's customer *a* wishes to make a payment to U's customer *r*, he sends him by post a cheque on his banker '; and *r*, on receiving it, has it carried to his account by U, who, having no direct communication with P, sends it to Y, who presents it to X through the medium of the Clearing-house. X debits ' with the amount, and advises him by the next post. Nothing could be more simple than this arrangement.

The institution of clearing-houses is spreading. They have them at Manchester and Newcastle, but, oddly enough, not at Liverpool, which has not adopted cheques, but prefers to use bank-notes and money. It is a local custom of the trade.

The New York Clearing-house dates from 1855, includes fifty-nine banks, and does an enormous business. A Clearing-house was established by some bankers in Paris on the 18th of March, 1872. The following is a table of its operations up to the 31st of March, 1880:—

	Francs.
1872–1873	1,602,584,727·51
1873–1874	2,142,902,845·48
1874–1875	2,009,740,692·50
1875–1876	2,213,724,860·58
1876–1877	2,598,607,894·42
1877–1878	2,199,593,418·67
1878–1879	2,628,243,743·21
1879–1880	3,222,745,255·48
	18,617,543,437·85

In 1842 Robert Stephenson and Morison established a sort of Clearing-house for settling accounts between railway companies.

In 1874 the London Stock Exchange Clearing House was started, for the purpose of balancing, not sums of money, but quantities of scrip between the various brokers. It must be observed that the amounts transferred represent only 10 per cent. of the business actually settled.

We see then that these institutions all aim at substituting for the use and transport of coin a simple transfer on paper. We may say that *the circulation of a country develops with the decrease of the use of money, in proportion to the extent of its business.*

It is one aspect of the fact we have already remarked, that *industrial progress consists in obtaining the greatest possible inverse proportion between the consumption of circulating capital and the return of fixed capital.*

We have just seen that banks fulfil three important functions; procuring good money, taking care of money, and economising the use and transport of money. In the performance of these three functions, they are aided by paper money in various forms:—bills of exchange, cheques, and bank-notes; a bank-note being a kind of cheque payable to the bearer without endorsement.

But banks have another important function, that of credit properly so called. They facilitate loans between A, who does not know what to do with his money, and B, who wants it for immediate use. For this purpose they use paper money, discounting drafts, and notes payable to order, which are promises to pay. And lastly, for some years past, they have absorbed as much capital as possible, have issued notes, subventioned large enterprises, and lent credit to embarrassed States.

The profit derived by the bank from all these transactions of every sort is a commission.

The bankers, rich as they are, do not work on their own resources.

The real source of their profits is the confidence they inspire. The banker is a broker between manufacturer and capitalist, and between trader and trader. His profits are in inverse ratio to the capital required. The capital itself is simply a concession to public opinion.

Discounting consists in cashing engagements contracted on account of actual industrial operations.

Discounting in London includes two functions, 1stly, the procuring money for country bankers, by discounting their paper when they are obliged to borrow, which seldom happens; 2ndly, the country bankers having almost always, on the contrary, too much money, the London bill-broker finds employment for it in discounting commercial bills. According to a statement of Mr. Richardson, one of the principal bill-brokers in London in the early part of this century, the second kind of business is fifty times as extensive as the first.

It is not necessary to go into the details of banking. We have said enough to indicate its two leading features. It now remains to consider the great question of the national banks of France and England.

The Act of 1844 divides the Bank of England into two branches; the Banking Department proper, and the Issue Department, whose sole function is to issue bank-notes not exceeding in the aggregate £15,000,000 on Government securities in the vaults of the Bank.

Nothing could be more unscientific than this distinction; for the use of bank-notes ought to vary with the discounting of bills of exchange.

I borrow the following balance-sheet from Mr. Bagehot's work; but it would be easy to draw up a similar table from the accounts published every Wednesday.

Issue Department.

Notes issued £33,288,640	Government debt . . .	£11,015,100
	Other securities	3,984,900
	Gold coin and bullion . .	18,288,640
	Silver bullion	0
£33,288,640		£33,288,640

Banking Department.

Proprietors' capital . . £14,553,000	Government securities .	£13,811,953
Rest 3,103,301	Other securities	19,781,988
Public deposits, including Exchequer, Savings Banks, Commissioners of National Debt, and dividend accounts . . 8,585,215	Notes	10,389,690
	Gold and silver coin . .	907,982
Other deposits 18,204,607		
Seven day and other bills 445,490		
£44,891,613		£44,891,613

Thus, out of the total number of bank-notes in circulation, £15,000,000, issued on the National Debt and other securities, are guaranteed by the State, and £18,288,640 are issued on gold coin and bullion. The Bank can in no way augment the circulation. All other notes issued by it must be guaranteed by specie. Such is the "iron system" "which ruins us," say its opponents, "which saves us," say its advocates.

Now, no bank in or out of London, except the Banking Department of the Bank of England, possesses any considerable sum in specie or negotiable securities, beyond what is required in every-day business.

On Dec. 29, 1869, the Debit Account of this department was as follows:—

Public deposits	£8,585,200
Private deposits	18,204,600
Bills at seven days and others . . .	445,480
	£27,235,280

The Credit Account showed a reserve in legal currency of:—

Bank notes	£10,389,690
Gold and silver coin	907,982
	£11,297,672

This is the entire reserve in legal currency, with which, according to law, the Banking Department faces a debit nearly three times as great. It has no other ready money.

All the other London banks deposit their principal reserve with the Bank of England. It is the bankers' bank. The reserve of the Bank of England (averaging, between 1866 and 1873, £10,000,000), is the whole of the money at disposal for meeting the debts of Lombard Street. Nay, more; as all the country banks send their money to London, the money in the vaults of the Bank of England forms not only its own reserve, but that of all the banks in the country. Nor is this all. Ever since the Franco-German war, London has become the clearing-house of Europe. The Bank of England reserve has therefore to face the contingency of a demand or immediate payment all over Europe.

All the banks depend on the Bank of England; all the merchants depend upon the banks; the reserve of the Bank of England is their sole guarantee; and this guarantee the directors of the Bank have a constant tendency to reduce in order to pay larger dividends to their shareholders.

The London and Westminster Bank holds a reserve of only 13 per cent. of its deposits. The Bank of England reserve is over 40 per cent. Hence it will be easily understood that there is a great difference in the rate of profits, and that the shareholders of the Bank of England are constantly complaining and urging the directors to diminish it. Thus the whole gigantic structure of English credit rests on the Bank of England. It is a pyramid standing on its apex. Besides, the interests of directors and shareholders clash with those of the public; while the mode of appointment of the directors themselves affords no adequate security for their competency.

Nevertheless, no one imagines that the Bank of England can fail. It is a sort of fetish. Its solvency is an article of faith. It makes no difference that in 1797 it suspended payment, that it very nearly did so again in 1825, and that in 1839 it was only saved by a loan from the Bank of France. Three times since 1844 Peel's Act has had to be suspended:—in 1847, because its reserve had fallen to £1,994,000; in 1857, because it had fallen to £1,502,000; and in 1866, because it had fallen to £3,000,000. But what does it signify? It is an accepted fact. The Bank can never fail.

We are here in presence of the same psychological fact which explains the existence of so many an old and abominable institution. People believe in it. People are used to it. It is the same force of custom which everywhere preserves so much that is bad and useless.

Mr. Inglis Palgrave, in his *Notes on Banking*, reckons that the sum total of bank-notes and specie in the hands of the bankers of the

United Kingdom does not amount to more than four or five per cent. of their engagements.

The entire credit of England is thus based on a fiction, though of course every one is convinced that the trading classes and their customers will never need to draw out at one moment the twentieth part of the money of which they are entitled to draw the whole.

In France, the law of 1791 proclaimed liberty of labour and of internal trade. Several banks were founded; they inspired confidence notwithstanding the terrible cataclysm of the assignats: credit was established; and they met with a success which proved their ruin. Their success tempted the Government. Bonaparte thought to manage business as he would manage a battalion. He wrote to Count Mollien, "The Bank must always discount bills at 4 per cent." To him banking seemed a department of Government, an engine of credit. The capital on which he started it was the privilege of coining money.

Such were the doctrines which inspired the law of the 24th of Germinal in the year XII. of the Republic, to which the Bank of France owes its origin. The Government converted a part of its capital into Government stock, which the Bank could not sell without its authority. It took possession of the rest, and gave drafts on the receivers-general in forced exchange. Out of an amount of 97,000,000 francs, discounted in 1805, 80,000,000 were composed of securities of this sort.

As long as the Empire lasted, the Bank was commercially useless. All its capital was engaged in Government funds, and was returned on deposit to guarantee loans at three months compulsorily renewed. While it had 128,000,000 francs thus absorbed, it had less than 18,000,000 francs in commercial bills.

On January 18, 1814, the Bank inflicted losses to the extent of 12 per cent. on the holders of its notes. As to its shareholders, they realised under the first Empire profits amounting to 90,000,000 francs.

Under the Restoration the Bank continued its relations with the Government, with the result that in 1818 it was obliged to reduce the date of maturity of its bills from sixty to forty-five days, and a crisis ensued. Still it continued its connection with the State. In 1825, the Duke de Gaeta expressed his great regret at "the deprivation of the extraordinary advantages which the Bank has derived in previous years from the service of the State." The Revolution of 1830 renewed these advantages. In 1833 M. Odier said in his report, "The Bank must seek every opportunity of extending its relations with the Government."

But now observe what took place. The Bank wished to remain a Parisian bank, doing important business with the State. But local banks were founded at Lyons, Marseilles, Havre, and Lille;

while Orleans, Amiens, Dijon, and Toulouse presented the statutes of their banks for approval. What was the Bank to do? It got the Council of State to sanction the principle that every local bank should be limited to its own locality, and no external communication allowed.

The Bank Charter expired in 1843, but was renewed for twenty-four years. Branches were established in various towns; but they were simply discount houses. The Bank made no increase in its capital in order to supply them.

The amount of business steadily increased. In 1846 the total money reserve consisted of current accounts belonging to the public and the Treasury, which were liable to be withdrawn at any time.

During this year the reserve fell to the extent of 172,847,000 francs. M. d'Argout ascribed this fact to the dearth of provisions; but the figures bear no relation to the importation of grain. M. Grandin explained the matter more correctly in the Chamber of Deputies. The Ministry had abruptly withdrawn its deposits. The Bank had sent out 110,000,000 francs in coin for the benefit of the bankers, who were using it to tender for foreign loans; and the public had withdrawn its money to invest in railways.

During the year 1847 the Bank was put to all sorts of shifts, none of which, however, proved prejudicial to its shareholders.

Then came the Revolution of 1848. Between the 26th of February and the 14th of March the reserve fell from 140,000,000 francs to 70,000,000; on the evening of the 15th there remained only 59,000,000. The vicious nature of the system became apparent. The Bank had 125,000,000 francs due to the Treasury, which required them. Its liabilities amounted to 305,000,000 francs, while its main asset was 1,170,000 francs of Rentes, which it could not negotiate without causing a panic. A forced currency was established, and a decree of the 27th of April united all the departmental banks with the Bank of France.

Fresh privileges were conferred by a decree of the 3rd of March, 1852, providing for the extension of the Charter, which was to expire in 1867; and in that year it was extended until 1897. The Bank will probably within the next five or six years propose a further renewal. The whole question will then have to be thoroughly dealt with.

In 1857 the Bank obtained the privilege of raising its rate of discount above 6 per cent. In 1861, it profited by this concession to raise the rate to 10 per cent. The Government then reassured public opinion by an inquiry, which has so far only resulted in six quarto volumes, entitled *Enquête sur la Circulation Monétaire*.

We must here briefly explain the operations carried on by the Bank, and the objections raised during the inquiry.

The business of the Bank of France consists in :—

1. Discounting bills on Paris or on towns where the Bank has branches, drawn at not more than three months, and bearing three endorsements—or two only where it is a *bonâ fide* trade transaction, but in that case accompanied by a transfer of Government stock, bank shares, or receipts for goods.

2. Making advances on French Government stock, payable within a fixed or an indefinite period ; on French railway shares and debentures ; on bonds of the Crédit Foncier and the city of Paris ; and on deposits of a value of 12,000 francs at least, in bullion or in gold and silver coin.

3. Issuing bills payable at sight and to bearer, and bills transmissible by endorsement.

4. Taking charge, on payment of a consideration, of national bills and securities, and French or foreign stock, and to receive payments on account of them payable in Paris.

5. Receiving on current account moneys paid into it and bills on Paris, and carrying out instructions respecting them to the extent of the amounts in its hands.

6. Issuing bills payable to order at the branch banks.

Now, what ought to be the chief object of a national bank ? To assist the operation of credit between individuals, and to facilitate exchange by negotiating bills.

But, advances on Government stock and other securities do less good to trade than to the speculators, who borrow on the securities they deposit, and with the advances thus obtained purchase fresh securities and begin again. When money is plentiful, the Bank advances freely, and its shareholders profit at the expense of the rate of discount. When money is scarce, the Bank finds it necessary to husband its resources, and raises its rate of discount.

It is a curious fact, and one which proves how little economic questions are understood, that several witnesses at the inquiry proposed that the Bank should have a uniform rate of discount !

The Bank has always opposed the issue of bank-notes for small sums. If it has now and then allowed the practice for a moment, it has always suppressed it on the first opportunity.

In an ordinary transaction only two signatures are necessary, the buyer's and the seller's. But the Bank requires three signatures. The real contracting parties have therefore to pay a third. It is true that a decree of 1868 facilitated the discounting of bills with two signatures, by authorising the Bank to accept as security, in lieu of the third signature, the deposit, not only of its own shares or of Government scrip, but also of any sort of securities on which it ordinarily makes advances.

The Bank has the right of curtailing the period which bills have to run. Such a right is absolutely revolutionary. It has also the right arbitrarily to refuse the paper of any house it chooses; and from this decision there is no appeal, though the motive may have been nothing but caprice, rancour, or political hostility. It is said that it never abuses these extravagant powers. Perhaps; but that would only show that the men are better than the system.

It is, of course, a bold thing to attack the Bank of France. We shall be told of the immense services it rendered during the war, and of the 1,485,000,000 francs it lent to the Government. But suppose the Bank had never existed, would France herself have been the less wealthy? Not in the least. The Government would have gone elsewhere for the money, that is all. We may rest assured that the Bank had the best of the bargain. For it is the peculiar advantage of this half-public, half-private institution, that it flourishes best during times of trial and disaster. A glance at its dividend will prove this.

In 1846, the shareholders received the highest dividend they had ever had, viz., 159 francs; in 1847 they had 177 francs. The dividend of 1869 was 107 francs; then came the war, and in 1870 the dividend was 114.

Troubles accumulated, and the dividend rose in 1871 to 300 francs, and in 1872 to 320. Prosperity returned; in 1878 the dividend had fallen to 95 francs; in 1879 it was 110.

M. Thiers said, in June, 1871, that "the Bank, by its services to the State, had covered itself with honour." We have seen that while deserving well of its country, it had deserved still better of its shareholders.

In reality, the Bank of France has no capital at all; for what capital it has is locked up or invested in Government funds. For meeting its engagements it has nothing but deposits of coin which may be withdrawn any day. Its reserve, which seems so large, may vanish at any moment. It is therefore purely fictitious.

This rapid sketch of the position of the national banks of England and France suffices to show on what an anomaly the entire credit—and consequently the whole industrial and commercial system—of the two countries rests. It is the monarchical idea applied to credit. The Government has thought proper to exercise a royal prerogative on the traffic in paper money. Its interference has done nothing but harm; for by concentrating all responsibility on a single establishment, by making it the sole reservoir of money in the country, and by inspiring the erroneous belief that no storm, however terrible, can ever sink it, the State has carefully paved the way for the very catastrophe it seeks to avoid. By mixing up public and private finance, it still further complicates the situation and adds to the danger.

Statesmen, who are rarely economists, have always been unwilling to admit this fact—that a bank-note is nothing more than an ordinary commercial bill or bond. It is not a substitute for money, but for other paper. The bank-note represents the endorsement by the bank of the note issued; only, as the bank's signature is at present good and universally known, the note is negotiable, on the sheer understanding that the bank is pledged to pay it in cash on presentation.

Now, as we have just seen, this obligation on the part of the national Banks of France and England is not enforced by any adequate sanction. Nevertheless, they go on, and it is only once in a decade or two that they fail to keep their engagements,—which, for a public institution, is not bad.

It is true they have a comparative stability; but what does it come from? Not from their capital, not from the money they have in hand; it rests entirely on their notes and on public opinion.

Accordingly, it is not the public who lean on the bank, as is generally supposed; it is the bank which leans on the public. When the bank is ruined, it is the public who save it.

This being so, what can be urged against freedom of banking?

A banker—a bill-broker if you will—thinks proper to issue notes payable at sight to the bearer. What risk is there? Since the notes are at sight, he is always bound to give cash for them, or he may as well close his bank at once; and banks are not usually opened to-day to be closed to-morrow.

The admirers of monopolies are always boasting of what monopolies have done; they take no account of what monopolies have hindered.

If with a reserve of £1,000 the banker can issue notes up to £4,000, he obtains from the public £3,000, for which he pays no interest, and puts it out at, say, 5 per cent. by discounting bills at that rate. It is his interest to keep as many notes as possible in circulation; and, as all other banks are similarly interested, there results a far greater extension of credit than could have been effected by a monopoly.

This monopoly is so contrary to the nature of things, that, notwithstanding all the protection enjoyed by the Bank of France, business tends to desert it, and to betake itself to the great financial companies, which accumulate deposits in their safes, and take up bills below the bank rate of discount.

On all accounts it is desirable to distribute the risks as much as possible; but the organisation of the national banks of England and France aims at concentrating them. The following remark of Mr. Bagehot's shows his appreciation of this: "The use of credit is, that it enables debtors to use a certain part of the money their creditors have lent them. If all those creditors demand all that money at once, they cannot have it, for that which their debtors have used is for the time being employed, and not to be obtained."[1]

Now, the bankers have come to regard reserves in cash as almost superfluous; there are scarcely any except at the national banks. If a panic supervenes, the entire strain is borne by the Bank. The least symptom is enough to disturb the Bank of France. Notwithstanding its enormous reserve, we have seen it raise its rate of discount in 1879 and in 1880; and the slightest rise impedes circulation.

We may therefore conclude that:—

The Bank of England and the Bank of France base the whole organisation of credit in the two countries respectively on a perilous fiction.

Freedom of issue by all banks ought to be substituted for the existing monopoly.

CHAPTER V.

PUBLIC COMPANIES AND ASSOCIATIONS.

IN primitive societies the strong impose their will on the weak, and compel them to minister to pleasures which they keep to themselves. All arrangements made by authority have been made in this spirit. The master is a military or religious chief. He commands, the rest obey. Women are the first slaves, captives are the next. Castes are formed. In India the Brahmin has a right "to all that exists." The Sudra owes him obedience, must keep nothing for himself, cannot accumulate. We are told that Joseph said to the Egyptians, "Behold, I have bought you and your land for Pharaoh." In all primitive civilisations we see authority imposed by the stronger or the cleverer—which comes to the same thing—on the weaker and more credulous.

As wants and capacities alike grow varied, the necessity of exchange is forced on the individual and the community. Exchange is a contract freely entered into. Little by little, by the force of things, contract takes the place of prescription. This characteristic appears very strongly amongst the Athenians—a nation of merchants and sailors. When an Athenian undertook to supply a native of Smyrna or Miletus, the one thing of importance was, that the engagement should be punctually and exactly carried out. It mattered not to the one contracting party who the other might be. Fidelity to engagements is the sole basis of trade; agreements and contracts have nothing personal in their character; they are absolutely *real*, using the word in its strict etymological sense.

[1] *Lombard Street*, p. 55.

Accordingly, in the ancient world it is in the Greek commercial cities, and especially in Athens, that we find the liveliest sense of individual rights.

In Rome, the individual was absorbed in the State ; his personality and his interests are ill-defined. Still, the associations which farmed the revenues appear to have had something in common with our joint-stock companies, whose distinguishing feature is the concerning themselves with interests irrespective of persons. But the object which the old revenue-farming companies had in view was neither commercial nor industrial; they were the mere agents of the State, taking upon themselves the ungrateful but profitable task of collecting the taxes.

The monks of the West were real industrial and commercial societies.[1] In times when public security was almost unknown, they placed themselves and their property under the protection of religion. Their capital and energy formed a common stock; they undertook public works, they cleared and cultivated large tracts of land. But in these communities men and things were not distinguished ; and often the abbey, instead of belonging to the community, was a mere appanage of the abbot, who, in the use of his discretionary power, openly made a profit out of the monks, while they in their turn as shamelessly traded on the credulity of the people.

The merchants of the Middle Ages organised themselves into leagues, to protect themselves against the barons. These defensive leagues, necessarily jealous and exclusive, were so firmly organised that they developed into actual States. Genoa, Pisa, and Marseilles banded themselves together, and traded with the infidel. Montpelier, which kept its consulship in the hands of merchants and traders, to the exclusion of doctors, advocates, and notaries, introduced the Arabian civilisation into France, and, with Narbonne, Agde, Nîmes, Béziers, and Cahors—then the centre of French commerce—served as a link between East and West. Rochelle was connected with the Hanseatic League, and the merchants of the Breton towns with those of Spain, Portugal, and Holland. Associations were formed by Avignon and St. Gilles; Nice and Pisa; Arles and Nîmes; Marseilles, Arles, and Avignon ; and Lyons and the towns of Champagne. The great London league included twenty-four towns. The Jews sought shelter from persecution in these centres.

The modern system of partnership seems to have originated with the Lombards. The citizens of Genoa, Florence, and Milan, even when their cities were at war with one another, still put their capital into a common fund. The liability of the partners to third parties was a constant theme of discussion among their lawyers. It

[1] See *Histoire des Prolétaires*, by Yves Guyot and Sigismond Lacroix, chap. viii.

was they who evolved the principles, still so imperfectly developed, of maritime law.

The Hanseatic League was founded by Hamburg and Lubeck in 1239, as a bulwark against the encroachments of Denmark. It at last included eighty-five towns, rose to a dominant position, and formed a federal republic, served by princes and administered by diets. It was one of the most powerful agents in the transformation of feudal civilisation. It was the Hanseatic League which abolished the right of wreckage, and which first gave a distinct form to the question of the respect due to contracts with foreigners.

The first joint-stock company that we hear of is the Russia Company, whose capital was composed of 240 shares, and whose regulations date from 1555 and were confirmed by Act of Parliament in 1556. The objects of another English trading society were sufficiently expressed by its title of Merchant Adventurers. In 1561 a company of shareholders was formed for the manufacture of iron by mechanical processes. Banks and marine insurance companies rapidly spread through England, Holland, the Hanseatic towns, and the commercial cities of the South; while the factories of Utrecht and Haarlem, and the sugar refineries of Amsterdam, were carried on by companies. Frequently the State intervened. The French East India Company was at once a corporation and a partnership with nominal shares.

In France, associations for working mills had been started as early as the sixteenth century; but joint-stock companies appear to have been unknown until the eighteenth century. The law of 1673 did not concern itself with them. The idea of association for commercial purposes was not originated till the time of Law. We find some important mining, insurance, and other companies, such as the Caisse d'Escompte, existing in 1788.

But there was as yet no clear distinction between financial and commercial associations like these, and those corporations whose characteristic principle was the community, not only of things, but also of persons. Such were the trade-guilds, in which the apprentice and journeyman were subject to the master. It was the aim of every branch of these guilds to assume to itself the monopoly of one of the products of human activity. They were less anxious to act, than to hinder others from acting. The spirit of protection invariably fosters a spirit of idleness. This must be the ruin of all associations of this kind.

The Revolution did well in breaking up the guilds, in the name of freedom of labour; but seeing or imagining in all other associations the same objectionable characteristics, it tolerated only one form, viz., the simple partnership. This distrust was perpetuated in our codes; and it was not until the law of 1867 that it showed some signs of abatement. It still reappears at intervals, in the tribune, in the press, and in the cabinet. It has its maxim—"There cannot be an *imperium in imperio.*" Accordingly, the citizens are to be kept apart; their energies are to be shut up in a sort of solitary confinement, lest their collective strength should prove too strong;—as if the power of a nation were not the sum of the power of its citizens, and as if the aim of the State should be to make a nation strong by stunting individual growth!

What has this famous system led to? The general tendency of economic progress has proved more powerful than legislative distrust. The State has been compelled to countenance the accumulation of a common capital, rather than go for ever without a railway. But, as the spirit of association has never been allowed to develop among us, it has been found necessary for the State to interfere in the formation and organisation of these societies; it has constituted itself their guardian, has guaranteed their credit, and, for fear of admitting an *imperium in imperio*, it has, with the perspicacity which distinguishes most of its precautionary measures, formed one itself, by creating monopolies such as the Bank of France, the Crédit Foncier, the Crédit Mobilier, and the great railway and insurance companies. It has thus taken upon itself the responsibility of all their faults and errors, and of all the disasters in which they may involve the public. Little by little, the Government perceives what it has done; reproaches are showered upon it; and it seeks to rid itself of its unpopular part by passing laws like those of 1863 and 1867, which, after all, are very inadequate safety-valves.

But what I wish to lay the greatest stress on, is the anti-progressive character of this legislation. For a long time it forbade all associations except those of a personal character, in which individuals as well as interests are bound up together. Now, if we glance at the process of human development, we observe that each step in advance has been marked by a sharper separation between persons and things. In the primitive tribe, man is linked to man; in the City-States of antiquity the individual is regarded as a molecule of the City; under the feudal system, every man is the vassal or serf of another; under a monarchy by divine right, men are simply the subjects of a king—subject himself to his confessor. As Sir H. Maine has shown, progress consists in the substitution of contract for prescription.

But how is this tendency displayed? The question throws us back on division of labour and distribution of functions.

In primitive societies, whilst the art of grouping interests is yet in its infancy, persons and interests are indiscriminately confused together. A man's master is the master also of his wife and children; he commands, and they obey. Association implies, not simply the pursuit of a common object, in view of which it exists, but also the possession of a common faith and common ideas, symbolisèd, in the classic civilisations, by a common altar. Even now, the same passion for confusion exists in the State and in private associations. Of the errors from which the State finds it so hard to free itself here in France we shall speak later on. Industrial and commercial associations in countries which have not yet had long and thorough experience are liable to similar misapprehensions. M. Courcelle-Seneuil [1] says, "In countries accustomed to association, commercial relations are completely separated from those of private life. It is not unusual for one partner not to know where the other lives, or whether he is married or single."

Under these conditions, partnership is simply an association of capital, in which individuals tend more and more to disappear and to become independent of each other. Personal piques and vanities, the rivalries of wives and children, find no place; we are united on the one point of securing the success of the matter in hand; for the rest, we have our own opinions in religion and politics, and on our own private concerns.

This separation of private from social life is the first rule in the art of grouping interests, an art hitherto little known and little observed.

Therefore,—

1st. *That form of association is the most advanced which most clearly distinguishes between interests and persons.*

2nd. *The power of association is in direct proportion to the clearness with which the interests associated and the end in view are defined.*

The highest expression of economic progress is the joint-stock company, whose action French legislation has so far striven to hinder. Until 1867 no joint-stock company could be formed in this country without the authorisation of the Government.

And yet, what progress has been made by this form of association! It has nothing to do with 'persons, it collects capital. This capital may belong to persons of different nationalities; but the sense of nationality is lost in the union for a common object, and thus the fusion of interests paves the way for the extinction of national hatreds.

Moreover, the management of capital in different countries does not greatly vary. Subject everywhere to the law of demand and supply, which is unaffected by circumstances or surroundings, its existence depends on its conforming to that law. Does not a true road to union lie here?

Liberty of person, solidarity of interests. Such should be the motto of all associations; and no association realises it so well as the joint stock company. It is not surprising therefore that legislators have so bitterly opposed it, even down to the present time.

---

[1] *Manuel des Affaires*, p. 133.

But then, we are told, joint stock companies sometimes conduct their affairs badly, and come to a frightful crash in the end. Yes. A train running off the line, the failure of a public company, is a public disaster; while the upsetting of a coach, the bankruptcy of a small publican, disturbs nobody very much. It is all a question of proportion.

But people can only learn by their own experience. The dupes who lose their money in such enterprises have relied on somebody's name, or on the look of a prospectus. They have had their *plébiscite,* voting their capital away in the hope of fabulous gains; then they have had their Sedan. It is their own fault.

Moreover, it is a great question whether the losses caused by these occasional catastrophes are not more than counterbalanced by the gains. The besetting fault of humanity is, not doing too much, but doing too little.

But here again we see the State appearing as an earthly providence, omnipresent, omniscient, regulating the life and acts of the ignorant, imprudent, unreasoning individual. Spite of the fact, proved by the history of social development, that all progress in the idea of law is marked by the increased predominance of the substance over the form, the legislator interferes to impede and trammel the form of contract.

Laws intended to affect the fluctuations of demand and supply are almost always useless, however well meant. On the Bourse, the *marché à terme* is prohibited,[1] and a dishonest debtor who wants to break through his engagements may plead its illegality; and yet, notwithstanding this risk, the practice has become habitual. The Penal Code forbids artificial rises and falls, under penalty of im-

---

[1] Speaking generally, the *marché à terme* may be said to be a form of sale, by the terms of which the merchandise is to be delivered at a time agreed upon, but still distant, while the price is fixed at once. The contract may, however, be either real or fictitious. It is *real* when the contracting parties have actually intended the goods to be delivered, and when proportionate damages can be claimed in case of non-delivery. This kind of contract is perfectly legal, and can be legally enforced. On the other hand, the bargain is fictitious when the parties arrange that, failing the delivery of the goods, the matter shall be settled by the payment of the difference between the price agreed on and the current market price at the time appointed for the delivery. Such a clause plainly shows that the buyer has no real wish to compel the vendor to fulfil the contract, and the whole affair is reduced to a speculation on the rise and fall of prices. When there is a difficulty in ascertaining whether the *marché à terme* is real or fictitious, the tribunals decide according to circumstances. If two men on the Bourse, who have no other occupation, were found to be carrying on a speculation of this kind, say in the wool trade, the bargain would be regarded as unmistakably fictitious. It is a simple case of gambling or betting, and as such the law refuses to recognise it (see Article 1965 of the Civil Code). It may be added, that betting on the rise and fall of the public funds is a misdemeanour provided against by Article 411 of the Criminal Code, while bets on merchandise are not punishable, but simply null.

prisonment varying from one month to a year; but this law is daily broken with impunity.

There is another disadvantage in laws restricting freedom of contract. They induce a feeling of false security. People fancy themselves effectually protected by the law, and neglect to look into the regulations and articles of the company, contenting themselves for the most part with reading reports, which, thorough as they may seem, are wholly fictitious. Almost all companies are controlled by a sort of Council of Ten, out of which only one or two members are initiated. These are usually persons whose attentions are divided among several financial companies, the interests of which are by no means necessarily identical. M. Emile Pereire was a member of nineteen boards of directors at once, and M. Isaac Pereire of twelve. They consult their own interests, rather than those of the public; the public must learn to defend its own, and not to put its money into the hands of financiers who are famous for their failures.

No sooner has one of these crashes taken place, than a number of Bills are brought in for preventing it by law. It is pretty well known how it came about, and every effort is turned to stopping that particular leak. The remedy comes a little late, but that does not seem to signify. Thus, even in England, after the fall of the City of Glasgow Bank, publicists of note demanded all sorts of useless measures with the most astonishing simplicity. The *Saturday Review* of the 28th of December, 1878, proposed that the banks should submit their affairs to official inspection every ten years. The *Saturday Review* must have forgotten the history of the *Crédit Foncier* and the *Crédit Mobilier*, both under the direct control of the State. The capital of the *Crédit Foncier*, intended to encourage French agriculture, was invested in Egyptian loans; and fictitious dividends were distributed under the guarantee of governors and deputy-governors appointed by the State. And this under a republican government.[1]

Up to the time of the Austrian crash, in 1873, joint-stock companies could not be formed without the sanction of the Government; and between 1867 and 1873 1,005 had been authorised, of which only 682 were ever able to make a start.

Herbert Spencer has demonstrated the uselessness of State interference with banks. The only real control is the control of the public. The more publicity the banks give to their affairs, the greater the confidence they will inspire. In proportion to the spread of sound economical opinions, they will be forced to submit to a diffused control, under penalty of provoking reasonable mistrust. As to the Glasgow failure, everybody knows that fear is a

---

[1] See the *Economiste Français*, May 10th, 1879.

bad counsellor; and the English Parliament did not allow itself to be carried away by panic. It simply passed a Bill facilitating the transformation of banks with unlimited liability into banks with limited liability.

The one good Bill bearing on company law was introduced by M. Emile Ollivier, of fatal memory. It is contained in a single clause :

"The law exercises control over commercial companies only in default of special agreements. All agreements are good as between the parties, provided they are not contrary to public order and morality. They cannot hold good as against third parties unless they are made public."

If this Bill had passed, we should not now see the organisation of societies framed on the most progressive lines impeded by State interference.

From time to time, violent outcries are raised against the distribution of wealth, as if all possible association of interests had uttered its last word, and locked itself up in its last formula. Far from it. The art of grouping interests is still in its infancy. A hundred years ago, people's minds had not even begun to distinguish between the corporation and the company; and certainly with some persons the distinction is not very clear yet. Only thirteen years ago,[1] a joint-stock company could not be formed in France without authorisation.

Yet, notwithstanding all these obstacles and inconveniences, it is to financial and commercial association that we owe the utilisation of a multitude of wasted forces, the construction of vast monuments of engineering skill, the piercing of mountains and isthmuses, the creation of co-operative societies like the Rochdale Pioneers. We look back on what it has already done, and cannot even guess what it may yet do when once it is freed from all those artificial guarantees which have warped its character and arrested its expansion.

---

[1] This was written in 1881.

BOOK VI.

THE FUNCTIONS OF THE STATE.

CHAPTER I.

STATE INTERVENTION IN ECONOMICS.

The foregoing examination shows that our existing economic organisation is purely empirical. We have seen what destructive prejudices and treacherous fictions lie at the root of great institutions like the Banks of France and England; we have passed rapidly in review a number of measures which, under pretext of enriching the country, only impoverish it.

Knowledge alone can dissipate these errors.

When the mistake is confined to individuals, the consequences, however deplorable, are circumscribed, and the reaction soon dies away. But when the error is collective, and strong enough to find embodiment in legislative measures, when it compels all the forces of society to serve its triumph, then it may do incurable mischief. It may check the progress of a nation, and reduce it to a level of permanent inferiority among the nations which surround it.

When we look impartially at human history, we see that the State has been the chief hindrance to economic progress.

In detail, this is undisputed. It is universally admitted that the State produces dearer and worse than private enterprise. Let us take a few chance instances.

It takes the Government 800,000 working days to build a ship of 8,000 tons; while private industry constructed the *Amiral-Duperré*, a ship of 10,487 tons, in 411,000. The Government built the *Redoutable* at a cost of 662 francs per ton, while the *Amiral-Duperré* cost only 562.[1]

---

[1] M. E. Farcy's speech in the debate on the Admiralty Budget for 1880. The figures have never been disputed.

When the persons included in the amnesty had to be brought home from Noumea, the adequate victualling of the ships was overlooked; and to this day the peculations on the sailors' rations go on just as they did a hundred years ago.

We have all read the astounding disclosures afforded by the inquiries into the administration of the War Department. All that was asked of it was, to be ready for war when it came. It comes at last, and then we are told that it is "an abnormal state of things;" as if, for the army at least, it were not the normal state of things!

So then it is discovered that the artillery is placed in parks where it cannot be got out; that there is no harness here, and no horses there; that supplies are missing wherever they are wanted; that the soldiers are now without food, now without ammunition. The incapacity and improvidence become almost ludicrous. The genius of Shakespeare never imagined a more sorrowful farce. And this sort of thing goes on.[1] The *caporal d'ordinaire* (mess-room corporal) has had to be reinstated, to prevent the grossest peculation in the contracts for meat. The War Department is obliged to confess that it turns out muniments of war at greater cost and of worse quality than private firms.[2]

The Department of Roads and Bridges is very proud of its science and skill. Nevertheless, it has perpetrated a series of sometimes disastrous mistakes. The population along the banks of the Loire complained in 1866 that their homes had been submerged by the floods. All the consolation the Ministry of Public Works could find to give them in its official report was, that they had nothing to complain of, for it was a wonder they had not all been drowned long before.

These shortcomings are not peculiar to France. From time to time some inquiry discloses the profound disorder which reigns in the English Admiralty; the number of ships which cannot sail, and of compasses which are only fit for an old curiosity shop. Everywhere the same astounding carelessness, the same egregious blunders. Did not the Indian Government overlook a little matter of a few millions in its budget?

We all know what a costly indulgence the Government mania for building has turned out. The Poor Relief Department has spent a great part of its funds in building. Then there is the Hôtel Dieu, the Empress's charity. Every one of its four hundred beds has cost 87,500 francs. Moreover, the patients, if they are well lodged, are ill fed; and there are said to be as many attendants as patients. And now the Ministry of the Interior is proposing to have penitential cells at the Conciergerie, which will come to 33,000 francs each.

[1] See *Journal Officiel*, November 27, 1878.
[2] *Journal Officiel*, November 30 and December 1, 1878.

Government is naturally prodigal, for it spends other people's money; and the more a department spends, the more important it is.

A new trade drives an old one out of the field. Those who carried on the old one must seek some fresh employment. The railway superseded the diligence; the guards and postilions had to take to other work. The State owed them no compensation, and gave them none. But had the diligences been in the service of the State, vested interests would have had to be recognised. At this moment, if you propose the abolition of indirect taxation, you are met with the unanswerable argument, "But what is to be done with the employés?"

Government is rigid; it cannot accommodate itself to new wants and difficulties. In order to act with regularity, it has had to bind itself by fixed rules. It can only act in a given direction and in a given manner. The necessity for order has given the spirit of control the predominance over that of initiative.

When Government has once made a blunder, it perpetuates it indefinitely. It is well known that the English Poor Law has never done the work it was meant to do; and yet from one day to another it could not be repealed without creating a catastrophe. In France we have thousands of decrepit institutions which go on in the same way. There is the monopoly of matches. Every one complains of it. No one defends it. Yet it will probably hold out another ten years.

We are always extending the system of Government inspection. In general, the results are just the opposite of what was looked for. Steam boilers are required to be of a certain thickness. It is, therefore, not worth the maker's while to improve the quality of the metal, and so make the boilers stronger and lighter. They are turned out according to regulation, receive the Government stamp, and—burst.

Laboratories are established and analysts appointed, and then it is found that the instruments used are not accurate. Is there any compensation for the victims? Everything goes by favour. Frauds go on unchecked, while things which have nothing fraudulent about them are punished as fraud. Fresh regulations are demanded; under the plea of the public health, every law is set aside; the importation of cattle and meat is forbidden; and whole classes of pariahs are created.

England, too, from time to time succumbs to the same craze; but she finds it no defence against adulteration. The publication in the *Lancet* of some facts as to the adulterations carried on by certain manufacturers and dealers, did more good than all the previous measures of the Government.

The State cannot be made responsible, it can always evade complaints. We see it in the postal and telegraph service. We see it in the bad cigars with which it thinks proper to supply the public. Ministers, magistrates, and police agents constantly violate the law, with the serene consciousness that they are above it.

I might quote many more examples of the deceptions created by the interference of the State, but I content myself with referring the reader to M. Menier's *Avenir Economique*.[1]

Official corruption is a subject of every-day conversation, and the vices,—for I will not say the shortcomings,—of the Government are even exaggerated. It is accused of theft and extortion, when it is guilty of nothing worse than idleness, indifference, neglect, and incapacity.

Everywhere disorder underlies the superficial order.

When it has thus been sufficiently proved that whatever the State puts its hand to, it does nothing but blunder; that the articles it makes for itself are dearer and worse than those made for it by private firms; that the irksomeness of State inspection outweighs its advantages; that its attempted reforms usually end in aggravated abuses; that in trying to avert one evil, it usually creates another; that it is commonly led to its decisions by considerations quite foreign to the matter in question; that its interference has the disastrous effect of discouraging private initiative; that it is at once prodigal of its resources and wanting in the power of adaptation; and that, notwithstanding a complicated system of supervision, its administration is rotten to the core—when the tribune, the press, the reports of Parliamentary Committees and official inquiries, are daily swelling the indictment against the State, what is the conclusion drawn from all this by the bulk of our publicists, deputies, politicians, and electors?

That the province of the State must be extended!

M. Emile de Laveleye says: "When one thinks on all the ills that bad Governments have inflicted, one can understand the desire to reduce their powers and to restrict their sphere." And two minutes afterwards he adds, with the *Catheder-Socialisten*, "History shows that the State is the most perfect agent of progress and civilisation." It is a somewhat naïve expression of a common inconsistency.

In 1863 and in 1869 the Republican party was opposed to centralisation; now it is in power, it talks of the rights of the State, and meets every proposal which aims at infusing some life into the commune with the reproach of disintegrating the country.

Whilst the Ministry itself admitted that the communes had made great sacrifices for the development of primary education, a future Minister of Public Instruction,—M. Paul Bert,—was annexing the communal funds and throwing them into a central fund which the State could distribute as it thought fit. The local authorities are

[1] Vol. II., Book I.

deprived of the control of instruction. The communes are not allowed to institute faculties of higher education. The education given by the University is now seen to be defective, and it is proposed to secure the monopoly for the State.

Complaints are made of the swarms of officials, and the abuse of offices in the gift of the Government at election times; and yet it is proposed that the State should not only buy up but work the railways, which would place fresh patronage at its disposal, and enable it, by an ingenious arrangement of tariffs, to favour one district at the expense of another.

The tobacco monopoly, advantageous as it may be to the Budget, is very injurious to French industry and agriculture. This being so, M. Alglave, Professor of Financial Science in the Faculty of Law in Paris, advocates the extension of the monopoly to alcohol.

I might multiply examples of these tendencies *ad nauseam;* every day some new law is proposed, some fresh regulation demanded, to hinder this, to superintend that, to draw a little tighter the gag that stifles and the bonds that confine us, as if what we want above all things were not air and freedom.

In spite of our old and varied experience, we still think that a change of rulers is all that is necessary. Every one thinks he could do better himself. He should ask himself whether he too has not made mistakes, whether he has never been too weak or too severe, whether he has never wasted his money in unsuccessful speculation, whether he has always managed his household affairs with prudence? And even if his conduct in these particulars has been irreproachable, it will not prove his ability to wield more extensive powers.

For perhaps he has, so far, had to deal with very limited matters, the elements of which are very simple and can be embraced in a single glance, their causes easily traced, and their consequences easily foreseen; while matters of State are so complex that Social Science is hardly now beginning to disentangle even a few of them. And while a private person, however intelligent, honest, and self-possessed, finds it hard to conduct himself with prudence, you are expecting the State, which, after all, is only guided by a few men, to be wiser, further-sighted, more intelligent than any one man by himself.

Despotism weakens the individual and narrows his capacities.

If a nation believes that the State can do everything, it will make it responsible for all the ills it suffers and all the blessings it goes without. It will attribute to it rain and fine weather, the phylloxera, and the Colorado beetle. Agriculturists will lay the blame of their bad harvests on it, and expect it to raise the price of corn, while the labourers are clamouring for it to lower the price of bread. Capitalists will at the same time ask for duties to protect them as producers, and for low prices to benefit them as consumers. Workmen will ask it to lessen their work and raise their wages.

Whoever cannot get what he wants will apply to the State. Some day they will break up the Government. Next day there will still perhaps be men rash enough to assure them that the State is an omnipotent providence, which can miraculously satisfy the most contradictory wants; and so on in a circle.

M. Guizot says, "It is a great mistake to believe in the sovereign power of the political machine." Yet he himself, while in power, helped to spread the mistake.

Faith in the State is a sort of adaptation of the religious idea. The State is regarded as a sort of earthly providence, which can create wealth and happiness, and confer a host of boons on the public or the individual. Then they pray, "Give me a good place. Hamper the industry of my competitors. Do me a favour. Give me privileges." As Bastiat says, "The State is the great fiction by means of which every one tries to live at the expense of everybody else."

The interference of the State in matters of Economy by means of regulations, protective duties, monopolies, and imposts, rests on the old idea of the omnipotence and omniscience of the governor, and the incapacity and ignorance of the governed.

It is justified under a rule by divine right; it is inadmissible under a government by discussion.

It is always costly.

CHAPTER II.

THE REVENUES AND EXPENDITURE OF THE STATE.

Those who seek to add indefinitely to the duties of the State forget that its services are not gratuitous. The following table, showing the expansion of our budgets, is a convincing proof of this.

The earlier budgets did not separate the expenditure of the State from the expenses paid out of special funds, such as the departmental and communal rates (*centimes additionnels*) and other accessory sources of revenue. These must be included in our table if we are to have an accurate comparison of the budgets of different periods.

Date.	Amount.
1789	531,440,000 francs.
1815	931,441,404 ,,
1828	1,024,100,637 ,,
1840	1,367,711,102 ,,
1852	1,513,109,997 ,,
1860	2,084,091,354 ,,
1865	2,147,191,012 ,,
1869	2,209,270,054 ,,

Date.	Amount.
1872	2,655,346,969 francs.
1874	2,945,034,736 ,,
1876	2,944,713,000 ,,
1877	3,051,766,000 ,,
1879	3,156,542,638 ,,
1880	3,145,000,000 ,,
1881	3,232,000,000 ,,
1882 (proposed)	3,294,000,000 ,,

To this must be added 559,000,000 francs more for outlay chargeable on special sources, the expenses of the *compte de liquidation*,[1] a series of charges which have just necessitated a loan of one milliard, and which will have to be supplemented by another before long.

Lastly, there must be added the expenditure of communes and departments. The octrois come to more than 250,000,000 francs. Communal taxes other than the *centimes additionnels* amount to about a hundred million francs, and the various items of the communal budgets to another hundred million, giving a total of some 4,200,000,000 francs, without reckoning the expenditure payable out of loans raised by the communes and departments.

Between 1789 and 1815 the budget had nearly doubled; in 1828 it reached a milliard; and under Louis Philippe, 1,600,000,000—an increase of 50 per cent. in seventeen years.

Almost every year expenditure has exceeded revenue; in 1840, by 138,000,000 francs; in 1847, by 214,000,000 francs; in 1854 by 186,000,000 francs; in 1860, by 119,000,000 francs; in 1861, by 164,000,000 francs. Out of the thirty years from 1840 to 1870, twenty years have shown a deficit; and since the war there have been deficits of 81,000,000 francs in 1872, 44,000,000 francs in 1873, and 64,000,000 francs in 1877.

According to M. Vacher's calculations, the convertible, or rather exchangeable, part of the total annual production of France is 9,400,000,000 francs—deducting taxes as far as possible. In round numbers, we may put it at ten milliards.

Suppose our expenditure for the year 1880 had amounted to less than 4,200,000,000 francs, the net income of France, according to present estimates, would be roughly 14,200,000,000 francs, out of which 30 per cent., or nearly one third, is consumed in public expenditure.

This proportion, while not excessive, is nevertheless considerable, the more so as we must look not only at the sum taken, but at the manner of taking it; and compare what has been done with it with what might have been done.

---

[1] This was a special fund, set apart after the late war, for replacing war material, building new fortresses, etc.

Out of the 2,836,503,223 francs of estimated revenue in the original budget prepared for 1882, there are,

Registration	552,096,000	francs.
Stamps	145,014,000	,,
Customs and Salt Duty	316,858,000	,,
Indirect Taxes	1,033,743,000	,,
Postal and Telegraph Service	138,204,000	,,
	2,185,915,000	,,

All these taxes are taxes on circulation; and they compose nearly four-fifths of the budget. The indirect taxes, properly so called, and the customs, amount to 1,340,000,000 francs—about half the budget.

Now M. Menier has shown in his book, *Théorie et Application de l'Impôt sur le Capital*, that all these taxes tend to check the development of wealth in France.

Adam Smith formulated four rules to serve as a test of the soundness of a tax. M. Menier, not from *à priori* considerations, but from observation of facts, gives nine. We quote them here, referring those who wish to see how they are worked out to M. Menier's book.

1st. Taxes should be levied on things, not on persons.
2nd. They should not affect circulation.
3rd. They should not impede freedom of labour.
4th. Taxation should be uniform.
5th. The assessment of taxes should be regular.
6th. Taxes should be levied on the capital of the nation; every man contributing in proportion to his capital.
7th. They should be stated, and not arbitrary.
8th. They should be levied at the time and in the manner most convenient to the tax-payer.
9th. They should be collected as economically as possible.

It is quite superfluous to attempt to show that all our taxes, as well direct as indirect, violate some one or other of these rules.

We may affirm that there is not one of our taxes that is proportionate. It has been repeatedly shown that the land-tax is 2 per cent. of the income in one commune, and 14 per cent. in another. As to licences, the duty is not levied on a source of income but on a charge—the value of the rent.

It is needless to speak of our indirect taxes; every one knows they are progressive in the wrong direction. They impede circulation; and we have already seen that wealth grows in geometric ratio to rapidity of circulation. They have another disadvantage, which indeed springs from this. We have said that the increase of wealth in a country is shown by the cheapness of circulating capital and the increasing value of fixed capital.[1] Now, what is the effect of indirect taxes on every article of production—wine, alcohol, salt, sugar, etc. ? To create a factitious dearness of circulating capital, and to check its natural fall. They are thus in flagrant opposition to the most significant indication of economic development.

They have the further disadvantage of falsifying the exact relations of the demand and supply of labour, and of interfering with its price; creating an apparent rise in wages, without benefiting the wage-earner. They heighten the price of production, and thus retard consumption, especially that of manufactured articles; for since they fall on the necessaries of life, they so far deprive the wage-earning classes of the power to purchase manufactured articles.

One would think that some Timon, swearing eternal hatred to the human race, was at the bottom of our financial system. It seems made on purpose to hinder the workman alike from producing and from consuming, and to compel every industry to hinder every other.

If there is a principle which is beyond dispute, it is that of freedom of labour. Now, indirect taxation strikes at freedom of labour in a thousand ways; it forbids work at a particular time or in a particular manner; it affects this product or that, according to the fancy of the legislator, who makes himself the judge of other men's wants. "We can tax alcohol," he says; "it is not a necessary. We must take the tax off wine and put it upon beer." M. Thiers made no secret of his opinion that indirect taxation ought to exercise a guiding influence on the industry of a country. Preconceived notions on the subject of taxation have prevented our seeing these anomalies. They are bound up with all our ideas on the constitution of society. They may be shown to have gone through the following phases :—[2]

In the primitive civilization, which rested on the idea of force and not of labour, it was the aim of every man to live at the expense of others. This idea clothed itself in various forms, of which the most distinct was that of conquest.

The conquered were to supply the wants of the conquerors; such is the origin of taxation. It is neither more nor less than tribute.

Taxation retained this form until the end of the French monarchy, and what was really meant by it may be described thus :—

Under the primitive system, taxation meant the *exploitation* of the oppressed classes by the oppressing class, of the conquered population by the conquering race.

[1] Page 109.
[2] What follows is a *résumé* of the early chapters of Menier's *Théorie et Application de l'Impôt sur le Capital*

Under the monarchic system, taxes were the *exploitation* of the people by the king.

In a word, the interests of those who pay and of those who receive are antagonistic, and the tax is the expression of this antagonism.

This view of taxation has been so general, that it pervades most of the definitions of economists. They have placed on the one side the individual, the subject, the tax-payer, and on the other the Government, the State, whose business it is to rule and restrain the individual,—as though their interests must needs be mutually opposed. But the State has always the best of it. It is the master of the citizens, instead of being simply the agent of the nation. It commands, and they must obey. The heads are counted, and each must pay. The tax is personal instead of being real. The man pays, not the thing. The citizens are the serfs and tenants of the State. They must pay so much per head for the right to live in the country.

This theory, which is the theory of Montesquieu, of J. B. Say, and of many others, is thus summed up by M. G. de Molinari. "Taxation has to meet the tax-payer in the very act of satisfying his wants."

This definition would justify imposts on consumption, the object of which is to arrange the taxes in such a way that whoever escapes one must pay another.

It is all very well to say, "But no one ought to be allowed to escape taxation." But you must confess that if you have to give back in poor relief—perhaps in the hospital or the prison—all that you took in taxes from those unfortunates to whom you have rendered life impossible, then your imposts are no gain to you, but a heavy charge.

Many other definitions of taxation,[1] while giving it a more extended meaning and attempting to indicate the mode of its application, still retain the old idea of antagonism between the tax-payer and the State.

The physiocrats understood it a little better. They did indeed maintain the idea of the antagonism between the Government and the community; but in their definitions the individual disappears; and moreover they try to point out the sources from which the revenue ought to be drawn.

Quesnay says,[2] "Taxes are a part of the revenue derived from the net produce of the landed property of an agricultural people."

Le Trosne says,[3] "Taxes are a portion of the annually renewed wealth of the country, charged on the net produce, and employed in the public service."

---

[1] See *Théorie et Application de l'Impôt sur le Capital*, Book, I., chap. iv.
[2] *Maximes Générales.*
[3] *De l'Ordre Social.*

Mercier de la Rivière says, "A sum drawn from the annual revenues of a nation to form the private revenue of the sovereign, in order to enable him to bear the annual charges of his sovereignty."

The definitions of Adam Smith and Ricardo are also generalisations. The former defines taxes as the revenue out of which the public expenditure and the necessary expenses of Government must be met; the latter, as that portion of the produce of the land and industry of a country which is placed at the disposal of the Government.

Rossi says, "Taxation is essentially a tribute imposed on the income of society, and it is based on the right of the State to claim a share in the distribution of the general net produce and income."

M. Courcelle Seneuil's definition is similar: "The taxes are a part of the general revenue raised by authority for the maintenance of the Government and its agents, and sometimes for other purposes deemed useful to the community."

These last definitions are incomplete, but they enlarge the question instead of narrowing it. They have one other great advantage, they make taxation a charge on property instead of on persons. And they point out the true source from which the taxes should be derived. They unequivocally assert that they ought to be raised on the national income.

But what is the national income? It is the sum of the private incomes of the citizens.

Now, according to Adam Smith, the sources of income are three: profits, rent, and wages. How are they to be reached? By analysing every income in detail. Here we see the inconsistency into which these economists have fallen. In their definitions they made the taxes fall on things; but in reality, as it turns out, they fall on persons. In order to reach the general income, we must ascertain from every one what his private income is. We have simply gone round in a circle and got back to the point from which we started.

Whether the tax is voted by the tax-payer or not, we come back to this, that it is a burden imposed by the State on the individual. Yet this definition is hardly consistent with the laws which regulate the production and distribution of wealth in a nation. A new definition seems to be required.

When, in 1789, the exhausted monarchy called on the nation to save itself, its representatives had an inkling, however vague, of a truth afterwards formulated by James Mill and others of the Bentham School; viz., that there must be identity of interests between the governing body and the community. This idea it is which is loosely expressed in the much-abused phrase, "the sovereignty of the people;" which is applied or mis-applied under every form of parliamentary government, and on which every democratic republic is based.

We may then distinctly affirm: That taxes cannot be a tribute paid by one class to another, as in the mediæval oligarchy or the classic republic; that they cannot be the dues imposed by the ruler on the nation, as in absolute monarchies; that they cannot be a bargain between two contracting parties, since the interests of the State and the people must be identical.

In the days of privilege, when whole classes were exempt from taxation, the State had to distinguish between the taxable and the non-taxable. It was as a protest against this system that the principle of taxation without exemption was asserted. But now that these privileges, however much they may be secretly coveted, can never again be professed as a principle, or form any sort of basis for legislation, the Exchequer has only to consider the national wealth in bulk. As far as the State is concerned, it is indivisible, like the capital of a manufacturer. There is no need to inquire to whom such and such portions of it belong. The State has nothing to do but to secure it every possible advantage. The State, in fact, has to deal with the capital of the nation exactly as I have to deal with my private capital.

A nation, regarded economically, is a unity in itself. It possesses a certain extent of territory, which has certain natural utilities; these natural utilities have been developed by labour or appropriated by man; *the capital of the nation is the sum total of the utilities it possesses.*

The nation, being a group of interests, forms a board, or *syndicate,* of which the State is the manager. In the case of France, this syndicate is composed of 86 individuals, viz., the departments; these again represent 362 arrondissements, which in their turn represent 2,500 cantons, representing 36,000 communes.

Such are the elements into which this syndicate resolves itself. But what are these communes, these cantons, these arrondissements, these departments? They too are combinations of interests; they are themselves syndicates. The mayor and prefect, then, are syndics, or directors; the government itself can be nothing more than the manager of the national syndicate. Now, just as there are not two systems of book-keeping, one for private individuals and the other for public bodies, so there cannot be two modes of management for the nation and for a company of private persons. Nay, I will push the analogy further still; I will add that there is but one mode of administering capital, whether it is done by an individual or by a body of individuals.

Now, if, instead of saying that these cases are analogous, we say they are identical, we shall get at the true definition of taxation, viz. :—

Taxes represent the general working expenses incurred in the employment of the national capital.[1]

The only tax which conforms to these rules and to this definition is a tax on fixed capital.

The following articles are the draft of a proposed law for creating such a tax.

Art. 1. Taxation is uniform. It is imposed on fixed capital.

Art. 2. Duties . . . are replaced by a tax, at the rate of so much per cent. on the selling value of fixed capital owned in France.

Art. 3. Fixed capital consists of all such utilities as do not lose their identity in the using, namely, the soil, mines, buildings, machinery, implements, ships, vehicles, beasts of burden, household utensils, furniture, and objects of art, when not regarded as commodities offered for sale.

Art. 4. The fixed capital owned within each commune shall be rated by the comptroller of the direct taxes. He shall be assisted by two delegates nominated by the municipal council. In towns consisting of several cantons, the municipal council shall nominate two delegates for each canton. These committees shall be empowered to add experts to their number.

Art. 5. In rating insured personal property, the policy of insurance shall be taken as the basis of the estimate.[2]

Art. 6. In rating real property the comptrollers of the direct taxes shall avail themselves of the official survey as it now stands, adopting, in place of the estimate of income, the real estimate of the saleable value, based on documentary evidence of sales in the neighbourhood within the preceding four years, on policies of insurance, and other like documents.

Art. 7. The tax extends to the whole of the capital, regardless of any debts and charges with which it may be encumbered.

Art. 8. Claims for exemption or reduction of the tax shall be referred to the mayor; and shall be presented, examined, and adjudicated upon, subject to the forms and delays prescribed in the case of indirect taxes. The lists of tax-payers shall be settled by the prefect at the end of the year.

Art. 9. All other regulations common to direct taxes shall be applicable to the tax on capital.

Art. 10. Departmental and communal expenses shall be met by means of *centimes additionnels*.[3]

---

[1] We are here speaking exclusively of that part of the work which belongs to the State. The total capital of the nation is partly under individual and partly under collective management. In the above definition of taxation, it is the collective part alone to which we refer.

[2] In France, all kinds of house property must by law be insured. (Translator.)

[3] See Menier's Bill for authorising the communes to turn the octroi duties into direct taxes, and the scheme for the suppression of the octrois by the author.

This bill has at least the advantage of being short and easily understood. It remains to examine the objections raised against it.

In order to soften the transition, it might at first be left to the option of the communes to test its operation. I need not go into these details here. All I have now to prove is the unscientific character of the present system of taxation, and of the fiscal doctrines of most economists.

And now, how are these funds employed, which, as we have seen, are raised on such questionable principles?

When the State has been in difficulties, it has borrowed. The French budget for 1882 assigns the modest sum of 1,083,304,000 francs for the service of the National Debt. This represents a capital of about twenty-seven milliards. Add to this, in round numbers, 50,000,000 fr. of interest for a departmental debt of about a milliard, and 200,000,000 fr. for a communal debt of more than four milliards, and we reach the sum of thirty-two milliards of debt.

Now, if we balance the millions which have been spent on administrative blunders, on buildings, monuments, and the like, unnecessary, unproductive, and often ill-fitted for their purpose, or on armaments and military enterprises, on our victories and our defeats, against those which have been spent in a really useful and reproductive manner, we shall find that it would take volumes to contain the first, while the second would go into a sheet of note-paper. The labour of doing it would hardly be thrown away, so long as there are people who wish to add to the functions of the State. Meanwhile, here is the expenditure of the budget of 1882.

	Francs.
The debt	1,083,304,000
Public worship	53,365,000
War (ordinary expenditure)	575,505,000
Marine (ordinary expenditure)	172,001,000
	Fr. 1,884,175,000

To which must be added:

War (extraordinary expenditure)	55,089,000
Marine (extraordinary expenditure)	35,184,000
	Fr. 90,273,000

Thus, out of an expenditure reckoned at 2,818,000,000 francs, more than two-thirds are consumed by the Debt, Public Worship, War, and Marine.

The Debt is almost entirely due to our mistakes; the budgets for War and Marine rather menace than guarantee our national security; while as to Public Worship, without entering here into any abstract questions, it is evident that, however productive of utilities it may be, its utilities are not of this world.

The other services cost:

		Francs.
Ministry of Justice		35,895,000
,, Foreign Affairs		13,758,000
,, The Interior		60,231,000
,, Algeria (civil service)		21,237,000
,, Finance (general service)		19,564,000
,, Marine (colonial service)		30,950,000
,, Public Instruction		69,909,000
,, Fine Arts		8,489,000
,, Agriculture and Commerce		21,534,000
,, Public Works	ordinary service	86,699,000
	extraordinary service	47,786,000
,, Finance (collection of revenues)		172,010,000
,, Posts and Telegraphs		111,136,000
,, Agriculture and Commerce		14,404,000

Admitting for a moment that all these services are useful, that Justice is not to be had at any lower price, that Foreign Affairs cannot be any more cheaply administered, that the expenditure of the Ministry of the Interior admits of no further retrenchment, that the money spent by the Ministry of Public Instruction is all logically employed in the intellectual development of the nation, we still see how comparatively small a place in our budget is held by the really useful services.

But I will cite just one instance of the prodigality of which a Government is capable. It is clear that no private enterprise, nor the most powerful financial body imaginable, could afford to despise a saving of 68,000,000 fr. per annum. Yet this is what our Government—a Republican Government—a Government by discussion—has been guilty of, in neglecting ever since 1876 to carry out the scheme for the conversion of the Five per Cents.[1]

The case is just this. The Government issues the Five per Cents. at 82 francs; that is, it says to its creditors, "For a sum of 82 francs you shall have a right to Government stock bringing you in 5 francs per annum." Only the Government reserves the right, if the rate of interest should fall, of either paying off its creditors at 100 francs, or of lowering the interest. Every subscriber to the loan knows the terms of the contract. The Five per Cents. have gone up to 120 francs, the interest amounts to 343,000,000 francs. Take one franc from every five, and you effect a saving of 68,600,000 francs per annum. Such would be the result of the conversion from five to four per cent. It might have been done

---

[1] The measure was successfully carried out in 1883. (Translator.)

in 1876, but it has been put off from year to year from political and electoral motives. It shows the grave defect of all State intervention in matters of economy. Governments concern themselves more with how things look than with how they are. They are guided in their decisions by other motives than the real interests involved.

One theory yet remains to be refuted. It prevailed very extensively under the old Monarchy: we find it repeatedly in Voltaire; and it is still reproduced now and again by some of our Deputies and State financiers. We give it here in all its simplicity.

The Government receives money; provided this money does not go out of the country, it will come into circulation again, and the country will be none the poorer.

At this rate, the Government may, without injury, absorb all the produce of the country, so long as it does not send it abroad. Logically or illogically, every one will recoil from this consequence. But if it be not true, the premiss must be false; and nothing is easier than to prove it so.

The State, the departments, the communes, absorb 4,200,000,000 francs a year. If the State did not absorb them, they would be put to other uses. Now, have they, when they leave the coffers of the State, any greater purchasing power than before they went in? By no means. Part has been employed in paying officials who consume, but do not produce; part has been used in founding cannon and providing rations; part has gone to pay the interest on the debt—which is robbing Peter to pay Paul; all this has been consumed. So far from being increased, its purchasing power has been diminished. The milliard thus used has been deflected from its natural course; and the very administration of the money has cost a good deal of unproductive labour.

The purchasing power of all the sums which pass through the hands of the State is less when they come out than when they went in.

"But," you will say, "how about public security at home and abroad? How about posts and telegraphs? and education? and public works?"

Here arises another question, as to what is the province of the State. Let us proceed to examine it.

CHAPTER III.

THE PROVINCE OF THE STATE.

IN entering on the study of this question, we must take into consideration some historical facts.

In the earlier civilisations the individual was the slave of the tribe, the *gens*, the clan, or the *mir*. His personality was absorbed in the community, and the community itself was embodied in a chief whose power was limited only by custom and religious tradition. The City-States of antiquity were so deeply impressed with this character, that they exercised an absolute control over the religious, moral, intellectual, and material life of every citizen. Moreover, as the city was organised only for war, defensive or offensive, and left productive labour to slaves, it was necessary to subordinate the private action of each of its members to the common action of all. Thus, even in liberal Athens, where ancient man was susceptible of the highest development, the law forbade celibacy; and Socrates was condemned to death because, in scoffing at the gods of the city, he had committed high treason. When the city came to be personified in Cæsar, it was to Cæsar that all freedom of action was subordinated, while he in turn was to supply the mob with bread and games, "*panem et circenses.*"

This conception of the omnipotence of the State has passed into our modern civilisation. The legists turned it to account for the benefit of the King; while the disciples of Rousseau transferred the same omnipotence to the State, which in theory was a kind of impersonal entity, but in fact always incorporated itself at last in one or more men.

The progress of civilisation may be measured by the emancipation of the individual. Luther claimed for man the right to choose his own faith. The great work of the 18th century, so magnificently recorded in the Declaration of the Rights of Man, was to eliminate more and more the intervention of the State. By proclaiming individual liberty, it checked individual caprice; by proclaiming liberty of religion and of the press, the right of public meeting, and the rights of labour, it acknowledged that it was not for the State to control the beliefs, the thoughts, the opinions, and the acts of the individual. Notwithstanding the retrograde steps which have been taken since then, and the caricatures of divine and human right which are constantly re-appearing in official speeches, in the press, and on the platform, it is to the carrying out of these ideas that all national effort for the last eighty years has been devoted.

If we cast an eye on the past as well as on the present, and consider the signs by which we know whether a measure is progressive or retrograde, we come to this—that we all accept as a criterion of progress the following law :—

Progress is in inverse ratio to the coercive action of man on man, and in direct ratio to the action of man on things.

This law points out the limits within which the action of the State must more and more confine itself, in spite of any temporary movement in a contrary direction.

The State will be less and less regarded as a director of conscience. Even so long as fifty years ago it was possible to say, "The law is of no religion." The words indicated a tendency rather than a reality; but the tendency cannot but grow. Recent experience has determined the State not to prosecute errors of opinion. In fact, it no longer has the right to choose between good doctrines and bad. It is in vain that it attempts to retain the control of the popular intellect; it is slipping away from it. Itself a Government by discussion, how can it impose its opinion without losing its character?

There is a profound difference, in idea if not as yet in law, between the ancient and the modern jurisprudence. In ancient times, persons were subordinated to things. A contract was called *nexum*, the contracting parties, *nexi*. They regarded it as a tie, bond; and this tie was knotted by religious formalities.[1] The odern idea of contract is different. Article 1101 of the *Code Civil* thus defines it: "A contract is an agreement by which one or more persons bind themselves to one or more others to give, to do, or not to do, a certain thing." And again, by Article 1126, "Every contract has for its object something which one of the parties binds himself to give, to do, or not to do." Contract can only relate to things, to specified services,[2] and may always be cancelled in consideration of damages (Article 1142). The further we go, the more marked is the distinction between persons and things. Private agreements tend to restrict more and more the sphere of the State; commercial bodies act independently of it; while the principle of exchange, by a sort of reflex action, is extended to all relations. Little by little the idea takes form, that in all the combinations of life there is only one fixed principle, namely, reciprocity of services. This reciprocity is determined by mutual consent, just as in a contract for sale. As industry and commerce are founded on the voluntary interchange of services, this principle becomes the basis of our productive civilisation.

The State should confine itself to the care of certain common and general interests. It should watch over the external security

[1] H. S. Maine, *Ancient Law*, p. 296.
[2] The provisions of the *Code Civil* with regard to the relations of the sexes are an infraction of these principles.

of the country, its army, its marine, its diplomacy; and over its internal security, in matters of administration, justice, and police. It should labour to increase the production of national capital, by means of education and of public works, and by the multiplication of the means of transport.[1]

"The bias indeed of most persons trained in political economy is to consider the general truth on which their science reposes as entitled to become universal; and, when they apply it as an art, their efforts are ordinarily directed to enlarging the province of contract and to curtailing that of Imperative Law, except so far as law is necessary to enforce the performance of contracts. The impulse given by thinkers who are under the influence of these ideas is beginning to be very strongly felt in the Western world. Legislation has nearly confessed its inability to keep pace with the activity of man in discovery, in invention, and in the manipulation of accumulated wealth; and the law even of the least advanced communities tends more and more to become a mere surface stratum, having under it an ever changing assemblage of contractual rules with which it rarely interferes except to compel compliance with a few fundamental principles, or unless it be called in to punish the violation of good faith."[2]

And again, "The word *status* may be usefully employed to construct a formula expressing the law of progress thus indicated, which, whatever may be its value, seems to me to be sufficiently ascertained. All the forms of *status* taken notice of in the Law of Persons were derived from, and to some extent are still coloured by, the powers and privileges anciently residing in the Family. If, then, we employ *status*, agreeably with the usage of the best writers, to signify these personal conditions only, and avoid applying the term to such conditions as are the immediate or remote result of agreement, we may say that the movement of the progressive societies has hitherto been a movement *from status to contract*."[3] That is, it has consisted in the elimination of absolute law, and the growth of the system of contracts.

The nation is to be regarded as simply a great public company, the members of which are free to act independently. The State is the manager of this company.

To govern, is to direct men; to administer, is to put life and order into things. The task of the State is becoming less and less that of government, more and more that of administration. It is the mission of the thinker rigorously to determine this formula; it is the mission of those engaged in public affairs to see it carried out in practice. Rising far above the question of the various forms of

---

[1] Many of these functions may be fulfilled by the communes.
[2] Sir H. S. Maine, *Ancient Law*, p. 305, 7th edition.
[3] *Ibid.*, p. 170.

government, this should be the legacy of the nineteenth century to the twentieth.

It remains to lay down the limits within which this action of the State should be confined. Ought it, for instance, to undertake public works, or to leave them to private initiative? Ought it to undertake the postal and telegraphic services, the railways and lighthouses? Can it hold monopolies?

We can here only point out some general rules, the result of manifold observation.

1st. In virtue of the principle that those who have an interest in a thing will do it better than those who have none, the Government should undertake nothing which can be done by private adventure.

2nd. The State should secure to every one the free use of his own faculties, that is, freedom of labour. It ought not to impede any form of human action which, being untainted by either violence or fraud, injures no one. It should, therefore, maintain freedom of trade, for without this the citizens are hindered in the use of their faculties. If it suppresses this, it is false to its mission. When it thinks to be a protector, it becomes an aggressor. And this is what it does when it establishes protective tariffs.

The same error appears in the creation of a crowd of factitious offences—offences not only of opinion, but of morals, which have in fact no other criterion than an uncertain public opinion. And it is for want of attention to this law that the State prohibits associations and meetings, and tries to secure to itself the monopoly of education.[1]

We have said that the State ought to provide for the security of its citizens by the administration of justice. But, in virtue of this rule, it ought not to impose its interference on citizens who prefer to have recourse to arbitration amongst themselves. It ought not to meddle with private agreements so long as they are free from violence and fraud. On the other hand, it ought to give an effectual sanction to the execution of contracts; and this is a mission it does not fulfil, for the sanctions of the law can be made effectual throughout the social scale only on condition of the absolute gratuity of justice; whereas, at the present time, justice is made a medium of taxation so that, in our land of professed equality, the poor man may always be victimised by the dishonesty of the rich.

The State must provide for personal and public security. All it has done so far has been to build luxurious prisons and keep a large number of persons confined in them. I suppose it is vain of its own machinery. As for the weak and unprotected, for ill-used and deserted children, they are sent to the House of Correction, and they come out—as a magistrate admitted—worse than they went in.

---

[1] See *Doctrines Sociales du Christianisme*, by Yves Guyot, 2nd edition.

Thus the State allows a number of living forces to be lost; and not only so, but, under pretext of protecting society and public order, it is constantly interfering with the inoffensive action of individuals.

The State must never become a speculator, seeking to make a profit out of its enterprises; it must never compete with private industry; it must undertake only works of public utility and the carrying on of the public services. It may assume the management of posts and telegraphs, so as to bind together all parts of the country, but it fails in its mission when it converts these services into sources of revenue. They should be conducted at cost price.

Article 538 of the *Code Civil* thus defines what is included under the term "public property": "Roads, high roads, and streets made at the expense of the State, navigable rivers, streams, wreckage and derelicts, ports, harbours, roadsteads, and generally all such portions of French territory as are not susceptible of private ownership, are considered as parts of the public property." Article 407 adds fortifications and their belongings. All these things are objects of public utility.

What is the test of public utility? It is plain that fortifications make no return; private persons would never think of erecting them with a view to profit; they are built only to meet the requirements of national security. The State alone can make them. But is this the case with the other objects comprised in Article 538? In England, roads, streets, ports, and roadsteads belong to corporations, counties, and even private persons; so that they are plainly not necessarily public property; while canals and railways are also private property, though under parliamentary sanction.

Now we cannot conceal from ourselves, that after the fall of the first Empire we had to send our engineers into England to study roads and canals; and they brought us back macadamised roads and the canal system of 1820.[1] England had been constructing railways for ten years when, in 1834, a lecturer on railways at the Ecole des Ponts et Chaussées itself advocated the employment of horse-power.[2] Fifty years ago we did not know what docks were, while Liverpool had had them ever since 1699. These facts prove that State intervention in the matter of public works is not indispensable; but they do not prove that it should be absolutely interdicted. The State might open them and keep them in repair, so long as it does not work them at a profit. Railways, for instance, should be regarded as roads, and handed over to private enterprise; there will then come a time when there will be competing services, both for passengers and goods, on the same line; neither passengers nor merchandise will have to pay the toll (*péage*) which at present forms the heaviest item of the tariff; there will be no charge except

---

[1] Dutens, *Histoire de la Navigation Intérieure de la France*.
[2] Isaac Pereire, *La Question des Chemins de Fer*, p. 69.

that of the transport itself, and this will be reduced to almost nothing.

Thus, *the chief economic function of the State is to provide the means of free circulation, and to establish between the different parts of the country a national solidarity.*

Here we have a positive duty of the State which seems scarcely to have occurred to those who at the same time wish to burden it with a host of other functions. At present this solidarity does not exist. Suppose a war to break out and a certain district to be invaded; your house is burned for purposes of defence; and yet you have to pay your share of the war indemnity just as if you had not already lost your house in the interests of the country. Then there are inundations. They are caused for the most part by the carelessness or clumsiness of an administration paid by the whole country. The cost to France of the inundation of 1855 has been reckoned at upwards of 155,000,000 francs. A credit of two millions was opened for the relief of the sufferers. In 1875 the ravages caused by the floods in the South were estimated at 149,000,000 francs; and the ridiculous sum of 48,539fr. 90c. was granted in aid. It is true there were private subscriptions, but they were quite inadequate. It was not a case for private charity, but for national insurance.

We may include as coming within the economical sphere of the State those services in which the general body of citizens are interested, and which cannot yield any immediate return, as certain scientific investigations, the maintenance of laboratories, and the higher education. I say the State, taking it collectively; but I think there would be great advantages in leaving the higher as well as secondary education to the initiative of the communes. As to primary education, I am in favour of the intervention of the State so far as this—that it should see to its being everywhere given. But recent facts have shown the action of the State to be less rapid and effective than that of the communes.[1]

As to the question of centralisation or decentralisation, there is no absolute criterion. Sometimes the links which unite the different parts of a country are too tightly drawn, and sometimes not tightly enough. In the latter case, a want of cohesion is felt, which has shown itself several times in Switzerland and the United States, and which, under the new German Empire, has resulted in the absorption of Germany into Prussia. In France, on the contrary, we are certainly over-centralised. But we may here call to our aid the rule before applied to mark out the relations of the State to the individual: what the commune or the district can do for itself, the State ought not to do for it. For instance, it is clear that there is a great advantage in the postal service being conducted by the State,

[1] See the statistics of primary education, published by the Ministry of Public Instruction.

this being beyond the sphere of the commune; but there is no such advantage in the intervention of the State to sanction the opening of a street, or to direct the local police.[1]

Lastly, the Government has to represent the interests of the nation in its relations with foreign countries.

In matters of economy, international policy must be guided by the following principles:—

The Government, so far from hindering international traffic and intercourse, must take all possible steps towards furthering it.

It must therefore favour all international agreements, such as treaties of commerce, and the assimilation of money, of weights and measures, and of railway and postal tariffs, etc.

It must never oppose a useful enterprise, however advantageous to a rival nation. This is a rule not only of interest to all nations, but of interest to each. I need name but one instance. England opposed the Suez canal. No nation has profited by it more than England herself.

The State must appropriate, construct, or maintain only the fixed capital indispensable to bring out the value of private property. It must never become a manufacturer of, or a dealer in, circulating capital. It must restrict itself to providing the freest possible circulation between the different parts of the country. Once admit the competency of the State to deal in tobacco, powder, or any other article, and there is nothing to prevent its turning baker the next day, and butcher the next, and hatter the day after. The sole manufacturer and the sole dealer!—the ideal of the communists and the monks.

CONCLUSION.

CHARACTERISTICS OF ECONOMIC PROGRESS.

We have only been able briefly to formulate the principles which govern the production and distribution of wealth, and to show that the art of co-ordinating the various interests is still in its infancy, and generally appears to be in direct contravention of the maxims of science. Bankers, financiers, merchants, and manufacturers all consider their own interests of the first importance, and enrich themselves often by doing the very reverse of what ought to be done. The economic organisation, even of the nations most advanced in wealth and civilisation, rests on the grossest empiricism, and on traditions dating from the earliest times. And yet we have shown how rapidly capital accumulates in England, in the United States, in France, and in Belgium. And this, although millions are

[1] See the scheme of municipal organisation voted by the Municipal Council of Paris, Nov. 6, 1890.

CHARACTERISTICS OF ECONOMIC PROGRESS.

thrown away every year in unproductive expenditure on military and marine armaments, and the energies of hundreds of thousands of men wasted during their best years, to the irretrievable ruin of their private career. The following table presents a calculation of the frightful waste of wealth occasioned by the wars of the last twenty years:—

	Fr.
Crimean War	8,500,000,000
Italian War (1859)	1,500,000,000
American Civil War, North	23,500,000,000
,, ,, ,, South	11,500,000,000
Schleswig-Holstein War	175,000,000
Austro-Prussian War	1,650,000,000
Expeditions to Mexico, Morocco, and Paraguay	1,000,000,000
Franco-German War	12,500,000,000
Russo-Turkish War	6,250,000,000
	66,575,000,000

A glance at the following table[1] will show (in millions of francs) the heavy charge to which Europe is put by its state of latent warfare:—

	Receipts.		Appropriation.			
	Gross.	Net.	Civil List.	War.	Debt.	Total Expenditure.
Germany	2,375	1,875	46	537	231	1,875
Austro-Hungary	1,712	1,531	30	303	531	1,640
France	2,781	2,717	...	732	1,062	2,717
Great Britain	2,100	1,812	16	675	700	1,812
Russia	2,187	2,100	35	795	425	2,225
Italy	1,562	1,412	14	228	457	1,412
Swiss Confederation	41	16	...	15	1·8	17
Belgium	250	235	3·2	43	65	235
Holland	227	212	2·2	78	56	212
Denmark	67	60	1·8	24	11	60
Sweden	122	107	2·6	38	12	107
Norway	68	62	·7	16	5·8	62
Spain	625	600	10	150	275	687
Portugal	143	125	3·2	29	62	137
Greece	37	33	1·7	9·7	15	37
Roumania	85	68	1	18	50	108
Servia	25	18	·5	4·3	0·7	22
Turkey	500	437	31	137	375	750
Total	14,812	13,426	200·0	3,839·0	4,339·0	14,121

[1] Kolb, *Statistique Comparée*, 1880. (The figures are approximate, fractions of millions being for the most part omitted in the several addenda, but reckoned in the totals.)

Those who, from temperament or classical education, attempt to carry the old Roman theories into the field of our productive civilisation may regard these commonplaces with scorn; but so long as these figures remain unreduced, and so long as some of those who are in power cherish the idea of recommencing the ravages of which we have just given an incomplete representation,—for in addition to all that appears in official statistics must be reckoned private losses, the check to production, and the waste of human capital,—so long it will not be useless to repeat that all these living forces, these millions of money, these energies spent in destruction, would have been better employed in production.

If we cast an eye on even the most productive societies, we are startled at the small number of persons whose activity is in any degree utilised.[1] I say, in any degree; for of those who do, or attempt to do, productive work—whether in the way of production, exchange, or transport—many, while putting themselves to the greatest pains, achieve only the meanest results. It is at the same time true that an inventor like Watt, Fulton, Stephenson, or Arkwright will add millions to the world's capital, and that, thanks to their discoveries, a stoker or an engineer may have a power of production which could not have been attained by the muscular strength of millions of labourers. It is true that the manager of a manufacturing concern may by some extremely simple expedient augment enormously the power of production of the instruments already in his hands. Yet even amongst such workers as these what an amount of time is lost! Where do we find any one devoting to his work the full force and energy of which he is capable? Even in the most industrious of our centres of civilisation, a very small fraction of human energy is employed in production.

It is the same with capital. The aim, of course, is, to produce well, to produce much, to produce cheaply. But a host of prejudices obstruct the realisation of this ideal. Few people have anything to be called a scheme, a method, a principle. On the contrary, people are, for the most part, slow to act, remiss in seeking out the best employment for their capital; and so it comes to pass that they let themselves be taken in by the claptrap of charlatans, and throw away millions on foreign loans, treating the whole thing as a sort of lottery, and leaving the result to chance or Providence.

The following is the result, as given in a table published by the *Economist* in its review of the state of commerce and manufactures for the year 1878.

---

[1] See Book IV. chap. ii.

Foreign Loans Issued in London since 1860.

Total Losses.

	£
Turkey	89,000,000
Peru	26,000,000
Mexico	16,000,000
Venezuela	4,600,000
Honduras	3,500,000
Uruguay	2,300,000
Paraguay	3,000,000
Bolivia	1,700,000
Costa Rica	3,400,000
Confederate States	2,400,000
Other States	5,200,000
	157,100,000

Partial Losses.

	£
Egypt	45,600,000
Austria	6,900,000
Alabama	1,000,000
Columbia	1,500,000
Argentine Confederation	1,400,000
Portugal	8,680,000
Hungary	700,000
Chili	700,000
Others	800,000
	67,280,000

To the list of partial losses must be added a Spanish loan of £109,000,000. Exclusive of this, however, we have a sum of £224,380,000 sterling invested on the London Stock Exchange in foreign loans between 1860 and 1878. Of this sum, £67,280,000 have been compromised, and £157,100,000 millions have completely disappeared.

In France it was once proposed to hold an inquiry into foreign loans; but no one has ventured to follow up the proposal.

No matter. Millions are thrown away every day on the Bourse in speculations that come to nothing. Then comes the waste of capital by the State itself—wasted, too often, in public works as well as in unproductive expenditure. In France we have a mania for building, and fasten up in unreproductive fixed capital large sums which are thus deprived for long enough of their purchasing power. In fine, we need only look at the mode of life of the wealthier classes in Paris, to convince ourselves of the immense amount of capital that is wasted day by day.

Yet even this waste is better than the narrow and petty inertia of the smaller French *bourgeoisie*. The English are now complaining of the frequency of early retirement from partnership. It is a vice which has long characterised French industry, though the existence of large companies is beginning to put a stop to it. Many people set before themselves a certain fixed goal, and the moment they have reached it they retire from business. They work only to earn the right to be idle. This goal attained, they take to speculation as an outlet for their surplus activity, then tire of it as aimless, and fritter away their savings on engrossing trifles. What a waste of force and of capital!

Even now, we are so ill-balanced that every now and then we are seized with a panic that takes us back to the year one. We took fright at machinery, and imagined it would ruin the working classes. Proudhon went so far as to propose that all new models should be shut up for several years in the Conservatoire des Arts et Métiers before they were allowed to be used. In 1873 some economists, more timid than prudent, announced that coal was going to run short, and recommended housewives to stint themselves in the use of it, in order to avoid the responsibility of condemning their great grandchildren three or four centuries off to die of cold, to eat their beefsteak in the Abyssinian manner, and to renounce tea and all other warm infusions and decoctions. Electricity stepped in and re-assured these alarmists; so then, in order not to be quite without a grievance, they predicted the ruin of the coal companies. In 1880 Mr. Brassey declares that gold is growing scarce; and while, up to that time, the fall of prices had been attributed to the abundance of gold, he ascribes it to the dearth of gold. And people take the alarm at once—just as they did thirty years ago, when M. Michel Chevalier predicted the depreciation of gold and the rise of the price of silver!

The Protectionists are especially liable to this depressing passion of fear. They periodically predict the ruin of France by the invasion of wool from Australia, pork from Chicago, beef from La Plata, corn from Russia or the United States, cotton and iron from England. They are seized with a chronic frenzy of persecution. For the last forty years, French industry has been expected to vanish altogether; our fields were to lie fallow, our population was to emigrate, wages were to be reduced to nothing, and all our factories were to be closed. None of all this has happened, and yet they go on with their prophecies; and the curious thing is, that they succeed in getting them turned into customs tariffs!

What a monstrous inconsistency! The genius of Invention triumphs over time and space, it throws its whole force into the effort to increase the speed of a train or a ship while economising a few kilogrammes of coal; it covers the globe with a network of telegraph wires, establishing an almost instantaneous communication between the inhabitants of its most distant regions; it creates ingenious contrivances for rendering the advance of capital almost gratuitous; and then, when it has made all these efforts, in comes the genius of Finance, of Administration, of Protection, and sets to work with quite another object in view. What is simple it finds bad; it multiplies formalities, it raises its customs barriers across harbour basins and railway lines, it lengthens time and widens distance, it separates Europe from America and Australia, it snatches away by its tariffs and imposts the benefits which the inventor has earned for mankind. And the people who do all this are men who have the reputation of being financiers and statesmen! They disdain the old adage of the Physiocrats, "Let be, let live," that is, let buy, let sell, let work. Their ideal is, no buying, no selling, no living, nor letting live.

Man has always been divided between the tendency to increase the number of the utilities he wants and the tendency to augment the value of those he possesses. In a word, every one wants to have the greatest possible number of utilities at his command, and to sell the utilities he has to others at the highest possible price. To this inconsistency are owing all the errors, all the false systems, the protectionist theories, and the appeals to the State.

Our interests are antagonistic only because each of us wishes to satisfy his wants without effort,—that is to say, without reciprocity. Hence the old notion that the best way to enrich oneself is to impoverish one's neighbour. Little by little the discovery was made, that peaceable exchange is more profitable than forcible conquest; and this exchange cannot take place without discussion, bargaining, and agreement. This discovery harmonises the interests which appeared to conflict.

It is the immediate interest of the manufacturer to produce cheaply and sell dear. If he has a monopoly, he can do this. If not, competition will compel him to produce in the best possible manner articles of the best possible quality while he reduces his profit almost indefinitely in order to extend his trade. But this compulsion results in the mutual advantage of himself and his customers.

There is an old prejudice which we sometimes hear repeated, and which appears in books where one would hardly expect it under this form:—It is the interest of England to ruin Spanish manufacturers, in order to force the Spaniards to buy her own products. Now, I do not say that this notion never existed in any English brain; but if it did, it has long ago disappeared. Every trader knows that his own prosperity depends on the prosperity of his clients, and that if his clients are poor, they cannot afford to buy. In this way he is led, by the mere force of facts, and without any sort of sentiment, to wish the maximum of prosperity to everybody; for the greater the general prosperity, the greater will be the general power to purchase, and consequently the greater the outlet for his goods. Thus the force of circumstances establishes solidarity of interests.

Again, the recognition of economic interests tends to do away with many of the causes of war. Wars have generally sprung from religious or dynastic questions, from national vanity, or from the idea that the way to enrich oneself is to impoverish others. But the improved means of communication and the abundance of disposable capital tend to increase international intercourse; the owners of property dread the risks that accompany every war; and little by little they will create so strong a public opinion that war will become absolutely impossible among industrial nations.

If we look back into history, we see men butchering one another for chimeras; abused by priests, who work upon their credulity by promising them happiness in this world and in a more or less indefinite future; deceived by heroes, whom they blindly follow and for whom they stupidly die; eager to let go the substance for the shadow; exasperating themselves about a word; hating one another for a dogma; and squandering on an illusion the whole force of their energies. All these are psychological phenomena. Now economic progress tends to effect a profound psychological change in those whom it touches.

Man in his primitive state has no means of defence against the forces of nature. The smallest satisfaction of his wants costs him considerable effort. But in our industrial civilisation he has domesticated these hostile forces, he has trained them to do his work; and the more he perfects his means, the less trouble he finds in securing their co-operation. His risks diminish; his certainties increase; he insures himself against fire, hail, accident, and death. With less effort, he is able to satisfy more wants. *Economic progress is in direct ratio to the action of man on things.*

A starving man can have no intellectual energy. If for a moment he ceases to be pre-occupied with this goading necessity, he takes refuge in dreamy introspection. Such is the story of the hungry Middle Ages.

The progress of science is teaching us to trouble ourselves no more about words and dogmas; to study realities in their complex relations; to substitute continuous observation for chance impressions; and these methods must in time cover the whole field of human action. The notion of morality based on reciprocal interests must govern our industrial civilisations, enforcing the recognition of reciprocal rights, respect for our plighted word, and fidelity to our engagements.

We are already beginning to reap these fruits of the industrial and scientific development of mankind; but by virtue of the law of survival formulated by Tylor, and in consequence of our false education, we are not yet freed from the traditions of military and sacerdotal civilisation, the source of all this waste of wealth, this fruitless expenditure of force, these wars, and this armed peace only less ruinous than war.

M. Courcelle-Seneuil has worked out the following ingenious parallel:—

Ancient, or Roman Ideal.	Modern, or Scientific Ideal.
1. Aim of social activity, war.	1. Aim of activity, peaceful industry.
2. Property founded on conquest.	2. Property founded on labour and saving.
3. Classes of persons:— free-born, freed, and slaves.	3. Citizens with equal rights.
4. Liberal and servile professions.	4. Functions morally equal, and tending to the same ends.
5. Political preponderance of the military element and of so-called public functionaries.	5. Political preponderance of the industrial element.
6. Absolute power founded on military force.	6. Empire of laws freely assented to by all.
7. Classification by privilege founded on tradition and the pleasure of the government.	7. Classification founded on personal merit, tested by free competition.
8. A stationary society, corrected from time to time by a reversion to the ancient type.	8. A progressive society, constantly improving itself by labour and invention.
9. A society ruled by laws, under the supervision of a public authority invested with compulsory powers.	9. A society living by the free initiative of the citizens, regulated by the observance of the moral law.[1]

We have undergone experiences sharp enough to make us aware of the prodigious errors we have committed in our mode of regarding and estimating our interests. We have learnt that peaceful solutions are better than violent ones, that blows are not arguments, and that foreign and civil wars cost dear and bring in their train certain evil and uncertain good.

The great internal problem which France has now to solve, is the substitution of peaceful for revolutionary means—of evolution for revolution.

The vague yearnings of the labouring classes, hitherto ill-defined, are beginning to shape themselves into opinions which may be grasped and discussed; and capitalists are beginning to understand that their claims must be investigated. Every one at last admits that a nation cannot be powerful while it is divided against itself, or while it is the policy of its government to strengthen itself at the expense of the individual citizen.

It is one of England's chief sources of strength, that her

---

[1] It would have been better to say "moral laws."

labouring classes know that through the free play of her institutions they can obtain, within a certain time, the reforms they demand. Surely the same conviction should exist à *fortiori* in France, the country of universal suffrage.

Our statesmen are timid, and dare not incur the responsibility of reforms, because they do not feel themselves urged on by any public opinion which knows its own mind. It is this public opinion which men who have any power of initiative, any faith in an idea, ought to set themselves to form.

Bentham rendered an immense service to England by sketching out for her a clear programme, which she has followed through various phases, and which her most eminent thinkers maintain and are still developing. France also must adopt a line of conduct, and give herself an ideal of action from which she must not allow herself to be diverted by passing political events; and this programme may be summed up in two words:—it is the substitution, in place of a military and sacerdotal civilisation, of a civilisation of science and production.

INDEX.

Adam Smith, Definition of Economic Science by, 12; Sympathy a motive equal to self-interest, 27; His definition of value contested, 35, 40; His definition of fixed and circulating capital, 50, 51; On different classes of banks, 250.

Administrative ability undervalued by working-classes, 175, 214.

Agricultural products, Fallacy of theory of fall in price of, compared with manufactured products, 99–101.

Amortisation, Definition of, 64.

Association for trade purposes, History of, 262–264; Wrongly opposed by the State, 180, 264; Advantages of, 266.

Association, Forbidden by French Revolution, 180; Distinguished from *coalition*, 201.

Bagehot, On credit, 62.

Balance of trade, Theory of, contested, 233–236.

Banks, Diverse functions of, 250–254; Vicious system of credit of Bank of England, 254–257; Evils of State interference with, 254–262; Short history of Bank of France, 257; Nature of business of Bank of France, 259.

Bastiat, His theory of value contested, 37; Definition of capital by, 49; On growth of national wealth, together with increasing cheapness of its constituent utilities, 69.

Blanc, Louis, Charges against economists by, 10; His scheme for organisation of labour criticised, 183–186.

Bonamy Price, Economic Science not a science according to, 7; His theory of commercial crises maintained, 240.

Capital, Divided by Garnier into material and non-material, 48; Various definitions of, 49; Defined, 50, 52; Fixed and circulating, varying distinctions between, 50; Fixed and circulating, articles composing, 54; Producing power of, increased by credit, 61; Fixed and circulating, relative values of, 94; Evidences of rise in value of fixed, and fall in value of circulating, 101–109; Increases faster than labour, 207.

Carey, His theory of rent approved, 219.

Catheder-Socialisten, Demands for State intervention by, 9.

Circulating capital, Definition of, 52; Consumption of, reduced by improvements in fixed capital, 57; Tends to be converted into fixed capital, 58, 60; Fall in value of, not to be prevented by protection, 106; price of, equalised by improved means of transport, 117.

Circulation, Definition of, 66; Rapidity of, instanced by Menier, 67.

Civilisation, Four stages of, 46.

Clearing-house, System of the, 252.

Coalition, Distinguished from *association*, 201.

Commerce, Part played by, in State economy, 230.

Committees of Inquiry, How constituted and conducted, 24–26; Herbert Spencer's estimate of, 25.

301

Competition, Advantages of, 232.
Comte, Auguste, his system of sociology deductive, 7.
Co-operation, Louis Blanc's views on, 183; Development of, in England, 212; Development of, in France, 213; Character of, 215.
Courcelle-Seneuil, Definition of a "want" by, 29; His definition of wealth, 31; Classic and modern social ideal contrasted by, 299.
Credit, Definition of, 60; Overcomes time, 61; Increases producing power of capital, 61; Views of various economists on, 60–63; As a function of banking, 254; Banks of England and France based on vicious system of, 254–262.

Demand and Supply, The regulators of value, 72; Operation of, how injuriously affected, 186; Evils of State interference with, 267–269.
Diagrams, Application of, to Economics, 23.
Discount, Varying rates of, in England, France, and Germany, 121; Rate of, not dependent on currency, 122.

Economic Science; Definition and defence of, by J. B. Say, 1–5; Inductive method applied to, 2; An experimental science, 3; Constituent parts of, 5; Disputes as to nature and scope of, 5–11; Bonamy Price's view of, 7; Position of, in Germany, 8–10; General ignorance on matters of, 11–13; Definitions of, by Adam Smith, J. B. Say, and Rossi, 12; Materials for formulating laws of, 20; Reasons for preferring this title to that of Political Economy, 41; Definition of, 44.
Economists, The, Charges against, by Ingram, 6; by Louis Blanc, 10; Held responsible for operation of laws they discover, 14; Their share in French Revolution, 16; Their influence on English history, 17; Power of discovering and of applying laws not always united in, 18; Not always impartial, 19.
Emigration, A constant check on over-population, 128; Gain and loss to mother-country through, 139.
Exchange, Definition of, 34, 64; Necessitated by multiplicity of wants and specialisation of aptitudes, 65; Is it productive of utilities? 231.

Fawcett, His definition of Political Economy, 42.
Fixed capital, Definition of, 52; Economy of human effort by improvements in, 55; Improvements in, reduce consumption of circulating capital, 57; Tendency of, to absorb circulating capital, 58, 60; Utility of, increased by improved means of transport, 117; Formation of, necessitates over-consumption, 243, 245; Proposal to render it alone liable to taxation, 282.
France, Ignorance of Economic Science in, 13; Causes of low birth-rate in, 130–139; Proportionate distribution of population among professions in, 147; Trades Unions illegal in, 200; Legislation demanded by trade syndicates in, 203; Excessive subdivision of land in, 225–228; Vices inherent in banking system of, 257–262; Unsoundness of present system of taxation in, 275–277.
Frugality, Disadvantages of, 212.

Gold, Advantages of, as medium of exchange, 80; Economists divided as to rise or fall of, 92.
Guilds of the Middle Ages, Oppression of working-classes by, 178; Suppressed by Turgot, 179.

Herbert Spencer, On general ignorance of Economic Science, 12; Influence of economists on English history, 17; His estimate of Committees of Inquiry, 25.

Inductive method, Application of, to Economic Science, 2.
Ingram, Views of, on Economic Science, 5; His charges against economists, 6.
Interest, Compounded of price of time and security against risk, 64; Rate of, not dependent on amount of coin in circulation, 117; Falls with rise of fixed and increase in circulating capital, 119; Rises with destruction or excessive formation of fixed capital, 120.

Jevons, S., On money and the coinage, 79; Enumeration of substitutes for metallic money by, 251.

INDEX.

Labour, Object of, to promote utility, 33; Not essential to wealth, 33; Definition of, 34; Advantages of short hours of, 188; Subject to same laws as other commodities, this theory opposed by both employers and workmen, 192; Capital increases faster than, 207.

Land, Peculiar economic character wrongly attributed to, 48, 217; Causes of increased value of, 96–100; Importance of, exaggerated, 217, 222–228; Property in, from being collective becomes individual, 220–222; Unequal distribution of, in England, 224; Excessive subdivision of, in France, 225–228; Land-law in Australia, 228.

MacCulloch, Definition of wealth by, 31; Definition of Political Economy by, 42.

Maine, H. Sumner, On social progress, 288.

Malthus, His law of population contested, 123–131.

Malthusian League, Principles of, 141.

Man, Three qualities universal in, acquisitiveness, egoism, dislike to trouble, 27; Progress of, in civilisation, through appropriation of matter and force, 45–47; A form of fixed capital, and consequently rising in value with increase of circulating capital, 152, 153, 172.

Menier, On circulation, 66; Principles of taxation according to, 277; His proposed law of taxation, 282.

Mill, J. S, His definition of wealth, 31; His definition of Political Economy, 42; His definition of capital, 46; On credit, 61; His definition of circulation, 66; On value, 73; His theory of commercial crises contested, 239.

Money, Amount of, in a country no criterion of its wealth, 77; Qualities essential to, 78; The common denominator of value, 79; Its value taken on trust, 79; Disadvantages of double standard of, 81–86; Substitution of paper, for coin, 81; General rise or fall in value of, a fallacy, 88–94; Economists divided as to rise or fall of gold, 92; No exception to general rule of rise of fixed and fall of circulating capital, 93; Commercial crises erroneously attributed to want of, 247; Substitutes for metallic, 251.

Natural agents all appropriated, 32.

Over-production, Its existence denied, 231, 240; Really over-consumption, 241–246; May exist in particular industries, 246.

Political Economy, Various definitions of, 41–43. See also Economic Science.

Population, Malthus' law of, contested, 123–131; Over-emigration, want of energy, a high standard of comfort, all checks to, 128, 130; Increase of, an incentive to progress, 140; Tendency of, towards concentration in towns, 142–145; French, proportionate distribution of, among professions, 147.

Practice not to be opposed to theory, 4, 15.

Price, Bonamy. See Bonamy Price.

Price, The nominal value of things, 75; Relation between rise in, and dearth of production, 75; General rise or fall in, a fallacy, 88–94.

Production increased by use of tools, 54; Relation between dearth of, and rise in prices, 75; Cost of, decreases with increase in amount of, 232, 238. See also Over-production.

Profits, Participation of workmen in, 209–211.

Protection no check to fall in value of circulating capital, 106.

Protectionists, Inconsistencies of, 182, 187, 239; Errors of, exposed, 231–239.

Proudhon, On growth of national wealth, 68.

Purchasing power, Extended effect of partial loss of, 242.

Reciprocity, Fallacy of, in commerce, 236–239.

Rent, Average, of English acre equals cost of transport of foreign corn equal in amount to yield of acre, 116; Ricardo's theory of, contested, 218–222; Carey's theory of, approved, 219.

Ricardo, His opinions on theory of exchange-value, 36; His theory of natural price of labour questioned, 174; His theory of rent contested, 218-222.

Rousseau, Mode of original appropriation of land, according to, 217.

Say, J. B., Definition and defence of Economic Science by, 1-5, 12; Distinguishes between capital productive of utility and capital productive of enjoyment, 49; On value, 73, 74.

Science, Progress in, entails subversion of previous opinions, 14.

Sciences, Two orders of, descriptive and experimental, 2.

Sismondi, His view, that labour has a value of its own, opposed, 34.

Smith, Adam. See Adam Smith.

Space, Gradual annihilation of, through improved means of transport, 59.

Spencer, H. See Herbert Spencer.

State, The, Mistaken view of functions of, shown in Constitution of 1848, 185; Mistaken opposition by, to trade associations, 264; Defects and abuses of State management, 270-273; Misapplication of its revenues by, 283; Action of, decreases with increase in civilisation, 286-288; Its true sphere of action, 289-292; While neglecting its own sphere, trenches on that of the individual, 289-291; Principles which should guide its international relations, 292.

State-intervention, Demands for, by Catheder-Socialisten, 9; Against and on behalf of the working classes, 180-182, 183, 188, 190, 200; With labour, how far beneficial, 188; Demanded by Trades Unions and workmen's delegates, 196, 203; Evils of, in banking, 254-262; Evils of, in demand and supply, 267-269; Demand for, prevalent, although its disadvantages recognised, 273-275.

Statistics, A descriptive science, 3; Unreliability of, 20-23, 235; Definition of, by Querry, 20; Averages sometimes misleading, 21; Compilers of, either interested or indifferent, 21; Reliability of, dependent on constancy of conditions, 22.

Strikes, Statistics respecting, 197; Waste occasioned by, 199; Sometimes useful, 199.

Summing up, 292.

Taxation, Unsoundness of present system of, in France, 275-277; Principles on which it should be based, according to Menier, 277; Evils of indirect, 277; Various definitions of, 279; True principle of, worked out, 280-282; Proposed law rendering fixed capital alone liable to, 282.

Theory, Practice not to be opposed to, 4, 15.

Time neutralised by credit, 61.

Tocqueville, A. de, Economists and the French Revolution, 16.

Tooke, On Credit, 62.

Torrens' Land Act (Australia), Provisions of, 228.

Trades Unions, Rise of, 193; Charges against, 194; Advantages and disadvantages of, 195; Their demands for legislation, 196; Illegal in France, 200; Regulate price of labour, 202.

Transport, Gradual conquest of space through improved means of, 59; Gradual decrease in consumption of circulating capital by means of, 109-112; Equalises prices of circulating capital, 112-117; Cost of, of foreign corn equals average rent of land in England yielding equal quantity of corn, 116; Increases utility of fixed capital, 117.

Utilities defined, 34.

Value, Previous theories of, inadequate, 35-40; Dependent on human relations, 37; Two conditions necessary to, in natural agent, 40; Definition of, 41; Résumé of constituents of, 67; Regulated by demand and supply, 72; No one source of, 73; Not constant but relative, 73, 74, 86.

Wages, Money not sole test of value of, 170; Proportion between, and price of food, 174; Modes of bringing about uniformity of, 201.

Want, A, Definition of, by Courcelle-Seneuil, 29.

Wealth, Definitions of, by Courcelle-Seneuil, MacCulloch, J. S. Mill, Hobbes, and Lauderdale, 30-32; Not exclusively material, 30; Defined, 32, 34; Not proportionate to amount of labour expended, 33; National, grows with increasing cheapness of its constituent utilities, various explanations of this phenomenon, 68–70; Author's explanation, 72, 109; Amount of money in a country no test of its, 77.

Women, Primary cause of subjugation of, 46; Improved pecuniary position of, 158, 169; Agitation for increased employment of, 190.

Working-classes, The, not injured by use of machinery, 152; Improved pecuniary position of, attested by figures, 154–170; Administrative ability undervalued by, 175, 214; Oppression of, in the Middle Ages, 178; Legislative interference with, 180–182, 200; Legislative interference on behalf of, 188; Legislative interference demanded by, 196, 203; Their demands and prejudices a counterpart of those of the *bourgeoisie*, 182, 184, 188; Compensation of, for injuries received in employer's service, 190; Relations between, and employers, 201, 203, 205, 207–210; Participation of, in profits, 209–211.

SOCIAL SCIENCE SERIES.
SCARLET CLOTH, EACH 2s. 6d.

1. **Work and Wages.** Prof. J. E. THOROLD ROGERS.
 "Nothing that Professor Rogers writes can fail to be of interest to thoughtful people."—*Athenæum.*
2. **Civilisation: its Cause and Cure.** EDWARD CARPENTER.
 "No passing piece of polemics, but a permanent possession."—*Scottish Review.*
3. **Quintessence of Socialism.** Dr. SCHÄFFLE.
 "Precisely the manual needed. Brief, lucid, fair and wise."—*British Weekly.*
4. **Darwinism and Politics.** D. G. RITCHIE, M.A. (Oxon.).
 New Edition, with two additional Essays on HUMAN EVOLUTION.
 "One of the most suggestive books we have met with."—*Literary World.*
5. **Religion of Socialism.** E. BELFORT BAX.
6. **Ethics of Socialism.** E. BELFORT BAX.
 "Mr. Bax is by far the ablest of the English exponents of Socialism."—*Westminster Review.*
7. **The Drink Question.** Dr. KATE MITCHELL.
 "Plenty of interesting matter for reflection."—*Graphic.*
8. **Promotion of General Happiness.** Prof. M. MACMILLAN.
 "A reasoned account of the most advanced and most enlightened utilitarian doctrine in a clear and readable form."—*Scotsman.*
9. **England's Ideal, &c.** EDWARD CARPENTER.
 "The literary power is unmistakable, their freshness of style, their humour, and their enthusiasm."—*Pall Mall Gazette.*
10. **Socialism in England.** SIDNEY WEBB, LL.B.
 "The best general view of the subject from the modern Socialist side."—*Athenæum.*
11. **Prince Bismarck and State Socialism.** W. H. DAWSON.
 "A succinct, well-digested review of German social and economic legislation since 1870."—*Saturday Review.*
12. **Godwin's Political Justice (On Property).** Edited by H. S. SALT.
 "Shows Godwin at his best; with an interesting and informing introduction."—*Glasgow Herald.*
13. **The Story of the French Revolution.** E. BELFORT BAX.
 "A trustworthy outline."—*Scotsman.*
14. **The Co-Operative Commonwealth.** LAURENCE GRONLUND.
 "An independent exposition of the Socialism of the Marx school."—*Contemporary Review.*
15. **Essays and Addresses.** BERNARD BOSANQUET, M.A. (Oxon.).
 "Ought to be in the hands of every student of the Nineteenth Century spirit."—*Echo.*
 "No one can complain of not being able to understand what Mr. Bosanquet means."—*Pall Mall Gazette.*
16. **Charity Organisation.** C. S. LOCH, Secretary to Charity Organisation Society.
 "A perfect little manual."—*Athenæum.*
 "Deserves a wide circulation."—*Scotsman.*
17. **Thoreau's Anti-Slavery and Reform Papers.** Edited by H. S. SALT.
 "An interesting collection of essays."—*Literary World.*
18. **Self-Help a Hundred Years Ago.** G. J. HOLYOAKE.
 "Will be studied with much benefit by all who are interested in the amelioration of the condition of the poor."—*Morning Post.*
19. **The New York State Reformatory at Elmira.** ALEXANDER WINTER.
 With Preface by HAVELOCK ELLIS.
 "A valuable contribution to the literature of penology."—*Black and White.*

SOCIAL SCIENCE SERIES—(Continued).

20. **Common Sense about Women.**   T. W. HIGGINSON.
   "An admirable collection of papers, advocating in the most liberal spirit the emancipation of women."—*Woman's Herald.*

21. **The Unearned Increment.**   W. H. DAWSON.
   "A concise but comprehensive volume."—*Echo.*

22. **Our Destiny.**   LAURENCE GRONLUND.
   "A very vigorous little book, dealing with the influence of Socialism on morals and religion."—*Daily Chronicle.*

23. **The Working-Class Movement in America.**
       Dr. EDWARD and E. MARX AVELING.
   "Will give a good idea of the condition of the working classes in America, and of the various organisations which they have formed."—*Scots Leader.*

24. **Luxury.**   Prof. EMILE DE LAVELEYE.
   "An eloquent plea on moral and economical grounds for simplicity of life."—*Academy.*

25. **The Land and the Labourers.**   Rev. C. W. STUBBS, M.A.
   "This admirable book should be circulated in every village in the country."—*Manchester Guardian.*

26. **The Evolution of Property.**   PAUL LAFARGUE.
   "Will prove interesting and profitable to all students of economic history."—*Scotsman.*

27. **Crime and its Causes.**   W. DOUGLAS MORRISON.
   "Can hardly fail to suggest to all readers several new and pregnant reflections on the subject."—*Anti-Jacobin.*

28. **Principles of State Interference.**   D. G. RITCHIE, M.A.
   "An interesting contribution to the controversy on the functions of the State."—*Glasgow Herald.*

29. **German Socialism and F. Lassalle.**   W. H. DAWSON.
   "As a biographical history of German Socialistic movements during this century it may be accepted as complete."—*British Weekly.*

30. **The Purse and the Conscience.**   H. M. THOMPSON, B.A. (Cantab.).
   "Shows common sense and fairness in his arguments."—*Scotsman.*

31. **Origin of Property in Land.** FUSTEL DE COULANGES. Edited, with an Introductory Chapter on the English Manor, by Prof. W. J. ASHLEY, M.A.
   "His views are clearly stated, and are worth reading."—*Saturday Review.*

32. **The English Republic.**   W. J. LINTON. Edited by KINETON PARKES.
   "Characterised by that vigorous intellectuality which has marked his long life of literary and artistic activity."—*Glasgow Herald.*

33. **The Co-Operative Movement.**   BEATRICE POTTER.
   "Without doubt the ablest and most philosophical analysis of the Co-Operative Movement which has yet been produced."—*Speaker.*

34. **Neighbourhood Guilds.**   Dr. STANTON COIT.
   "A most suggestive little book to anyone interested in the social question."—*Pall Mall Gazette.*

35. **Modern Humanists.**   J. M. ROBERTSON.
   "Mr. Robertson's style is excellent—nay, even brilliant—and his purely literary criticisms bear the mark of much acumen."—*Times.*

36. **Outlooks from the New Standpoint.**   E. BELFORT BAX.
   "Mr. Bax is a very acute and accomplished student of history and economics."—*Daily Chronicle.*

37. **Distributing Co-Operative Societies.**   Dr. LUIGI PIZZAMIGLIO. Edited by F. J. SNELL.
   "Dr. Pizzamiglio has gathered together and grouped a wide array of facts and statistics, and they speak for themselves."—*Speaker.*

38. **Collectivism and Socialism.**   By A. NACQUET. Edited by W. HEAFORD.
   "An admirable criticism by a well-known French politician of the New Socialism of Marx and Lassalle."—*Daily Chronicle.*

SOCIAL SCIENCE SERIES—(Continued).

39. **The London Programme.** SIDNEY WEBB, LL.B.
 "Brimful of excellent ideas."—*Anti-Jacobin.*
40. **The Modern State.** PAUL LEROY BEAULIEU.
 "A most interesting book; well worth a place in the library of every social inquirer."—*N. E. Economist.*
41. **The Condition of Labour.** HENRY GEORGE.
 "Written with striking ability, and sure to attract attention."—*Newcastle Chronicle.*
42. **The Revolutionary Spirit preceding the French Revolution.**
 FELIX ROCQUAIN. With a Preface by Professor HUXLEY.
 "The student of the French Revolution will find in it an excellent introduction to the study of that catastrophe."—*Scotsman.*
43. **The Student's Marx.** EDWARD AVELING, D.Sc.
 "One of the most practically useful of any in the Series."—*Glasgow Herald.*
44. **A Short History of Parliament.** B. C. SKOTTOWE, M.A. (Oxon.).
 "Deals very carefully and completely with this side of constitutional history."—*Spectator.*
45. **Poverty: Its Genesis and Exodus.** J. G. GODARD.
 "He states the problems with great force and clearness."—*N. B. Economist.*
46. **The Trade Policy of Imperial Federation.** MAURICE H. HERVEY.
 "An interesting contribution to the discussion."—*Publishers' Circular.*
47. **The Dawn of Radicalism.** J. BOWLES DALY, LL.D.
 "Forms an admirable picture of an epoch more pregnant, perhaps, with political instruction than any other in the world's history."—*Daily Telegraph.*
48. **The Destitute Alien in Great Britain.** ARNOLD WHITE; MONTAGUE CRACKANTHORPE, Q.C.; W. A. M'ARTHUR, M.P.; W. H. WILKINS, &c.
 "Much valuable information concerning a burning question of the day."—*Times.*
49. **Illegitimacy and the Influence of Seasons on Conduct.**
 ALBERT LEFFINGWELL, M.D.
 "We have not often seen a work based on statistics which is more continuously interesting."—*Westminster Review.*
50. **Commercial Crises of the Nineteenth Century.** H. M. HYNDMAN.
 "One of the best and most permanently useful volumes of the Series."—*Literary Opinion.*
51. **The State and Pensions in Old Age.** J. A. SPENDER and ARTHUR ACLAND, M.P.
 "A careful and cautious examination of the question."—*Times.*
52. **The Fallacy of Saving.** JOHN M. ROBERTSON.
 "A plea for the reorganisation of our social and industrial system."—*Speaker.*
53. **The Irish Peasant.** ANON.
 "A real contribution to the Irish Problem by a close, patient and dispassionate investigator."—*Daily Chronicle.*
54. **The Effects of Machinery on Wages.** Prof. J. S. NICHOLSON, D.Sc.
 "Ably reasoned, clearly stated, impartially written."—*Literary World.*
55. **The Social Horizon.** ANON.
 "A really admirable little book, bright, clear, and unconventional."—*Daily Chronicle.*
56. **Socialism, Utopian and Scientific.** FREDERICK ENGELS.
 "The body of the book is still fresh and striking."—*Daily Chronicle.*
57. **Land Nationalisation.** A. R. WALLACE.
 "The most instructive and convincing of the popular works on the subject."—*National Reformer.*
58. **The Ethic of Usury and Interest.** Rev. W. BLISSARD.
 "The work is marked by genuine ability."—*North British Agriculturalist.*
59. **The Emancipation of Women.** ADELE CREPAZ.
 "By far the most comprehensive, luminous, and penetrating work on this question that I have yet met with."—*Extract from* Mr. GLADSTONE'S *Preface.*
60. **The Eight Hours' Question.** JOHN M. ROBERTSON.
 "A very cogent and sustained argument on what is at present the unpopular side."—*Times.*
61. **Drunkenness.** GEORGE R. WILSON, M.B.
 "Well written, carefully reasoned, free from cant, and full of sound sense."—*National Observer.*
62. **The New Reformation.** RAMSDEN BALMFORTH.
 "A striking presentation of the nascent religion, how best to realize the personal and social ideal."—*Westminster Review.*
63. **The Agricultural Labourer.** T. E. KEBBEL.
 "A short summary of his position, with appendices on wages, education, allotments, etc., etc."
64. **Ferdinand Lassalle as a Social Reformer.** E. BERNSTEIN.
 "A worthy addition to the Social Science Series."—*North British Economist.*

SOCIAL SCIENCE SERIES—(Continued).

65. **England's Foreign Trade in XIXth Century.** A. L. BOWLEY.
 "Full of valuable information, carefully compiled."—*Times.*
66. **Theory and Policy of Labour Protection.** Dr. SCHÄFFLE.
 "An attempt to systematize a conservative programme of reform."—*Man. Guard*
67. **History of Rochdale Pioneers.** G. J. HOLYOAKE.
 "Brought down from 1844 to the Rochdale Congress of 1892."—*Co-Op. News.*
68. **Rights of Women.** M. OSTRAGORSKI.
 "An admirable storehouse of precedents, conveniently arranged."—*Daily Chron.*
69. **Dwellings of the People.** LOCKE WORTHINGTON.
 "A valuable contribution to one of the most pressing problems of the day."—*Daily Chronicle.*
70. **Hours, Wages, and Production.** Dr. BRENTANO.
 "Characterised by all Professor Brentano's clearness of style."—*Economic Review.*
71. **Rise of Modern Democracy.** CH. BORGEAUD.
 "A very useful little volume, characterised by exact research."—*Daily Chronicle.*
72. **Land Systems of Australasia.** WM. EPPS.
 "Exceedingly valuable at the present time of depression and difficulty."—*Scots. Mag.*
73. **The Tyranny of Socialism.** YVES GUYOT. Pref. by J. H. LEVY.
 "M. Guyot is smart, lively, trenchant, and interesting."—*Daily Chronicle.*
74. **Population and the Social System.** Dr. NITTI.
 "A very valuable work of an Italian economist."—*West. Rev.*
75. **The Labour Question.** T. G. SPYERS.
 "Will be found extremely useful."—*Times.*
76. **British Freewomen.** C. C. STOPES.
 "The most complete study of the Women's Suffrage question."—*English Wom. Rev.*
77. **Suicide and Insanity.** Dr. J. K. STRAHAN.
 "An interestesting monograph dealing exhaustively with the subject."—*Times.*
78. **A History of Tithes.** Rev. H. W. CLARKE.
 "May be recommended to all who desire an accurate idea of the subject."—*D. Chron.*
79. **Three Months in a Workshop.** P. GOHRE, with Pref. by Prof. ELY.
 "A vivid picture of the state of mind of German workmen."—*Manch. Guard.*
80. **Darwinism and Race Progress.** Prof. J. B. HAYCRAFT.
 "An interesting subject treated in an attractive fashion."—*Glasgow Herald.*
81. **Local Taxation and Finance.** G. H. BLUNDEN.
82. **Perils to British Trade.** E. BURGIS.
83. **The Social Contract.** J. J. ROUSSEAU. Edited by H. J. TOZER.
84. **Labour upon the Land.** Edited by J. A. HOBSON, M.A.
85. **Moral Pathology.** ARTHUR E. GILES, M.D., B.Sc.
86. **Parasitism, Organic and Social.** MASSART and VANDERVELDE.
87. **Allotments and Small Holdings.** J. L. GREEN.
88. **Money and its Relations to Prices.** L. L. PRICE.
89. **Sober by Act of Parliament.** F. A. MACKENZIE.
90. **Workers on their Industries.** F. W. GALTON.
91. **Revolution and Counter-Revolution.** KARL MARX.
92. **Over-Production and Crises.** K. RODBERTUS.
93. **Local Government and State Aid.** S. J. CHAPMAN.
94. **Village Communities in India.** B. H. BADEN-POWELL, M.A., C.I.E.
95. **Anglo-American Trade.** S. J. CHAPMAN.
96. **A Plain Examination of Socialism.** GUSTAVE SIMONSON, M.A., M.D.
97. **Commercial Federation & Colonial Trade Policy.** J. DAVIDSON, M.A., Phil.D.

DOUBLE VOLUMES, 3s. 6d.

1. **Life of Robert Owen.** LLOYD JONES.
2. **The Impossibility of Social Democracy: a Second Part of "The Quintessence of Socialism".** Dr. A. SCHÄFFLE.
3. **Condition of the Working Class in England in 1844.** FREDERICK ENGELS.
4. **The Principles of Social Economy.** YVES GUYOT.
5. **Social Peace.** G. VON SCHULTZE-GAEVERNITZ.
6. **A Handbook of Socialism.** W. D. P. BLISS.
7. **Socialism: its Growth and Outcome.** W. MORRIS and E. B. BAX.
8. **Economic Foundations of Society.** A. LORIA.

SWAN SONNENSCHEIN & CO., LIM., LONDON.

www.ingramcontent.com/pod-product-compliance
Lightning Source LLC
Chambersburg PA
CBHW021208230426
43667CB00006B/603